# India and the World Bank

# India and the World Bank

## The Politics of Aid and Influence

Jason A. Kirk

ANTHEM PRESS
LONDON · NEW YORK · DELHI

Anthem Press
An imprint of Wimbledon Publishing Company
www.anthempress.com

This edition first published in UK and USA 2011
by ANTHEM PRESS
75-76 Blackfriars Road, London SE1 8HA, UK
or PO Box 9779, London SW19 7ZG, UK
and
244 Madison Ave. #116, New York, NY 10016, USA

*British Library Cataloguing-in-Publication Data*
A catalogue record for this book is available from the British Library.

*Library of Congress Cataloging-in-Publication Data*
The Library of Congress has cataloged the hardcover edition as follows:
Kirk, Jason A.
India and the World Bank : the politics of aid and influence / Jason A. Kirk.
p. cm.
Includes bibliographical references and index.
ISBN-13: 978-1-84331-850-7 (hardcover : alk. paper)
ISBN-10: 1-84331-850-4
ISBN-13: 978-0-85728-951-3 (ebook : alk. paper)
ISBN-10: 0-85728-951-9 (ebook)
1. Loans, Foreign–India. 2. World Bank–India. 3. Economic assistance–India.
4. India–Economic conditions–1991– I. Title.
HG3971.K57 2010
336.3'4350954–dc22
2010003315

ISBN-13: 978 0 85728 412 9 (Pbk)
ISBN-10: 0 85728 412 6 (Pbk)

This title is also available as an eBook.

For Deepa

# TABLE OF CONTENTS

# LIST OF ILLUSTRATIONS

# ACKNOWLEDGEMENTS

This book would not have been possible without the support and assistance of family and friends, mentors and colleagues, and dozens of Indian and World Bank officials who spent time with me for formal interviews and informal conversations.

First, I thank my wife Deepa, to whom this book is dedicated. Her support, through years of study and multiple trips to India and Washington, has never wavered, in spite of her demanding career and our shared responsibilities of caring for our two wonderful children, Arun and Uma.

I thank my father and mother, Bill Kirk and Debbie Durdel, for understanding my budding interest in India, thirteen years ago, as an undergraduate at the University of North Carolina. I thank my parents-in-law, T.L. and Anjana Devi Perumallu, for their encouragement and support. I also deeply appreciate the hospitality of their relatives in India, K.L. Krishna and the late Indira Krishna in Delhi, and G.R.K. Murthy and Puspha Valli Murthy in Hyderabad, who opened up their homes (and kitchens) to me.

This project began when I was a graduate student in the Political Science Department at the University of Pennsylvania. It would not have taken shape without the critical early mentorship of Francine Frankel, who taught me so much about India's society and political economy, and Tom Callaghy, who inspired my interest in the evolution of the international financial institutions. Rudy Sil, whose early outreach was directly responsible for my decision to attend Penn, provided the essential foundations for my interest in comparative politics. Avery Goldstein modeled what I still consider an ideal life-work balance, and this has been every bit as much an inspiration as the more directly substantive contributions of other mentors. I also would like to thank other Penn mentors for developing various interests and habits of inquiry that have shaped this work in some way: Tulia Falleti, Marie Gottschalk, Ed Mansfield, Rogers Smith, and Bob Vitalis in Political Science, Surendra and Vijay Gambhir in South Asian Studies, Alan Heston in Economics, David Ludden and Bob Nichols in History, and E. Sridharan at the University of Pennsylvania Institute for the Advanced Study of India (UPIASI) in

New Delhi. Douglas Verney, Professor Emeritus, York University, was an energetic and encouraging "unofficial" Penn mentor at an early stage of my interest in Indian federalism. A special thanks is due to Frank Plantan, who saw fit to employ me as a lecturer in the International Relations Program in 2005–6, after I had completed my doctorate but before my wife's training in Endocrinology at Penn had concluded. In addition to faculty mentors, I would like to thank several of my grad school classmates at Penn for their intellectual companionship at early stages in this project: Ahmel Ahmed, Cheng Chen, Michele Commercio, Todor Enev, Ferdous Jahan, Matt Tubin, Stacey Philbrick Yadav and especially Vikash Yadav.

A number of colleagues at other institutions have been important sources of intellectual inspiration, scholarly critique or simply friendship. I would like to thank the following for our interactions during various phases of this project: John Echeverri-Gent at the University of Virginia, Sumit Ganguly at Indiana University, Devin Hagerty at the University of Maryland-Baltimore County, Sunila Kale at the University of Washington, Peter Katzenstein at Cornell University, Peter Kingstone at the University of Connecticut, Atul Kohli at Princeton University, James Manor at the School of Advanced Study, University of London, Rahul Mukherji at the National University of Singapore, Irfan Nooruddin at the Ohio State University, Aseema Sinha at the University of Wisconsin, and Erik Wibbels at Duke University. I also thank my colleagues at Elon University, especially Laura Roselle and Ryan Kirk (no relation), and my former colleagues at Virginia Military Institute, especially Jim Hentz and Dennis Foster.

I would like to thank several sources for their financial support at various stages of this project, beginning with the most recent and going back to the earliest stages: at Elon University, I thank the Faculty Research and Development Committee for the Hultquist Award and for a Summer Research Stipend; at VMI, the Dean's Office for a Grant-in-Aid in support of summer research; at Penn, the School of Arts and Sciences for a Dissertation Fellowship, and the Christopher H. Browne Center for International Politics and the Political Science Department, both for Summer Research Grants. I also would like to thank the US government, under the auspices of the National Security Education Program administered by the Academy for Educational Development, for support in the form of the David L. Boren Graduate Fellowship.

This project would not have been possible without the generous devotion of time by many hardworking Government of India, Government of Andhra Pradesh, and Government of Karnataka officials, along with staff members at the World Bank and other informed sources in India and Washington. A number of these individuals are cited as sources in this book's Bibliography; I would like to thank this group collectively and not repeat their names here.

Citing sensitivities, not all of the persons with whom I spoke in the course of gathering information for this project wished to be named, but let me also thank collectively these anonymous sources (which I have endeavored to keep to a minimum number). Let me thank several individuals who made important contributions, and who are not already listed in the Bibliography: in Delhi, Shankar Acharya, Sanjeev Ahluwalia, Balveer Arora, Sanjaya Baru, Vikram Chand, Bibek Debroy, Mohan Guruswamy, Zoya Hasan, Pauline Hayes, Stephen Howes, N.J. Kurian, Ajit Mozoomdar, Hiranya Mukhopadhyay, M. Nagarajan, Jairam Ramesh, D.K. Srivastava, and Sujata Viswanathan; in Hyderabad, Rajen Harshé, Vijay Kumar, Gautam Pingle, C.H. Hanumantha Rao, Balwant Reddy, J. Mahender Reddy, T.L. Sankar, R.S. Sharat, Radhika Sridhar, and B.P.R. Vithal; in Bangalore, M. Devendra Babu, Teresa Bhattacharya, S.C. Khuntia, M. Govinda Rao, Hemlata Rao, N. Sivanna, and Vinod Vyasulu; and in Washington, Montek Singh Ahluwalia (then at the IMF), and Mark Sundberg.

Finally, though I count myself as a constructive critic of the World Bank, I frequently disagree with some of the institution's most strident detractors in the US, Indian and transnational NGO and activist communities. Nevertheless, I owe them an enormous debt of gratitude for pushing the Bank toward greater openness and transparency during the years in which I have undertaken this research.

J.A.K.<br>
Chapel Hill, NC, USA<br>
December 2009

# Introduction

# UNDERSTANDING THE BOND BETWEEN THE WORLD BANK AND ITS LARGEST BORROWER

*It was six men of Indostan*
*To learning much inclined,*
*Who went to see the Elephant*
*(Though all of them were blind),*
*That each by observation*
*Might satisfy his mind.*

*The* First *approached the Elephant,*
  *And happening to fall*
*Against his broad and sturdy side,*
  *At once began to bawl:*
*"God bless me! but the Elephant*
  *Is very like a wall!"*

John Godfrey Saxe ("The Blind Men and the Elephant," 1873)

*India is large for the World Bank, but the World Bank is small for India.*

World Bank Country Strategy for India, 2009–12

## Overview

India has been the World Bank's single largest borrower since the institution's inception over six decades ago. As of mid-2009, India's cumulative borrowing stood at around US$74 billion (Press Trust of India 2009) in combined assistance from the International Bank for Reconstruction and Development (IBRD, chartered at Bretton Woods in 1944) and the concessionary International Development Association (IDA, established in 1960 for the world's poorest countries).

No other country comes close to this level of cumulative borrowing from the World Bank (informally, "the Bank," and comprising both IBRD and IDA). More populous China has borrowed more than India in some fiscal years, but it began borrowing from the Bank only in 1981. China passed the per capita income cutoff for access to IDA aid a full decade ago – "graduating," in Bank-speak, to IBRD-only status. Altogether, it has borrowed about two-thirds as much from the Bank as India has. In most recent years, the two Asian giants have alternated as the Bank's largest and second-largest current borrowers.[1]

Recent annual World Bank lending to India has been in the US$3–4 billion dollar range – not a negligible number. However, when looked at in relation to other key indicators – such as government spending, total investment, or the size of India's rapidly growing economy – the World Bank's financial contribution to India's development is minuscule. The Bank contributes only about 3.3 percent of the central government's development spending, and its loan volume is only about 0.2 percent of India's Gross Domestic Product (GDP) (World Bank 2008b). In the past several years, India has experienced single months when private portfolio investment inflows topped US$6 billion – roughly double the entire *annual* volume of World Bank lending.

This is an unusually low level of official development assistance for a low-income country. In per capita terms, most countries of similar income levels utilize a much higher share of external assistance. And while India is poised to cross the middle-income threshold in the near future (which likely will make it, like China, ineligible for IDA borrowing) its self-reliance is not new. It has been a low relative aid outlier for decades, partly for demand-side reasons and partly for supply-side constraints on aid to the largest countries generally.

India was not always so well positioned to access alternative resources for development. During the first couple of decades after Independence in 1947, external assistance from the World Bank and other sources represented a significant share of development spending. Especially in the late 1950s and early 1960s, India's economic plans were underwritten – substantially and ironically – by external assistance, as the Cold War superpowers both took a strategic interest in this leading "Third World" country. India depended on external assistance both for food and financing, even as its leadership pursued one of the most centrally planned and autarkic development strategies outside the communist bloc: central planning and public sector dominance in heavy industry and infrastructure; control over private industry in other sectors through licensing and interventionist policies; and relatively little emphasis, at least initially, on agricultural modernization despite the sector's employment of the great majority of the population.

But at least since a major economic crisis in the mid-1960s – which rendered India vulnerably dependent on aid, and made it susceptible to pressure from the

US and international financial institutions to alter its economic policies – Indian leaders have sought to minimize the country's reliance on external assistance. Even as the Green Revolution eventually ended India's food aid dependency, the determined stockpiling of foreign exchange reserves helped break the habitual reliance on external assistance for balance-of-payments support, and enabled the country to avoid a repetition of a humiliating 1966 rupee devaluation and "aborted liberalization" episode (Mukherji 2000). Though it experienced subsequent economic crises in 1973–4, 1979–80, and, most seriously, in 1990–1 – each triggering interventions by the Bank, the International Monetary Fund (IMF), or both – India has avoided the kind of structural dependency on external assistance that characterized its earlier position, and which characterizes the predicament of some African states even now. New Delhi also has vigilantly and, in the main, successfully safeguarded India's policy autonomy even during economic crises. And especially since the mid-1990s – the period that is the main focus of this book – India has been the indisputable senior partner in its country assistance relationship with the World Bank. Simply put, the borrower is in a position to dictate terms of assistance to the lender, not the other way around.

For the World Bank, too, the aftermath of the 1960s Indian economic crisis ushered in a concern – which has persisted ever since – with its own relevance in India, and a related special sensitivity toward the sovereignty concerns of the Indian leadership. The Bank was badly stung by Indian accusations that its role in the 1966 devaluation drama had been that of an unwitting instrument of a bullying American aid policy, personally imposed by President Lyndon Johnson. So tarnished was the relationship that for years afterward the Bank evinced an "exaggerated reticence" (Zanini 2001) to push major policy reforms in India, even after it embraced what came to be known as a pro-market "structural adjustment" agenda in Africa, Latin America, and much of the developing world. And after the mid-Cold War phase, neither the US nor other major outside powers took much of an interest in pushing for economic reform in India. With the diminishment of bilateral aid, World Bank loans took on a larger share of India's external assistance – but as noted, in the context of generally diminished reliance on aid. The 1966 experience cast a long shadow over the Bank-India relationship, and a deference toward India became ingrained in the Bank's culture – a somewhat surprising legacy in an organization that often is criticized for its limited institutional memory. Even after the Bank's return to major policy-based lending in India in the context of the 1990–1 balance of payments crisis, and India's acceleration of liberalization since that time, the Bank has tread rather gingerly in its reform advocacy – ever aware that it cannot really push the Indian leadership any further than it is already willing to go.

## "The Bank Needs India More than India Needs the Bank"

In New Delhi and Washington, it has become a commonplace in aid policy circles that "the World Bank needs India more than India needs it." For some Indian officials and analysts, it is a point of nationalist pride, whereas for others it is simply a pragmatic truism. For World Bank officials, it is a source of some frustration and anxiety about the future direction of the relationship. There is a good deal of truth to this insider axiom. But as clichés tend to do, it also oversimplifies a deep and multifaceted relationship.

N.K. Singh, a prominent Indian commentator and longtime government official, entitled a 2005 *Indian Express* column "The World Bank Needs India as Much as We Need It." But beyond this slogan (which was, itself, a more modest phrasing of the point), he went on to offer a more nuanced interpretation of the relationship's evolution:

> India's relationship with the World Bank can be seen in three phases. In the first phase, as a source of project financing to support large capital expenditure at a time when access to external credit was limited [...]
>
> In Phase II, notwithstanding liberalisation efforts, in the 1980s, our balance of payments remained fragile and an external crisis loomed large. The economic crisis in 1991 obliged seeking World Bank resources along with the IMF facilities to finance critical imports and honour debt obligations [...] access to these funds was contingent on significant changes covering trade, industrial regulation, banking and financial sector reform apart from fiscal prudence to ensure macro-economic stability.
>
> In Phase III, beginning from the mid-1990s, the World Bank has become an active development partner and has even tried to mainstream policies in state governments with the national objectives. For Central sector projects, *its policy prescriptions have increasingly mirrored what we have ourselves adopted* in the Ninth and Tenth Five Year Plans. They have increasingly realised the limitations of pre-conceived development paradigms in the so-called Washington Consensus [...] (Singh 2005, emphasis added).

"So what does the World Bank now mean to India?" Singh asked. First, he suggested, "it continues to be a valuable source for long-term external credit," at competitive costs compared to domestic or other external borrowings, "for infrastructure like roads, power, ports, airports, rural roads." Second, concessionary IDA assistance is valuable, given the high poverty ratio in India, "for sustaining the social sector, particularly health, education, rural sanitation," and related objectives. Third, the Bank can facilitate "creative financial engineering" for public-private partnerships during India's process of market deregulation. Finally, "the Bank's engagement with state governments" has evolved from a concentration on "the better performing states" to a newer emphasis on "poor performing states" – "an experiment whose outcome would be keenly watched."

Singh suggested that the notion that the Bank imposes "conditions which circumscribe our economic sovereignty" was a "somewhat misunderstood concept":

> India is a success story and the Bank among others would like to be seen as part of this success. We need not grudge it this comfort. In the 57 years of interaction, our needs and their predilections have undergone tectonic shifts. There are not too many borrowers with large demands and a credible record. We need the Bank but the bank needs us as much (ibid.).

A recent column in *The Economist* demonstrates the almost comical disconnect between this insider perspective and a popular view in India, particularly on the left, that puts the World Bank at the head of a sinister neoliberal cabal that has eroded Indian sovereignty from within. Dominic Ziegler, the author of the magazine's "Banyan" column,[2] offers this vignette:

> While sipping syrupy tea and watching television in a Mumbai slum, Banyan was once cheered to see the kindly face of Manmohan Singh, the prime minister, appear on screen. What a gift to India he is: honest, accomplished, wise – a leader-sage. But not to everyone. "World Bank gangster!" one tea-drinker hissed (Banyan 2009: 40).

Indeed, those who ascribe a virtually unchecked hegemonic power to the World Bank often make much of the "revolving door" linking senior economic posts in New Delhi to the Bretton Woods institutions in Washington, as typified in the careers of officials such as Montek Singh Ahluwalia and Shankar Acharya (both of whom, it should be acknowledged, granted interviews for this book). Some analysts contend that the prominence of such high-profile technocrats in India's policy formulation reflects a conscious design on the part of the international institutions to insinuate a neoliberal agenda (Sengupta 2008) – essentially colonizing the Indian state from within.

Taking this criticism head on, Acharya has "outed" himself and colleagues with similar career stints at the international financial institutions:

> What do the following have in common: I.G. Patel (former governor, RBI [Reserve Bank of India]), S. Venkitaramanan (former governor, RBI), Bimal Jalan (current governor, RBI), Arun Shourie (minister for disinvestment and commerce and industry), V.K. Shunglu (former comptroller and auditor-general), Ashok Mitra (former finance minister,

West Bengal), Montek Ahluwalia (former finance secretary), Arjun Sengupta (former member, Planning Commission), Raja Chelliah (former member, Finance Commission), A. Vaidyanathan (former member, Planning Commission), Rakesh Mohan (deputy governor, RBI), Ashok Lahiri (chief economic advisor), Prodipto Ghosh (additional secretary, PMO [Prime Minister's Office]) and (in the interests of transparency) myself (former chief economic advisor)?

[…]

They have all served for several years as a staff member of at least one of the world's three largest international financial institutions (IFIs), the World Bank, the IMF and the Asian Development Bank, before serving in the top tiers of India's economic and financial administration (2003: 173–4).

"Why should this be a problem?" Acharya asks. In fact, he suggests, there may not be *enough* people with such experience in India's centers of economic and financial policy formulation. Even if one does not agree with this particular point, it seems strange that it should surprise anyone that Indian technocrats with specialized skills and country-relevant experiences would cycle through the IFIs, and stranger still to assume that this would somehow weaken India's capacity for upholding its sovereignty and economic interests in its engagements with the institutions. Influence just as well may operate in the reverse: Indian technocrats can play a role in encouraging more realistic analytical frameworks, and appropriate assistance strategies, on the part of the external institutions.

A distinct but related point, less frequently noted, is that in the case of the World Bank, the administration of its operations in India has been brought almost entirely *inside* the country – in a very practical sense, it becomes ever harder to define the Bank as an "external" institution at all. The Bank literally has "been in" India longer than in any other country, maintaining a continuous in-country presence since 1957. But much of this evolution follows from relatively recent managerial reforms within the World Bank overall. In the 1990s, under the James Wolfensohn presidency, the institution pursued significant decentralization initiatives, and the India Country Director – the top-level staff position for the country assistance relationship – was one of the first of such posts to be moved permanently from Washington to the borrower country capital. The Bank's offices in the leafy Lodi Estate district of New Delhi, on a site it has occupied since the early 1990s, employ almost 200 professional staff. Over 90 percent of them are Indian, including senior economist positions and other top jobs – suggesting a significant "indigenization" of the institution's country operations. (So far, though, there has not been an Indian national as country director; the current director, the fourth since the mid-1990s, is Roberto Zagha, a Brazilian with previous experience in India).

The Bank, as many analysts have noted, is much more than a provider of IBRD loans and IDA credits for infrastructure and social development projects, though its lending function remains central to its mission. It is also, for better or worse, the leading multilateral public sector international institution in the field of development – so predominant in development research, for example, that its former chief economist, Nobel prize winner Joseph Stiglitz, suggests, "were it involved in the production of an ordinary commodity, it might be accused of anti-trust violation, dominating an industry" (Stiglitz 2007: 1; cited in Weaver 2008: 10).

Ngaire Woods argues that the Bank pursues nothing less than a "globalizing mission" – encouraging integration into the world economy with "a determination to ensure trade liberalization, privatize state-owned enterprises, open up developing countries to foreign investment, and deregulate labor markets in member countries" (2006: 1). The Bank deploys more than just loans in pursuit of this vision of unleashing global market forces: its tremendous data and research output, its technical assistance and policy advice to borrowers, all have become as important as its financial role. Moreover, the "knowledge bank" and the "Bank as a bank" functions are mutually reinforcing: the Bank learns and synthesizes development knowledge from its intensive and extensive field experiences (though there are limits to the originality of its thinking; Gavin and Rodrik 1995). Its financial resources and "brand" also make it a highly influential propagator of ideas, whether generated from its own experiences or drawn from the broader theories and practices of the epistemic development community (Gilbert and Vines 2000: 19).

Though economists dominate the Bank's operations and research staffs, and though economic rationality is generally the dominant perspective of its prodigious knowledge products, many analysts have noted the inherently political nature of much of its lending and advisory work. An "apolitical norm" may be "an important part of the Bank's identity and legitimacy in the eyes of the international community" – and in the self-perceptions of its more than 12,000 professional staff in Washington and worldwide – but it is also an "organizational myth" that serves the interests both of influential member states and of the Bank itself (Miller-Adams 1999: 23). Particularly as it has taken on anti-corruption and good governance agendas since the 1990s, the Bank has become necessarily enmeshed in politics in many of its borrower countries.

This study treats the World Bank as a political actor, both in the global political economy and in the politics of economic reform in its borrower countries. It employs a theoretical perspective on the Bank that treats it both as an instrument or "agent" of states – more precisely, an international intergovernmental institution bound in a layered nexus of relationships to its major shareholder states, both rich country donors and developing country borrowers – but also as a large and often unwieldy actor in its own right in the global political economy. Much existing scholarship on the Bank stresses the power of its major donor members in shaping its lending and knowledge operations, and emphasizes the Bank's powers of persuasion or even coercion in its conditionality relating to borrowers' economic policies. Some of the literature treats borrower power – if it considers it at all – mainly as a passive-resistive trait, a tendency to promise market-oriented reform in exchange for aid with no genuine commitment to follow through. This may be a rational strategy for borrowers, given that the Bank's own incentives to continue lending lead it to enforce conditionality only partially in most situations (Killick 1998). Some scholars have taken the power and influence of borrowers more seriously, and not surprisingly have found that generalizations about the Bank and its borrowers can be misleading, given the very different contexts of its relations with countries as diverse as Mexico, Russia, and Senegal (Woods 2006).

This book focuses on the critical case of India – a county whose relationship with the Bank defies easy categorization and generalization, and yet which is among the very most important and influential of the Bank's members. The Bank's bond with its largest client, this study will show, does not conform either to leading scholarly conceptualizations of the Bank and its borrowers, or to popular perceptions of the Bank-India relationship (including within India). To misunderstand the Bank-India relationship is to substantially misunderstand both the Bank, as an organization, and India itself, as one of the most important crucibles in the world-historical processes of economic transition and poverty reduction. These are the very missions at the center of the Bank's burgeoning agenda, and given the historical and financial depth of its involvement in India's development, the Bank's own self-image and broader legitimacy are closely bound to India's developmental achievements and shortcomings. Yet India has pursued its market reform and pro-growth strategy largely on its own terms, retaining the prerogative to articulate its own developmental priorities (though in the complex playing-out of its increasingly fragmented domestic politics, "articulate" would seldom seem to describe policy outcomes). In this *internal* political transformation, the Indian leadership has left only limited room for the World Bank (or any outside actor) to influence its economic reform process, and in any case has demanded that such interventions generally conform to its own predilections.

To slightly reframe the dictum about the asymmetry of need in the World Bank's relationship with India, it might be more useful to think in terms of *relevance* than material need. Indeed, in interviews with dozens of World Bank staff and Indian officials since 2002, the notion of "relevance" has arisen repeatedly: how does the Bank make an impact in India, with respect to policy and institutional change (which are immediate and intermediate goals)? Over the longer term, how does it contribute to economic growth and poverty reduction? Simply put, the World Bank perceives that it wields only marginal influence in India, and this perception is essentially correct. The Bank desperately wants to increase and safeguard its relevance in India, though it recognizes that it is swimming against the tide.

India, on the other hand, appears largely ambivalent about its changing relationship with the World Bank – the institution that B.K. Nehru, India's Ambassador to the US, referred to as "our international banker" more than 50 years ago. The Bank since then has become both less *and* more than this description would imply: *less*, in that India's economic model and sources of investment capital have changed so profoundly that the notion of a one-stop financial concierge seems quaintly anachronistic; *more*, in that the Bank has become much more than a lender and aid coordinator, now serving as advisor and partner to Indian policymakers both at the Centre and increasingly at the state government level.

## An "India of States": Does Sub-national Engagement Resolve the Bank's Relevance Dilemma, or Exacerbate It?

As this book will argue, the adoption of a *sub-national lending and analytical concentration* has been the single most important strategic shift by the Bank in India over the past dozen years. This new approach – essentially, engaging a federal "India of states" – began with a so-called "focus states strategy" of selective assistance for purportedly reform-committed states in the late 1990s. As we will see, the state-level results of this roughly half-decade experiment were mixed. More recently, at New Delhi's behest, the Bank has shifted to a special emphasis on "lagging states," where widespread poverty and weak human development indicators persist.

It is important to note that there has been a global trend, in the Bank's lending and analytical work over the last decade or so, to unpack large federal countries by focusing on sub-national development policies and institutions. But this evolution has gone considerably further in India than in other federal borrowers such as Brazil, Mexico, Nigeria, Pakistan, or Russia. In India, the impetus for the selective sub-national engagement initially came from the Bank, as a bid to enhance its relevance to India's economic reform process.

Most importantly, however, the strategy's acceptance, institutionalization, and evolution have depended on the demands of the Indian leadership. State governments, for their part, have pursued an engagement with the Bank for a variety of reasons: some appear to view a World Bank reform program as a vote of confidence in their investment climate – a kind of "seal of approval" – as they compete with other states to attract private capital. Others seem less interested in the substance of reforms than in reform rhetoric, but still seem to view engagement with the Bank as a mark of prestige as they assert greater autonomy from the central leadership in New Delhi. In some cases, distressed states simply need the money: though it is an extreme example, a recent Development Policy Loan (DPL) for Bihar represented about *20 percent of the state's own revenue for the year* (World Bank 2008b: 13). Simply put, against the all-India story of rapid economic growth and diminishing aid reliance, there is a more complex story at the sub-national level, reflecting the increasing disparities between what some observers are calling "the two Indias" – one a middle-income country and rising global power, the other home to millions of poor people and among the densest agglomerations of deprivation anywhere in the world.

Some observers of the sub-national lending focus by the Bank (and by other development assistance providers, such as the Asian Development Bank, or ADB, and Britain's Department for International Development, or DFID) have suggested that the direct engagement of Indian states with international institutions represents an end-run around the central government, a diminishment of New Delhi's authority over economic policy (Sridharan 2003). But if we trace the origins and evolution of the Bank's state-level engagement – and this will be one of the principal purposes of this book – the record does not confirm this "diminished central authority" hypothesis.

A better way of understanding the change is what Lloyd and Susanne Rudolph (2001) call the emergence of "shared sovereignty" between India's central government (commonly referred to as "the Centre") and its states, in the context of an evolving "federal market economy." With the liberalization of trade, investment, and industrial policies, and the concomitant declining importance of central planning, the states have become much more important actors in the development process. Some states have embraced the reform ethos, and the most successful have attracted substantial private capital and have experienced rapid economic growth. So-called lagging states have seen little or no growth acceleration, or improvement in their human development indicators, after liberalization. Though the relationship between economic growth and poverty reduction is complex (and there are vigorous methodological debates over pre-and post-reform poverty estimates; Deaton and Drèze 2007 [2002]), there has been a dramatic divergence in official poverty indicators across the states.

As the map "Percent of State Population Below Poverty Line, 2004–5" shows, states with relatively low poverty headcounts (i.e., below 20 percent) are fairly well distributed across the country, whereas a dense concentration of poverty runs through north-central India – encompassing much of eastern Uttar Pradesh, Madhya Pradesh, and interior Maharashtra, and especially the contiguous states of Bihar, Jharkhand, Chhattisgarh, and Orissa. The states with

**Map.** Percent of State Population Below Poverty Line, 2004–5

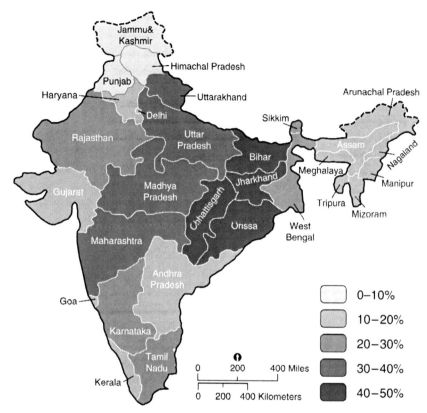

Note: National boundaries as indicated are not intended to represent a position on disputes with China and Pakistan.
Source: World Bank 2007a: Annex 2, p. 1, which drew data on poverty headcounts from "Poverty Estimates for 2004–05," Press Information Bureau, Government of India, March 2007. Map created by Ryan Kirk, Department of History and Geography and Department of Environmental Studies, Elon University.

lower poverty ratios are, for the most part, the same states that have exhibited relatively strong growth performances in the post-reforms period. Conversely, the extremely poor states have been some of the slowest growers since the 1990s. There are anomalies: it is noteworthy that Maharashtra, one of the fastest-growing states, also exhibits considerable poverty in the context of regional disparities within the state. It is sometimes forgotten that although Maharashtra includes the booming Mumbai metropolitan area, the city itself is home to the largest number of urban poor in the country (Tatke 2009), and the state also encompasses extremely poor inland districts. The situation in Uttar Pradesh (UP) is similar, in that western UP is more oriented toward dynamic Delhi, whereas the eastern part of the state is more comparable to notoriously "backwards" Bihar. Punjab and Haryana were breadbasket beneficiaries of the Green Revolution in earlier decades, and their poverty ratios are the lowest in the country even though, beginning in the 1990s, their growth rates were slower than those of other high-income states Gujarat and Maharashtra. Some additional dimensions of state-level reform, growth, and poverty will be discussed in later chapters.

Thus, it certainly appears to be the case that state-level policies, institutions, and overall governance have become critical determinants of investment and growth. Even so, the new dispensation of India's political economy is a *shared* sovereignty: the states do not possess the autonomy of independent countries, and India's Constitution and federal fiscal regime place explicit constraints on their external borrowing, among other developmental prerogatives. The Centre still controls their relations with the World Bank and other external assistance providers, as represented in Figure 1. In fact, it is critical to note that the Government of India is the formal "borrower" on all state-designated loans from such lenders, and it transfers the rupee equivalent sum to the respective "beneficiary" state government. The Bank, for its part, requires a sovereign guarantee on its loans, which would keep the Centre on the hook for state debt even if New Delhi itself did not insist on being the formal borrower.[3] In formal-legal terms, then, these provisions mean that the states and the Bank *cannot* circumvent the Centre. They still might try to do so in practical-political terms, given that coalition governments at the Centre – the "new normal" pattern in Indian politics for nearly all of the last two decades – often depend on regional or single-state parties for support, stability, and even survival.

In other words, state leaders might demand access to World Bank borrowing in exchange for their ruling party's support or cooperation at the Centre. Does this strategy work? The answer, as the case studies presented in this book will show, is "sometimes yes, and sometimes no." This is not surprising, given that both scholarly and Indian media accounts have shown that *other* types of central resource transfers to states are subject to partisan allocation (Khemani 2003, 2002; "Ransom State" 2002). What needs to be recognized in the case of the Bank's state-level loans, as distinct from other forms of centrally allocated budgetary support to the states, is the three-sided nature of the transaction. The Bank itself – because of its interest in remaining engaged and relevant in India – may have its own incentive to partner with states that enjoy particular political clout at the Centre. Thus, there is a fundamentally trilateral political economy – Centre, states, and World Bank – to the innovation of selective sub-national assistance that has evolved in India over the last fifteen years.

The key case of Andhra Pradesh, the Bank's flagship "focus state" from 1998 to 2004, offers the clearest demonstration of this kind of politics – but also of its

**Figure 1.** Flow of World Bank Assistance to India and Its States, Traditional Approach and Selective Approaches

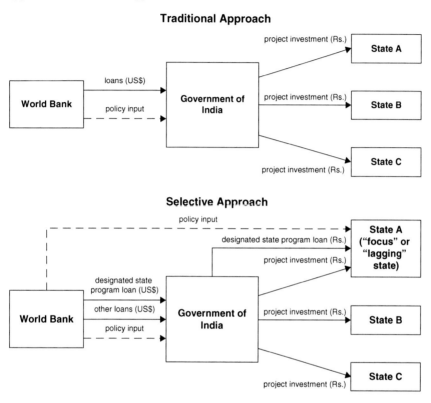

limits. Andhra Pradesh (AP) was led by a key supporter of the central coalition government at the time, Chief Minister N. Chandrababu Naidu of the AP-based Telugu Desam Party (TDP), who briefly overreached in the early 2000s to claim a highly disproportionate share of India's external assistance for his state. But central officials moved quickly not only to reassert their authority over AP's relations with the Bank (and its DFID partner in the assistance program), but also to rationalize the entire strategy of selective sub-national assistance.

Thus, if there was a brief possibility that the Bank's engagement with states had gotten out ahead of the Centre's supervision, the finance ministry in New Delhi quickly caught up with the politics. Ever since, it has kept a careful watch over such borrowing, and it essentially directed the Bank's shift in selective lending from a "leading reformers" strategy that invested in states like AP, Karnataka, and Tamil Nadu beginning in the late 1990s, to a more recent "lagging performers" concern for states like Bihar (with the Orissa and Uttar Pradesh programs falling somewhere in between the two rationales).

But even though the Government of India ultimately holds most of the cards in the three-sided relationship, the central officialdom seems more interested in reacting to and restraining Bank-state relations than in proactively asserting its own preferences. To use another metaphor, if the Bank is attempting to punch above its weight in India, then New Delhi sometimes seems not to know its own strength with respect to the Bank – or at least, not to fully appreciate how deferential the Bank is willing to be in the relationship. Within very broad limits relating to its basic financial model and formal governance, the Bank is willing to adapt its Country Assistance Strategy (CAS) in just about whatever way its Indian "client" wants it to. The clearest evidence of this almost obsequious willingness to adapt to Indian preferences is the shift, around 2004, from the "focus states" to "lagging states" paradigm of selective sub-national assistance – a shift leveraged by the central finance ministry, as its priorities for the Bank's state-level engagement and for aid generally underwent dramatic changes.

## The Indian Central Leadership's Changing Priorities: From the Two-Level Game to "the Two Indias"

From the late 1990s to the early 2000s, the priorities of the Government of India for external assistance and internal development changed in ways that significantly impacted its stance on the Bank's state-level lending programs, and the Bank-India relationship more broadly. In the 1990s, the Centre's interest had been to give a general impetus to state-level reforms that would complement its own liberalization initiatives. Particularly in the mid-1990s, a relatively fragile coalition government at the Centre recognized that burgeoning budgetary problems in many states portended a broader fiscal challenge for India as a whole, and also sought ways to encourage state-level policies that would lead to market-driven growth. But it would be very difficult politically for state leaders to undertake necessary reforms, such as restructuring public sector enterprises and reducing popular consumption subsidies. The central leadership recognized that India's complex fiscal federalism was part of the problem, since the existing regime created perverse incentives for state-level fiscal discipline – encouraging too much current spending and too little investment in infrastructure, primary education and health, and other sectors critical to development.

In what the international relations literature calls a "two-level game" strategy (Putnam 1988; Evans, Jacobson et al. 1993; Drezner 2003) the Government of India essentially decided to use selective state-level engagement by the World Bank to encourage reform goals that the Centre wanted to pursue anyway – especially, the restructuring of India's complex fiscal federalism toward a more performance-based resource allocation – but could not bring about on its own given its dependence on state-level parties for coalition support.

The Bank's experiences in the focus states of AP, Karnataka, and Uttar Pradesh were mixed, but by the early 2000s a broader embrace of reform (or, at least, the rhetoric of reform) had taken on a critical momentum. As well, the Centre was experiencing some success in reforming the federal fiscal regime with the introduction of a Fiscal Reforms Facility. The central leadership increasingly was interested in projecting the image of India as a rising power on the world stage, and announced new aid policies calibrated to reposition India less as an aid recipient and more as an international donor. Finally, there emerged a renewed political concern for interstate disparities in economic growth and poverty reduction. A reinforcing narrative of "reforms with a human face" took root after the 2004 elections, which led to leadership changes at the Centre and in key states – including the Bank's star reformers AP and Karnataka. All of these factors coalesced to produce a shift in the Bank's sub-national strategy from the focus states phase – which deliberately encouraged strong performers and shunned non-reformers – to an explicit emphasis on the lagging states.

Thus, the Bank has become a participant in India's federal and coalition politics of reform. Its assistance strategy has followed the Indian government's evolving developmental agenda, rather than the other way around. When the Bank's literature speaks of a "partnership" with the Government of India, it is not just development bureaucracy boilerplate. And it is *India* that is the senior partner and ultimate arbiter of the Bank's assistance strategy.

This helpmate function – which complements but transcends the Bank's financial contribution – has connoted India's primary interest in its relationship with the Bank for about a decade and a half now. India doesn't need the Bank's money so much as it want its influence (limited as it is) to tilt outcomes in the complex political processes of reform. But the Indian government's interest in seeing the Bank play a part in reforms is conditional, not absolute. The Bank cannot exceed the mandate that the central leadership gives it.

At the same time, it would be an overstatement to say that India has little use for the Bank's loans, or that the financial function is not important to retaining its interest in the Bank. Though, as noted, the Bank's financial contribution is only a fraction of private investment, India is still happy to utilize the Bank as a lender. The IDA credit share in the Bank's assistance "blend" for India makes its loans relatively cheap, even considering the so-called "hassle factor" of the extensive safeguards and conditions carried by the Bank's loans. India's IDA eligibility may soon end – and if it does, its relationship with the Bank likely will undergo a profound transformation, eventually coming to resemble the Bank's even more limited relevance in China, Brazil, and other IBRD-only middle-income borrowers.

It is a profound contradiction that even as India as a whole inches ever closer to the per capita income cutoff that will end its "low-income" designation for World Bank purposes, and will end its eligibility for concessionary IDA borrowing, the Indian government itself has encouraged a Bank assistance strategy that places special emphasis on lagging states. There is a vast "other India," or *Bharat* (the Hindi name for the country, colloquially suggestive of the north-central heartland), which has been left largely untouched by the country's recent economic achievements. States such as Bihar, Orissa, and UP contain massive concentrations of the world's poor, and are far more populous than many African states that have become eligible for enhanced debt relief (and whose access to IDA likely will continue as long as the facility exists). The coming IDA endgame between India and the Bank will be perhaps the most fascinating chapter yet in their long shared history, and its outcome will have important implications for global development assistance. Moreover, as India continues its transition from borrower to donor and seeks an expanded role in global governance, its influence in the World Bank is likely to become even more important, with consequences for other member countries – donors and borrowers alike.

## Scope and Argument

This book is about power, influence, and the politics of reform in the "country assistance" relationship between the World Bank and India. A more specific focus of this book is the emergence and evolution, over the past fifteen years or so, of a selective sub-national assistance strategy for the World Bank in India. Significantly, other lending institutions have pursued similar state-level engagements, but the Bank's programs have been the largest and highest-profile. Thus, this book does not analyze in any detail similar approaches by the ADB, DFID, or other lenders, though it will note their occasional partnerships and generally friendly competition with the World Bank in particular states. (A similar but distinct point should be made about the Bank's Bretton Woods sister: this book is not about India and the IMF, though the latter's interventions up to the 1991 liberalization will be noted where relevant).

The World Bank's state-level engagement emerged out of its long-running interest in encouraging economic liberalization in India, based on its conviction that market-led growth offers the most effective means to reduce poverty in this country that is so very important to the Bank's financial operations, self-image, and broader legitimacy (for a comprehensive discussion of the Bank's perspective on India's "development challenges and policies," see World Bank 2006a). The new approach has coincided with a period of rapid political and economic change in India, and though the Bank had proposed the strategy as a way of gaining a firmer grip on its assorted activities in the country, it increasingly has found itself drawn into India's complex politics of reform. The Bank has been used as an instrument to pursue a variety of interests at the central and state government levels, and it has been forced to retool quickly as these interests have evolved and occasionally conflicted. Thus, the Bank does not lead India in the way of economic reform so much as it is forced to follow India's own incremental, deliberative process of change. It must tread carefully so as to not affront an Indian leadership that still jealously safeguards its sovereignty, even as it embraces the self-image of an important global power.

India's leaders, it has been said, have sometimes appeared to be "counting chickens before they have hatched" with respect to India's great power ambitions (Luce 2007: 7). Even so, access to alternative sources of development financing has greatly diminished their dependence on World Bank loans. Therefore, India can say no to the Bank – and it has done so, in high-profile instances during the history discussed in this book. And *because* India can say no, it does not have to do so very often: the Bank proactively looks for ways to retain India's interest in keeping up a high lending volume. As the Bank has come under attack from critics on the left and right in recent years, it has become that much more important to remain engaged in large, relatively reliable borrowers such as India – in fact, especially in India. In contrast to its relationship with China, which has borrowed relatively little from the Bank during its three-decade march to the market, the Bank can claim India as a borrower for fully six decades, and can claim with at least some narrative credibility (if not certain empirical evidence) to have contributed to India's economic achievements. Moreover, even if its legitimacy were not at issue, the Bank would have an interest in what India does for its financial model, and therefore for its (limited) autonomy from donor countries. India's unblemished repayment history on its unmatched volume of borrowing has been, and continues to be, a major contributor to the institution's cash flow. In short, for both material and ideational reasons, and particularly in view of India's great size and rising global profile, the Bank needs India as a borrower – and this need, in turn, gives India both influence over the Bank and the ability to resist the Bank's efforts to influence it.

Thus, the central argument of this book is that *the World Bank's enduring search for relevance in India requires it to be receptive to the Indian leadership's changing priorities for development assistance – so much so that India itself has become the primary author of the Bank's Country Assistance Strategy, especially with respect to the Bank's selective sub-national engagements.* Far from the image of a national state "in retreat," the Indian government is firmly in command of its relationship with the Bank, even as the processes of democratic and economic change are transforming the state. As Baldev Raj Nayar has recently argued, there is a pervasive "myth of the shrinking state" about India. In fact, he argues, liberalization, the resurgence of the private sector, and rapid economic growth all have "empowered and enabled" the state (2009). Debates over the diminishment and decline of the state miss the point, when the real questions concern how the various constraining *and* enabling faces of globalization make possible both change and continuity in national governance (Weiss 2003).

As this book will also argue, India possibly could be getting even *more* out of its relationship with the Bank – more effective uses of funds, more appropriate analytical work, and perhaps most importantly, more low-cost loans for its lagging states – if it adopted an even more assertive advocacy for its continuing interest in development assistance, while (paradoxically) giving the Bank greater freedom to experiment, especially at the state level. The Centre, understandably, wants to keep a careful eye on the states' external borrowing. As recent scholarship on fiscal federalism shows, the expectation that a central government will bail out fiscally wayward regions in the event of a crisis has encouraged proliferating sub-national debt, and contributed to significant financial problems, in several federal countries in recent years (Rodden 2006). Argentina is perhaps the most notorious poster-country for the perverse incentives that some kinds of federal arrangements can create for fiscal discipline and market reform (Wibbels 2005). But control is not always what it seems to be: as the analysis here will show, the Government of India's formal-legal authority over the states' borrowing has sometimes led the World Bank to engage in a kind of "insurance" lending to politically important states – as a way of incentivizing the Centre's continued support for state-level assistance generally – even to the point where the Bank itself has acquiesced to profligate policies and dubious reform commitment on the part of state-level leaders.

But while the Bank's state-level experiences have been mixed, sustained engagement and learning in states such as Andhra Pradesh and Orissa have brought some encouraging results – even if reform lessons have not traveled across states as readily as the Bank once hoped. As already noted, the Bank's recent engagement with India's lagging states has brought it to a contradictory juncture. States such as Bihar and Uttar Pradesh are poorer and far more populous than many low-income countries. It would be unfortunate if the Bank's recent engagement (or, in the case of UP, re-engagement) with these states were to be neglected within a few years. Yet as India as a whole verges on crossing the middle-income threshold, these states will lose eligibility for IDA credits, their cost of borrowing will rise considerably, and India's central government may have less interest in encouraging their relationships with the Bank. If any country could make the conceptual case for a reform of IDA that would provide continued access to concessionary loans for the poorest regions of the largest countries – where the fight to achieve the Millennium Development Goals (MDGs) will be won or lost – it is India.

## What this Book is *Not* About

It is important to make clear what this book is not intended to be. As already noted, it is about the Bank, not any other international financial institution or development assistance provider. It is about India, not any other large World Bank borrower, though it might be read with some interest by specialists on countries such as Argentina, Brazil, China, Indonesia, Mexico, Nigeria, Pakistan, and Russia – all large countries exhibiting sharp regional differences in developmental achievement and federal or quasi-federal institutional arrangements. But even though the World Bank itself has become increasingly interested in common challenges of federalism, there is an implicit conviction in this investigation that federal political economies are all so unique, in at least some key respects, that they must be closely studied on their own terms. Rob Jenkins, who takes a similar interest in how federalism and globalization interact in the Indian context, has pointed out that "federalism has never been a single, clearly definable entity, either in theory or practice" (2003: 600).

This book is not a thorough history of the Bank-India relationship – though it does seek to put its subject matter in a broader context. Surprisingly, given the depth of the Bank's engagement in India, no general history of the relationship has been written. But two comprehensive histories of the World Bank, the authoritative volume by Devesh Kapur, John P. Lewis, and Richard Webb (1997) and a similar earlier work by Edward Mason and Robert Asher (1973), both encompass extensive discussions of the Bank's experiences in India and attest to how deeply the country has influenced the institution. (In addition to these histories by outsiders, the Bank's own Operations Evaluation Department presents a concise and surprisingly self-critical analysis; Zanini 2001). Such histories help make sense of the Bank's bond with its largest borrower – why the relationship has been unique, how it has led the Bank to expand its mission and functions in ways that have impacted its work elsewhere, and where it might be headed as India now transitions to middle-income status.

On the borrower side, too, it is enlightening to note the Bank's role in the evolution of economic policy in India – the episodic appearances it makes in general works on India's political economy and development (e.g., Frankel 2005 [1978]; Nayar 2001; Panagariya 2008]. What is most striking, though, is how modest the Bank's contributions have been over the past couple of decades. The emphasis here will be on developments from about 1994 to 2009 (coincidentally, picking up about where the Kapur, Lewis, and Webb general Bank history leaves off).

This book is not a comprehensive analysis of democratic politics and economic reforms in India, though again, it seeks to situate the Bank-India relationship in the context of several interrelated transitions: toward regionalized coalition governments at the Centre, increased policy autonomy at the state level, reform of federal fiscal institutions, and liberalization of the investment regime across states. India's economic reform politics are so complex, especially when state-level experiences are considered, that a thorough discussion would require a book in its own right – if not several books.

This book is not about the ground-level impact of particular Bank-supported projects in India. Some readers, and particularly critics of the Bank, will be disappointed at the relative inattention to project impact (the limited discussions here rely on existing accounts, and break no new ground). There is already a fairly extensive literature in this area, and a main goal of this book is to re-conceptualize India's relationship with the Bank at a more aggregate level. The Bank's own evaluations of its project and program impact in India vary. On the one hand, in spite of incentives to be self-congratulatory, the Bank periodically does admit to poor outcomes. On the other hand, it tends to perceive project implementation and loan performance in India as better than in many other borrower countries. Independent scholarly accounts vary, and there is a strand of criticism that sees Bank interventions as having worse than indifferent impacts – as actually accentuating poverty, inequality, insecurity, and deprivation.

No doubt the Bank has contributed to some spectacular disasters in India, such as the infamous debacle over dam development on the Narmada River in the early 1990s, or more recently, the inexcusable corruption and fraud in several health projects that came to light during 2006–8 (both episodes are discussed in this book). Disappointing outcomes in some of the Bank's recent interventions in India, particularly related to privatizations in electricity and water, have been starkly at odds with its seemingly sure-footed (and, critics would say, arrogant) advice. But the Bank has also contributed, however modestly, to important successes in India's development. For example, even though methods associated with the Green Revolution in agriculture have created new ecological challenges (from groundwater depletion to excessive uses of fertilizers and pesticides), and even though the benefits have been spread unevenly across India's regions and social groups, the ending of chronic food shortages has been a transformative achievement. Similarly, the Bank's research, assistance, and advocacy should be credited for helping to bring greater attention, over the years, to the "social sectors" of primary education and health, and to the policy and institutional dimensions of growth. But arguably, the relationship between growth and poverty reduction remains insufficiently understood, and the Bank has given too much credence to the "science" of development and given too little heed to its "art" – failing to acknowledge, as Jessica Einhorn has put it, that "much is serendipitous about development" (2001: 30).

The Bank has no shortage of critics, both on the left and right, both Indian and non-Indian, both activist and academic in bearing. Among independent studies of the Bank, especially by non-economist social scientists, critical perspectives may well outnumber more favorable views. (This is an informed impression, not a formal count). The Bank's diverse detractors can be quite passionate in their beliefs. Given the charged atmosphere, there is a risk that polemicists on different sides of the "World Bank wars" will seize upon any new work, such as this book, to support their arguments. This book will try to offer a suitably objective analysis to be equally disappointing – and hopefully equally informative – to the Bank's left and right critics, and to the Bank's apologists. The nature of the research questions it pursues implies a closer engagement with officialdom than with civil society perspectives, or with the citizen subjects/objects of Bank-assisted development in India. To that extent, this is an "insider's" book, written by an outsider with some empathy for elite interests on both sides of the Bank-India relationship.[1] This book is not meant to engage with or refute existing accounts so much as to offer a different perspective, which corresponds more closely to how many World Bank and Indian officials themselves perceive their relationship. None of this is to suggest that such official views of the relationship are necessarily "truer" than outsider or subaltern perspectives. But as this book will show, official views do have real consequences – which is why the shortage of attention to them in much existing literature is so surprising and problematic.

On the subject of the Bank's critics, it is worth making two of this book's assumptions clear from the outset. One assumption is that the Indian state would pursue many of the same policies and actions it takes in the name of "development" even without the World Bank's assistance. Indeed, this is not a hypothetical claim: India's continuing pursuit of dam development on the Narmada River, more than a decade after the Bank's withdrawal from the socially and environmentally damaging scheme, should acquaint even the most casual observer with this point – which is why it has been so absurd to see protestors with "Save the Narmada" placards outside World Bank-IMF meetings in recent years. Put simply, some critics of World Bank projects commit a fallacy in assigning blame, responsibility, or merely causal impact to the Bank, when in fact they are "seeing the state" in action (to borrow a phrase from Corbridge, Williams, et al. 2005).

Note that the claim here is that India would do much of what it does in pursuit of development with or without World Bank *assistance* – *not* that state action would be the same in a world in which the Bank did not exist. That is a much more difficult counterfactual to ponder. Clearly, the Bank has played a leading role in proselytizing for liberalization and globalization the world over; trans-nationally, it is "the leading proponent of the 'project of development'," as Michael Goldman puts it. But Goldman significantly overreaches in calling the Bank "the world's most powerful international institution" (2005: xii).

Kenneth Surin makes an even more hyperbolic claim in calling the Bank an "unaccountable planetary executive" (2003).

To insist, almost by definition, that everything the Bank touches is part of a "grand illusion of development" and a "hegemonic" power structure (ibid., xvii, xviii)[5] is to fail to take seriously state power in the Indian context. And the misunderstanding of the relationship might have particular consequences for democratic debate and participation in India, to the extent that it shifts attention away from the state and toward its accomplice (to reverse the accusatory discourse). From an activist standpoint, such an approach might be understandable – indeed, as Margaret Keck and Kathryn Sikkink have shown, local non-governmental organizations (NGOs) and "transnational advocacy networks" have sometime found it easier to move international organizations than to leverage changes in state policies (1998). But the state must be kept in view, whether the goal is activism or academic understanding.

The Bank's more rightward critics tend not to have a problem perceiving state power – for them, it is often the root of all pathologies in Bank-supported development projects. If the signature concept for the Bank's left critics is its neoliberal hegemony, on the right it is more often seen as abetting a pathologically statist model of development, at best extraneous to the miracle of the market that is globalization, and at worst coddling bloated bureaucracies in borrower countries that would be better off subjected to the discipline of market forces. Shyam Kamath holds foreign aid, and especially World Bank assistance, responsible for "financing the leviathan state" in India throughout the Cold War, and continuing to give misplaced support to statist development to the detriment of the private sector (1992).

The bête noire for this anti-aid camp is corruption – the Bank itself is supposedly shot through with it, and it abets its insidious persistence within the governments and public sectors of its borrowers. Though recently there have been high-profile disclosures of significant official corruption in Bank-assisted projects in India, some perspective is in order. One does not have to condone corruption to concede that to some extent, it seems to be endemic to capitalist political economies, and that the "use of public office for private gain" may be particularly "rife during the period of early capitalist development" – as experiences elsewhere in Asia, from South Korea to China, have shown over the past half-century (and as the history of capitalism in the West also attests; Khan 2002: 165).

Again, this is not to apologize for the Bank's failures to exercise due diligence with respect to the use of its funds, but simply to suggest that the nature of private-public intercourse in India's economic transition would sustain significant levels of corruption even if the World Bank did not exist. And from another perspective, though there may be a compelling moral imperative behind the highly publicized anti-corruption initiatives that the Bank has pursued since the 1990s (however tinged in hypocrisy these can be seen to be), such interventions are likely to have limited impact and may be misguided. Former Bank official David Phillips argues succinctly, "It is by no means clear that corruption fighting is susceptible to Bank intervention" (2009: 131).

In sum, as Mushtaq Khan has articulated so well,

> Without excusing corruption, international agencies have to face up to the fact that the construction of capitalism, although it may be necessary for the long-term prosperity of poor counties, is itself an ugly and conflictual process. Attempts to attain a corruption-free, representative and accountable system of governance at this stage may not only not be achievable, but may divert attention away from what actually needs to be done to improve the quality of state intervention to accelerate the transition and make it more socially acceptable (2002: 165).

Finally, let us reemphasize that this book is about power and influence in the country assistance relationship between India and the World Bank: it is primarily about who sets the terms for the Bank's lending and analytical work *in India*. To some extent, it is also about how India's needs and preferences, and the Bank's own interpretations of experiences in India, have shaped the Bank's broader perspectives and operations in the field of development.

This book is not primarily about India's role in the World Bank's *overall* governance. In particular, it is not about India's (still quite limited) decision-making power within the Bank's formal governance structures – the Board of Directors or the more remote Governors. There is a substantial literature on official governance in the Bank, much of it highly critical of the weighted voting arrangements that vest considerable formal authority in rich donor countries (especially the US). There have been numerous proposals for reform of the Bank's governance, some of them quite inventive and persuasive (e.g. Jakobeit 2005; Woods 2006, 2005). This book makes no serious effort to engage with this kind of work – not because it is unimportant, but because such grand designs tend to run up against the same quandary that has quashed reform proposals for other key global governance institutions: significant formal changes would have to be worked out through the existing system.

Formal governance in the Bretton Woods institutions is at least somewhat more flexible than in, say, the UN Security Council, in that weighted voting can adjust a bit to reflect new participation patterns in the financing of the institutions – which is why countries like Brazil, China, and India have been working to reposition themselves less as borrowers and recipients and more as donors and contributors. Major changes probably will be incremental and slow, however, and China's influence probably will continue to expand well ahead of India's. But at least as important as formal governance is to recognize that India exercises significant *informal* influence in the World Bank. In fact, its influence may be even greater than that of the other Asian giant, given what the Bank's work in India – the longest-running client and a democratic crucible in the global challenge of poverty alleviation – contributes to its broader legitimacy.

### The World Bank's Story, or India's?

To insist that this book is a study of the assistance relationship between the World Bank and India might be to beg the question, "But is it really the World Bank's story, or really India's story?" Again, it is an analysis of the *relationship* between borrower and lender. This is not an evasive answer. In the discipline of sociology, for example, it is a commonly accepted analytical practice to treat the relationship as a "unit of analysis," giving attention both to material exchanges and to mutually constitutive processes of identity formation. In political science, which studies power relations converging around the state, there is a similar growing consensus that power must be understood both as material capability and as influence – an inherently relational concept.

### Plan of the Book

Chapter One, "The First Half-Century: From Bretton Woods to India's Liberalization Era," will establish the background for understanding the relationship through the 1990s (the remainder of the book will focus on the last fifteen years). This history will show how in many ways, India and the World Bank have grown up together. Yet it also will make clear that for most of their shared six decades, the Bank has confronted significant challenges in terms of its influence on India's economic policies. Even India's 1991 macroeconomic liberalization, while supported by stabilization and structural adjustment loans from the IMF and the Bank, proved to be something of a false start for the renewed relevance of the Bank.

Chapter Two, "Remaining Relevant: The Reform Strategy for an India of States," will analyze a major innovation in the Bank's country assistance strategy for India, beginning in the mid-1990s. The Bank resolved to disaggregate the large federal country, and to focus its assistance on India's lead reforming states with a view to encouraging powerful "demonstration effects" that would lead non-reforming states to embrace similar changes in policies, institutions, and governance. From the Bank's perspective, such "selectivity" was a concession to the maxim, "India is too big for the Bank." Though the Bank pursued focus-state lending as a way of enhancing its relevance in India,

New Delhi was an integral partner – ultimately, the senior partner – in the strategy.

Chapter Three, "Reasserting Central Government Control, Reorienting Aid Toward 'Lagging States'," will discuss an impasse that would confront the focus states strategy by around 2004, and the reasons for yet another significant shift in the Bank's approach. Having begun to address the challenge of state-level reforms and fiscal deficit reductions, the Indian government turned attention to a different concern: the widening gaps in per-capita income and poverty rates among India's richest and poorest states. At the behest of the Indian government, the World Bank's Country Assistance Strategy embraced the new concept of "lagging states," and proclaimed that the Bank's state-level lending would place a special emphasis on those states with the highest concentrations of poverty and the lowest human development indicators.

Chapter Four, "A Bittersweet Graduation. Can IDA hold on to India, and Will India Let It?" will discuss the critical juncture now confronting the Bank-India relationship. The Bank's new emphasis on lagging states has brought into sharp relief "the two Indias," in which the per-capita incomes between the wealthiest states, such as Gujarat and Maharashtra, and the poorest states, such as Bihar and Jharkhand, diverge by as much as five to one. But on the wings of its recent rapid economic growth, India as a whole now stands at the cusp of ineligibility to borrower from the Bank's IDA facility for low-income countries. Some of the donor countries that fund IDA appear especially eager to devote a greater share of its resources to the group of Heavily Indebted and Poor Countries (HIPC), concentrated largely in sub-Saharan Africa. Were India to "graduate" from IDA,[6] its relationship with the Bank would likely become more like that of Brazil, China, and other large middle-income countries who borrow from the Bank on market terms, and who increasingly have turned to alternative sources of financing that carry less stringent conditionality than the Bank's safeguard- and procedure-laden loans. This penultimate chapter will discuss the material reasons why the Bank would stand to suffer a significant loss of financial and operational autonomy if it loses India as its largest borrower, as well as what the implications of such a change might be for the Bank's self-image and legitimacy. The chapter will also discuss India's own ambivalent perspective on its possible graduation out of IDA.

The concluding chapter, "India's Changing Relationship to Global Development Assistance," will discuss what could be a pivotal global governance arena for India as an emerging power in the years ahead. New Delhi is intent on repositioning India in the development assistance regime, moving from the role of borrower to donor and partner, following a similar transition that China has made over the past decade or so. This impulse is understandable, but it may place too much emphasis on formal decision-making in the Bretton Woods institutions, and may lead India to give up some of the more subtle forms of power and influence it has possessed as a leading borrower – not to mention the loss of cheap money. This final chapter will also reflect on the long and winding road that is the Bank-India relationship, and how their shared experiences enhance our understanding of some of the most profound forces shaping the global political economy today – the relationship between democratic change and economic reform, the uneasy balance between growth and equality, and the aspiration to voice and influence of emerging powers.

## Methodological Note and Literature Discussion: An Integrated Perspective

The remainder of this introduction will briefly discuss the theoretical foundations for the empirical analysis presented in this book. This study is primarily a close analysis of what Harry Eckstein (1975) calls a "crucial case."[7] As Timothy McKeown suggests,

> Cases are often more important for their value in clarifying previously obscure theoretical relationships than for providing an additional observation to be added to a sample. In the words of one ethnographer, a good case is not necessarily a "typical" case, but rather a "telling" case, in which "the particular circumstances surrounding a case serve to make previously obscure theoretical relationships sufficiently apparent."
>
> Case studies are often undertaken because the researcher expects that the clarification of causal mechanisms in one case will have implications for understanding causal mechanisms in other cases. […] Whether a causal account that fits one historical circumstance will fit others is an open question (2004: 153; in-quote from Mitchell 1984: 239).

Ultimately, it is my contention that the evolution of the assistance relationship between the World Bank and India is worth understanding on its own terms, but it may also have broader implications for change in the international financial institutions (IFIs), states in the global economy, and the political economy of reform in federal democratic countries.

### The World Bank and its Borrowers

Broadly speaking, research in international political economy has tended to approach the international financial institutions in one of two ways. Traditional state-centric theories of international relations (IR), of both the neorealist and neoliberal varieties, are skeptical that international organizations generally should be understood as "actors in their own right" in the international political economy. At best, international organizations are instruments through which sovereign states, the most important actors in an anarchic international system, can somewhat mitigate uncertainty by coordinating to manage collective action problems. As Stephen Krasner argues, international organizations are "only one small step removed from the underlying [state] power configurations that support them" (1985: 28). Hence, state-centric accounts have tended to focus on the power and influence of the major shareholder countries – particularly the United States – in the international financial institutions and development banks.

This focus on the most powerful member states continues to engage analysts, even if more recent studies have given somewhat greater attention to civil society influences and internal organizational dynamics. Scholarly attention to rich country influence in the IFIs is not limited to works in conventional state-centric IR theory. For example, Robert Wade, a specialist on the political economy of development, argues that "American values and interests" are of "determining importance" to the functioning of the Bank (1996: 35). More recently, a book by Sarah Babb (a sociologist and a specialist on the evolution of economic policymaking in Mexico; 2004) breaks new ground by going "inside the beltway" to investigate how US domestic politics, such as congressional wrangling over aid allocations, influence the ideas and activities of the World Bank (and its regional multilateral development bank counterparts). In essence, she argues, "Washington politics" shape US policies toward the multilateral development banks, and US policies in turn shape the banks' "organizational trajectories" (2009: 3).

However important donor country preferences and politics might be, a thorough conception of the World Bank must also come to terms with other influences on its ideas and activities. The second major approach to research on the IFIs has been rooted in organization theory, occupying a cross-disciplinary space at the intersection of political science and sociology. The approach owes much to the great pioneer of that field of study, Max Weber, and his concepts of rational-legal authority and the "indispensability of technically expert administration" (Bendix 1977 [1960]: 465). Michael Barnett and Martha Finnemore argue that international organizations such as the World Bank should be understood as bureaucracies, and "can become autonomous sites of authority, independent from the state 'principals' who may have created them, because of power flowing from…the legitimacy of the rational-legal authority they embody, and… [their] control over technical expertise and information."[8] International organizations, in this perspective, may also develop their own goals – or their own interpretations of goals handed to them by states – along with their own distinctive modes of functioning based on their internal divisions of labor and organizational capacities. They may effectively adapt and learn in response to new, or newly defined, problems (Haas 1990), but they also may be prone to dysfunctional, self-defeating, even "pathological" and "hypocritical" behaviors (Barnett and Finnemore 2004; Weaver 2008). In sum, international organizations may be chartered by states to serve state interests, but once born, they assume a life of their own – refining and reinterpreting their missions, developing expertise and capabilities that may confer on them significant authority in their specialized domains, and evolving an organizational culture and interest in self-preservation.

Both the state-centric and organizational approaches to the World Bank help to illuminate important aspects of its sprawling operations, and the question is not "which approach is better" but rather "how does putting the two together help us to understand patterns of continuity and change" in the Bank's agenda and actions. As Michelle Miller-Adams points out, in an innovative study of the Bank's private sector, civil society, and governance agendas in the 1990s,

> The World Bank is a prominent actor in the international system, created by states to help govern that system and subject to the kind of state-centered analysis that has dominated the study of international relations. Yet it is also a large and complex institution that enjoys significant autonomy in its operations and goal-setting; hence, it can be analyzed using the tools of organization theory. Each of these approaches provides only a partial picture of the dynamics that drive institutional change at the World Bank" (1999: 9).

Recent scholarship employing principal-agent theory can be seen as an effort at bridge building between the state-centric IR approach and the organizational sociology approach (Hawkins, Lake et al. 2006). While there may be promise in the continued development of principal-agent theory for the study of the World Bank and related institutions, early attempts at constructing formal models have produced relatively limited insights, with clear applicability only in particular issue areas (such as environmental reforms; see Nielson and Tierney 2005, 2003). This is not to criticize the approach, but rather to suggest that a more inductive case-study approach might contribute just as much to our understanding of interactions between states and international organizations.

So far a deficiency in much of the principal-agent work on the IFIs has been an inattention to borrower countries. Most of the theoretical work has equated "principals" with the countries holding the largest shares of formal voting power in the governance of the institutions, and misses the possibility that borrower governments, too, might "delegate" certain functions to such organizations.[9] This is an odd omission, given that there is a well-established perspective in IR known as "two-level game" analysis (as noted earlier in this introduction), which argues that state leaders sometime use commitments to international institutions to help overcome domestic political constraints that might otherwise thwart their ability to implement preferred policies. For example Robert Putnam, who first suggested the two-level game concept, argues that IMF stabilization programs are often "misleadingly criticized as externally imposed," when in fact reform-minded state leaders use IMF "pressure" as an excuse to enact austerity measures that they would not be able to push through in the course of normal domestic politics (1998: 457; Vreeland 2003 makes a similar point).[10] As we shall see here, during the mid-1990s the Indian government embraced the World Bank's state-level reform lending strategy for similar reasons.

Thus, the literature on states and the international financial institutions should be attentive to the possibility that borrowers, too, might view the organizations as working "for them." Certainly, large developing countries such as China, India, and Brazil perceive their relationships with the lenders in this way, at least in certain contexts. But in much of the literature, to the extent that borrowers are seen as having any significant power vis-à-vis the Bank, it is generally a passive-aggressive trait at best – the ability to borrow money while agreeing to, but ultimately failing to adhere to, the policy "conditionality" attached to the loans. Miles Kahler (1992), Paul Mosley and colleagues (1995), and Tony Killick (1998) have described how the Bank's own interest in continuing to lend can weaken the credibility of its threats to withhold assistance if borrowers fail to follow through on reform commitments. This may be an adequate way of conceiving of the power of borrowers that are highly dependent on development assistance, such as many African states.[11] But there is a world of difference between the Bank's relationships with such borrowers as compared to the clout of the Asian giants. The latter do not need to borrow from the Bank – however useful they may still find its financial and non-lending services. Mega-borrowers such as China and India do not need to engage in the "ritual dance" (Callaghy 1989) of pro forma promise-making to secure access to World Bank loans, because if they do not agree with the Bank's policy advice, they simply ignore it, and if the Bank threatens to withhold assistance, they simply make do without it.

Some analysts have acknowledged the differences in borrower power between, say, Chad and China. Miller-Adams suggests,

> The limited voting power of borrowers understates the influence they can wield. Borrowing countries have a say in Bank policies, although theirs tends to be a 'negative' power, the power to say no rather than to place a new issue on the institution's agenda. This source of influence has its roots in the Bank's steady expansion and historical equation of success with higher lending levels. In order for the Bank to grow, and before it can request a capital increase, demand for its loans must rise, and that demand

comes from borrowers. Thus, borrowers exert control over the Bank by their willingness or unwillingness to accept the conditions of Bank lending. Those borrowers that have access to other sources of capital (such as middle-income countries that can now borrow on private markets) and large countries in which the Bank needs to do business in order to maintain its loan volume (such as China) are more powerful than the smaller and poorer developing countries (1999: 10–11).

But even this more differentiated perspective may understate the influence of mega-borrowers such as China and India. Even if they are not directly "placing a new issue on the Bank's agenda" (and a decade later, this contention seems less credible), they are forcing the Bank constantly to innovate new assistance strategies in a bid to stay relevant. In a very real sense, then, it is the Bank that is the supplicant in its relations with such countries, not the other way around. It faces strong material and ideational incentives to remain engaged in these countries, so it must innovate its assistance programs in ways that appeal to state authorities. And as suggested earlier, this is even more the case for India than for China or any other large-volume borrower, given the unparalleled depth and breadth of the Bank's engagement in India.

Probably the best single volume on the IFI's relationships with their borrowers, in terms of offering a balanced theoretical perspective and rich empirical analysis, is Ngaire Woods' *The Globalizers: The IMF, The World Bank, and Their Borrowers* (2006). Notwithstanding that Woods analyzes both Bretton Woods institutions, her study, more than any other, complements the integrated perspective on the World Bank in this book. Woods offers the image of a World Bank "riding three horses at once" – first, held accountable to powerful donor governments and influenced by their political preferences; second, influenced by the economistic and technical orientation of its staff as well as internal bureaucratic politics; and third, relying heavily on relationships with borrowing governments (2006: 4). Woods well might have added a fourth horse in the form of pressures from civil society, nongovernmental organizations (NGOs), and transnational activists, since her nuanced and thorough analysis offers evidence of their influence. But it is in taking borrower power, in particular, more seriously than most studies that Woods makes a significant contribution to our understanding of the Bretton Woods "globalizers." She offers rich case studies of relations between the institutions and a diverse set of borrower case studies: Mexico, Russia, and the region of sub-Saharan Africa (with a particular focus on Senegal and Zambia).

But valuable as it is, Woods' book says almost nothing about the Bank's relationship with India, apart from discussing the mid-1960s economic crisis (which will be discussed here, in the following chapter). There is essentially no discussion of Bank's relationship with India during the last forty-five years. The discussion of China is also quite limited. This is not to single out for criticism one of the best books on the World Bank in many years; the inattention to its relations with India (and China) is widespread in the scholarly literature.[12] This is a significant lacuna, for surely these two rising powers are now among the most influential actors in the global political economy, and will continue to demand greater voice in global governance arenas. The World Bank will be an important component of that agenda, and to understand what kind of Bank they will want, it is important to understand what their experiences with the Bank have been.

### The Political Economy of Reform in India

The two-level game concept pivots our analysis of the Bank-India relationship into the domestic political arena of the world's largest democracy. The complex political economy of development and reform in India has spawned a substantial body of scholarly literature (e.g. Bardhan 1998 [1984]; Desai 2005; Frankel 2005 [1978]; Jenkins 1999; Mooij 2005; Mukherji 2007; Panagariya 2008; Nayar 2007a, 2001; and many others). India's economic transition has transpired amid a great transformation in its democratic politics, which itself has been the subject of a rich descriptive and explanatory literature (e.g. Chakrabarty 2006; Chandra 2004; Chhibber and Nooruddin 2004; Corbridge and Harriss 2000; Ganguly, Diamond et al. 2007; Jayal 2006). One of the most interesting lines of research has attempted to understand the interaction of economic liberalization and federalism in India (Jenkins 2003; Rao and Singh 2005; Sáez 2002; Sridharan 2003) and to explain that variations in development across India's states that have become even more pronounced during the reforms era (Jenkins 2004; Kennedy 2004; Sinha 2005).

Rather than attempting to summarize this vast corpus here, it will suffice, for the moment, to relate a concise list compiled by Lloyd and Susanne Rudolph – easily the most versatile American political scientists specializing in India's politics, political economy, and international relations – of the "challenges and changes" confronting India's democracy since the 1990s:

1. *A more prominent role for federal states in India's political system.* The states are making themselves heard and felt politically and economically more than they ever have in the half-century since India gained its independence from Britain.
2. *The transformation of the party system.* The era of dominance by the Indian National Congress has ended. Congress remains a major party, but it must now operate within a multiparty system that includes not only the nationally influential BJP [Bhartiya Janata Party], but a host of significant regional and state-based parties as well.

3. *Coalition government.* Stable central governments based on parliamentary majorities have given way to coalition governments that must depend on constellations of regional parties. In this regard, India has become like Italy or Israel, both places where small parties can make or break governments and thereby affect the whole nation.

4. *A federal market economy.* Economic liberalization has been marked by a decline in public investment and a rise in private investment, the displacement of the federal Planning Commission by the market, and the emergence of the states as critical actors in economic reform and growth. The result has contributed to a transformation of India's federal system.

5. *The central government as regulator.* Despite what the above points might suggest, India's central government is not fading away. The Centre is holding on, but its role has changed. The Centre had previously acted as an intervenor; now it acts as a regulator. In the economic realm, it monitors the initiatives of the several states. It tries (albeit mostly without success) to enforce fiscal discipline. In the political realm, the Centre acts – through regulatory institutions such as the Supreme Court, the presidency, and the Election Commission – to ensure fairness and accountability. Since the emergence of the first coalition government in 1989, this role as 'policeman' or honest broker has grown, while the interventionist institutions, the cabinet, and parliament, have waned in significance.

6. *A social revolution.* In most states, and to a significant extent at the Centre as well, there has been a net flow of power from the upper to the lower castes. Indian politics has experienced a sociopolitical revolution that, in varna terms, has meant a move from a Brahmin (priests, intellectuals) toward a shudra (toilers) raj.

7. *Centralism has held against extremism.* The imperatives of centrist politics have checked the momentum of Hindu fundamentalism. India's diverse and pluralist society, the rise of coalition politics, and the need to gain the support of the median voter have transformed the Hindu-nationalist BJP from an extremist to a centrist party" (2008 [2002]: 313).

The confluence of all these political trends – decentralization, party regionalization, lower-caste mobilization, religio-cultural nationalism, and, cutting across all of the others, two decades' worth of coalition government – has had untold implications for India's economic liberalization. Simply put, it is impossible to make sense of the recent course of economic policy, reform, and development in India without an appreciation for how it has been "embedded" in a web of political and social change.[13] India's complex democratic process has constrained the scope and speed of economic reforms, but it has also helped to legitimize liberalization by giving voice to interests previously subordinated during the earlier decades of dominance – by the Congress Party in the political sphere, and central planning in the economic sphere.

Not all analysts would agree with this perspective. Prabhat Patnaik, for example, has consistently argued that India's economic reforms have been brought about through the abridgement of democracy (2003, 2000; Patnaik and Chandrasekhar 2007, 1998). He argues that the support base for reforms is narrow, and makes much of the fact that many of the people involved in economic policymaking have worked previously at the IMF or the World Bank. He even suggests that globalization has been responsible for the intensification of divisive, distracting politics of communalism, fundamentalism, regionalism, and secessionism.

Of particular salience for our purposes is the recurring contention that India's economic liberalization was somehow imposed by the Bretton Woods institutions and their agents within the Indian central ministries. Amit Bhaduri and Deepak Nayyar (1996) emphasize the role of IMF and World Bank pressure in bringing about the 1991 economic reforms. They recognize that a severe balance-of-payments crisis had to be addressed, but maintain that it need not have been interpreted as an indication of fundamental flaws in India's developmental model. It is perhaps understandable that the Bretton Woods institutions would loom large in accounts written not long after the early 1990s crisis, which triggered their interventions in the form of stabilization and structural adjustment loans. But Suresh Tendulkar and T.A. Bhavani note, with some bemusement, "The socialists and the Left parties still refuse to accept the legitimacy of liberalization and globalization calling them as 'Fund-Bank policies' – a good thirteen years after the Fund-Bank package of 1991 was successfully completed in 1993" (2007: 163).

Jos Mooij, a Dutch political scientist, offers a sensible rejoinder to the view that India's liberalization was externally imposed:

> …there was a significant amount of willingness, if not eagerness, among Indian policymakers as well… Moreover, it is also important to keep in mind that, although the economic policy changes may seem huge in India, as compared to many other developing countries that went through an adjustment process, India's experience is one of gradualism, with the national government very much in charge (2005: 25).

As noted earlier, Baldav Raj Nayar takes this line of argument even further, contending that globalization and liberalization have augmented and empowered the Indian state. We will return to this theme later in the book.

The most significant political economy changes, in terms of India's relationship with the World Bank, have been the rise of regional parties, the "new normal" mode of coalition government at the Centre (and in many states), and the sharing of decision-making authority between Centre and states in the new "federal market economy." Later chapters will discuss in some detail the federal and coalition government challenges confronting the reform-minded leadership in New Delhi.

But first let us turn to what was, at least on the face of it, a simpler era.

# Chapter One

# THE FIRST HALF-CENTURY: FROM BRETTON WOODS TO INDIA'S LIBERALIZATION ERA

*Policy was not "formulated." It was formed. It evolved. It resulted from events.*

Leonard Rist, head of the World Bank's Economic Department, 1961[1]

*India was the Jewel in the Crown of the World Bank [...] The reputation of the Bank tended to be measured in terms of what it could do for India.*

A senior World Bank official, ca. 1995 (Caufield 1996: 23)

*The India Department has one job – to lend money to India. Of course, every country department pushes its own country, but for years, during the Cold War, India held a special position as the largest nonaligned democracy. The donor community treated it with kid gloves for years – and the India department still thinks that way.*

A World Bank staff member, ca. 1995 (ibid., 23)

*India has always been a reluctant partner.*

Edwin Lim, World Bank Country Director for India, 1996–2002 (2005: 108)

India and the Bank have grown up together. Edward Mason and Robert Asher, in a history of the Bank's first three decades, say simply, "It is no exaggeration to say that India has influenced the Bank as much as the Bank has influenced India" (1973: 675). Catherine Caufield, writing in the mid-1990s, remarked of the then half-century that the Bank and India had traveled together, "As greater and greater sums of money passed between them, the Bank succeeded in putting its imprint on India, but India's imprint on the Bank is just as deep" (1996: 23). A more recent report by the Bank's own semi-independent Operations Evaluation Department (OED) puts it succinctly and incisively: "India was one of the Bank's founding members, is still one of the Bank's main borrowers, and has had a major influence on the Bank's understanding of development" (Zanini 2001: 9).

This chapter will discuss the evolution of the Bank-India relationship, from the Bank's origins and India's independence in the mid-1940s, until India's early-1990s embarkation on a course of economic liberalization. It is not a comprehensive history of the lender-client connection; the range of Bank activities relating to its largest cumulative borrower would provide enough material to fill many volumes. Rather, the approach here is thematic and episodic, focusing on key issues in Bank-India relations during different historical phases, and on critical junctures that pushed their association in new directions.

India's influence on the World Bank – on both its understanding of development, and on its organization and operations – comes through clearly in comprehensive histories of the institution (see for example Kapur et al. 1997; Mason and Asher 1973). Similarly, the general literature on India's political economy and development policies also makes clear both the importance and the limits of the Bank's role in the country (see for example Frankel 2005 [1978]; Panagariya 2008; Nayar 2001). Recently, Bank-sponsored studies, such as the OED report noted above, have focused directly on understanding the relationship with India (Zanini 2001).

But whereas the existing scholarly literature has emphasized either the Bank perspective or the Indian perspective on their exchanges, and the Bank's own analyses are meant to offer direct policy lessons for its operations, the purpose of this chapter is to show more generally what both Bank and borrower bring to the table, and how their partially overlapping but also divergent incentives have interacted to shape their relations over the years.

The Bank faces strong internal incentives – both ideational and material – to conduct itself with a special deference toward India. As one of the giants of the developing world, as the first major decolonization case, as a paradigmatic model of import substitution industrialization (ISI) and central planning when many development economists held a favorable regard for these approaches, and as a country that has remained democratic for almost its entire post-Independence history, India has occupied an incomparable position in the Bank's understanding of development and poverty reduction. At times, especially early on in their shared history and more recently during India's liberalization era, Bank and Indian views on economic policies have been fairly closely aligned. During other periods, especially from the mid-1960s through the 1980s, their perspectives diverged. What is remarkable about the divergent phase, however, is the Bank's reluctance to confront the Indian leadership, and its willingness to subordinate policy disagreements to the ongoing task of project lending in India, given the significant role of the country portfolio in sustaining the Bank's overall operations and subjective understanding of its own global relevance.

For its part, India has engaged the Bank from a complex and shifting combination of motivations, which have ranged from an idealistic view of the Bank as a servant and advocate for the developing countries, to an indifferent or even hostile reaction to the Bank's advice (especially when such counsel is seen as reflecting rich country pressures), to the instrumental utilization of the Bank's resources and technical authority to tip the balance in domestic political competition over the direction of India's economic policy. Only a few other large borrowers – China perhaps, or Brazil – are so consistently in command of their interactions with the Bank, and *no* other country has experienced the same depth of continual engagement with the Bank as India has.

The first part of the chapter examines the early years of the Bank-India relationship, when the Indian leadership became fixed in its view of an active role in the Bank's management and determined not to be a passive recipient of aid. In the 1950s, Bank assistance to India played a significant role in helping to underwrite the country's capital-intensive ISI strategy. During that decade, as the US Cold War doctrine of Containment expanded to focus increasingly on Asia, India came to be seen as strategically important and Western aid sustained it through repeated food and foreign exchange shortages. Rich countries supported the innovation of new institutions to meet India's needs, in particular the Aid-India Consortium and the International Development Association (IDA) under the World Bank's aegis.

But as India's food and foreign exchange problems persisted, and as its foreign policy of nonalignment sometimes shaded into criticisms of US policy and closer relations with Moscow, the donors took an increasingly critical view of India's Plan approach and sought to condition aid on significant agricultural, industrial, and trade policy reforms. In 1966, on the understanding that the Bank would arrange for continued balance of payments support and other assistance through the Consortium, India undertook the first devaluation of the rupee since 1949 amid considerable internal debate. When the devaluation proved politically explosive, India backtracked from other reforms – with the notable exception of agriculture – and embarked on a path of intensified state control over industry and trade through the 1970s.

In the wake of India's aborted liberalization, the World Bank found itself in a struggle it has been fighting, with only fleeting respites, ever since: a struggle to remain relevant to an Indian leadership determined to minimize the country's dependence on external assistance, and vigilant of its sovereignty in economic statecraft. The specific tactics employed by the Bank to curry favor with the Indian leadership have evolved over the subsequent decades; through the 1970s and 1980s, the Bank's operative principle was to lend India as much as possible, and to avoid any policy discussion that might turn contentious – even as the Bank's guiding philosophy and lending elsewhere evolved toward neoliberalism and structural adjustment.

In the early 1990s, the Bank engaged a more pro-market Indian leadership in a genuine reform dialogue while experimenting with new ways of targeting its lending portfolio. India's 1990–1 balance of payments crisis was even more serious than the situation a quarter century earlier had been, and this time the Indian government embarked on a much more comprehensive and elite-consensus-driven liberalization program. For a time, it looked as though the Bank would be closely involved in India's reforms, but after an initial run of three quick-disbursing Structural Adjustment Loans (SALs) in the early 1990s, the Indian leadership became more sensitive to the need to maintain a broad political consensus in favor of liberalization, India's politics became increasingly fragmented, and the government made it clear that it would follow its own pace on policy change.

For the Bank, the alternative to a major programmatic role in Indian policy-making historically has been a steady stream of investment projects (though the line between "project lending" and "program lending" often blurs). However, as India's liberalization has expanded its borrowing options, the Bank has had to work harder to retain its appeal to the Indian government, particularly with respect to large-scale infrastructure investment. The chapter will conclude with an examination of a critical case, the Sardar Sarovar scheme on India's Narmada River, which became one of the most controversial projects in the Bank's history after Indian and Western nongovernmental organizations (NGOs) called attention to significant social and environmental problems associated with it. The activists lobbied donor governments to pressure the Bank to commission an in-depth independent investigation, which resulted in a recommendation that the Bank reconsider its lending for the project. Ultimately, rather than submit to Bank pressure to address the resettlement and ecological problems, India withdrew its loan request and pressed ahead without the Bank's assistance.

In sum, this selective survey of the history shows how the basic problem of "relevance" – a word heard repeatedly in conversations with dozens of Bank staff in 2003–8 – has been a defining challenge in the Bank's relationship with its largest borrower. All of this experience would lead up to a profound sense of frustration and lack of direction on the Bank's part by the mid-1990s. The next chapters will show how the Bank has attempted to break out of this pattern through significant changes to its assistance strategy since that time.

## The Early Years: An Era of Good Feelings

Though India was still three years away from Independence, it was an active participant at the 1944 Bretton Woods Conference, consistent with the internationalist goals of Jawaharlal Nehru and other leaders of the Indian independence movement. The Indian delegation sought to shape the Articles of

Agreement of the IBRD and its sister institution, the IMF, in ways that would favor the interests of developing countries.

While its influence on the Fund was more limited, India did succeed in pressing for a specific reference to the needs of the "less developed countries" in the Bank's charter (Kapur et al. 1997: 60). New Delhi's delegates pushed to give "due regard" to the "fair representation to the nationals of member countries" in the organization's staff. This wording was rejected by the Anglo-American sponsors of the conference; in its place, the Bank's Articles of Agreement promised to give "due regard to the importance of recruiting personnel on as wide a geographical basis as possible," with the caveat that staffing would be "subject to the paramount importance of securing the highest standards of efficiency and technical competence."[2] By 1971, India's contribution of 59 nationals to the Bank's professional staff was surpassed by only four countries – the US (370), Britain (198), France (88), and West Germany (77) (Mason and Asher 1973: 69).

India did not achieve all of its goals for the IBRD. At the inaugural meeting of the Board of Governors in Savannah, Georgia in early 1946, India backed Britain's John Maynard Keynes in the view that the Bank (and the Fund) should be located in New York, like the new UN General Assembly, so as not to be too closely associated with the capital of one nation. The American preference for locating the Bretton Woods institutions in Washington, DC – just blocks from the White House and US Treasury – prevailed (ibid., 37).

India scored a serendipitous victory at Bretton Woods by virtue of the smoldering tension between the Soviet Union and the West, as the United States and Britain took the lead in steering the conference agenda. Originally, the five member countries entitled to appoint an Executive Director (ED) were to have been the US, Britain, the Soviet Union, China, and France. When the Soviets declined to ratify the Bank's Articles, however, India moved into fifth place (ibid., 29). While the Executive Board has since expanded, and India's share power has declined, it retains effective control of an ED (who also represents several of its South Asian neighbors). Most importantly, its membership on the very first Board reinforced its leaders' belief that they had an important role to play in shaping the emerging international financial architecture. India has always seen itself as an active and important governing member of the World Bank, and not merely a "client."

For the first two decades (the mid-1940s to mid-1960s), the Bank's relationship with India was quite amiable. India's economic policies – import substitution industrialization, or ISI, with a heavy emphasis on state-owned enterprises in key "commanding heights" sectors such as heavy industry, railways, and energy – were generally supported by prevailing intellectual currents in the new field of development economics.[3] India, the thinking went, needed external assistance as a supplement to domestic savings, to finance capital-intensive projects such as roads, power plants, and dams. This fit well with the Bank's own need to establish a strong credit rating for the bonds it offered on private capital markets, and to retain the confidence of the wealthy member countries that provided the guarantees behind its paper.

The early Bank was particularly interested in lending for specific projects, which, it sought to convince investors, would be sound investments. In 1949, the Bank's first loan to India – for a railways project – was preceded by a lengthy discussion in the Executive Board over whether it was "safe" to lend US$100 million to a developing country (ibid., 181). Still, the Bank's rich country members perceived loans for "brick-and-mortar" infrastructure projects as carrying lesser risks than lending to support a borrower's general development "program" or balance of payments. As Devesh Kapur, John P. Lewis, and Richard Webb explain, "Visibility, verifiability, and apparent productivity were the touchstones for projecting an image of supervised, controlled, safe 'quality' lending" (1997: 122). Roads, power plants, and dams were "tangible." But Lewis also suggests, "Some of the rationale for the bias in favor of projects was illusory: it was not, in fact, possible to insulate project performance from the national policy environment" (1993: 17).

India could generate plenty of projects. But India also desired the Bank's dollar-denominated loans as a source of precious foreign exchange for the import of capital goods – factory equipment and machine tools, for example – needed to establish self-sufficient industries. The Bank's "project focus," Indian officials felt, was "too rigid" and would not give India sufficient flexibility with respect to imports. B.K. Nehru, India's Commissioner General for Economic Affairs (and the nephew of Prime Minister Jawaharlal Nehru), complained to the Bank's Davidson Sommers at the time of the 1949 railways loan, "We're going to have to pick so many projects… it will just take too damn long to get the total [lending volume] that we need." Sommers replied that so long as the Bank could formally dress up its loans as for particular projects, then for practical purposes India could consider the assistance as being "just as flexible as a balance of payments loan" (Kapur et al. 1997: 123).

Thus, from the very beginning, the Bank has sought to accommodate Indian needs and preferences, even as it has pursued its own agenda in order to shore up its finances and institutional viability. Reflecting on the Bank's early lending to developing countries, Kapur, Lewis, and Webb observe,

India was to become the Bank's steadiest and largest borrower. Impressed by the moral and intellectual qualities of India's leaders and civil service, the Bank developed an unusually respectful and constructive relationship with that country. Though most lending to India has taken the form of project loans, the Bank's supportive and respective attitude to the Indian government meant that, in effect, lending to India took on the characteristics of program lending (1997: 101).

*Sub rosa*, the possibility of sharper differences of opinion lurked. For example, when World Bank President Eugene Black (1949–63) first visited India in 1952, he was "vexed by what he considered India's doctrinaire and unrealistic discrimination against private capital and its unjustifiable preference for industrializing through investment in the public sector" (Mason and Asher 1973: 372). In 1956, he wrote to Indian finance minister T.T. Krishnamachari, "I have the distinct impression that the potentialities of private enterprise are commonly underestimated in India and that its operations are subjected to unnecessary restriction" (ibid., 372).

The comments were relatively minor points in an overall friendly letter, but when they made their way into a Calcutta newspaper, an outcry rose up against Black's "hidden threat" and "humiliating conditions" (ibid., 372). Krishnamachari responded coolly, "I am aware that your views and ours about private and public enterprise do not altogether coincide though the differences are not quite as great as seem in public debate. We are, of course, not convinced that the motive of private profit is the only one which can ensure efficient operation of an industry; nor do we believe that private enterprise is inherently superior to state enterprise" (ibid., 373). The Bank essentially dropped any such attempt at dialogue over India's approach to development for the better part of the next decade.

By the end of the 1950s, the Bank's bonds had secured the AAA rating, and it could afford to relax its project focus somewhat to lend for a borrower's balance of payments. The timing was fortuitous, as India's need for foreign exchange became more acute after a series of failed monsoons and a crisis in agriculture that forced it to draw on foreign currency holdings in order to purchase food from overseas. In fact, India's Second Five-Year Plan (1956–61), as Baldev Raj Nayar argues, "was beset with problems from the very beginning," and as colonial-era Sterling reserves began to draw down, "the planners hurriedly sought to save" the Plan by "restricting investment to a 'core' plan, consisting primarily of its heavy industry component" and placing little emphasis on the rural sector (2001: 93).

By expanding aid, external actors paradoxically "acted to save a plan that had as its aim economic independence from those very actors," and enabled Indian planners to avoid "more radical thinking about the very viability of the economic strategy and their approach to economic policy" (ibid., 94). New Delhi thus avoided addressing the fundamental "inability of agriculture to deliver sufficient supplies of food for a rapidly growing population," reinforced "dependence on foreign powers for food and finance," and risked creating a cycle whereby India would be "bailed out from crisis to crisis" (ibid., 95, 93).[4] However, the external aid providers, and India itself, would only grasp the full dimensions of the relationship between aid and India's economic policies some years later.

In 1958, the Bank convened a special meeting of India's major bilateral aid providers – Austria, Belgium, Britain, Canada, Denmark, the Federal Republic of Germany, France, Italy, Japan, the Netherlands, Norway, Sweden, and the United States – to address the foreign exchange shortage. The donor countries formed the Aid-India Group, with the Bank as coordinator (the body was later renamed the Aid-India Consortium, and was a precursor to the Consultative Groups that the Bank now chairs for many other borrower countries and issue-areas, to coordinate multilateral and bilateral aid efforts). From New Delhi's point of view, the choice of the Bank as coordinator was desirable: given India's overarching objective of economic self-reliance and its nonaligned foreign policy, going through the Bank allowed it to ask for help without appearing subservient to any bilateral donor (though, in reality, the US exercised significant leverage within the Consortium, as soon would be clear). B.K Nehru recalled,

> It was decided that this immediate rescue operation should not be handled through [bilateral] diplomatic channels to avoid any political flavor being brought into it but should be regarded as a simple banking operation. The World Bank was our international banker. We were going to go to it and place our difficulties before it, tell it that we wanted a large loan and ask it to raise the finance for us from whatever sources it thought proper... [It was] demanded by me and agreed to by him [World Bank President Black] that we would not directly ask any government to help us and we would not even be present at meetings the World Bank might arrange of governments who it thought would be willing to finance us. Mr. Black demanded and I agreed that we would explain to governments what our difficulties were, but that would be the limit of our activity (quoted in Mason and Asher 1973: 14).

The Consortium began to critically evaluate the ability of existing aid arrangements to meet India's needs. India's need for longer-term, lower-cost, more flexible financing was a key impetus for the creation of IDA, as a concessionary World Bank facility, in 1960. A former member of India's Planning Commission, reflecting a view of the Bank-India relationship shared by many officials in New Delhi, quipped in 2003, "You know, IDA was created for us."[5] The remark is substantially true, though the emergence of newly independent countries in Africa was also a major reason for IDA, and the institution was only launched after the US dropped its initial opposition.[6]

The creation of IDA was a watershed for the Bank: it enshrined it as the premier multilateral development agency. With IDA in play, World Bank lending to India increased fivefold between 1958 and 1960; it was during this period that India became the Bank's largest annual borrower (a position it would hold until the 1980s, when mainland China began borrowing, and has recently regained). In the early 1960s, India and Pakistan's combined share of IDA credits rose to almost three-fourths of the total for all countries, leading some to joke that it was really the "India-Pakistan Development Association" and prompting other member countries – in particular, Latin American borrowers – to press for an agreement that not more than half of IDA commitments in any given year should be for the two South Asian countries (Mason and Asher 1973: 401, 92).

Mild resentment from other borrowers notwithstanding, Mason and Asher suggest that the late 1950s to early 1960s "represented the high point in cordial relations between India and the [World] Bank Group" (ibid., 676). As preparatory work got underway for India's Third Plan (1961–6), India took for granted that the Bank and the Consortium donors would provide the funds necessary to finance its foreign exchange requirements. I.G. Patel, an economist and government advisor, recalled that Indian officials were "encouraged by our [aid] experience during the Second Plan," and asked the Bank to work with the Consortium "to underwrite in advance our requirements of foreign exchange during the Third Plan period."[7] On behalf of the Consortium, the Bank sent a team to India in 1960 to evaluate the Third Plan. Patel later described the Bank team's report, which essentially endorsed India's projected Plan requirements, as "one of the most heart-warming documents in the annals of international relations."[8]

## Cold War Politics, Asian Drama, and the Aid-India Negotiations[9]

The late 1950s and early 1960s also marked the height of American interest in India during the Cold War, as Washington's doctrine of Containment expanded to regard Asia as a vital arena in the competition between authoritarian socialism and democratic capitalism. Not coincidentally, Moscow's interest in India also peaked during this period (Chaudhry and Vanduzer-Snow 2008: 48). It should be pointed out that from India's independence until the Soviet Union's demise, Moscow provided 16 percent of all aid received by India – almost double the bilateral US share of 8.6 percent through 1988, though this figure does not include US contributions through multilateral sources such as the World Bank.[10] As Gilles Boquérat's recent history shows, "Although India's foreign policy was based on the refusal to recognize the logic of blocs, the Indian government did not hesitate to take advantage of the East-West confrontation to mobilize aid from both superpowers, implying that if assistance was lacking or taking too long to come, it might rely for support on the opposite camp" (2003: 401).

Nick Cullather shows that "while India barely registered on the list of US interests in 1949, within a decade it had assumed a pivotal position in Cold War strategy" as "US officials came to see India and China as contenders in a symbolic race for economic development" (2007: 59). By 1959, the US Department of State would be producing memoranda with ominous titles such as "Soviet Economic Offensive in India."[11] With China's "fall" to communism and the onset of the Korean conflict, the Truman and Eisenhower administrations warily came to regard nonaligned India as important for its size and democracy, and gradually began to send food aid as an instrument of US diplomacy. America's first loan to India was in 1951, for the purchase of two million tons of wheat (Chaudhry and Vanduzer-Snow 2008: 49). In 1956, the US launched a major "food for peace" program under Public Law (PL) 480, which allowed India to pay for food in rupees, on concessional loan terms. India's imports of American wheat grew from 200,000 tons in 1954 to over 4 million tons in 1960 (Cullather 2007: 70).

Both Truman and Eisenhower had difficulty getting past the aloof and sovereignty-sensitive line of Nehru and the Indian foreign ministry; these qualities encouraged suspicions about India among conservatives in the US Congress, as well. But gradually, Cold War liberals advanced an image of "the future of Asia, and eventually the world balance of power" hinging on "the competition between democratic India" and China, as it was put by US Congressman and two-time Ambassador to India Chester Bowles (ibid., 64). This narrative was repeated and shaped by the media, the US State Department and Agency for International Development (USAID), and institutions such as the Ford Foundation, and ultimately rang through the rhetoric of the Democratic presidential candidate in 1960.

John F. Kennedy's campaign criticized Eisenhower for neglecting what Cullather (2007: 72) calls the "food gap" in India (even as Kennedy sounded the alarm that a "missile gap" between the superpowers favored Moscow, though US intelligence would contradict the latter claim). Just as the arms race dominated US-Soviet competition, a kind of "development race" between China and India shaped American perceptions of its interests in Asia, and the new administration "came into office with a bold pledge 'to those peoples in the huts and villages across the globe struggling to break the bonds of mass misery'" (ibid., 82).

The American aid policy also reflected domestic political interests, muddled concepts, and muted doubts about whether India was entirely up to the challenge, however. Food aid served the interests of American wheat producers, even as it distorted prices and production incentives for Indian farmers (Cullather 2007; Kamath 1992). As noted above, development economics was burgeoning during this period, but was also unsettled amid various theories of modernization. There was particular uncertainty about the role that agriculture should play in the critical early "Big Push" or "take-off" phases of rapid industrialization (ibid., 73–8). While some analysts stressed the need for simultaneous and interlocking investments and productivity gains across the industrial and agricultural sectors, others, including the influential W.W. Rostow (later a Kennedy advisor), countered that "only manufacturing, engineering, power generation, and mass communications could attain growth rates fast enough to outstrip rising populations. Derivative sectors, such as agriculture, would be carried along behind" (ibid., 76). In this view, it did not much matter if US food aid substituted for Indian self-sufficiency in agriculture in the short run, if such assistance provided the means for India to undertake the investments necessary to achieving industrialized "maturity" over the critical early decades.

Even so, a shadow of uncertainty about India's prospects in the great Asian race hung over such intellectual exercises. Rostow's self-described "non-Communist manifesto," *The Stages of Economic Growth*, confidently predicted in 1960, "By 2000 or 2010 – which is not all that far away – India and China, with about two billion souls between them, will be, in our sense, mature powers," meaning "they will have the capacity to apply to their resources the full capabilities of (then) modern science and technology," even if they were not yet "rich in terms of consumption per head" (Rostow 1990 [1960]: 127). Though Rostow conceded "it is by no means assured that Communism will then dominate China, and democracy India," he suggested that "if China maintains forced draft and solves the food problem," it might achieve "maturity" in fewer than three generations (ibid., 127). By implication India, employing presumably less coercive means, would follow somewhat behind.[12] (Though Rostow's version modernization theory was overly deterministic, it is worth noting that his basic prediction for 2000–10 has proven correct).

India's role in this Manichean competition was, in some ways, more imagined than real. Cullather points out that "the mirage of a democratic-capitalist versus communist race faded the closer one came to New Delhi" (ibid., 65), given Nehru's commitment to socialist central planning and his vision of joint Indian-Chinese leadership on behalf of Asia and the less developed countries. Nehru himself repeatedly dismissed the notion of a rivalry – at least until the Chinese attacked and routed India in an October-November 1962 border conflict. This short war, which ran partially concurrent to the US-Soviet Cuban missile crisis, led a despondent Nehru to disregard nonalignment in a desperate plea for American military assistance – including fighter aircraft, air defense radar, and American pilots (Kux 1993, 207). But when the Chinese announced a ceasefire before Kennedy reached a decision, India's distrust of the US was reinforced. The administration in Washington, for its part, was now more than ever convinced of India's importance (though its alliance with Pakistan and the nettlesome Kashmir dispute would complicate efforts to pursue a strategic engagement with India after the Sino-Indian conflict) (ibid., 208–18).

Meanwhile, India's economic situation only became more challenging, even before the security calamity materialized. The crisis in agriculture persisted, and India's exports (rather paltry to begin with) stagnated, even as it imported more and more capital goods in support of its ambitious industrialization objectives. As noted above, though the World Bank nominally steered the Aid-India Group/Consortium after its formation in 1958, in fact Washington was its most powerful force during the early 1960s (Muirhead 2005: 1), relegating the Bank to a co-piloting role that sometimes found the institution in an awkward relationship both with India and with the other lender countries.

The US was more willing than some other Consortium members to help underwrite India's Third Plan needs – perhaps not surprising, given its deeper pockets and its leadership position among the Western powers. Still, the US Congress in 1961–2 "was becoming increasingly hesitant" (ibid., 5), constraining the Kennedy administration to "the position that the United States should merely *match*, all other [bilateral] contributions [by the Consortium], excluding those of the World Bank" (ibid., 6). The US coaxed Canada, France, and Japan to slightly increase their aid for India during a 1962 pledging session; Britain and West Germany remained committed to previous pledges (though in fairness, the UK at this time confronted its own balance of payments situation, and Bonn had already pledged a substantially higher share than the other Europeans or the Japanese) (ibid., 6).

Particularly after the India-China war, US officials found this "deterioration of the aid-giving climate with respect to India" alarming (ibid., 6). But they also began to recognize the futility of expecting others to ante up without assurances that aid would be put to good use. William Gaud, assistant administrator for the Near East and South Asia at USAID, informed the World Bank that the US would like to see "pressure" applied to India to make its policies "comply with the views of [Consortium] members."[13] This implied a much closer scrutiny of India's record and Plan framework.

At least some Bank officials in the field were only too happy to oblige. Benjamin King, the resident representative in New Delhi, offered a private set of observations about Indian interlocutors that was particularly acerbic, and focused as much on personalities and processes as on the Plan framework itself:

*Civil Service*
Not geared to development problems.
Scared to death of decisions.

Excessively hierarchical.

Unwilling to collect, analyze or reveal factual information leading to possible criticism, even self-criticism (pathological).

Committees – no staff work.

*Planning Commission*

Pathetic leadership.

Inadequate system of establishing criteria.

Overly concerned with day-to-day operations.

Wholly unable to keep track.

*Government and economic policy*

Motivation – economic development and economic relief, but both hopelessly confused. Result "sentimental planning."

No real overall policy-making body or mechanism capable of ascertaining facts and presenting issues squarely.[14]

Though few involved in the formal aid negotiations would ever state their views in terms so stark and impolitic, the Consortium's 1963 meetings "marked a new criticism of India's economic policies" (ibid., 2), as the repeated bailing out of India led some donors to be concerned that they might be "throwing good money after bad" (ibid., 1) in the absence of a significant rethinking of the fundamental model embodied in New Delhi's Five Year Plans. Consortium countries were concerned that during the first part of the Third Plan, India had failed to meet its targets:

The Plan had as one of its aims raising real income at the rate of 5.5% per year. As the population was growing at a rate of nearly 2.5% per year, the implied increase in per capita income would be about 3% per year. In fact, up to mid-1963, the overall rate of growth during the first two years of the Plan was probably only about 2% per year. Consequently, per capita income had remained more or less constant or declining since the end of the Second Plan. As well, India's export earnings were not keeping pace with requirements for foreign equipment and food... With respect to agriculture, the production index actually fell... Finally, industrial production for 1962–63 went up by 8%, as against a 6.5% increase the previous year. While that was an encouraging development, the figure remained well below the 11% annual average target put forward by the Third Plan (ibid., 5).

If there was a general consensus that India needed to do more on the policy front to help itself, Consortium member views on specifics diverged somewhat. In general, the Bank and the US pushed in the direction of expanding assistance, while Britain and Germany were the first to raise criticisms of Indian policies for being insufficiently committed to private enterprise (though in Britain's case, aid reluctance likely was dictated as much by its own economic troubles as by conservative ideology at The Bank of England, and as noted above, Germany, whatever its misgivings, continued to pledge relatively substantial aid sums in view of India's political-strategic significance). But as Consortium meetings increasingly became venues for questioning India's development model, Bank and US officials began sharpening their criticisms and pro-market arguments as well.

There were other fissures within the Consortium: the US, Canada, and the Bank pressed for more concessionary aid against other members' desire for loans carrying interest rates at near-market-terms; on the other hand, the Bank and the US disagreed over the share of program versus project assistance, as well as over whether India's slow utilization of a previous year's aid commitments should count against new pledges (Washington's position, reflecting conservative pressures in the US Congress, favored project lending and treating undisbursed sums as new aid in year-on-year pledge accounting). Meanwhile, Bank President George Woods (1963–8) criticized Consortium countries for the practice of "tied aid," the self-interested lender requirement that "constrained the Indians from getting the best deal by linking aid to procurement of products and expertise from the country providing assistance" (ibid., 10).

Given the range of issues and competing political impulses – among and even within the Consortium countries – it was perhaps inevitable that what had been relatively friction-free aid negotiations a half-decade earlier, when the group was first constituted, became by 1963–4 much more laborious and drawn-out affairs. Still, India publicly complained that it found the Consortium's scrutiny unreasonable, and its aid pledges inadequate. Such criticism, in turn, merely served to irritate member countries:

> Hans Henckel, the chief of the German delegation to the pledging session, rejected this [Indian expression of dissatisfaction] out of hand… Henckel wanted the fact publicized that during the first three years of the Third Plan, the consortium had provided about 75%, US$3.28 billion of the US$4.4 billion, that had been cited by the World Bank and India as the latter's requirements for *all five* years of the Plan. Why, Henckel asked, had there been an unanticipated increase of almost 50% in the foreign exchange requirements of the Third Plan? That had come about, he was informed, because of external factors, including… export performance and the recent emergency situation caused by the People's Republic of China invasion. The Germans were also irritated by what seemed to be the Bank's

unqualified support of India – they relied on Bank guidance in developing their own Indian aid program because, as they admitted, they knew nothing about the subcontinent. And that guidance, they increasingly believed, was flawed (ibid., 12; emphasis in original).

As the aid negotiations grew increasingly contentious, the Bank's prestige as Consortium coordinator – and as the ultimate institutional embodiment of the entire case for development assistance – came under threat. The new climate put the Bank on the defensive, and the "good feeling" and harmony of interest that had characterized the early Bank-India relationship gradually began to dissipate. India still preferred that the Bank play the lead role in coordinating its aid needs – New Delhi much preferred this multilateral arrangement to the direct exercise of rich country power – but as Consortium preferences and Indian prerogatives increasingly diverged, the Bank found itself pulled in competing directions.

## The 1966 Devaluation Drama and "Aborted Liberalization"

In 1964, the Bank sent a mission to India, headed by outside economist Bernard Bell, to study extensively the economic situation and to report back with policy recommendations. Indian officials were somewhat reluctant to submit to such external scrutiny, but Bank staff persuaded them that if it undertook such a study, the Bank would command greater authority as Consortium coordinator and would be able to mobilize additional assistance from the donors (Mason and Asher 1973: 196).

Instead of endorsing existing policies, as the Bank's 1960 work had done, the Bell mission's massive 14-volume report, offered in 1965, called for a number of structural reforms to India's economy. "Its major concern," economist Arvind Panagariya recently has written, "was the low level of foreign exchange reserves and, therefore, 'maintenance' imports including agricultural products and fertilizer. It made two major policy recommendations: a shift away from heavy industry toward agriculture, and devaluation of the rupee accompanied by an end to the licensing on the bulk of intermediate inputs (but not consumer goods and machinery) and export subsidies. The Bell mission also recommended substantial nonproject aid for maintenance imports until the reform secured the necessary improvement" (2008: 56). The rupee devaluation, which would be the first since 1949, became the most symbolically important recommendation, though the exhaustive Bell report went on to recommend that India should also adopt policies to increase private and foreign investment, modernize agriculture, and strengthen price incentives to farmers, among other measures.

Bank officials told Indian policymakers that if they adopted such reforms, "a substantial increase in development assistance would be justified" (Mason and Asher 1973: 196). Though the Bank's pledge was informal – since it could not commit Consortium members to increased bilateral aid – Indian officials understood a *quid pro quo*: India would devalue the rupee and implement other reforms recommended in the report, and the Bank would see to it that India's foreign exchange needs were met. Ultimately, in May 1966, Indian Planning Minister Ashok Mehta presented a draft of the country's Fourth Plan to George Woods, who pledged the Bank's "best effort" to increase Consortium assistance to US$1.2 billion for 1966 and US$1.5 billion for 1967 (Kux 1993: 251–3).

The reform recommendations came at a time of unprecedented Indian vulnerability to external pressure. By mid-1965, India's foreign exchange reserves had plummeted to US$500 million, from a high of US$1.87 billion a decade earlier (Chaudhry et al. 2004: 62). As Rahul Mukherji suggests, "The need for food imports at reasonable prices and the foreign exchange shortage made India critically dependent on the US, the World Bank, and the IMF" (2000: 380). An informal division of labor within the Consortium emerged: the Bank took the lead role in dialogue with Indian officials on the devaluation and liberalization (on the former, the IMF also would be involved), and USAID took the lead on the agricultural policy aspects. But whereas early on in the episode the Bank and US positions were reasonably well aligned, the ultimate denouement would see their aid relations with India diverge dramatically.

The political context preceding and during this devaluation and "aborted liberalization" episode was very important (Mukherji 2000). On the Indian side, the recommendation for far-reaching reform came at an awkward time. After Nehru's death in May 1964, Lal Bahadur Shastri, a pragmatist committed to a greater emphasis on agriculture (Panagariya 2008: 49), first succeeded him as prime minister. But Shastri himself died unexpectedly on a diplomatic visit to the Soviet Union in January 1966, throwing India's politics into disarray as intra-Congress Party rivals jockeyed for power. A group of state-level leaders known as "the Syndicate" and steered by the Tamil politician and Congress Party President Kumaraswami Kamaraj, elevated Nehru's daughter Indira Gandhi to the premiership over a fierce rival, former finance minister Morarji Desai. These party leaders were powerful figures in their own states and could deliver crucial vote blocs to the party, but since none of them enjoyed a national profile – Kamaraj, for example, spoke neither English nor Hindi well – they had agreed to promote Mrs. Gandhi in the expectation that she would be rather pliant. However, Mrs. Gandhi and her closest advisors negotiated the devaluation and reform program with the external lenders behind closed doors, without including Kamaraj (who was particularly committed to traditional socialist goals) or other party bosses (Frankel 2005: 96; Mukherji 2000: 382).

Moreover, American actions in 1965 had placed additional pressure on the Indian leadership, as US President Lyndon Johnson held India to a "short tether" policy by which he personally authorized food aid on a month-to-month basis, contingent on India's continued willingness to submit to policy scrutiny.[15] As well, the United States had temporarily suspended military and economic assistance to both India and Pakistan following their 1965 war, even though Pakistan had initiated the conflict. Washington's botched attempt at even-handed diplomacy left an opening that Moscow would skillfully exploit by initiating closer ties with India (Kux 1993: 238–9).

In part, the "hard new look" at aid to India taken by the US president reflected "growing unpopularity for foreign aid with his former congressional colleagues, especially aid to South Asia which loomed large in the overall figures" (Kux 1993: 240). At the same time, according to Rostow, Johnson "felt deeply... about getting the Indians to do a better job in producing food."[16] Robert Paarlberg argues that the US policy community was divided over how to assist India, with the departments of State and Agriculture advocating more food aid and less conditionality, against the White House's more critical and coercive posture (1985: 144–57). In any event, "What the US executive seemed not to understand was that the more strongly they pushed the Indian government to submit on economic policy, the more the Indian government had to prove that it was not kowtowing to the United States" (Woods 2006: 38).

Initially, during a March 1966 visit by Indira Gandhi to Washington, it looked as if the president and the new prime minister would restore the relative goodwill that had marked the two countries' aid relations just a few years earlier. Johnson urged Congress to approve 3.5 million tons of emergency food aid, saying, "India is a good and deserving friend. Let it never be said that bread should be so dear and flesh and blood so cheap that we turned in indifference from her bitter need."[17] But Johnson also took a dim view toward Indian criticism of the American war in Vietnam. In July, shortly after India accepted the devaluation, Mrs. Gandhi visited Moscow and agreed to a joint communiqué criticizing US military actions in that Southeast Asian nation. According to Dennis Kux,

> Although American officialdom did not expect India to endorse US policy toward Vietnam, Washington was clearly annoyed by Mrs. Gandhi's less than nonaligned remarks. Ambassador Bowles wrote that when he commented [that] Mrs. Gandhi was not saying anything more than the Pope or the UN Secretary-General [had said], the curt response he got from Washington officials was, "The Pope and U Thant don't need our wheat" (1993: 255).[18]

If Kennedy's perceived perfidy at the time of the China-India war had reinforced India's doubts about the US as a friend, Johnson's erratic and overbearing style was an even greater source of frustration. Panagariya characterizes Johnson's politicization of aid as "excessively intrusive" (2008: 48), and Stephen P. Cohen suggests, "Since America was then deeply enmeshed in Vietnam, many Indians came to see the policy not as well-meaning but the behavior of a bully, and one that had Asian blood on its hands at that."[19] Moreover, Washington's coercive aid diplomacy raised questions in New Delhi about whether the World Bank's critique of Indian economic policies was being dictated by the Johnson administration.

Under different political circumstances, the rupee devaluation might not have become so explosive, though some opposition was inevitable. As it happened, among Indian officials, a contingent of technocrats favored economic restructuring. The agricultural reform program, in particular, received strong support from Minister of Agriculture C. Subramaniam, and pro-liberalization advisors to the finance ministry, such as the young Jagdish Bhagwati, endorsed the industrial reforms and currency devaluation. L.K. Jha, a principal participant in the dialogue with the World Bank, later described the Bank's pressure as "leaning against open doors,"[20] as by 1966 a number of Indian officials had been persuaded by the repeated crises of the need for significant policy changes.

On the other hand, as Francine Frankel points out, "The package of economic reforms recommended by the World Bank, taken together, represented a fundamental departure from basic principles of planning laid down by Nehru" (2005: 271), and as such it was bound to encounter resistance among some old hands. Krishnamachari, again serving as finance minister, had resigned from Shastri's cabinet in December 1965, at least in part over his opposition to the Bell Report's call for devaluation (ibid., 287). That he remained close to Kamaraj only sharpened the fault lines between the Syndicate and the Indira Gandhi government (Mukherji 2000: 382). Commerce Minister Manubhai Shah was not convinced either, and Planning Minister Asoka Mehta pledged to Parliament in February 1966 that there was "no question" of the government considering devaluation (Mukherji 2000: 383). Ambassador B.K. Nehru, closest to the pulse in Washington, favored the "aid-cum-devaluation" deal (ibid., 384).

Mrs. Gandhi herself was something of an enigma; she kept her own counsel as she listened to conflicting advice from economic experts and relied on a close circle of confidants, a pattern that would intensify throughout her premiership. Mukherji characterizes her as ambivalent on devaluation and argues, "She was not a convinced liberalizer nor an ideologically driven person. Her twin objectives in her early days as prime minister in 1966 were to get out of the foreign exchange crisis and to consolidate her power" (ibid., 381).

In the final analysis, Jørgen Pedersen suggests, external pressure "tipped the balance… between proponents of different policies" in this divided political context (1993: 106). On June 6, 1966, Minister of Finance Sachin Chaudhuri announced in a special radio broadcast the government's decision to devalue the rupee by 36.5 percent – or equivalently, revalue the dollar 57.6 percent – thus raising the prices of imports quite substantially (Frankel 2005: 289; Panagariya 2008: 56). He described the devaluation as "one of a number of economic decisions of great consequence to the health and progress of our economy."[21] Other policy changes would include some liberalization of intermediate imports for fifty-nine "priority" industries, and reductions to export subsidies (Panagariya 2008: 56–7).

The backlash against the announcement was severe, and "cut across ideological lines," with different sections of the Congress Party and opposition parties from both the socialist left and nationalist right attacking Mrs. Gandhi (Frankel 2005: 299). "Even the major industrial and business groups were skeptical, welcoming the step only if it paved the way for the complete dismantling of government regulations and controls over the economy" (ibid., 299), which it did not. Vested industrial interests opposed the liberalization of imports and reduction of export subsidies, and organized labor was divided (Mukherji 2000).

The left parties, in particular, castigated the government for surrendering to imperialist pressure and condemned the World Bank as Washington's handmaiden. Hiren Mukherjee from the Communist Party of India told Parliament, "It should be common knowledge here that the decision to force India down to her knees had been made by the cloak and dagger aid givers of America long ago."[22] Circumstances appeared to vindicate this view. Frankel observes,

> Although it would take some time for the potential benefits to the Indian economy from all these measure to take effect, one gain was immediate and glaringly apparent. Within ten days of the finance minister's announcement of devaluation and the liberalization of foreign exchange controls, the United States announced resumption of economic aid to India. The implication was unmistakable. The government had devalued in response to pressures by the major aid-giving nations in order to get further assistance (2005: 299).

John P. Lewis, the director at USAID at the time, later suggested that many Indians interpreted the devaluation as "a blow to national pride. Lowering the rupee lowered the flag" (1995: 142). B.K. Nehru later admitted that the government had failed to prepare the ground politically, and in particular had failed to appreciate the psychological importance that the rupee exchange rate had assumed after remaining unchanged for nearly two decades. He remarked, "It was as if devaluation had castrated India."[23] Nayar suggests,

> Devaluation failed to generate a larger liberalization process because of its foreign authorship. The questioning of Nehru's economic strategy no doubt existed within India as well, at even the highest levels… Yet, India could not genuinely claim ownership of the liberalization program. Instead, Western powers were recognized as its authors… in view of their highly intrusive participation in India's economic decision-making (2001: 103).

The fallout would extend to the 1967 elections, in which the Congress Party's traditional dominance in Parliament was reduced to a narrow majority. In eight states – Bihar, Kerala, Madras, Orissa, Punjab, Rajasthan, Uttar Pradesh, and West Bengal – the party failed outright to win legislative majorities (Frankel 2005: 307), driving a wedge between Mrs. Gandhi and the state-level leadership and ultimately sowing a formal split in the Congress Party.

As she lost the support of her patrons in the senior Congress Party establishment, Mrs. Gandhi sought support from the party's more radically socialist elements and reached out to smaller left-leaning parties in the Parliament. On liberalization, Mrs. Gandhi turned about-face, abandoning the reform program negotiated with the Bank – apart from agricultural sector components – and instead launching an aggressive expansion of the public sector including new licensing requirements and other restrictions for industry, and nationalizing the country's major banks. By the end of the 1960s, the reversal of liberalization would be complete, and India's policies as *dirigiste* and protectionist as ever.[24] It was, in short, a "radical revolt against liberalization" (Nayar 2001: 104). Moreover, Mrs. Gandhi's government resolved never again to become so "vulnerably dependent" on aid, and painstakingly began building up substantial foreign exchange reserves (Lewis 1995: 139, 182), though this cushion would not last forever.

Following this formative 1966 episode, "relations between the Bank and India were visibly tarnished" (Mason and Asher 1973: 679). Even the pro-liberalization contingent in the government harbored serious resentment toward the Bank, after the latter proved unable to deliver on the assurance of additional aid through the Consortium. Though the Bank itself provided India with US$900 million for 1966 (against the expected US$1.2 billion), it could not mobilize the donor governments to increase their bilateral contributions, which instead fell precipitously over the next several years. Thirty-five years later, a report by the Bank's Operations Evaluation Department still cited the devaluation debacle as a critical juncture in the Bank's relationship with

India: "While the government accepted the need for reform, Bank pressure caused resentment… The Bank and India became estranged, with the notable exception of agriculture… the government emerged from this episode wary of liberalization and determined to lessen the country's dependence on foreign assistance" (Zanini 2001: 10).

For its part, the Bank came away from the episode convinced that "economic liberalization remains a sound, and indeed necessary set of policies for development; the power to grant or to withhold aid money can be used, and should be used, to induce governments to liberalize their economies; but not, perhaps, in India" (Mosley et al. 1991: 29). Indeed, within months, Bell and the Bank took some of the policy proposals worked out in India and adapted them to a major aid and reform program for Indonesia, where the authoritarian Suharto regime did not confront the same domestic constraints that dominated India's decision-making (Kapur et al. 1997: 467–71).

Even more importantly, this episode has been cited as an early experiment in the kind of policy-based lending that the Bank would later formalize in the Structural Adjustment Loan (SAL) instrument in 1979, and would utilize extensively in Latin America and Sub-Saharan Africa after the 1980s Third World debt crisis. To be sure, "the Bank's experience in India helped it to clarify policies regarding balance-of-payments support for countries during a foreign exchange crisis" (Lele and Bumb 1995: 74). The 2001 report by the Bank's Operations Evaluation Department notes that "for the Bank, the [1966] policy dialogue represents an early attempt to use the leverage of its lending in a major member country" to elicit far-reaching policy changes (Zanini 2001: 10). In fact, some of the very same Bank personnel involved in the dialogue with India in the mid-1960s, such as Stanley Please, would go on, a decade-and-a-half later, to serve as key architects of the structural adjustment loan instrument.[25] However, as will be discussed later in this chapter, the Bank would not attempt such policy-based lending again in India for a quarter of a century.

## Eliciting Goodwill: A "Lending Push in a Poor Policy Environment"

As noted above, in the early 1960s, the United States provided fully half of the total assistance from the Aid India Consortium. A decade later, US-India relations had deteriorated over a range of issues, including Vietnam, Indira Gandhi's warming to Moscow, US President Richard Nixon's support for Pakistan (and use of mild gunboat diplomacy in 1971, in opposition to India's alliance with Bangladeshi separatists in East Pakistan),[26] and India's developing nuclear program. American bilateral aid to India plummeted.

After the 1966 crisis, the Bank assumed a lending posture that was deliberately independent of Washington's aid policy toward India. It increased its IBRD and especially IDA assistance to India to fill the gap created by the decline in US and other bilateral aid. The Bank had been stung badly by accusations of its complicity in the US effort to humiliate India, and it went out of its way to mend the client relationship. By "stepping up its aid without attaching any strings to it," the World Bank "elicited much goodwill from Indian officials" after the withdrawal of bilateral assistance (Pal 1985: 263; Zanini 2001: 10). By the end of the 1980s, the World Bank would be providing about 65 percent of India's aid, and the US bilateral share would plummet to low single digits (less than Moscow's share, prior to the Soviet Union's demise) (Kamath 1992).

During the long presidency of Robert S. McNamara (1968–81), the former US Secretary of Defense, the Bank intensified its poverty focus and expanded its worldwide lending commitments tenfold.[27] India became even more central to the Bank's mission, as the McNamara Bank downplayed reform advocacy in favor of meeting expanded lending targets. Greg Votaw, a Country Director for India who had been an advocate of pushing for liberalization of India's economic policies, was replaced by Ernst Stern, who "quickly won the approval of McNamara for hitting loan targets and eliminating all unpleasantness about policy disagreements with the Indian government" (Kamarck 1996: 124).

As the Bank's OED notes, after 1966 "the Bank's activist attitude gave way to an exaggerated reticence to advocate policy change. Instead, the Bank focused on narrow issues directly related to its operations' success" (Zanini 2001: 10). While it continued balance-of-payments lending for a few more years after the 1966 crisis, and temporarily turned up the volume again during another, milder foreign exchange crisis in 1973–4, "conditionality was used sparingly and common ground between the Bank's objectives and the government's was continuously stressed" (ibid., 10). To a considerable extent, this retreat from conditionality in India – even as the Bank developed structural adjustment lending for other clients – reflected reverberations from the 1966 devaluation.

But the Bank also began to reorient its mission and goals not long after the mid-1960s experience in India. With the arrival of McNamara in 1968, the Bank became much more focused on targeted poverty reduction. The sheer scale of deprivation in India made it a central front in this new war on poverty, especially since McNamara placed a heavy emphasis on meeting country-specific lending targets, which were treated as indicators of progress in the campaign. Martha Finnemore, who describes McNamara as a "norm entrepreneur" for so personally imprinting new goals on the Bank, notes that from his first speech to the Board of Governors McNamara demonstrated that he "understood his central mission to be doing something about world poverty" (1996: 107). But McNamara's antipoverty thrust echoed and amplified a new concern in development economics for poverty not just as a condition confronting countries, but also more directly as a predicament of poor *people* within developing countries; the Bank's own Pearson Report, published around the time of McNamara's arrival, "made it abundantly clear that the benefits of growth were not 'trickling down' to the poorest" in the Bank's client countries (ibid., 109).

In lending operations, the anti-poverty norm led to a 1970s emphasis on new kinds of projects, focusing on agriculture and rural development, family planning, and the "social sectors" of primary education and health. Finnemore argues that the Bank's antipoverty focus did not develop in reaction to specific demands from either lender or borrower countries, though she does suggest that India's emphasis on "minimum needs," dating from the Third Plan, had made an impression on the Bank leadership. Mahendra Pal notes that early in his presidency, McNamara gave a speech acknowledging India's "truly exceptional importance in the global developmental efforts," and in particular "the fact that for more than two decades the nation has been a center of developmental thinking and experimentation designed to add the newer dimensions of social progress to economic expansion" (1985: 215, 219).

The fight against poverty would provide a common narrative for the Bank and India during the 1970s, as *garibi hatao* ("eliminate poverty" in Hindi) became the populist slogan of the Indira Gandhi government, attempting to reach out over the estranged elite of the Congress Party to court the electorate directly (Kohli 1996: 116; Thakur 1998: 604). It is noteworthy that during the Emergency regime (1975–7), when Mrs. Gandhi came under harsh criticism in Western capitals, McNamara visited India and kept extensive notes that make no suspension of the *de facto* suspension of democracy but characterize the country's priorities as essentially "sound" (Kamarck 1996: 124). Lloyd and Susanne Rudolph suggest that the Bank's (and the IMF's) praise for Emergency-era economic performance was rooted in a lurking suspicion that India's unwieldy democracy had held back its development (1987: 222).

There was one minor issue that led to disagreement between the Bank and India, but it proves the larger point: When Mrs. Gandhi's government proposed, in 1973, to reduce net foreign aid to zero in pursuit of "self-reliance," "McNamara told M.G. Kaul, India's secretary of finance, that such a policy was 'dangerous and counterproductive' and that 'it was unrealistic to expect that India could be able to continue her development efforts at a reasonable pace without a positive transfer of foreign aid'" (Kapur et al. 19997: 297).

Though foreign aid barely amounted to 1 percent of India's GNP during the 1970s, "there was still much room for improvement in Indian export and savings performance and for the substitution of domestic efforts for foreign aid" (ibid., 297). As noted above, the Bank continued to provide balance-of-payments support to India for several years after the 1966 crisis, including during another, smaller crisis in 1973–4 (which followed the OPEC oil price spike after the 1973 Arab-Israeli war). This ongoing relationship led some within the Bank, particularly senior economists, to call for greater scrutiny of India's trade and industrial policies concomitant to continued "program lending," though McNamara put his considerable clout behind the project lending approach and avoidance of macro-conditionality (Mosley et al. 1995: 29).

After 1975, the Bank moved away from program lending altogether in India, and retreated to lending for specific projects only, albeit with a heavier emphasis on poverty reduction than during the earlier concentration on capital formation. This renewed project focus deprived the Bank of any significant influence mechanism with respect to macroeconomic policies in India, even if it had been inclined to pursue such conditionality again with the client.

Ironically, though Indira Gandhi's premiership is probably better remembered for the sharply socialist turn India's economic policy took in the late 1960s and early 1970s (noted above), the government later inducted incremental "liberalization by stealth" (Nayar 2001:120), especially during Mrs. Gandhi's second, post-Emergency tenure in 1980–4 (Panagariya 2008: Chapter 4). Nayar suggests that Mrs. Gandhi began to listen more to the advice of reform advocates in her government and, with little fanfare, "resorted to a set of more [market-] orthodox policies... the hallmark [of which] was pragmatism" (2001: 115, 117). By linking the rupee to a weak Sterling, India effectively devalued it while managing to avoid the kind of uproar that had occurred in 1966. It also decreased public expenditure and liberalized import restrictions, albeit modestly and without fundamentally rejecting the ISI model.

In 1981, after a second oil shock and a severe drought led India to again seek external assistance, it favored a US$6 billion dollar loan from the IMF's new Extended Fund Facility (the creation of which India had advocated, much as it had helped lead developing country efforts to establish the Bank's IDA facility two decades earlier). At the time, this was the largest ever IMF loan to a developing country. Praveen Chaudhry, Vijay Kelkar, and Vikash Yadav show that India preempted any effort by the Fund to link major policy reform requirements to this loan, by deploying a strategy of "homegrown conditionality" whereby the government would "formulate and pace the reforms in such a way that democratic institutions would not be compromised" (2004: 64) and a 1966-style political backlash would be avoided. "Convinced that the existing [Five Year] Plan was strong enough to meet the Fund's conditions for an extended arrangement," Finance Ministry, Planning Commission, and Reserve Bank of India officials received Mrs. Gandhi's approval for negotiations with the Fund, and made clear to the latter that any departure from the Plan would have to meet with parliamentary approval (ibid., 66).[28] The IMF accepted this arrangement. As Suresh Tendulkar and

T.A. Bhavani characterize its position, the Fund "wanted it to be a stabilization-cum-structural adjustment loan while India agreed only to the balance-of-payments stabilization support" (2007: 157). The US, for its part, opposed the major assistance package on the grounds that India would unduly burden the IMF and limit access for other developing countries, but in the end it abstained from the otherwise unanimous approval vote by the Fund's Executive Board in November 1981 (Chaudhry, Kelkar et al. 2004: 68–70).

Ultimately, in yet another signal that it would have the last word on its economic prerogatives, India never drew on the loan's third tranche, and it repaid the IMF ahead of schedule. This announcement elicited goodwill from the Fund in 1984–5 for the improvement to the latter's liquidity position (ibid., 74–5) at a time when it was becoming increasingly involved in lending for stabilization and structural adjustment in other developing countries. However, Nayar notes that "behind the vaunted claims of self-reliance lay the real reason – the intent (in [I.G.] Patel's words) 'to escape from the discipline of the IMF,' which would have accompanied the [third] installment" of Fund assistance (2001: 137), coming as it would have during a new context of global debt crisis. For political reasons that will be discussed later, India did not wish to submit to Bretton Woods discipline to address its piling up of fiscal deficits, at the central and state government levels, during this period (ibid., 137).

The World Bank's involvement in the 1981–2 IMF-India transaction was minimal; it tendered no complementary program assistance (Guhan 1995b: 74) and one Bank official told a Fund counterpart that he thought India's loan proposal was "a joke" (Chaudhry et al. 2004: 67). The episode caught both the Fund and the Bank in periods of transition, the latter's following McNamara's departure in June and his replacement by the Ronald Reagan appointee A.W. Clausen (1981–6), a former BankAmerica president. In any event, by this time the momentum of Bank-India relations had been moving away from policy-conditioned lending for well over a decade. For the Fund, EFF-style lending was a new undertaking, and Indian officials possibly predicted that its conditionality would be relatively weak.

Soon after, in the wake of a major financial crisis that rocked the developing world – triggered by Mexico's threat of default on its external debt in 1982 – both the World Bank and the IMF moved toward a neoliberal orthodoxy that would come to be known, to supporters and detractors alike, as the doctrine of structural adjustment. This "meant that a debtor country applying for financial assistance from the IMF and/or World Bank had to commit itself to a number of stringent economic and structural reforms," essentially reflecting what economist John Williamson would call, infamously, "the Washington Consensus" in favor of "free markets, trade liberalization, and a greatly reduced role for the state in the economy" (Gilpin 2001: 314–5).

As noted above, though India began to liberalize, modestly, during Indira Gandhi's latter premiership – and under her son Rajiv Gandhi's government (1984–9) – its economic model retained a statist impetus squarely at odds with the Bank's evolving pro-market orthodoxy. It was still one of the most closed and heavily regulated economies in the non-Communist world (Joshi and Little 1996: 63). The OED notes the increasing divergence between the Bank's general disposition and its business-as-usual approach in India:

> Throughout the 1980s, the Bank was more concerned with the transfer of resources [to India] than with whether those resources were put to effective use. Despite widespread recognition that India needed to adopt a new model of economic management, Bank management did not address India's disappointing policy record for fear of jeopardizing a strong lending relationship with a sensitive client...
>
> While the Bank was actively promoting structural adjustment in many of its member countries, high-level discussion of necessary policy adjustments in India – to say nothing of an explicit link between the Bank's lending and policy reform – was largely avoided (Zanini 2001: 10–11).

The report notes that even at decade's end, just before macroeconomic crisis hit India in 1990, the Bank sent a country brief to its Executive Directors enthusing about India's growth prospects and the soundness of its development strategy (as Panagariya notes, India *did* experience a growth spurt of 10.5 percent of GDP at factor costs in 1988–9, though this was largely on the back of a jump in agricultural growth following four years of virtual stagnation in the sector, along with expansionary fiscal policy and foreign borrowing; 2008: 100–1). According to the OED, "Mild warnings about the increasing stress in the balance of payments and public sector finances were overshadowed by the extensive coverage of the positive achievements of the government's policies in the late 1980s and the implicit endorsement of the institutional and policy framework underpinning them" (Zanini 2001: 60, *n*2). This was in spite of predictions of impending crisis from some *Indian* economists.

India avoided the kind of austere, off-the-shelf structural adjustment programs that the Bretton Woods institutions would require of other borrowers as conditions for assistance during the 1980s, in part because its own 1981–2 balance of payments difficulties, "homegrown conditionality," and sizeable IMF commitment had (only barely) preceded the global debt crisis. But the World Bank's bitter past experience in India, and the continued importance of India in the Bank's overall portfolio, militated against conditionality in their relationship. India remained an essential borrower for the number of projects it could field, for its share of the world's poor, and for the steady repayment stream on its accumulated borrowings. Despite occasionally voiced internal concerns about India's economic policies, the Bank kept expanding its portfolio, ensconced in the pattern of project and sector-specific lending that had dominated the relationship since the end of its balance of payments support in the mid-1970s. The IDA share in new assistance began to decline, but IBRD lending for investment projects expanded, so that annual Bank commitments to India reached an unprecedented US$3 billion in 1989–90. The Bank's India staff did not relish the avoidance of policy dialogue, but the modalities of the assistance strategy did not offer much scope for it, and in any case they were not willing to run the risk of ruffling sovereignty-sensitive Indian officials.

## The Early 1990s: A False Start for Renewed Policy Influence?

In 1990–1, India experienced a severe balance of payments crisis – a more serious economic emergency, in some ways, than even 1966. The new crisis was linked to external shocks from the Persian Gulf War (following Iraq's August 1990 invasion of Kuwait), as the double-whammy of a price spike for oil imports and shrinking remittances from Indians working in the Gulf region strained the current account. More fundamentally, though, analysts have argued that the crisis stemmed from structural imbalances and unsustainable policies, including large current account deficits throughout the 1980s and a rapid accumulation of foreign debt, accompanied by a deterioration in the "quality" of debt as current government expenditures rose and public investment fell (Panagariya 2008: 101–3; Nayar 2001: 132–5). Persistent inflation fed back into the balance of payments situation as "it made exports increasingly uncompetitive, which then had to be supported with higher export subsidies from the state" (Nayar 2001: 133).

Even before the Gulf crisis, in July 1990, India's deteriorating position led it to withdraw US$660 million from its reserve tranche with the IMF (ibid., 138); this was followed by an emergency loan of US$1.8 billion in January 1991, which was quickly depleted (Weinraub 1991). At the height of the balance of payments crisis, in mid-1991, India's foreign exchange reserves fell to alarmingly low levels, and the government's credit rating was downgraded. Frankel notes,

> India's credit rating was so low that the government could no longer raise loans from foreign banks to finance essential imports, and, as foreign exchange reserves fell to the equivalent of two weeks' worth of imports, transferred gold to British banks as collateral to stem speculation about an imminent default. Under such circumstances, it was much easier to argue that the only recourse was the International Monetary Fund (2005: 590).

In July 1991, India sought stabilization assistance worth US$2.3 billion from the IMF, followed by its first SAL from the World Bank in the amount of US$500 million. In fact, reciprocal conditions made the Fund and Bank assistance essentially interdependent (Dhar 2003: 232). The attendant policy reforms, discussed below, were much more systematic than the "piecemeal reforms of the 1980s" (Panagariya 2008: 95) and constituted "a watershed in India's economic history" (Nayar 2001: 129). As Panagariya observes, "The IMF program and the World Bank SAL initiated a process of liberalization that has continued to move forward at a gradual pace until today" (ibid., 103).

Some opposition politicians and critical theorists, both then and even now, have interpreted this to mean that the Bretton Woods institutions imposed a neoliberal orthodoxy on India – that the Bank and the IMF, perhaps in concert with captured Indian elites, were the true authors of the reform program. The Communist Party of India (Marxist) (CPM) lion E.M.S. Namboodiripad characterized the government's argument that there was no alternative to Bank-Fund assistance as "like a thirsty man taking a cup of poison on the plea that there is no alternative with which he can quench his thirst."[29] Political scientist Ashis Nandy told *The New York Times* in June 1991, "We are very uneasy about the conditions imposed on us. This will be seen as a kind of interference in India's autonomy" (Weinraub 1991).

Prabhat Patnaik and C.P. Chandrasekhar note the "great historical significance" of India's 1991 transition (2007: 52). However, they reject the notion that India's existing economic model had "collapsed" and argue that a "'liberalization' lobby, consisting of both the Fund and the Bank as well as elements within the Indian government and business class… considered [the crisis] a heaven-sent opportunity to tie the country down to structural adjustment, to jettison altogether, and not just rectify, the dirigiste regime which had prevailed since Independence. In other words, the event of historical significance was achieved as a silent coup, behind everybody's back [*sic.*] as it were, by trapping the country into structural adjustment" (ibid., 52, 55). Even more sweepingly, Patnaik and Chandrasekhar hold rich country governments and "metropolitan capital generally" – with "the Bank and the Fund as its chief spokesmen" – responsible for India's "retreat" from the Nehruvian legacy (ibid., 63).

This view does not hold up to scrutiny, either in light of events leading up to the 1991 structural adjustment episode, or the subsequent course of India's reforms and relations with the external lenders. A broad official consensus underpinned the new, pro-market direction in 1991 – and has continued to support reform, albeit at a measured pace, ever since – even in spite of leadership changes that might have thrown the program off track.

In the absence of acute crisis, India's leaders may have remained "immobilized by ideological and social divisions from moving on to new principles of competition and greater integration with the global economy," as

Frankel suggests (2005: 588). But by early 1991, the severity of the impending emergency had broken the remaining ideological impasse and the constraints imposed by vested industrial and bureaucratic interests. A short-lived non-Congress coalition government, led by socialist Prime Minister Chandra Shekhar and Finance Minister Yashwant Sinha,[30] argued that "a comprehensive package of macro-economic adjustment would be the only sustainable solution to the fiscal crisis," in an interim budget it presented for 1991–2 (ibid., 589). When that disparate coalition fell apart amid infighting over identity politics, corruption, and other issues not directly related to the economic crisis (Chakrabarty 2006: 138–43), the Congress Party returned in June 1991 after a campaign that saw its original prime ministerial candidate, Rajiv Gandhi, assassinated by a Sri Lankan Tamil extremist, and the veteran Telugu Congressman P.V. Narasimha Rao called out of near-retirement to lead the party to power on a wave of voter sympathy.

Rao chose as his finance minister Dr. Manmohan Singh, an Oxford-trained economist who, as early as the mid-1960s, had criticized India's ISI model for what he saw as its unwarranted export pessimism (Singh 1964). Singh had been part of India's technocratic establishment since the 1970s, and had served as the Governor of the Reserve Bank of India (1982–5) and Deputy Chairman of the Planning Commission (1985–7). Alongside other key officials such as Commerce Minister Palaniappan Chidambaram and Commerce Secretary Montek Singh Ahluwalia, Singh's finance ministry now ushered in the most sweeping and comprehensive economic reform program in India's history.

Francine Frankel summarizes the "first stage" of reforms beginning in mid-1991, "an integrated package of policies to go beyond crisis management and set the economy on a sustainable growth path of 7 percent per annum":

> The government drastically cut back the number of industries reserved for the public sector; removed compulsory licensing on the private sector for starting and expanding new enterprises in virtually all industries; devalued the rupee; introduced current account convertibility to pay balances on the current export and import (trade) account; removed quantitative quotas on imports; steadily reduced tariff levels on imports; lifted restrictions on majority foreign investment in a wide range of industries; allowed foreign companies to borrow funds in India, raise public deposits and expand their operations by creating new businesses and taking over existing businesses, and permitted foreign financial institutions to make direct portfolio investments in India's two stock markets (2005: 591).

For a market enthusiast, it was a "golden summer" (Das 2002: 213). A cover feature in *The Economist* called India "a tiger uncaged" (ibid.). The World Bank itself would remark in a report, "India has fundamentally altered its development paradigm" through reforms that "have ended four decades of planning and have initiated a quiet economic revolution."[31]

The reforms were also basically homegrown. Panagariya argues that India's internal reform advocates had learned from the patchwork approach to liberalization in the 1980s, and had begun to perceive that a more comprehensive program "was politically feasible as long as it was packaged as necessary for the good of the common man" and consistent with India's national interests (2008: 95). While some criticized the Rao government for failing to bring out a white paper and not taking the opposition into confidence regarding the reforms (Patnaik and Chandrasekhar 2007: 55), Jalal Alamgir credits the leadership with fashioning, both for itself and for the broader polity, a well-planned "enabling narrative" that he describes as a kind of "nationalist globalism." Singh, Chidambaram, and others advanced a coherent argument that treated enhanced material capabilities rather than moral suasion, and economic openness rather than the autarkic Nehruvian model, as the keys to India's realization of Nehru's own cherished goal of a global influence commensurate with its civilizational grandeur (Alamgir 2007).

A major policy statement, *The Economic Survey 1991–92*, argued, "Self reliance does not mean isolation. We live in a world of great variety – of people, resources, of knowledge and behaviour. It is there for us to cooperate with, trade with, learn from, and contribute to. It is there for us to measure ourselves against."[32] The world around India was also changing dramatically. The demise of the Soviet Union and "the spectacular success of outward-oriented policies in China" dealt great blows to "the view that India could steer itself out of poverty through investment and import controls" (Panagariya 2008: 95). The Chinese model presented a particularly compelling challenge, given that it was even more populous than India. The notion of a kind of development competition between the two Asian giants had decades-old roots, as we have seen – even if the market-oriented reforms launched by Deng Xiaoping's regime had rewritten the game's rules.

Panagariya (who, it should be noted, was a staff member in the World Bank's Research Department at the time) offers an account of the Bank's role in India's early 1990s reforms that perfectly captures the realization that SAL assistance might have been a false start for the Bank's increased relevance to the formation of economic policy in India. He argues,

Contrary to the assertions by many, the influence of the IMF and the World Bank was confined to the first set of actions. After the World Bank structural adjustment loan of December 1991, which concluded in December 1992, the government of India was back in the driving seat. From then on, it was the World Bank that needed India rather than the opposite. It wanted to maintain the appearance of being involved in India's liberalization process, and therefore continued to lend money. For example, the trade and investment liberalization loan that followed the SAL was an entirely opportunistic move on the part of the Bank and came without conditions (ibid., 95).

He offers a remarkable personal anecdote about a mission by the Bank, for this trade and investment liberalization loan, in March 1993. The narrative's informal nature leads him to place it in a footnote, but it is worth quoting at length:

> Senior officials in the India Department of the Bank had told the mission team that if the Bank were to offer this loan, the government of India would have to take action on the liberalization of consumer goods imports. Soon after the mission arrived, India announced its new export-import policy, which took no action toward the liberalization of consumer goods. The mission leader discussed the matter with the officials in the Finance Ministry and was told that the prime minister had decided against further liberalization until the elections in some key states, due in June 1993, were over. The following evening, the chief of the India Country Operations Division arrived and told the mission that if there was no action on consumer goods, it was "no go" on the loan. The next morning, the chief went to the Finance Ministry and spoke with the senior officials there. Upon returning to the hotel, he informed the mission that the loan could perhaps still go forward on the basis of the actions already taken by the government of India. In the event, that is just what the Bank did – the $300 million loan was based entirely on the actions the government had already taken. As a postscript, India liberalized consumer goods imports almost a decade later, on April 1, 2001, upon losing a World Trade Organization dispute settlement case brought by the United States. In the meantime, the World Bank continued to loan money to India without so much as a hiccup! (ibid., 468–9, n1).

With a pro-liberalization team steering India's economic program, the Bank might have hoped that it could move beyond the awkward avoidance of policy dialogue that had defined its relationship with India for so many years. Emboldened by its early supporting role in India's macroeconomic adjustment, the Bank began to take a harder look at its project and sector lending, and decided to discontinue support for certain public enterprises such as India's State Electricity Boards (whose inefficient operations were contributing to ballooning state budget deficits, as the next chapter will discuss). At the same time, the Bank sought to expand lending for health, education, and rural development projects. But the decrease in public enterprise lending meant that some of the most finance-intensive areas of the Bank's India portfolio were cut off; the increased emphasis on human development lending required fewer assistance dollars but was more demanding of Bank staff time since it required close study of India's institutions and governance (Zanini 2001: 12).

Despite the initial exuberance over liberalization, when the Bank's lending to India began to shrink – new commitments dropped to under US$1 billion for 1994–5 (ibid., 12) – the Bank's country team began to fear adverse consequences for its "relevance" and ability to "maintain a seat at the table" of economic policy formation (Chassard 2002). India's substantial "second generation reforms" agenda (discussed in the following chapter) remained uncompleted, but the return to a more comfortable resource position, accelerating economic growth, and new influx of private investment meant that India did not depend on the Bank's assistance as during 1990–1 and could follow its own reform agenda and pace. One senior Bank official believed that India's acceptance of conditionality in the structural adjustment loans had been "an historical accident" made possible only by the severity of the 1990–1 balance of payments crisis; he now sensed that the Bank's ability to engage Indian officials in significant policy dialogue might be slipping (Zagha 2002). The Bank's Country Assistance Strategy (CAS) risked becoming "not really a 'strategy' at all," just sundry projects with no integrating framework (Chassard 2002). During discussions toward an updated CAS in 1995, "the government made it clear to the Bank, as well as to the IMF, that it preferred to follow its own pace in reforming the economy and that it did not see a role for the Bank in framing the agenda" (Zanini 2001: 12).

If the India Department staff worried about its relevance to the client, senior management worried about the implications for the Bank's general financial health and operational autonomy if its ability to retain India's high levels of IBRD borrowing for project assistance were jeopardized. Just one year before this precipitous fall-off in lending volume, the Bank had to pull out of a major dams project in India, ending what to this day remains one of the most acrimonious controversies it has ever weathered over any project, anywhere. If the Bank had perceived project lending as a means to avoid policy confrontation with the Indian government, the Narmada issue demolished this illusion. Before concluding this history, let us turn briefly to this critical episode.

## Dam Debacle: The "Narmada Effect" on Bank and Borrower

The Sardar Sarovar Dam and Irrigation Project on India's Narmada River was to have been one of the flagship infrastructure achievements of the Nehru era.

One of India's major river systems, the Narmada and its tributaries flow through the central and western states of Madhya Pradesh, Maharashtra, and Gujarat before draining into the Arabian Sea. Traditionally, Hindus have held that the Narmada (from Sanskrit, "giving mirth or pleasure"[33]) sprang from the body of Lord Shiva, and in spiritual importance it is surpassed only by the Ganges.[34] It has sustained many villages that dot its banks through a largely arid region. After independence, Indian planners were determined to tap it for irrigation, hydropower, and drinking water, and in 1961, Prime Minister Nehru laid the foundation stone for what was to become on of the most debated development projects in history.

In addition to its principal dam at Sardar Sarovar,[35] the project was designed to encompass a network of 30 other major dams and a multitude of minor ones spread across the three states. Planners proposed to irrigate some 5 million acres, generate 1,200 megawatts of electricity, and provide drinking water for 30 million people (Caufield 1996: 8). But soon after ground was broken, the three states became locked in a dispute over the distribution of these benefits, and construction was halted for two decades – though not before some villagers in the project zone were forced to move.

Catherine Caufield, who conducted extensive interviews in India and at the World Bank in 1994–5, provides a detailed account of the Narmada saga (1996). Caufield demonstrates that the Bank long had taken an interest in the Narmada project, and moved quickly to extend assistance when the three state governments finally reached an accord. During the mid-1980s, the Bank sent a series of four missions, ostensibly to "maximize [the project's] financial and technical viability and minimize its negative side effects" (1996: 11). The Bank and Indian planners had always known that like other large dam projects, this one would involve the resettlement of local residents – many of them peasants and *adivasis* (tribals, literally "original inhabitants") – from reservoir areas. Caufield (1996: 8, 11) cites figures implying that upwards of half a million people would have to move; other sources put the total closer to 200,000 (Guha 2007: 612). In fact, as later became clear, there was no firm understanding of the total impact at the time of the Bank's engagement (Morse 1992: Introduction).

Yet none of the four Bank missions conducted any substantive assessment of the likely social impacts of displacing so many people – even though an Indian government-appointed tribunal, which ruled that the states should compensate farmers on a "land-for-land" principle, did *not* mandate redress for the many peasants and *adivasis* who held no deed of title to the land they worked (Miller 1992: 4). This was in spite of the fact that in the early 1980s, the Bank had adopted general resettlement and rehabilitation policies providing that displaced persons should "regain at least their previous standard of living," as well as specific safeguards for tribal peoples whose "customary usage of land should be respected" (Morse 1992: xv). The Bank, according to Caufield, sent a lone consultant to investigate the social dimensions of the massive project (1996: 13). This individual reported back that the state governments had no resettlement and compensation plans, nor had they made any real efforts to collect the data necessary to create such plans. In short, by supporting the project, the Bank was disregarding its own policies.

From early on in the Bank's engagement, internal dissenters criticized the project. The Bank's environmental department was perhaps the most vocal, arguing that in addition to the social concerns, important ecological considerations (discussed below) were being ignored. But Bank managers, keen to lend to such an important client for such a large project, sent a loan proposal before the Executive Board anyway, which approved the full US$450 million in project assistance. This sum, while not insubstantial, represented only about 10 percent of the projects' total cost (Shihata 1994: 10), with the remainder coming from the Asian Development Bank, several bilateral aid providers including Japan, and India's own resources.

From the recommencement of construction, the resettlement of the local population was a disaster. With no real plan in place, the states' task was left to contractors and work crews. Caufield's narrative movingly conveys a sense of the human tragedy:

> Construction workers and company officials pressured the villagers to affix their thumbprints to deeds of sale, or to blank sheets of paper to be filled in later. Some relinquished their land this way; others refused. The homes of those who resisted were demolished. When some villagers appealed to the Gujarat High Court for a stay against forcible removal, the contractors stepped up the pace of demolition so the stay, when granted, was useless. A few of the four thousand [initial] oustees were paid for their property according to a formula that a World Bank-sponsored study says "invariably undervalues land." Three-quarters, however, received no compensation at all. Years later, the Bank reported that many of them "could be seen camping in extreme poverty at the edge of what remained of their lands" (1996: 13).

In 1989, an Indian social worker named Medha Patkar founded a citizens' activist group called Narmada Bachao Andolan ("Save the Narmada Movement") to protest the project on social and environmental grounds. Using Gandhian civil disobedience tactics such as a week-long march to the river's mouth in Gujarat, the Andolan succeeded in placing the Narmada issue in an international spotlight. Patkar's group forged ties with human rights and environmental NGOs in the West, which in turn began to lobby their governments in protest of the project. Authorities in India tried to repress the movement, detaining protestors for days or weeks at a time (Miller 1992: 4), but this only upped the ante and encouraged activists to focus their efforts on the World Bank and its donors. Patkar testified before a US House of Representatives special hearing on the Bank's role in the project, and the Japanese government withdrew its pledge of US$200 million for the project.

The upsurge of criticism caught the Bank on the back foot, and the controversy over the project cast the Indian government in a distinctly unflattering light. Though the Bank's own researchers had called attention to the project's serious problems, Bank managers – eager to lend and hesitant to ruffle the Indian government – suppressed criticisms. Finally, in 1991, World Bank President Barber Conable (1986–91) commissioned an independent review of the Bank's involvement in the project. Never before had the Bank hired an outsider to critique a Bank-funded project so comprehensively. Bradford Morse, a former Republican congressman and retired administrator for the UN Development Program, agreed to head the review, on the condition that his team be granted total autonomy, a million-dollar budget, and full access to all documents related to the project (Shihata 1994: 10; Caufield 1996: 25–6).

In June 1992, Morse delivered a 385-page report citing wide-ranging deficiencies in the Narmada project. It described ecological problems including downstream salinization, destruction of fisheries, and increased risk of malaria (owing to enlarged water surface area in reservoir zones); a Bank consultant who had studied the Sardar Sarovar site just six months previously was quoted as saying it would create "ideal breeding sites" for mosquitoes and "take Malaria to the doorsteps of the villagers" (Morse 1992: xxiii). The most biting criticisms, however, related to the project's lack of a credible resettlement and compensation program. Embarrassingly for the Bank, the report said that almost all of the project's problems had been documented before, and suppressed or ignored by Bank managers. A review team member recalled, "Morse told Lewis Preston [Conable's successor as Bank President, 1991–95] they could have saved a lot of money just looking in their own files" (Caufield 1996: 26). The report concluded with the suggestion that the Bank should "step back from the project and consider it afresh" (Morse 1992: xxv).

The Morse Report was careful not to disparage India or the three state governments, saying that ultimate responsibility for clarifying compensation policies "appears to us to rest with the Bank" (ibid., xx) which, after all, had commissioned the investigation. Cognizant of the sovereignty subtext of this formulation, the report also maintained – presciently, it turned out – that "every decision as to the Sardar Sarovar Projects has always been, and will continue to be, a decision for India and the states involved" (ibid., xxv). To the extent that the report rebuked India, it only pointed out that the government, like the Bank, had failed to act consistently with its own "comprehensive structure of policies for environmental protection and assessment of environmental impact" (ibid., xxi). It was more difficult to call out India for failing to live up to its own policies on resettlement and compensation, since India had no such national standards, viewing the issue as a subject for the state governments. In this area, the report could refer only to the jurisprudence of the Narmada Water Disputes Tribunal, which had laid down some conditions regarding resettlement and rehabilitation (though, as noted above, not for oustees lacking formal land title) but had been primarily concerned with the interstate distribution of benefits.

Though it focused fastidiously on the specific social and environmental problems plaguing the project, the Morse Report also evinced an astute understanding of the broader political context:

> We are well aware of the scale of the development task facing India, of the importance India places on irrigation in increasing production in the agricultural sector, and of the longstanding partnership between India and the Bank in this endeavor. But our Terms of Reference… require us to consider the Bank's policies, India's environmental regime, and the credit and loan agreements. These emerge from the context of Bank-India relations just as surely as does the longstanding partnership in the enhancement of agricultural production between the Bank and India. If there was no intention of following Bank policy or India's regulatory regime, it would have been appropriate to acknowledge this (ibid., xxiv).

The report also suggested that misguided enthusiasm might be to blame for the "failure to incorporate Bank policies into the 1985 loan and credit agreements and subsequent failure to require adherence to enforceable provisions of these agreements":

> How did this happen?
> It is apparent that there has been, and continues to be, deep concern among Bank officers and staff that India should have the means to enhance agricultural production. The Sardar Sarovar Projects were seen as offering enormous benefits, especially in terms of delivery of drinking water and irrigation. *There developed an eagerness on the part of the Bank and India to get on with the job. Both, it seems, were prepared to ease, or even disregard, Bank policy* and India's regulations and procedures dealing with resettlement and environmental protection in the hope of achieving the much-needed benefits (ibid., 353–5; emphasis added).

But if the Bank and India ultimately shared responsibility for the failures, their courses of action after the report's appearance would diverge sharply.

Ten weeks after Morse submitting his findings, the Bank issued its initial reply, "Narmada: Next Steps," which claimed that India had given assurances that it was taking measures to address the problems highlighted by the report, so there was no need to "step back." Interpreting this as a non-response, an international assemblage of some 250 activist organizations took out a full-page advertisement in the *Financial Times*, publishing an open letter to Bank President Preston that demanded, "the World Bank must withdraw from Sardar Sarovar immediately." If the Bank failed to pull out, it would show itself to be "beyond reform," and the NGOs would spearhead an international campaign to pressure donor countries to cut the Bank's funding (Caufield 1996: 27).

In October 1992, the Bank's Executive Directors met to consider the project's future. Australia, Canada, Germany, Japan, the Scandinavian region, and, in particular, the US, all called for a suspension of Bank support, but many borrower country Executive Directors sided with India and the board voted to give it until 1 April 1993 to demonstrate compliance with the relevant social and environmental covenants.

India never did acquiesce to the Bank's newfound sensitivities on these subjects, and on 31 March 1993, one day before the compliance deadline, it asked the Bank to cancel the remaining loan disbursements and to withdraw from the project. According to Caufield, "This was a face-saving maneuver, agreed ahead of time with the Bank, which otherwise would have had to cancel the loan the following day on the grounds of noncompliance" (ibid., 28). But the Bank may have been more concerned than India with saving face.

India forged ahead with the project without Bank assistance, at least until 1995 when its Supreme Court issued an injunction that brought a temporary halt in construction. In 1999 the Court's stay was lifted and work resumed. A highly-charged decade later, the struggle against the project continues, though as construction marches on the activists appear to be losing a war of attrition. Patkar and Narmada Bachao Andolan – flanked by a phalanx of allied Indian and transnational groups – have continued to protest the development scheme, invoking tactics including "drown pledges" and hunger strikes. For the anti-globalization movement, the Narmada issue has taken on mythical proportions: at the World Bank-IMF Spring Meetings in April 2000 in Washington, D.C., a late-to-the-party activist could be seen carrying a placard reading "Save the Narmada River," years after the Bank's withdrawal.[36]

The Narmada debacle had significant ramifications for both Bank and borrower, though the former bore the brunt of the impact. In 1993, the Bank established an Inspection Panel to investigate complaints about its lending operations. This semi-independent body would be "empowered to investigate complaints from people directly affected by Bank projects regarding violations of World Bank policy, procedures, and loan agreements."[37] Ibrahim Shihata, Vice President and General Counsel of the Bank and an architect of the panel, called Sardar Sarovar "the single most important case to draw attention to the issue of the Bank's accountability" (1994: 9). Michael Goldman argues, "This episode was important not only to social activists around the world, who could now see their potential power, but for the World Bank itself. The 'Narmada Effect,' as it has come to be called, is invoked regularly inside the Bank and reminds staff that the Bank must 'reform or die'" (2005: 152–3).

India took a different lesson from the episode: doing business with the Bank could be more trouble than it was worth (as the decision to press on without its assistance so vividly shows). This point was not lost on the Bank, either. Simply put, the Bank is conflicted. It retains a strong portfolio interest in continuing to lend for such works in its largest borrower countries. But as it submitted to ever-expanding safeguard demands from NGOs in subsequent years, the Bank began to box itself into a "standoffish posture," as Mallaby puts it, toward massive infrastructure projects generally.

If there were any doubt, in what might be seen as a postscript to this episode (and a similar 1999 controversy over a smaller dam project in China's Qinghai province), India and China's Executive Directors drove the point home in February 2003 when they issued "their first-ever joint statement," a "rebuke of the Bank's managers and all staff members who worked on infrastructure" and a demand that the Bank in this sector "needed to respond more energetically to their poor clients" – in this case, two borrowers who "spoke for" more than two billion people.[38]

Who did "speak for" the Indian poor that would be impacted by a project like Narmada: the Indian NGOs and transnational activists, the donor countries, or the Indian state? The question poses a profound dilemma for the Bank. In a generic sense, this is a dilemma that it faces in all of its client countries, but India's democracy – and above all its size in the Bank's portfolio – render the Bank's dilemma there particularly acute.

## Conclusion

A comprehensive history of relations between India and the World Bank could fill volumes. The intent of this chapter, a selective survey of key phases and critical junctures in the relationship, has been to show how deeply impacted the Bank has been by its work in India, and how the importance that the Bank attaches to its largest borrower has led it continually to evolve its lending strategy in an effort to remain relevant to India's development. The Bank has gained much of its understanding of growth, poverty reduction, and what it deems sound development strategy in India, and when its judgments in all such matters have evolved over the years, it has often been on the basis of lessons learned in India. This is not even to mention the role that India has played, directly or indirectly, in the establishment of new World Bank institutions such as IDA and the Inspection Panel.

The chapter has also provided insights into the role of the Bank in India's development over the years: its influence, but also its limits. The Bank's project and balance of payments assistance, alongside its role as coordinator of the Aid-India consortium, provided India with much-needed financial resources in the early part of this history. As this pattern shaded into aid dependency in the 1960s, India came to resent external scrutiny of its economic policies, and endeavored to end the addiction. It has since used the Bank more strategically and instrumentally, sometimes to tip the balance in domestic struggles over the direction of economic policy. But the Bank has never been India's tutor or taskmaster – with the arguable exception of the 1966 devaluation, and even then, a section of the Indian policy elite favored the course of action. India has followed its own developmental path (and continues to do so). This, along with its sheer size and importance to global development and poverty reduction efforts, has made it a client of considerable attraction – and frustration – for the Bank. The allure of India is simply existential; like the British mountaineer George Mallory reportedly said, when asked why he wanted to summit Mt. Everest: "Because it's there."

As an early decolonization case, as a country with a distinctive development strategy, and as an uncommon democracy in strategically important Asia, India became important both to the Western allies and to the World Bank – the latter's "apolitical norm" notwithstanding – during the early Cold War. Initially, India's central planning model and ISI strategy were seen as models for the developing world, and its democratic regime gave it a special status in a perceived race to modernization against an authoritarian-socialist "peer" such as China. But India's economic record proved disappointing to the West and to the Bank – in part, at least, because of the great expectations thrust upon it. As persistent food and foreign exchange shortages made India vulnerably dependent on foreign aid, donor countries led by the United States used the Bank to pressure India to change its economic policies, culminating in the politically explosive devaluation of the rupee in 1966, well more than a decade before the formalization of structural adjustment lending by the Bank.

In the wake of the bitter fallout from India's devaluation and abandoned liberalization, the Bank's policies diverged sharply from those of the US. This challenges the conventional wisdom about donor country influence over the Bank's operations; one remarkable aspect of this history is how *insignificant* the US was in influencing Bank-India relations after the 1960s. The Bank stepped up assistance to fill the space vacated by bilateral aid, and it scrupulously avoided any policy controversy with India, even as it became more neoliberal in its relations with other borrowers,[39] and even though India remained wedded to its autarkic state-led development model (with only piecemeal reforms) through the 1980s.

In 1991, a quarter-century after India's first major balance of payments crisis, another economic emergency led to the Bank's first structural adjustment loan in the country, and the launch of a major liberalization program by a committed Indian leadership. But even though the Indian government and the Bank's market philosophies were now more closely aligned, India's relatively quick return to stability – and eventual burgeoning foreign exchange reserves and private investment – sharply reduced its material need for the Bank's resources. As the leadership moved on to the challenging task of maintaining a broad consensus behind liberalization – amid seismic changes to India's political system in the direction of party fragmentation – India successfully resisted the Bank's attempts to play a part in framing the liberalization agenda. India, to the Bank's frustration, would reform on its own terms. The Bank's challenge in post-liberalization India was to remain relevant to the reform process, and to package its material resources and development expertise in a way that would continue to draw a steady stream of Indian borrowing even as New Delhi enjoyed other options.

Everest eluded Mallory. By the mid-1990s, the realization had begun to dawn that India was too big for the World Bank. Perhaps the resolution to the Bank's relevance dilemma lay in dividing the leviathan state.[40]

## Chapter Two

# REMAINING RELEVANT: THE WORLD BANK'S STRATEGY FOR AN INDIA OF STATES

*There was always agreement between the two partners that the Bank should make a greater contribution to Indian development than it actually had. The disagreement was over whose fault it was. Like many arranged marriages, however, the relationship has endured and grown stronger over time, despite the absence of romance in the beginning and the persistence of irritating behavior on both sides over the decades. [...] In 1996, there were some reasons for optimism that the Bank could finally make a difference in India. [...] Some states were breaking out of the pack by pursuing aggressive reform and growth policies, led by a new generation of politicians.*

Edwin ("Ed") Lim, World Bank Country Director for India (1996–2002)
(Lim 2005: 108–9)

*Being chief minister in contemporary India is a tough proposition. States can no longer look to the Centre for resources, they have to fend for themselves. [...]*
  *A politician who wants to deliver cannot have an ego. He has to lobby with the Central government for funds, using every persuasion he can think of.*

Nara Chandrababu Naidu, Chief Minister of India's Andhra Pradesh
state (1995–2004) (Naidu and Ninan 2000: 6–7)

*I consider your money to be my money.*

Palaniappan Chidambaram, Finance Minister of India (1996–8,
2004–8) to the World Bank's Ed Lim, 1996 (Lim interview, 2003)

In the mid-1990s, the World Bank evolved a new assistance strategy for India. Its core innovation has been policy-based lending relationships with select state governments in India's federal system.[1] Though the Bank's involvement with India's states was not new – the states had always played an important role in project implementation – the new strategy departed from the traditional arrangement in two important ways. First, in the past, the Bank made no real attempt to influence how its assistance would be allocated across the states, leaving that to the central government. Second, to the extent that the Bank engaged in comprehensive policy dialogue with India (and the previous chapter demonstrated the limited and episodic nature of such engagement) it essentially was confined to the central government level.

Under India's Constitution, the states have powers in a number of areas critical to development, including the "social sectors" of primary education and health, physical infrastructure provision and capital maintenance, agriculture and allied functions such as irrigation, industrial promotion, and more. However, prior to the 1991 liberalization, the central government in New Delhi ("the Centre") had encroached significantly on the states' authority through its various ministries and especially through the Planning Commission. The latter also had dominated decision-making with respect to investment allocation across the states.

Virtually since the beginning of its relationship with India, the World Bank has invested in particular projects in the states – first mainly in infrastructure, then later in rural development and the social sectors as well – but the meting out of projects across the states had been determined by a combination of technocratic decisions made in New Delhi and political bargaining between the Centre and the states. In short, the Bank had engaged the state governments as implementing agencies for development projects that were largely designed and allocated at the Centre.

Under the new approach, the Bank has taken the view that the overall policy and governance environment – encompassing a wide range of fiscal, sectoral, and institutional factors – is much more conducive to economic growth and poverty reduction in some states than in others. The Bank aims to maximize the impact of its assistance – both in terms of intermediate policy outcomes and longer-term growth and poverty outcomes – by focusing on select states. Summing up the contrast with the Bank's old way of doing business, one Bank official suggested, "In portfolio terms, we've gone from investing in a sort of all-India 'mutual fund' to picking individual 'stocks'."[2]

This book's introduction depicted the basic conceptual contrast between the Bank's traditional (pre-1998) and selective (post-1998) approaches to India's states. Technically, as previously noted, the Government of India (GoI) is the "borrower" for the Bank's state-level loans, with the state governments designated as "beneficiaries." This reflects the Indian government's preference to carefully manage state government borrowing. In other federal countries, the Bank has lent directly to sub-national governments in recent years, though its charter does require a sovereign central guarantee on such loans (Article III, Section 4(i)). In the Indian arrangement, the Centre agrees to on-lend the rupee equivalent of the Bank's dollar-denominated loans/credits to the states.[3]

The Bank's criteria for choosing states have evolved considerably since the strategy first emerged in the 1990s. During an initial "focus states" phase – mainly involving operations in Andhra Pradesh, Karnataka, and Uttar Pradesh – the Bank emphasized states whose leadership purportedly had demonstrated a strong commitment to reforms. Between 1998 and 2003, the Bank's lending to these three states comprised a little more than one-third of its total assistance to India, consisting of both investment and adjustment lending (another third went to fund central government projects and programs, and the remaining third went to projects in other states).

A brief technical note is in order here. World Bank lending, both IBRD and IDA, comes in two forms: investment lending and adjustment lending, also known as "project" and "program" assistance (the latter is sometimes also referred to simply as "budget support"). As Howes and colleagues explain, "A typical investment loan has a 5–7 year duration, and it finances goods, works, and services in support of economic and social development sectoral projects. On the other hand, an adjustment loan has a relatively shorter duration (1 to 3 years), and it provides quick-disbursing financing to support policy and institutional reforms. Over the past two decades, adjustment loans have accounted for about 30 percent of total Bank lending [worldwide]" (Howes, Mishra et al. 2008: 43, n1).

Since adjustment lending is general budget support, it may be considered a more flexible form of financing than project assistance, which disburses against specific expenditures (for example, depending on the nature of the project, paying contractors for land surveys, technical planning, construction costs, medicines, and so on). However, there are also more comprehensive policy conditions associated with adjustment lending, which often get at key fiscal and budgetary issues such as deficit reductions and expenditure restructuring (for example, lowering or eliminating consumption subsidies and increasing investments in infrastructure and the social sectors). Formally, the World Bank in 2004 established a new label, Development Policy Loan (DPL), for the instrument formerly known as the Structural Adjustment Loan (SAL). Here, to facilitate the narrative and to provide conceptual consistency across the mid-1990s to present period, I will use the more informal terms, "policy-based lending," "adjustment lending," and "program lending" interchangeably to indicate both DPLs and SALs (as well as special cases, such as the Bank's first comprehensive reform loan package for Andhra Pradesh in 1998, which "bundled" project support in several sectors under broad policy agreements between the state and the Bank, so constituted because it preceded the World Bank executive board's approval of a sub-national structural adjustment loan instrument).[4]

More recently, the Bank's sub-national emphasis has shifted from "focus states" to "lagging states" – those with high rates of poverty and low human development indicators. This shift has taken the Bank into policy-based lending for states like Bihar, widely perceived as having some of the *weakest* policies and institutions among all states. In other words, the focus has shifted from what some critics characterized as "picking winners," to pulling along the states that have the farthest to travel. This chapter will explain the origins of the sub-national emphasis in the World Bank's assistance strategy for India, and will discuss the initial "focus states" phase of its implementation. The following chapter will discuss the shift toward "lagging states."

The Bank's increased sub-national emphasis, over the last fifteen years, has been the single most important innovation in its country strategy for India – which, we have seen, is its largest cumulative borrower and one of its largest annual borrowers. Yet the strategy has received almost no attention from outside analysts, either in the literature on India's political economy or on the Bank itself. Stephen Howes, Deepak Mishra, and V.J. Ravishankar – all World Bank economists during the strategy's implementation – offer the only systematic analysis of the new approach (Howes, Mishra et al. 2008), apart from this author's own work on some of its aspects (Kirk 2007, 2005). They note, "policy-based lending by the World Bank to the states of India […] is one of the largest policy-based lending experiences in the world, and certainly the largest at the sub-national level" (Howes, Mishra et al. 2008: 41). But though their analysis is quite valuable, and based on first-hand experience, they readily concede that theirs is not an independent perspective. The purpose of this chapter is to provide a more comprehensive political economy perspective on the strategy.

The genesis and early implementation of sub-national reform lending is a somewhat complicated story to tell, since it requires an explanation of the role of India's states in the economic liberalization and the changing political economy of federalism in India, as well as a discussion of state-level political contexts that vary enormously. Indeed, as this chapter will demonstrate, one of the reasons for the Bank's mixed record so far in its state-level relationships in India might be an initial underestimation of just *how* significant are the political economy and developmental differences across the states.

The story also attests to how the economic reform impulses of India's central government are constrained by federal and coalition politics. The post-1991 liberalization has coincided with the end of single-party rule in India, and *federalized coalition governments* have become the "new normal" in New Delhi. Neither the Congress Party nor its only major challenger for "national party" stature, the Hindu chauvinist Bharatiya Janata Party (BJP), have been able to form governments without the support of other, smaller parties. Such coalition partners (or outside supporters) are parties whose bases are restricted to regions or even single states, lending an implicitly "federalized" quality to central coalition politics.

The emergence of such a fragmented political environment, alongside the diminishment of central planning after liberalization, has led some analysts to argue that the capacity of the central government to coordinate investment with the states has been diminished (Sáez 2002). Certainly, the states have pursued increasingly independent and differentiated strategies with respect to private and foreign direct investment, with important implications for their growth rates in the liberalization era (as the next chapter will discuss). In a similar vein, some observers have speculated that the World Bank's new sub-national lending approach reflects the diminished capacity of the central government to manage relations between the Bank and the state governments. By allowing sub-national policy dialogue and lending, Kripa Sridharan suggests, the Centre "has removed itself from the picture in a sense" (2003: 477).

This is an oversimplification. The central government still formally and legally controls the states' external borrowing – and as this chapter will demonstrate, the Bank itself is only too aware of its role. Historically, as we have seen, India has sought to retain maximum policy autonomy vis-à-vis the Bank and other international financial institutions; in fact, the Bank's original incentive for the new state-level focus was to make itself more relevant to India's reform process.

Against this backdrop, the Centre's support for sub-national policy-based lending presents an intriguing puzzle. This chapter will argue that while the Bank *was* the initial force behind policy-based lending to the states, the strategy met with the Centre's approval because it complemented the Indian government's *own* interest in encouraging state-level reforms. Simply put, this suggests that the incentives that impact the Bank's state-wise lending choices in India are not necessarily the same ones that drive private investors, even if the Bank and private actors may look for broadly the same indicators of "market-friendliness" in state-level policies. The Bank still is bound by a highly centralized – and still inherently political – external assistance regime in India, even if decentralizing logics drive other kinds of investment allocations.

It necessarily is a nuanced story. In one respect, the "diminished central capacity" hypothesis is right: the central government that originally approved the Bank's new strategy, the United Front (1996–8), was an especially fragile coalition of parties whose main common interest was their shared antipathy both toward the Congress and the BJP. The particular importance of regional parties to this coalition inherently limited the central government's policy leverage over state leaders, who were reluctant to undertake politically unpopular fiscal and public enterprise reforms. But the political and bureaucratic leadership in India's finance ministry at the time was also critical to the Centre's approval of the new assistance strategy: the World Bank's interlocutors were among the most reformist leaders in the country.

Finance Minister Palaniappan Chidambaram told the Bank's Country Director, Ed Lim, "I consider your money to be my money," and the two men and their senior staffs shared many of the same ideas about the state-level reforms and the changes in India's fiscal federalism that would be necessary to consolidate the liberalization launched in 1991 (which Chidambaram, as commerce minister, had helped to implement). The Bank, the finance minister recognized, could help catalyze state-level reforms that the Centre wanted to see anyway, but which it could not coerce out of state leaders given its political dependence on their support.

Chidambaram's statement is instructive for what it says about India's control over its relationship with the lender. If the Bank was being permitted to do something revolutionary, it was only because the strategy aligned with the Centre's own interest in tackling the "second-generation reforms" agenda. The Indian leadership's embrace of sub-national reform lending by the Bank signifies its ability to adapt to the new federalized coalition politics, and to devise novel ways of pursuing its economic reform goals in spite of the states' greater capacity to resist pressure from New Delhi. State governments might enjoy the new financing opportunities presented by the World Bank, but the Centre would retain ultimate – even if arm's length – discretion over relations between the Bank and the states. The Bank was a mere instrument; the Indian government was its manager.

If it is tempting to dismiss Chidambaram's statement as mere posturing, then it is also revealing that in implementing the new strategy, the World Bank has acted in ways that demonstrate that it, too, understands that it serves at the pleasure of Indian authorities. The Bank, concerned that the Centre might rescind its support for the focus state strategy, was compelled to seek "protection" against this possibility by making Andhra Pradesh the flagship beneficiary of the new strategy. This state's ruling Telugu Desam Party (TDP) and mercurial Chief Minister N. Chandrababu Naidu (1995–2004) provided critical support to the central government coalitions through successive elections (Naidu helped convene the 1996–8 United Front, and offered outside backing to the 1998–9 and 1999–2004 National Democratic Alliance led by the BJP). The World Bank perceived that the state's political clout made it harder for the Centre to rescind support for the focus states program once it was set in motion.

Eventually, the Centre *did* begin to rethink its support for the strategy – ironically, at least in part because the overwhelming focus on Andhra Pradesh led some other states to complain that the selection process was arbitrary and politically biased. More fundamentally, the Indian government became more concerned about widening inter-state disparities, and asked the Bank to shift its strategy from "lead reforming states" to "lagging" ones. That shift in India's rationale for state-focused lending, which began in the early 2000s and was reinforced by the perceived message of the 2004 elections, is the subject of the next chapter.

This chapter begins with a discussion of both the "supply-" and "demand-side" factors that led to a meeting of minds between the Bank and India on sub-national policy-based lending in 1996. The analysis then moves on to the early implementation of the strategy, tracing the selection process for the Bank's inaugural class of states and comparing some aspects of its policy dialogue and the politics of reform in Andhra Pradesh, Karnataka, and Uttar Pradesh. The comparison of the state-level experiences focuses on political economy and treats fiscal reforms as the main priority of their programs with the Bank, though power sector and governance issues will also be discussed.[5] The last part of the chapter assesses some aspects of the "focus states" experiment against its original goals, in particular the Bank's goal of remaining relevant in India and India's goal of addressing state-level fiscal aspects of its ongoing economic reforms program.

## A Marriage of Interests: Shifting the Focus of Policy-Based Lending to India's States

### Supply Side Incentives and Organizational Factors

Though state-level policy-based lending could not have been initiated without the express support of the Government of India, the story behind the strategy begins with the Bank rather than at the Centre – and within the Bank, at the level of the India department rather than with senior management or donor country preferences. While it ran parallel to a developing interest on the Bank's part in fiscal decentralization and the special reform challenges confronting federal countries generally, the focus-states strategy for India was fundamentally a bottom-up response to the particular challenge of engaging such a large, proud, and relatively self-reliant borrower. It was a logical evolution for an assistance strategy in a country "too big for the Bank."

According to officials on both sides of the Bank-India relationship, the idea of the Bank establishing comprehensive and direct policy dialogue with India's states – possibly linked to lending operations – first emerged around 1994. At the October 1994 IMF-World Bank annual meetings (held in Madrid that year), Bank officials floated the idea in sideline discussions with Indian finance ministry representatives. While Finance Minister Manmohan

Singh did not rule out the possibility, he did not consider the proposal to be detailed enough to warrant action.[6] The Bank did manage to include in its 1995 *Country Assistance Strategy* a proposal to focus more attention on state-level sectoral and fiscal reforms, which the Indian government approved (Howes et al. 2008: 45). But the link between reform-oriented analytical work and lending operations was not nearly as explicit as it would become in the next iteration of the strategy.

There was a cross-national context for sub-national policy-based lending by the Bank, though its role in shaping the India strategy was at best indirect, not causal. The Bank employed a form of sub-national policy-based lending in Brazil beginning in 1994, in response to a request by federal authorities there concerned with burgeoning state-level budget deficits and debt. During 1995-7, the Bank conducted a policy dialogue with several Brazilian states, and proffered a series of four loans for the privatization of state banks and public infrastructure enterprises, accounting for about 10 percent of its country commitments during this time. A report by the Bank's Operations Evaluation Department (OED) characterizes these transactions as "de facto adjustment loans that had to be constructed as investment loans because there was no appropriate lending instrument at the time" (OED 2004: 10) (The Bank's Executive Board had not been presented with any proposal for a "sub-national adjustment loan" instrument; the Bank's India team would confront the same procedural constraint in its early policy-based lending to Andhra Pradesh, discussed below). Similarly, in 1995–6, Bank staff and Argentine authorities agreed on policy-based loans for a set of that country's provinces.

But in the mid-1990s, the Bank's India Department was "barely aware" of its counterparts' parallel experiments in Latin America (Zagha 2002). The country team came to its own understanding of the role of India's states in the reform process, through on-the-ground experience.

There also was a new, ready-made vocabulary for what the Bank was proposing to do in India: *selectivity*. In the mid-1990s aid literature, something of a paradigm shift was underway from "conditionality" to "selectivity," based on findings that *ex-ante* reform requirements were seldom effective in encouraging borrowers to change their policies. Rather, a growing consensus suggested, policy-based lending should employ *ex-post* selectivity. As Paul Collier argued, "Conditionality should be used not to induce policy change but to ensure that aid goes to environments where it can be effective" (1997: 64). In other words, policy-based lending should reward and encourage demonstrated reformers, rather than attempting to "buy" reform up front. Though Collier and others meant selectivity to apply to a cross-national context – his focus was on aid to sub-Saharan African countries – the Bank would modify the idea to rationalize selective sub-national engagement in India.

Additionally, it should be noted that around this same time, other external assistance providers developed sub-national policy based lending in India. The Asian Development Bank (ADB) made such a loan to Gujarat in 1996. Though the ADB would later claim to have pioneered such lending in India (Asian Development Bank 2007), this seems to be another case of the parallel development of similar strategies. The ADB was able to fashion an appropriate sub-national adjustment lending instrument before the World Bank did, but this likely reflected organizational differences between the two lenders (the greater diversity of country interests on the World Bank's executive board, along with the greater visibility of its operations, led it to take more time to approve a new sub-national SAL-type loan instrument; in the meantime the Bank improvised in India, using state-focused investment lending for Andhra Pradesh in 1998).

As it turned out, the World Bank occasionally would cross paths with the ADB in the states (Karnataka, we will see, had the luxury of choosing between the two lenders), but the Bank's scale and resources led its sub-national policy-based assistance to dwarf that of the ADB and other comers such as Britain's Department of International Development (DFID).[7] On the other hand, the ADB's lower profile may have facilitated a more productive dialogue with some of its "focal states," such as Kerala and West Bengal. These two states traditionally have had strong Communist parties, and even though they have become much less doctrinaire in recent years – the left leadership in West Bengal, in particular, has aggressively courted private investment – the "imperialist" World Bank might have been somewhat more awkward a patron for them.[8] DFID's state-level approach was to partner with either the World Bank or the ADB, sometimes piggy-backing grant aid onto the multilateral lenders' programs, though it began to move away from its "partner states" model after 2004.

At least as important as any cross-national idea diffusion or lender competition-*cum*-coordination within India was another organizational factor: the World Bank's appointment of a new Country Director for India in 1996, the first to be stationed permanently in New Delhi rather than in Washington (following a managerial reform initiative under World Bank President James Wolfensohn). Not only did this proximity create new possibilities for engagement with the states, but the personality and experiences of the new director were also important. Edwin ("Ed") Lim had served as Chief of Resident Mission for the World Bank in Beijing from 1985 to 1990, where he oversaw some of the Bank's earliest lending to mainland China and drew lessons from its rapid growth experience.

Lim quickly took the temperature of Bank-India relations, and appraised the political context of India's economic reforms. "Compared with the relationship with China, the Bank's relationship with India was actually deeper, more solid, and based on a high degree of knowledge – if not always understanding – of each other," he later reflected (2005: 108). Lim also perceived that whereas India's political leadership could be touchy regarding its relations with the Bank, finance ministry technocrats such as Montek Singh Ahluwalia – a professional economist and former World Bank manager – "by and large shared the same views on what was needed to accelerate reform and growth, as well as on the frustration in persuading the politicians to act" (2005: 108).

When he became country director for India in late 1996, Lim recalled, "There were persuasive long-term as well as short-term reasons for a new approach for the World Bank in India":

> From a long-term perspective, few in the Bank or in India would disagree that the Bank's contribution to development and poverty reduction in India over the preceding five decades had been disappointing relative to India's needs and potential. A short-term reason also existed. When the worst of the 1991 crisis was over and the first wave of reforms focusing on the external sector was under way, the need for balance-of-payments financing from the Bank began to fade. However, India's economic performance continued to be hampered by unsustainable domestic policies (for example, power, food, and fertilizer subsidies, as well as civil service wages), which in turn fed large fiscal deficits at both the central (federal) and state levels. However, we were unable to articulate a program of assistance that would provide an effective and coherent response to those policy issues, thus greatly diminishing India's appetite for borrowing from the IBRD for what was a relatively disparate program of isolated operations. As a result, our lending to India dropped and softened considerably (two-thirds IDA, one-third IBRD). This situation began to concern some of our major shareholders, prompting them to call for India – as they had for China – to graduate from the IDA (2005: 113).

Thus, Lim confronted both the shadow of the past – India's post-1966 wariness at Bank efforts to influence its economic policies – and the coming possibility of India's ineligibility for the Bank's lowest-cost IDA aid. Ratcheting up the IDA share in assistance to India was not going to work, given donor positions, so the Bank would have to find another way of remaining relevant to the borrower. The Bank, as Lim understood it, would have to find a new way of appealing to India's leaders that would increase the attractiveness of standard-term IBRD loans and give the Bank "a seat at the table" in India's reform process (Chassard 2002).

Lim's transition from leading the Bank's lending in China to overseeing operations in India significantly shaped his ideas for engaging the Indian leadership. Noting that the Chinese growth miracle had benefitted some of its provinces much more than others (basically, the coastal areas over the interior), Lim invoked a Deng Xiaoping dictum, "If we all want to be rich, we have to let some become rich first" (Lim 2005; Lim 2003). India's states were a highly varied lot, he observed, not only in their starting points at the time of the 1991 liberalization, but also in the commitment of their leaders to market reform and pro-growth policies. The Bank's ability to do very much about the states' initial conditions was inherently limited, but its engagement with select state leaders – those who were committed to growth-supporting policy reforms – might make a difference.

Lim thus put a new spin on the as-yet unfulfilled Bank idea of going sub-national with policy-based lending: the Bank should be "deliberately anti-egalitarian" in lending to India's states; it should lend heavily to the most reform-committed among them to encourage them to achieve their full growth potential. Their success, he reasoned, would present powerful "demonstration effects" to the rest of the country that would be more influential than whatever material resources the Bank could provide. By practicing "selectivity" and concentrating lending in a handful of states, Lim argued, the Bank could leverage greater policy influence throughout India (Lim 2003). Reform laggards could take lessons from the focus states, or stew in the juice of their own misguided policies.

The idea of "deliberately anti-egalitarian" assistance to the states, on the basis of their economic policies, was revolutionary in the context of India's existing regime for transferring central resources to the states. Though in practice partisan and political considerations have influenced Centre-state transfers (Khemani 2003; see below), normatively, at least, the idea that resources should be allocated objectively to promote balanced regional development has been a defining attribute of India's federalism for decades.[9] When the Planning Commission was established in the mid-1950s, in support of the Nehruvian development strategy, it "was enjoined to reduce poverty and work to minimize inequalities in income, status, facilities, and opportunities" across India's diverse population, including economic disparities across states (McCarten 2003: 258).

As the incoming World Bank country director in 1996, Lim's interactions with the outgoing Manmohan Singh finance ministry were limited; Lim said he did not enjoy good access to ministry officials in comparison to his earlier experiences with the Chinese leadership, and he found the "protocol fixation" of the ministry "amazing" (Lim 2003). However firm Singh's convictions were about the need for India to continue its liberalization process, he was equally committed to protecting India's prerogative to reform on its own terms and at its own pace. Soon, however, Lim was to encounter a new finance minister less concerned with protocol, and willing to partner with the Bank to accelerate reform in the states, even if it meant greater regional inequality.

## Demand Side Incentives and Political Context: Coalition Government and Fiscal Federalism

In April-May 1996, India's general election produced an unstable situation. No party emerged with a majority in the 545-seat parliament to form a government. The BJP, which had won a plurality of seats (at 161), tried to form a government, but it lasted less than two weeks when it could not demonstrate the support of the chamber's majority. The Congress Party, which had led India since mid-1991 and had ushered in economic liberalization, performed relatively poorly (140 seats) and declined to partner with the left parties to head the government. Instead, the Congress and the left parties (led by the Communist Party of India-Marxist) offered outside support to a hurriedly convened "United Front" coalition of parties, which collectively held 192 seats, with the Janata Dal and its leader H.D. Deve Gowda of Karnataka leading the government. Not only did the United Front encompass stridently regionalist parties, but it also straddled a range of economic perspectives, making the prospects for continuing liberalization difficult.

That autumn, Ed Lim called on the new Minister of Finance, Palaniappan Chidambaram, to secure approval of the Bank's strategy for selective, policy-based lending to India's states. Lim offered the "demonstration effects" rationale, and sweetened the proposal by suggesting that state-level policy-based lending could become a vehicle for significant expansion of the Bank's total assistance to India, from the mid-1990s annual average of about US$1.5 billion up to US$3 billion (Lim 2003).

Lim later reflected that India's 1996 embrace of what would come to be known as the Bank's "focus states" strategy had depended both on the political context of a constrained coalition government, and the "configuration of specific people" in the Indian finance ministry at the time. Though Lim and the Bank encountered early support for the new strategy among ministry technocrats and advisors (such as Montek Ahluwalia, Shankar Acharya, and Jairam Ramesh), the stance taken in favor of the approach by the political leadership (Chidambaram) was the most decisive (ibid.).

Chidambaram, it should be noted, has twice served as India's finance minister (1996–8 and 2004–9), and has been a consistent advocate of pursuing market-led economic growth. As commerce minister, he had supported Manmohan Singh's Finance Ministry in the major liberalization program of 1991, and some observers have suggested that his reform enthusiasm even exceeded that of his predecessor. Shekhar Gupta, the editor at *The Indian Express* who worked with

Chidambaram when he penned a regular opinion column for the paper from 2002 to 2004 (while the NDA government was in power), suggests that he is "the most prominent, persistent, committed – and successful – of a handful of instinctive reformers in our political system" (Gupta 2007: ix). Chidambaram, who holds a Masters in Business Administration (MBA) degree from Harvard, has consistently articulated pro-market views and the conviction that a rising tide lifts all boats: "it is sustained economic growth – and the consequent reduction in levels of poverty – that will empower millions of people of India [...] when India emerges as an economic powerhouse, it will be unstoppable" (Chidambaram 2007: 1–3).

But apart from personal inclination and background, what political economy factors led Chidambaram to embrace such a significant change in India's relationship with the Bank beginning in 1996? The potential doubling of annual Bank lending was not decisive. As Lim conceded, by the mid-1990s India had returned to a much more comfortable foreign exchange position – about US$60 billion in reserves – so that the dollar incentive that had accompanied earlier Bank conditionality was not as important. Moreover, budding private investment was expanding the government's options for project financing.

On the other hand, Chidambaram had come to recognize by the mid-1990s that for India to proceed beyond the first stage of liberalization, the state governments would have to effectively complement the Centre's initiatives by committing to a wide range of "second stage" budgetary, institutional, and governance reforms in their domains. Chidambaram and his fellow reformists apparently had a reasonably clear understanding, through their immersion in India's political economy, of some of the sub-national and intergovernmental dimensions of reform that the academic literature only recently has caught up to.

A somewhat technical discussion of the state government's reform incentives – and their relationship to India's fiscal transfer regime – is necessary to make clear the central government's motives in embracing a sub-national focus for the World Bank. Narratively, this risks falling down a rabbit hole into the maddening complexity of India's diverse state-level politics and fiscal federalism. The excursion will be brief, but it will shine some light into the deeper context of centrally managed resources in India, of which World Bank loans to the states are just one relatively minor component. The World Bank could not be just an outside spectator to India's fiscal federalism: it is also a participant in the system (World Bank 2004c). The upshot of this analysis is a more multidimensional picture of the reform challenges that India and the World Bank were plunging into by way of sub-national reform lending.

Note that the discussion here generally employs past-tense verbs, meant to suggest that this was how India's fiscal federalism and states' reform incentives looked from the perspective of the central government and World Bank in the latter 1990s. As we will see in the conclusion of this chapter, the period since 2000 has seen some modifications to the intergovernmental transfer regime.

In many respects, the importance of India's states to its economic development was nothing new.[10] Many key policy areas – including aspects of rural development, education, health, industrial, infrastructure, and tax policy – are subjects in which the states have always held important powers, either by Constitutional writ or by historical convention. But the planning apparatus had also distorted the picture for many years. Sanjeevi Guhan, a public finance specialist and former state-level finance secretary, articulated what many analysts were beginning to perceive in the mid-1990s. While "the federal dimensions of the new economic policies [had been] relatively neglected so far," he said, they were "bound to assume increasing importance as these policies gain momentum" (1995a: 241). With the shift from plan to market, the states' constitutional powers and economic policies would become much more significant:

> Why is the role of the states important in the structural adjustment that has been initiated? The obvious answer is that under the division of responsibilities in the Indian Constitution, most of the key sectors salient to the adjustment process lie within their primary jurisdiction: industrial infrastructure; power development; agriculture, its allied sectors and irrigation; roads, other than national highways; social sectors such as education, health, and medical services, nutrition, water supply, and urban development.
>
> This explanation may seem to be inadequate for it might be argued that, after all, for nearly four decades it was possible for the central government to dominate economic development in India through the planning process and other instrumentalities. The short answer is that, essentially the NEP [new economic policy] involves the dismantling of detailed planning and of the pervasive regulatory system which was its corollary. The implication of this process is a shift in the role of government from activities hitherto controlled at the center – notably, industrial regulation – to those which mainly fall within the sphere of the states such as social welfare and infrastructure for agriculture and industry. *The space vacated by central planning has to be filled by the private sector and by the states.* To a much greater degree the states will have to shoulder the full potential of their constitutional responsibilities *and to do so they need to be encouraged and enabled to act* (ibid., 241; emphasis added).

Complicating this picture were electoral incentives in many states, and India's byzantine regime of intergovernmental fiscal transfers. Many of the most politically vexing of India's "second generation" reforms would have to transpire at the state level. Beginning in the 1980s, increasingly competitive electoral politics in many states had followed the rise of new regional and single-state parties as challengers to the Congress Party. This trend was accelerating in the 1990s, just as India's national leadership was attempting to pursue market-oriented economic reforms. As Niraja Gopal Jayal observes, "Since 1989, India's party system has become increasingly fragmented with the number of national parties remaining more or less constant, while the number of state parties have more than doubled" (2006: 195). These developments encouraged the abandonment of what had been, until the 1980s, an "Indian tradition of fiscal prudence" (Joshi 1998: 147).

By the mid-1990s, liberalization advocates recognized that key second-generation reform goals might founder on India's increasingly fractured politics. Stabilizing the states' budget deficits and shifting spending toward infrastructure and the social sectors would require that state governments raise tax revenues, cut popular consumption subsidies, painstakingly restructure or privatize loss-generating state-owned enterprises such as the State Electricity Boards (SEBs), and reduce public sector payrolls – estimated to carry as many as 1,000,000 redundant workers (Frankel 2005: 591). Some states, such as Uttar Pradesh, were even said to carry significant numbers of deceased or fictitious employees on their rosters.

The political challenges presented by such a reform agenda were daunting. Oftentimes, the very policies that were breaking the states' budgets had comprised key campaign promises by their political leaders. Farmers, a key constituency in many states, were not likely to back incumbents who rescinded cut-rate electricity, fertilizer, and irrigation provision. Nor would many middle-class voters, inured to policies intended for the truly poor, embrace an end to subsidies for rice and other staple foods. Subsidized provision and outright theft of electricity were siphoning state resources away from capital maintenance and investment; physical capacity in the power sector was literally breaking down under the strain in some states. State employees' unions, often closely linked to political parties, would oppose public enterprise restructuring and privatization that threatened to eliminate jobs.[11] Indeed, political party leaders often had treated the entire public sector as all-purpose patronage for their functionaries and voters. And yet if they failed to reverse many of these policies, the states might be faced with insolvency, as interest payments claimed a growing proportion of their revenue expenditure and investment in infrastructure and the social sectors declined.

Along with the domestic electoral compulsions leading states to carry large budget deficits, India's fiscal federalism undermined their incentives for fiscal discipline. There is a growing consensus in the comparative political economy literature that fiscal federalism generally can create soft budget constraints for sub-national governments. Depending on the particular institutional arrangements, states/provinces in federal countries may expect that the national government can be made to "accommodate and share in excess expenditures" through fiscal transfers and bailouts (Rodden et al. 2003: 6; see also Rodden 2006).

According to this perspective, the sub-national governments put their electoral interests ahead of the fiscal stability of the federation as a whole, leading them to run budget deficits with the expectation that they can shift the cost burden to the central government. For reasons ranging from formal-legal obligations to political dependence on regional allies, the central government may find it impossible *not* to rescue sub-national governments from the consequences of their profligacy. As Jonathan Rodden explains,

> The peril of fiscal federalism is ultimately driven by politics… If the center is merely a loose, logrolling coalition of regional interest groups, it has a hard time resisting bailout requests or firmly regulating the fiscal behavior of local [i.e. sub-national] governments. Furthermore, intergovernmental grants and loans from the center to the lower-level governments are likely to be highly politicized. The central government party or coalition will be tempted to use its discretion over the allocation of grants strategically, attempting to shift resources to allies or districts with electoral importance (2006: 10–11).

Wibbels (2005) makes the case that federal democratic countries in which intergovernmental transfers fund a high share of sub-national government spending face special challenges in coordinating the policies – especially fiscal policies – necessary to support a coherent program of market reform. In India, this issue is potentially significant because central transfers historically have funded a relatively high share of state government expenditures: India exhibits what public finance specialists consider high degree of *vertical fiscal imbalance*, meaning there is a significant asymmetry in the assignment of revenue powers and expenditure responsibilities across the Centre and the states. During the 1990s, India's states accounted for 55–60 percent of total government expenditures, but only about one-third of total revenues (McCarten 2003: 251). In certain sectors, the states accounted for almost all government spending: 97 percent of irrigation maintenance, 90 percent of public health expenditure, and 86 percent of public education expenditure in 2000 (Howes et al. 2008: 43). Among developing countries, only China surpasses India in the share of general government expenditure carried out by sub-national governments (ibid., 43).

In effect, the states' incentives to spend on electorally popular budget items – such as free electricity for farmers, consumption subsidies, and worker salaries – were not sufficiently checked by the political costs of raising revenues to pay for the expenditures, since the system places the revenue onus on the Centre. Historian Dietmar Rothermund notes, "State governments are often admonished to do more about mobilizing resources, but the tax structure does not permit them to do so. They would also hesitate to commit political suicide by burdening their voters with taxes" (2008: 42). It should be pointed out, also, that the states historically have not taken full advantage of the revenue bases available to them. The minimal collection of agricultural income tax, which rural elites resist, is a noteworthy example (Rao and Singh 2005: 352).

A detailed discussion of India's complicated federal fiscal regime is beyond the purview of this study, though a number of recent works have discussed its various technical and political economy aspects.[12] To simplify, the system encompasses three main channels of current fiscal transfers (as opposed to loans and/or guarantees) and investment allocation. The first is the constitutionally mandated Finance Commission, which is a quasi-independent body of technical specialists that convenes every five years to set rules for the devolution of central revenues to the state governments. The second is the Planning Commission, which is an intrinsically political (and extra-constitutional) body that determines Plan investment across the states. Third are the various central government ministries that control the budgets of "Centrally Sponsored Schemes" mandated to the state governments.

Despite rules and formulae, which ostensibly ensure that objective principals govern the allocation of resources across states, India's fiscal federalism is an inherently political regime. The prime minister chairs the Planning Commission, and its decisions are subject to oversight of the National Development Council, which includes the central government cabinet ministers and the chief ministers of the states – who, naturally, lobby for their share of resources. Though the Planning Commission and the central ministry budgets historically afforded the most direct opportunities for political discretion in allocating resources to the state governments, Finance Commission transfers also offered discretionary opportunities at the margin (Rao and Singh 2005; Kletzer and Singh 2000).

World Bank researcher Stuti Khemani, using data from 1972 to 1995, shows that partisan ties between the Centre and state governments correlated with higher state budget deficits and current intergovernmental transfers. In other words, central authorities took a more permissive view of fiscal policies, and were more generous with transfers, for states governed by the same party in power at the Centre (the study found no significant variation in these patterns whether the central government was led by the Congress Party or a non-Congress coalition,

as the latter, too, apparently incline toward constituent and allied parties;
Khemani 2003, 2002).

While the Planning Commission still plays a role in investment allocation, its
importance was diminished after the 1991 liberalization. In 1992–3, 58.9
percent of total central transfers were subject to the rules of the Ninth Finance
Commission, as compared to only about 21 percent subject to Planning
Commission control (Rao 1997: Table 7). By the mid-1990s, this left the
Finance Commission as the main focus of political debates over the principles
that should guide resource allocation: should the Centre favor states with the
best fiscal management, or should it continue the norm of using centrally
managed resources to promote regionally balanced development? Often the
two goals were in tension.

Devolution formulae had changed somewhat from one Finance Commission
to another, but they had generally followed a "gap-filling" methodology to meet
shortfalls in the states' budgets. Some analysts suggested that this approach
reduced the states' tax effort and even encouraged them to inflate budgetary
projections – incurring strategic deficits to maximize their share of central
transfers. According to Gurumurthi, it was "not unusual to see states tending to
incur a large amount of expenditure in the base year prior to the constitution
of a [new] Finance Commission" (1995: 35).

A final area of central support to the states consisted of central government
loans, guarantees for state borrowing from other sources, and allocation of
assistance from external providers such as the World Bank.[13] Right up to the
mid-1990s, the allocation of World Bank loans to support investment projects
across India's states had been controlled by Centre, with the same basic
discretion afforded by other aspects of the federal fiscal regime. A study by
World Bank researchers found that in passing on earmarked external assistance
to the states, the Centre had tended to make reductions in other transfers to
states (Swaroop et al. 2000).[14] It was precisely this resource channel over which
the World Bank itself now wanted to gain more control, via the strategy of sub-
national policy-based lending that Ed Lim was proposing to Chidambaram's
finance ministry.

Simply put, from the standpoint of prudent fiscal practices, much of the
allocation to states under India's fiscal federalism was "based on measures of
policy failure more than on success" (Mukherji 2002: 70). Chidambaram
understood much (if not all) of this. He, and other reform advocates at the
Centre, recognized that in order for the states to undertake the range of reforms
necessary to consolidate the macro-liberalization, India would have to transform
its fiscal federalism – from a labyrinth of soft-budget constraints, perverse
incentives, and favored resource access for politically-connected states – into a
more rule-bound and performance-based allocation. But the especially fragile

hold on power by the United Front government would make it very difficult politically to take up what essentially amounted to regime change in India's fiscal federalism. The coalition at the Centre was too dependent on the support of regional parties holding power in many states. Not only would the formal rules of the game (such as the transfer principles adhered to by the Finance Commission) have to change in order to stop giving the states incentives to run budget deficits, but the Centre also would have to tie its own hands in order to prevent politicized transfers from undermining the states' fiscal policy accountability.

This is where the World Bank could come in. Chidambaram viewed Lim's proposal for selective state-level engagement as a marriage of interests for the Bank and India. He thought it would "do the states some good to expose them to the conditionalities of external lenders" (Chidambaram 2003). In a classic two-level game strategy, Chidambaram proposed that the Bank could help encourage state-level reforms that the central government itself wanted to bring about, but could not force on the states given its own tenuous position and need to retain regional allies.

Selective World Bank assistance could be used to give reforming states access to a kind of "incentive fund," outside of the normal allocation, rather than simply substituting for other central transfers (as generally had been the case in the past). This would help avoid framing the move toward performance-based resource allocation in zero-sum terms, since the Centre would not be "taking away" resources that the non-reforming states perceived as entitlements. Though this aspect of "additionality" to state budgets later would be seen as problematic both by the Bank and the Indian government (Howes et al. 2008: 64), both appear to have looked upon it favorably at the time. Further, if non-reforming states did complain about their lack of access to Bank loans, the Centre could respond, if somewhat disingenuously, that its hands were tied: if the states did not like the Bank's policy conditions, they could take their complaints to the Bank.

In short, the finance ministry's view was that since the Bank did not depend on the political support of state leaders – as the central government did – it would be in a better structural position to enforce fiscal discipline and to hold state governments to reform commitments. The Bank, as an external actor, could enforce conditionality that the Centre itself could not impose on the states. Over the longer term, for Chidambaram as for Lim, the goal was a "demonstration effect": if enough states became socialized through their engagement with the Bank in fiscally responsible governance – and came to identify their economic and electoral interests with market reform – it could create political space for reforming India's fiscal federalism to encourage the same objectives.

Chidambaram made it clear, however, that India was the senior partner in this marriage. "I consider your money to be my money," he told Lim (Lim 2003). The idea for selective state-level lending may have originated with the Bank as a way of enhancing its influence, but the central government had hardly "removed itself from the picture," nor would it permit the Bank to "bypass" its authority, as some analysts speculated (Sridharan 2003: 477; Reddy 2002: 874). To the extent that the Centre would permit the Bank to engage with the states at a "retail" rather than "wholesale" level (Howes et al. 2008: 42), it was only because the Indian government shared with the Bank the goal of encouraging the states to align with its liberalization agenda. The Centre would not relinquish its ultimate control over the states' external borrowing (as the on-lending arrangement noted in this chapter's introduction demonstrates) and it did not perceive the new arrangement as a retreat. The Centre was in control; the Bank would be on a short tether.

And yet, from the Indian government's perspective, the strategy depended on a sleight-of-hand. The Centre would have to convince the states that there was no end run around the Bank's policy conditions for access to increased lending. Reconciling these goals – remaining in control while reducing discretion – would be a fine balance.

## Selecting and Engaging the Focus States: Politics and Policy Dialogue

After the Finance Ministry signaled its approval of the Bank's state-focused strategy in 1996, the Bank moved quickly to put it into practice. Almost from the beginning, however, the strategy had to be adjusted to account for changing circumstances, particularly as the states' fiscal situations worsened and sheer desperation – as much as "demonstrated reform commitment" – led them to seek policy-based loans from the Bank.

The World Bank Group's *Country Assistance Strategy (CAS)* document is the "the central vehicle" for identifying "the key areas in which Bank Group support can best assist a country in achieving sustainable development and poverty reduction" (World Bank 2007b: 54). Every four years, following discussions with the government and civil society "stakeholders," an updated *CAS* establishes the framework for Bank operations in India based on a "comprehensive diagnosis of the development challenges facing the country" (ibid., 54). The Bank's December 1997 *CAS* for India led off with an emphasis on reforming states: "As the focus of the reforms has shifted to the states over the past few years, the Bank Group's assistance strategy is itself being reoriented to focus mainly on those states that have chosen to embark on a comprehensive program of economic reforms."[15] The document was unsentimental about the implications for non-reforming states, and for equity: World Bank lending would "end in states where commitment to reform does not exist. These may include some of the poorest states in the country."[16]

Also in 1997, the Bank halted a rural water supply investment loan for Punjab, following the state government's announcement of free power and irrigation water for farmers. According to Howes et al. (2008: 46), "These totemic populist measures did not directly impact on rural drinking water, but the Bank's refusal to go further with the project was a clear demonstration of its willingness to take into account the 'general policy framework' when making lending decisions to states." Similarly, when the Left Front government of West Bengal would not agree to a World Bank analysis of its fiscal situation (and would not commission such an analysis by another party), several Bank projects under preparation for the state were shelved in 1999 (ibid., 46). Lim later suggested that the Punjab pullout was calculated to send a message (Lim 2003); he maintained that while the Bank "never gave these decisions any publicity, [...] this being India, the media and the public soon became aware that the Bank was increasingly allocating its resources to reforming states and withdrawing from non-reforming states" (2005: 115).

But by far the biggest bang for the state-focused strategy was the initiation of a close relationship with Andhra Pradesh, which would come to be seen as the flagship focus state owing both to the volume of Bank assistance and to the high national and even international visibility of the state's chief minister. Details of the Bank's engagement with this state are discussed below, but it is worth noting more generally that Andhra Pradesh was the first of several states whose initial interest in the Bank's policy-based assistance was driven by an acute state-level fiscal crisis that struck in 1997–8 – brought on in part by the central government's own actions.

In 1997, the Fifth Pay Commission[17] recommended a substantial increase in compensation for central employees. The United Front (then led by Prime Minister I.K. Gujral) buckled under the threat of a massive strike by government workers, and accepted the pay hike against the counsel of economic advisors. Though the state governments were not formally obligated to raise pay for their own workers, many did so under similar pressures (Kurian 2002). Very quickly, the "slow secular deterioration in fiscal performance over the 1980s and 1990s was catalyzed into a state-level fiscal crisis" as a declining state revenue trend ran headlong into a nearly 30 percent increase in real wages for civil servants (Howes, Mishra et al. 2008: 43). Several years later, Shankar Acharya cited the Fifth Pay Commission effects as "the single largest adverse shock to India's strained public finances in the last decade" (2003: 111). The sub-national fiscal situation was already precarious, and the pay increases triggered an acute crisis in some states, including Andhra Pradesh and Uttar Pradesh. When these states came to the World Bank for assistance in the late 1990s, their leaders may have had the reform religion, but they were recent converts.

The 2001 *Country Assistance Strategy* was even more explicit about the Bank's sub-national strategy for India, listing Andhra Pradesh, Karnataka, and Uttar Pradesh as the focus states for the period and leaving open the possibility that other reform-committed states could join them. The Bank's Executive Board had by then approved of the first Sub-national Adjustment Loan (SNAL) in an early 2000 package for Uttar Pradesh, and this new instrument was envisioned as the key tool for pursuing the focus states strategy. The CAS suggested that state-level adjustment lending could accelerate to as much as US$500–900 million a year (one-sixth to one-third of total annual lending of up to US$3 billion for India) (ibid., 46), and this range did not even include the complementary investment loans that states might avail. The 2001 CAS hinted that the focus on reforming statements might risk leaving some of India's poorest states behind, but the adoption of UP as a focus state mitigated this concern. (The Bank also pursued a broad reform dialogue with Orissa, a low-income state, but this engagement would not lead to an adjustment loan for several more years).

The 2001 CAS ran until 2004, and this period would turn out to be the high-water mark of the "focus states" strategy. By coincidence, 2004 was also to be the year of an Indian general election and several parallel state elections, and the incumbent coalition at the Centre (the BJP-led National Democratic Alliance since 1998) was ushered out in what many analysts interpreted as a rebuke of its tone-deaf campaign theme, "India Shining." In Andhra Pradesh and Karnataka, two of the Bank's star reformers lost control of the governments. In the former, the chief minister's "surrender to the World Bank" was a campaign theme for a rival candidate who promised free power to farmers, and delivered it as soon as he took office. Meanwhile, Uttar Pradesh's program with the Bank had long since gone off track, following a confrontation between its leadership and the Bank in 2002.

The late 1990s through 2004 thus marks the fascinating "focus states" chapter in the Bank-India relationship. Let us now turn to the Bank's very different experiences with Andhra Pradesh, Karnataka, and Uttar Pradesh during this period.

### Andhra Pradesh

Andhra Pradesh (AP) emerged in 1998 as the foremost focus state, following a period of sustained interaction between the Bank and its government, led by Chief Minister Nara Chandrababu Naidu, beginning in 1996. A major, multi-sector loan package for the state in 1998, the US$543 million Andhra Pradesh Economic Restructuring Project (APERP), marked the operational onset of sub-national policy-based lending (even though this package was an investment

**Table 2.1. World Bank Group Investment and Adjustment Loan Commitments to Andhra Pradesh, 1998–2009**

| | | |
|---|---|---|
| 1998 | AP Economic Restructuring Project | $543 mn |
| 1999 | AP Power Sector Restructuring Project | $210 mn |
| 2000 | AP District Poverty Initiatives Project | $111 mn |
| *2002* | *AP Economic Reform Loan / Credit* | *$250 mn* |
| 2002 | AP Community Forest Management Project | $108 mn |
| 2003 | AP Rural Poverty Reduction Project | $150 mn |
| *2004* | *AP Economic Reform Loan / Credit II* | *$220 mn* |
| *2007* | *AP Economic Reform Loan / Credit III* | *$225 mn* |
| 2007 | AP Community-Based Tank Management Project | $189 mn |
| 2007 | AP Rural Poverty Additional Financing | $65 mn |
| 2009 | AP Rural Water Supply and Sanitation | $150 mn |
| 2009 | AP Road Sector | $645 mn |
| | *Total Adjustment Loans* | *$695 mn* |
| | GRAND TOTAL | $2.86 bn |

Note:   Italics indicate adjustment loans (see endnote 4). All figures are US$.
Source: Various loan documents. Online. <http://go.worldbank.org/63DY8HX2R0>. Retrieved on 06 July 2009, 04 November 2009.

rather than an adjustment loan, it was bound by a fiscal framework and public expenditure management agreement, in addition to sector-specific reform content; World Bank 1999). Beginning with APERP, the Bank has invested heavily in the state (nearly US$3 billion in investment and adjustment loans through 2009; see Table 2.1), sometimes directly supplemented by aid from Britain's DFID and other sources. During the 1998 to 2004 "focus states" period, Andhra Pradesh, with about 7 percent of India's population, claimed about 12 percent of World Bank lending commitments for the country. At the high point of the engagement, during 2001–3, this single state laid claim to nearly one-third of all external assistance commitments to India (World Bank, ADB, and bilateral sources).[18] DFID's grants to AP in 2002 exceeded British aid to any other *country*.

Andhra Pradesh was the public face of the Bank's focus states strategy, and Naidu was the public face of Andhra Pradesh. Before Naidu, it was implausible that AP's economic prospects would be described in the superlative terms that became commonplace in media coverage at the height of his tenure. India's fifth most populous state and the northeastern state of India's distinctive southern region (comprising AP, Karnataka, Kerala, and Tamil Nadu), AP had a per capita income below that of neighboring Karnataka and Tamil Nadu, and well below that of India's richest states (such as Punjab, Haryana, Gujarat, and

Maharashtra), placing it in the lower-middle income tier among India's states overall. Its infrastructure penetration was relatively low, and it lagged behind in key social indicators such as literacy and infant mortality. Its 1980s economic growth rate had been about the same as the national average (5.5 percent), but this was underpinned by recurrent deficit spending that had driven the state to an unsustainable fiscal position. Further, aggregate economic indicators masked considerable variations within the state, between the better-off "coastal Andhra" region and the much poorer interior regions of Telengana and Rayalaseema.

In his early career, Naidu had supported the two-pronged attack that his father-in-law N.T. Rama Rao ("NTR"), a former cinema icon, had used to establish the TDP as a major force in regional politics beginning in 1983, ending the Congress Party's dominance in a state that had been one of its most consistent bases. First, NTR had appealed to Telugu "self-respect" and stoked popular anger at perceived indignities inflicted upon the state by successive Congress-led central governments. Second, he had used mass-appeal welfare policies – India's largest public housing program; a consumption subsidy on rice that, according to a World Bank estimate, eventually came to cover 85 percent of the population; cut-rate power provision; and even free clothing – to pull together an electorate fragmented along caste and regional lines.[19]

Such policies were electorally potent, but broke the budget – rapidly turning the state's budget surpluses into deficits.[20] A return to power by the Congress Party in 1989–94 did not stem the fiscal deterioration, since it too now embraced the logic of competitive populism. Thus, Karli Srinivasulu has described the history of AP politics from 1983 until the late 1990s as the "NTR regime" (1999: 210). After the Congress-led government at the Centre ushered in macroeconomic liberalization in 1991, NTR repeatedly attacked the Congress government in AP for its association with "anti-poor" policies, and won the 1994 state election. As NTR's finance minister in 1995, Naidu professed, "If there is one distilled lesson out of our development experience spanning nearly a half-century, it is that 'trickle-down' theories of growth do not work… The most effective and possibly the only way to alleviate poverty is by direct income transfer methods such as the rice subsidy programme" (quoted in Suri 2005: 140).

But Naidu modified this stance after wresting power from NTR in 1995, following a familial controversy.[21] The state's fiscal stance was unsustainable. The rice and power subsidies in particular had placed tremendous strain on the budget, and another NTR policy that Naidu had supported, prohibition of alcohol, deprived the state of excise taxes. The state began resorting to overdrafts on its account with the Reserve Bank of India just to cover its administrative costs. As a former AP finance official put it, "We were firefighting on a day-to-day basis" (Subbarao 2002). Naidu took some steps to address the crisis, raising the price ceiling on rice and weakening the ban on alcohol sales.

In mid-1996, the government issued a White Paper on the state's finances, which made the case that current trends were unsustainable and that the state would have to undertake challenging fiscal reforms.

Around this same time, Naidu developed a keen interest in the growth achievements of Southeast Asia, and was particularly taken by the Malaysian model.[22] In 1991, Mahathir Mohamad's government had produced a document called *Vision 2020*, which proclaimed a goal of "full development" by the year 2020. Malaysia had also worked with the consultancy McKinsey & Company on a plan to position Kuala Lumpur as a "knowledge economy" hub. Naidu was enthralled by ideas such as "leapfrogging" the traditional agriculture-to-industry transition, and exploiting the potential of information technology (IT) to move AP directly into an advanced, globally networked service economy. Eventually, Andhra Pradesh would work with McKinsey on its own *Vision 2020* plan,[23] which, along with his ubiquitous laptop computer, became Naidu's leitmotif.

A forceful if not conventionally charismatic politician, Naidu proclaimed to investors and the elite media his determination to set AP on a new course, as a model of globally integrated, high-tech, market-led development. He cultivated the image of an able administrator – "the CEO of Andhra Pradesh" – outside the stereotypical mold of the state-level political class in India, which he criticized for "too much politicking and too little governance" (Naidu and Ninan 2000: 17).

The makeover was largely successful. Bill Gates visited, and Microsoft established its first-ever international software development center in Hyderabad, the state capital. In March 2000, US President Bill Clinton's trip through India skipped buzz-worthy Bangalore in favor of more humble Hyderabad. By the time of his successful reelection bid in 1999, if he had not yet pulled AP into the ranks of the high-growth states, he had certainly created a new perception of its prospects through a combination of business-friendly policies and savvy public relations. In an annual *Business Today* survey of CEO perceptions about states as investment destinations, AP's rank rocketed from twenty-second (out of 26 states) in 1995 to third in 1999.[24]

The close partnership between Andhra Pradesh and the World Bank began in October 1996, with a meeting between Naidu, Jim Wolfensohn and Ed Lim that would become legendary in Indian bureaucratic circles. Wolfensohn's first trip to India set a precedent in that it began with overnight visits to the state capitals of Karnataka and Orissa, and concluded with three days of talks in New Delhi (Ramesh 2002). This itinerary was intended to signal the states' importance in the Bank's new strategy – but Andhra Pradesh was not on it. Undaunted, Naidu used a connection in the central finance ministry to arrange for an unusual meeting with Wolfensohn before the Bank president returned to Washington.[25]

Naidu flew to New Delhi and captivated the Bank leaders with a PowerPoint presentation on his vision of transformation for Andhra Pradesh. Wolfensohn,

Lim recalled in 2003, went with his "gut instinct" in responding to Naidu's pitch, and the two men from the Bank both agreed that they should "seize the opportunity to deliver in a big way" on the Bank's state-focused assistance strategy for India. After the meeting, Wolfensohn turned to Lim and asked, "How soon can you go to Hyderabad?" (Lim 2003).

Within weeks, Lim took a Bank team to the state capital, and in December agreed in principle on an assistance program that could run up to US$3 billion over a period of several years, depending on the pace of reforms (Lim 2003). While the timeframe was somewhat open-ended, the US$3 billion figure was significant because this was about the same total that the Bank then envisioned in annual lending to India overall. In January 1997 the Bank produced a report, *Andhra Pradesh: Agenda for Economic Reforms*, outlining steps the state should take to achieve its "developmental potential": introducing policies to attract private investment; restructuring or privatizing loss-making state enterprises such as the AP State Electricity Board; increasing investments in physical infrastructure, basic education, and health; levying new user charges for public services; and further reducing or eliminating consumption subsidies for rice, electricity, and other items (World Bank 1997a). Lim said he pushed the staff for a fairly wide-ranging analysis in the *Agenda* report, believing it was important not to conceptually "ring-fence" problems in particular sectors from the broader fiscal challenges confronting the state (ibid.).

Naidu's government pressed ahead with a bill proposing to split the State Electricity Board into separate entities for generation and transmission, and establishing an independent regulatory authority for the power sector. The TDP's two-thirds majority in the State Assembly passed the bill in April 1998, over a boycott from the Congress Party and sharp criticism by the other opponents. In June, the Bank consummated its new partnership with the state government in the US$543 million APERP investment loan package, followed in February 1999 by a US$210 million Power Sector Restructuring Project.

The Naidu public relations machine shifted into high gear as he prepared to seek reelection in 1999, and sleepy Andhra Pradesh suddenly grabbed headlines in national English-language publications such as *India Today* and *Business Standard*, as well as in international media such as *Time* and *The Wall Street Journal*. The World Bank, apparently pleased at its association, issued press releases heralding AP as India's "lead reforming state" (World Bank 1998). *The Economist* proclaimed AP's as "the election to watch in India" and portrayed it as a defining test of fiscal prudence and good governance against politics-as-usual:

> Despite almost a decade of liberalization, chief ministers in India continue
> to believe that elections can be won by promising ever-bigger subsidies, jobs

reserved for certain castes and other forms of patronage. Mr. Naidu is a rare exception. If he is elected, it will show that it is possible to stress productivity and decentralization, rather than subsidies, and still win. What is at stake is not just Mr. Naidu's future but *a change in the prevailing political thinking among India's states* ("Booting Up" 1999; emphasis added).

When Naidu's TDP emerged victorious, the verdict was hailed a mandate for economic reforms. However, this narrative overlooked two important points. First, the TDP's victory actually depended on an eleventh-hour deal with the Bharatiya Janata Party (BJP) that traded the Hindu nationalist party's alliance in the state election for Naidu's support at the Centre. According to the Election Commission of India, the TDP won 43.9 percent of the vote share with the BJP bringing an additional 3.7 percent, against the Congress Party's 40.6 percent. Under "first-past-the-post" representation rules, the victors' seat advantage in the State Assembly far exceeded the popular vote margin: the TDP took 180 seats and the BJP 12, against 91 seats for the Congress Party (of a total 294 seats; the balance went to other small parties). But the TDP-BJP alliance also entailed an agreement by the BJP not to put up candidates in certain districts; without this concession, it likely would have cut into the TDP's vote share. Some analysts contended that if the election had been a three-way contest among the Congress Party, the TDP, and the BJP, then Congress would have won (Manor 2004; Srinivasulu 2003; Suri 2002).

Second, and more fundamentally, the Naidu encountered by the state's voters bore little resemblance to the one in the narrative favored by some in the elite media. On the stump, the "CEO" never really rejected the paternalist welfarism of NTR. Nor did he marshal the broad consensus behind reform that he claimed to believe was necessary. Rather, he tried – and failed – to hold in balance the overall reduction of the state's budget deficits with the creation of new welfare programs targeted to elicit support from key groups: free cooking gas cylinders for one million rural women, toolkits for "backward caste" tradesmen, and so on.[26]

In fact, Naidu so thoroughly coated his reform policies with "sweetening doses of populism" that he earned a censure from India's Election Commission, which took issue with his announcement of new spending programs in the run-up to polls ("He Knows" 1999). If anything, when speaking to voters, Naidu reinforced the NTR conception of state-as-provider, even similarly giving the impression that benefits flowed directly from the chief minister – and raising expectations that they would continue to do so (Manor 2004). As Suri observes, "Like a political wizard, Chandrababu Naidu pulled out one welfare scheme after another from his hat, averaging one every week" (2005: 147).

It was this populist side of Naidu that caught the attention of *The New York Times*, reporting from the village of Atmakur:

> A central riddle of Indian politics was about to be answered here as the cyber-savvy chief minister of one of India's largest states, the country's most dynamic economic reformer, rose to address a huge, raucous political rally in this hard scrabble farm town.
>
> The riddle is this: How does a politician – in this case, a darling of the World Bank who slashed popular food subsidies early in his term – sell his vision for economic growth to a mostly rural, illiterate electorate that is just struggling to survive day to day?
>
> The short answer: he didn't really try.
>
> As the chief minister, N. Chandrababu Naidu, faced the whistling, cheering throng, this self-proclaimed CEO of Andhra Pradesh, a man whose Web-site biography pictures him sitting at his laptop, made no mention of his successful courtship of Bill Gates and other corporate executives or his efforts to restore fiscal balance to the southern state's budget.
>
> Rather he spoke the traditional language of social programs: marriage halls for Muslims, irrigation canals for farmers, free hand tools for artisans, matching grants to poor women who save money.
>
> "This government is for the poor," thundered Naidu, the son of a modest farmer. "I lay down my life for them" (Dugger 1999).

Significantly, the *Times* article also noted a survey conducted by the New Delhi-based Centre for the Study of Developing Societies, which found that five out of six prospective voters in AP had never even heard of the government's economic reforms program (ibid.).

The World Bank was not ignorant of Naidu's Janus-faced tendencies, or of the special political relationship between the TDP and the BJP. It believed that the former might ensure the political survival of its star reformer, and that the latter augured well for the Centre's continued support for the Bank's state-level lending strategy. Lim perceived that Naidu's clout at the Centre – poised to carry over from the United Front to a new BJP-led coalition – was a kind of "insurance policy" for the Bank (Lim 2003).

What the Bank might *not* have grasped fully were the incentives that Naidu's approach created for his political opponents in the state. If Naidu emphasized electoral sops and made no real effort to articulate a new paradigm for the role of the state in economic development, then it made sense for the Congress party simply to raise him one in the competitive populism game – as it did with promises of free electricity in the 1999 campaign. Moreover, the steps that

Naidu's government did take in the name of "people's participation" were often fig-leaves for the TDP's partisan circumvention of local elected *panchayati raj* institutions: as analysts have noted, new water users' associations, village school committees, and the like were often dominated by local TDP cadres (Mooij 2003). The Bank's "partnership" was with the ruling party, the opposition could argue, not with the state's people.

The government's insistence – at the Bank's urging – on passing the electricity reform act in 1998 over the opposition's objections had set the stage for an intense confrontation when reforms in that sector began to take hold in mid-2000. Not long after the election, the new electricity regulatory commission convened a series of ostensibly public hearings on the subject of tariff revision, which Naidu described as "engaging stakeholders in dialogue." The hearings may have done more harm than good, however. Farmers' groups, flatly opposed to any revision, dominated the proceedings.[27] Further, the news media were barred from attending a major hearing in Hyderabad – implausibly due to "lack of adequate space" at the meeting hall (Harshe 2001) – and retaliated with critical coverage of the issue.

When the commission endorsed an increase in electrical tariff rates across nearly all user categories – including a 54 percent raise for domestic users – there was an overwhelmingly hostile reaction, according to press reports in *Frontline*, *The Hindu*, and other local sources. The opposition parties along with several trade unions led rallies against not only the power tariff increases, but against the government's reform program more generally. The opposition staged a walkout from the State Assembly and led a series of hunger strikes and public marches – one of which, on 28 August 2000, crammed an estimated 25,000 people into Hyderabad's Basheerbagh Chowk. Violence erupted, and police fire killed one union member and one Congress Party supporter. Naidu alleged that the Congress had brought in Naxalites (Maoist guerillas) to incite mayhem; the opposition denied this and shot back that the chief minister had issued orders encouraging police brutality.

An even more effective rhetorical weapon, which the Congress would wield tenaciously through the remainder of Naidu's tenure, was criticism of the chief minister for surrendering AP's economic sovereignty to the World Bank. The Bank played right into the opposition's hands when Wolfensohn casually told Indian press correspondents in Washington that the "not dramatic" power tariff increase should have gone even further (Prasad 2000). Political parties that had never been so united behind any issue in the state's history came together to denounce Naidu's government for "bartering the state's interests to the Bank" (Jafri 2000). A joint opposition statement called Wolfensohn's remarks "evidence of gross interference in the policies of the state government and an affront to the self-respect" of its people. The Communist leadership claimed to have unearthed "secret" documents on the agreement between the Bank and the government.[28] The state BJP leadership – supposedly TDP allies – accused Naidu of becoming a "puppet" in the hands of the Bank, "borrowing indiscriminately," and taking the state on the road to "economic slavery" (Sridhar 2000). Even some members of the chief minister's own party turned hostile. The deputy speaker, Chandrasekhar Rao, wrote to Naidu imploring him "to allow the common man to at least retain his underwear" ("Riding Two Horses" 2000). (Rao later broke ranks with the TDP to form a new party advocating separate statehood for Telengana).

It might be tempting to dismiss these proceedings as merely partisan histrionics, but the opposition had simply tapped the rhetorical wellspring of Telugu "self-respect" that the party of NTR itself had pioneered. Thereafter, Naidu's government fumbled for a way to frame its relationship with the Bank for voters, but by then the opposition had defined the reform program as a violation of AP's economic sovereignty and an attack on its most vulnerable citizens.

The TDP, rather crudely, tried to promote its relationship with the Bank using populist tactics. In November 2000, when Wolfensohn paid a visit to the state, he and Lim joined Naidu on a helicopter jaunt to the villages of Medchal and Mahbubnagar, where they met a gathering of women participating in a self-help credit cooperative funded partly by the Bank. According to a press report, the district's TDP legislator had told the women they "would get big [personal] loans from the big bank." A few women even named the exact amount they expected to receive as a result of the visit: Rs. 500,000 each (about US$11,550) (Messias 2000).

Naidu's reform program also ran up against a miserable situation in the rural sector. In 2001–3, rainfall in AP hit 40-year record lows. Farmer suicides, already a distressing occurrence in the state, exploded to shocking proportions with several thousand deaths (estimates ranged from 3,000 to 7,000) through mid-2004.[29] The drought's first year coincided with local elections, which foreshadowed the TDP's declining fortunes. The low point of a rough ride for Naidu was an assassination attempt on his motorcade by Naxalite insurgents in October 2003.

While the opposition in AP continued to press the theme that Naidu and the Bank were squeezing the poor, critics outside the state saw the TDP leader as a master of the bargaining game for centrally allocated resources. Indeed, Naidu epitomized the different political economy impulses confronting state leaders in India under liberalization. On the one hand, as much as any other chief minister, he articulated the view that states now had to compete vigorously to attract private investment by presenting market-friendly policies.

In his 2000 book *Plain Speaking* (part political biography and part management treatise), he expressed,

> Being chief minister in contemporary India is a tough proposition. States can no longer look to the Centre for resources, they have to fend for themselves. At the same time the demands made of a state are increasing. As populations continue to grow, and the aspirations of an expanding middle class continue to rise, people are becoming more aware of their rights and less willing to put up with shoddy governance. They demand better civic amenities. [...]
>
> There has been a dramatic change in the role chief ministers have been called upon to play. Gone are the days when industrialists had to wait upon the government to get licences. Today states are competing aggressively with each other to attract industries to their states (Naidu and Ninan 2000: 6).

In the same breath, however, Naidu maintained that a modern state leader "has to lobby the Central government for funds, using every persuasion he can think of" (ibid., 7). Naidu was also a forceful advocate of a "performance-based" federal resource allocation, saying the system was still "over-centralized" and that for too long, "Planning Commission and Finance Commission formulae have been heavily loaded in favour of population and poverty" (ibid., 36–8).[30] Politics, too, had played too prominent a role in the transfer of resources to states:

> It is not healthy in the long run for regional parties to merely acquire political clout at the Centre so that they can cash political cheques in a situation where all states are competing for bigger slices of a fast-dwindling Central pie. [...]
>
> Coalition partners should not be seen as holding the government of the day to ransom (ibid., 34, 39).

Yet that is essentially what Naidu did, first by brokering the formation of the United Front coalition in 1996, and then by strategically offering "issue-based" outside support to the BJP's National Democratic Alliance after 1998 and 1999 general elections. The TDP's pivotal support for successive central coalitions enabled Naidu to hold the Centre to ransom for resources. He openly boasted, "The Telugu Desam Party's role in the United Front government contributed to better Centre-state relations [...] and led to the flow of a record quantum of funds under various sectors to Andhra Pradesh" (ibid., 33). Naidu maintained that this was due to "improved financial devolution to the states," but given his state's unimpressive budget position at the time, it was patently not true that performance criteria over politics accounted for the state's share.

The same could be said about the TDP's relations with the subsequent NDA government. As a 2002 story in *India Today* put it, "The shrewd Andhra Pradesh chief minister cashes in on the NDA's fragility to squeeze national resources for his state" (Aiyar and Menon 2002: 21). During the drought – which also hit hard in some of India's other states, as well – it was particularly galling that Naidu demanded and received a much larger rice allotment than any other state under the centrally administered Food for Work Programme. As the *India Today* report pointed out, "That the state has cornered a lion's share of resources is proved by just one statistic: while Central grants to all states increased by only 2.6 per cent between 2000–1 and 2001–2, Andhra Pradesh's share rose by 34 percent" (ibid., 22). Finally, as the next chapter will show, Naidu's special relationship with the BJP eased the state's access to its 2002 adjustment loan from the Bank, which would have been held up by finance ministry bureaucrats had he not appealed over their heads to the union finance minister.

The resource bounty was not enough to ensure the survival of Naidu's government, however. When the state scheduled its election for early 2004, to run concurrent to the national parliamentary polls, the Congress Party under the leadership of Y.S. Rajasekhara Reddy (popularly known as "YSR") launched a state-wide campaign that again promised free power supply. This time, YSR pledged not to raise electrical tariffs for at least three years. Naidu protested to voters that such promises would ruin the sector: "If this is done, there will be no electricity left to supply," he warned. "You can use electric wires as clotheslines" ("Electricity" 2004). Thus the 2004 election came to resemble what some had imagined five years earlier: a campaign pitting the opposition's incredible profligacy against plainspoken reformism on the part of the chief minister. But the opposition owned the narrative that the state's economic reform program was externally imposed and anti-poor; all that was left was for Naidu to plead for more time for reforms to pay off.

In the April–May 2004 State Assembly elections, an alliance among the Congress, Telengana party, and left parties swept 48.7 percent of the state's popular vote, against 40.4 percent for the TDP-BJP alliance (giving the former 230 seats in the State Assembly against a mere 49 seats for the latter). The challengers also won a solid majority of AP's parliamentary seats in the concurrent national elections, contributing to the ejection of the NDA government at the Centre and its replacement by the Congress-led United Progressive Alliance. The state's new chief minister, YSR, immediately signed an order granting free power to farmers, per the central campaign pledge. He considered his mandate to be relief to the rural sector.

For its part, the World Bank appeared somewhat chastened by the defeat of its star reformer. In August 2004 the Bank released a report on AP that hedged on its achievements to date, calling it "a leader in reforms, but not yet in growth." It also went much further toward a kind of political economy analysis of the state that the Bank had previously avoided, noting "deep-seated structural rigidities in the economy, like the state's colonial legacies, geographical endowments, and caste-based disparities," and a "skewed distribution" of public goods that "has led to social unrest and ethnic violence in rural AP, making the growth process erratic and higher growth rates unsustainable in the long run" (World Bank 2004d). The report offered a new round of recommendations for policy and institutional reforms, and said that a consultation draft had been "well received" by key officials in the state government. But at the same time, Bank officials in New Delhi threatened to cut off adjustment loans to state governments that provided free power (Bhattacharjee 2004) — a clear warning to YSR's government — and suggested that if states wanted to aid poor citizens, they should do so in a more direct and targeted manner. With Naidu, its poster reformer, relegated to the opposition bench, the Bank's eight-year love affair with Andhra Pradesh appeared to be on the rocks.

Yet in October 2004, the state finance minister Konijeti Rosaiah felt obliged to appear before a civil society event called the Forum to Save Andhra Pradesh from the World Bank to insist that the state government "did not consider the World Bank as an enemy" ("No Conditional Loans" 2004). The new government, he said, would consider borrowing from the Bank, but only as a last resort and only for "productive purposes" – *not* for reform-linked budget support. But by May 2005, Reddy would begin to broach the idea of borrowing for budget support, trying to rationalize this about-face by maintaining that he would not accept any "specific conditions" and even claiming to have "convinced the Bank of the merit" of schemes such as free power ("Heels" 2005). Still, the Bank seemed unsure of the new government (Kurmanath 2005).

After a respectable interim, the relationship resumed, and the Reddy government availed a US$225 million adjustment loan in 2007, similar in size and policy content to the previous two reform operations between the Bank and the Naidu government. Andhra Pradesh also continues to borrow for infrastructure and poverty projects, and though the rate of assistance has slowed since the Naidu era, the state remains an important focus for the Bank in India, even if the "focus state" rationale has given way to the more recent "lagging states" paradigm. Indeed, as the overall justification for the Bank's state-level engagement has evolved, so have the Bank's descriptors for Andhra Pradesh; though it still credits the government with a reformist orientation, it now places more emphasis on the state's regional poverty and lagging human development indicators, which, despite recent growth around Hyderabad and along the coast, remain persistent challenges.

YSR was reelected in May 2009 (just as the Congress-led coalition at the Centre was also returned to power), but he died in a helicopter crash the following September and was succeeded by Rosaiah as caretaker chief minister. It was too early to know what the implications of the leadership change might be for one of the Bank's most important state-level relationships; Rosaiah's previous service as finance minister (and de facto leadership of the cabinet in late 2008 and early 2009 as YSR took to the campaign) suggested at least short-run policy continuity. But almost immediately after YSR's death, loyalists began calling for the installation of his son Jaganmohan Reddy, a newcomer to politics and apparently not favored for the state's top job by the national Congress leadership in New Delhi ("YSR Death Triggers Ugly CM Race" 2009). In November 2010, Rosaiah stepped down and Nallari Kiran Kumar Reddy, a YSR protégé hand-picked by the national Congress leadership, took over as Jaganmohan left the party.

The leadership struggle may have been managed, but a larger crisis has engulfed AP since late 2009 with the reinvigoration of demands for Telangana statehood. This presents a serious governance challenge for the Congress Party, both at the state level and nationally as it looks to retain support in AP ahead of the next elections (due in 2014). The Centre has courted discontent both from Telangana opponents and champions, first by indicating support for separate statehood, then by appearing adrift after a centrally appointed committee recommended that AP remain united. As of this writing, the situation remains volatile. The TDP, still led by Naidu, now supports Telangana statehood. Meanwhile, a charismatic former film star, Chiranjeevi ("the immortal one"), has taken to the political stage—recently merging his upstart Praja Rajyam Party with Congress—to proclaim themes of social justice and statewide unity. Future scenarios in AP politics could give the World Bank a strong sensation of having "seen this movie before."

### *Karnataka*

Against the backdrop of the Andhra Pradesh experiment, the Bank's experience in neighboring Karnataka presented a surprisingly different picture. For a time, Karnataka looked to be a more likely focus state for the Bank than its neighbor. The Bank's involvement there never attracted as much opposition inside the state – or attention outside of it – but it was precisely this low-key atmosphere that might have facilitated a slow and steady engagement. The partnership started out amiably, but it later went off track for reasons that still seem somewhat arbitrary. In the focus-states phase of the Bank's sub-national strategy, Karnataka was the one that got away.

In the mid- to late-1990s, Karnataka in some respects presented a more promising picture than AP. A solidly middle-income state, its recent economic growth rates had been somewhat higher than the national average, and its capital Bangalore was already well ahead of AP's Hyderabad as a global technology and services center. Its budget position, if not a model of fiscal prudence, was a far cry from the impending disaster that drove Naidu's interest in the World Bank.

James Manor, a political scientist at the Institute of Development Studies (Sussex, UK) who has closely studied both Karnataka and AP, points out that they exhibited remarkably similar trajectories – "unmatched by any other pair of Indian states" – from the 1950s into the 1990s (Manor 2004: 256). Both states started out as bastions of Congress Party support; both gave rise to strong regional parties in the 1980s as anti-Congress interests gathered (the TDP in AP and the Janata Party in Karnataka); both alternated governments between the Congress Party and regional challengers during the 1980s and 1990s, always trending in the same direction in simultaneous elections until 1999.[31]

However, the apparent parallels in party system development and electoral outcomes obscured deep and long-standing differences in the two states' political cultures and institutions. Historically, Karnataka's politics have tended to be more developmentalist and cooperative than AP's, with less partisan, regional, or group conflict (more recently, this relative serenity has been disrupted somewhat as the BJP has made inroads in Karnataka). Some of the contrast can be traced to colonial-era legacies; at least 80 percent of Karnataka's farmers owned their land (a much higher share than in AP), and though its agricultural growth rate had been modest, regional disparities were smaller than in AP (Manor 2004).

In the late 1990s, Manor served as a consultant to the World Bank, overseeing a set of governance studies for eight Indian states – including Andhra Pradesh, Karnataka, and Uttar Pradesh – as the Bank's sub-national strategy was developing. The studies were internal documents, and Manor's contract with the Bank did not permit him to discuss in detail their "sensitive" contents. He did, however, share the overall judgments about the states that he conveyed to the Bank, while maintaining that his input was merely one strand among "lots of other information" that shaped the Bank's choice of focus states. Karnataka, Manor told the Bank, was a "dead reliable place," and what its leadership lacked in Naidu-style panache, it made up for with "a great deal more care, more institutionalization, liberal governance, and common sense" (Manor 2002).

Indeed, the Bank took an early interest in Karnataka as a focus state candidate. But the state's government at the time did not reciprocate the interest. Chief Minister J.H. Patel (1996–9) was an old socialist and the former leader of a state employees' union. When the Bank sounded him out on a program loan to support power sector, fiscal, and governance reforms, his response was nonchalant: "I'll come to you when I need the medicine" (Bhattacharya 2002).

The relationship changed after a Congress Party government led by S.M. Krishna came to power in October 1999. Krishna immediately approached the Bank to express interest in an assistance program similar to that of AP (this was just when the Naidu government's involvement with the Bank was beginning to attract press attention, but before the anti-reform backlash set in). According to Howes, Mishra, and Ravishankar, "The element of competition with AP was clear and often explicit. Karnataka felt that AP was threatening it, and that it was in danger of being left behind" (2008: 52).

The initial meeting between Krishna and the Bank went very well (Ramesh 2002), and put the state on a fast track for assistance. Around this same time, the state government also explored the possibility of an adjustment program with the Asian Development Bank (ADB); the state's former Chief Secretary, B.K. Bhattacharya, recalled, "We were put in the rather fortunate position of being able to choose our development banker" (2002). However, both the World Bank and the central finance ministry insisted that the state could not enter into reform programs with both lenders. Krishna's government ultimately went with the World Bank in view of its greater financial and technical resources (Bhattacharya 2002).

Krishna ordered a White Paper on the state's finances. The Bank insisted on this step as a precondition to an adjustment loan; by 2000, the opposition in AP had begun to assail Naidu for "surrendering" to the Bank, and the Bank wanted to avoid a repeat of this experience by ensuring that Krishna's government initiated a broad public dialogue on reforms before the issue of Bank borrowing ever came up.[32] The government selected M. Govinda Rao, a public finance specialist and director of the Bangalore-based Institute for Social and Economic Change, to supervise the analysis. Though the main thrust of the document was similar to the diagnosis in AP – Karnataka needed to restructure its expenditures toward infrastructure and the social sectors, in order to induce private investment as "the prime mover of economic activity" (Government of Karnataka 2000: 3–4) – Rao maintained that he was given a free hand in drafting the report; "I typed it myself," he recalled with a laugh (2002). Significantly, he pointed out, the Krishna government insisted to the Bank that an independent local analyst should undertake the study, and that it did not wish to use an international consultant with little knowledge of the state (implicitly rejecting the kind of McKinsey association adopted by Andhra Pradesh). Krishna also seemed to understand, more than Naidu, the political imperative of paying heed to the distributive dimensions of economic change, proclaiming in 2000 his commitment to "the eradication of poverty through economic growth tempered with equity" (Menon 2004a). Thus, if Krishna's initial interest in the Bank was driven in some part by a sense of competition with neighboring AP, the subsequent controversy of the reform program there also affected the engagement between his government and the lender.

Even more fundamentally, however, the Karnataka government's initial outreach to the Bank was more proactive, and not driven by the desperation that had led Naidu to court its assistance. Though the White Paper noted a "steady deterioration in fiscal conditions in Karnataka [...] the situation [had] not yet reached a crisis point" (2000: 8, 12). This lesser urgency meant that the state government would not be as dependent on the Bank's assistance as its counterpart in AP was. At the same time, the Bank's more limited engagement in the state would mean that it had less at stake, too – in terms of sunk resources and audience costs – if the relationship turned sour.

The Bank's arms-length distance enabled Krishna to consistently stress that the government was in the driver's seat; even in the presence of senior Bank officials, he publicly asserted that there was "nothing like a fixed frame" for the reforms and that they were simply "an ongoing process" (though in spite of this insistence, the Bank's loans would be based on policy "triggers" and would contain fixed fiscal targets). He avoided the kind of popular backlash that Naidu encountered, and the opposition did not perform theatrical denouncements of Krishna's "selling out." This seemed to reflect both a different strategy than Naidu employed in AP, as well as the underlying differences in the state's political traditions.

The Bank's contrasting approaches and reception in Karnataka and AP were plainly evident during Wolfensohn's visits to both states in late 2000. At a press conference, Wolfensohn praised Krishna for a "good record for the first year," but also quipped that "it would become problematic" if the Bank "over-complimented" him. He stressed that the Bank had not forced the government to take on the reform agenda, saying, "It is for the states to decide what they want to do." He remarked that since he was "not the elected chief minister of any state," he would prefer to leave any detailed policy discussion to Krishna, but noted that in Karnataka, "no one had complained" about terms being laid down by the Bank. Local press reports neatly summed up the contrast between Karnataka and its eastern neighbor: upon leaving the genial conference with Krishna, "Mr. Wolfensohn began his two-day visit to Andhra Pradesh amid tight security and protests against the conditions the multilateral organization was forcing on the state" ("A Blend of Reforms" 2000; see also "India: States' 'Admirable' Plans" 2000).

In 2001, the Bank tendered the First Karnataka Economic Restructuring Loan/Credit (KERL), worth US$150 million. Subsequent program and project loans put Karnataka's total share of Bank assistance at US$1.4 billion through 2007 (see Table 2.2), a significant sum but well behind AP.[33]

The 2002 and 2003 monsoons were not so obliging to the state. In fact, even before those two drought years, policy disagreements between the state government and the Bank emerged during the KERL transaction, which was originally discussed as a US$250 million adjustment loan but reduced to US$150

**Table 2.2. World Bank Group Investment and Adjustment Loan Commitments to Karnataka, 2001–7**

| | | |
|---|---|---|
| 2001 | *First Karnataka Economic Restructuring Loan/Credit* | *$150 mn* |
| 2001 | Karnataka Watershed Development Project | $100 mn |
| 2001 | Karnataka State Highways Improvement Project | $360 mn |
| 2002 | *Karnataka Structural Adjustment Loan II* | *$100 mn* |
| 2002 | Karnataka Community-Based Tank Management Project | $99 mn |
| 2004 | Karnataka Urban Water Sector Improvement Project | $40 mn |
| 2006 | Karnataka Municipal Reform Project | $216 mn |
| 2006 | Karnataka Panchayats Strengthening Project | $120 mn |
| 2006 | Karnataka Health Systems Development and Reform Project | $142 mn |
| 2007 | Karnataka Community-Based Tank Management Supplement | $64 mn |
| | *Total Adjustment Loans* | *$250 mn* |
| | GRAND TOTAL | $1.39 bn |

Note: Italics indicate adjustment loans (see endnote 4). All figures are in US$.
Source: Various loan documents. Online. <http://go.worldbank.org/63DY8HX2R0>. Retrieved on 06 July 2009.

million "when the state government refused to implement an agricultural power tariff increase recommended by the state's Electricity Regulatory Commission" (Howes, Mishra et al. 2008: 52). This sticking point notwithstanding, the differences appeared reconcilable at first, and within the same fiscal year the Bank disbursed the remaining US$100 million in a second adjustment loan (ibid., 52). But this would turn out to be the last program loan for Karnataka.

The situation in AP had shown how politically explosive reforms in the power sector could be, but according to Howes, Mishra, and Ravishankar, "The reason given by the Government for not moving forward with the tariff increase [in 2001] was heavy rains which had led to bumper harvests and depressed agricultural output prices," making farmers with electrically-driven pump sets especially sensitive to any increase in their cost basis. "Ironically," they note, "the next two years were ones of drought, which made it even more difficult to implement power tariff adjustments" from a political standpoint (ibid., 52). The same drought that plagued AP affected 23 of Karnataka's 28 districts (Menon 2004b), and similar reports of farmer suicide emerged, though in much lesser numbers. The government, forced to mobilize relief funds from its own resources and to petition the Centre for emergency aid, faced a difficult dilemma, since continued budgetary support from the World Bank depended on the state's adherence to deficit reduction targets.

Under the circumstances, Krishna decided to follow a middle path by cutting expenditure, but at a pace short of the targets, essentially slowing down the reform process as the state rode out the adverse conditions. In September 2001, the cabinet put on hold a power rate increase and asked the Bank to "relax its conditions… in view of the difficult situation" in the countryside ("India: Cabinet Decides" 2001). The state also put on hold a plan to privatize power distribution. Still, the chief minister continued to espouse prudent budget management, as in his 2002–3 budget speech where he said:

> We have to cut unproductive expenditures so as to be able to provide enhanced allocations for social sectors like health, education, and social justice and infrastructure sectors including agriculture, irrigation, and roads. This would pave the way for speedier economic growth and employment generation in rural areas. Resources raised by the state, both revenues and borrowings, have to be put to optimum use (Krishna 2002).

The Bank initially responded to the moderated reform pace by expressing empathy with the government in public, while privately stating its concern that the program was going off track. Even though Krishna's government arguably was doing more than Naidu's, the Bank held Karnataka to a stricter standard.

On 11 March 2003, Lim's successor at the Bank, Country Director Michael Carter, announced that Karnataka's fiscal adjustment had been "slower than expected" and that the state did not qualify for a third adjustment loan (Sreedharan 2003). Thus, whereas in AP the Bank offered a US$150 million Rural Poverty Reduction Project loan in 2003 and a second Economic Reform Program loan worth US$220 million in 2004, its only new commitment to Karnataka during the same period was a US$40 million investment loan for an urban water sector project.

What accounted for the contrast? Krishna himself complained that the central government must have pressed the Bank to lend more to AP on account of Naidu's support for the NDA coalition, and insinuated that the stepmotherly treatment of Karnataka reflected his Congress Party's place at the head of the opposition in parliament.[34] There may be some truth in this, though the politics behind the allocation were too opaque to say so with certainty. Howes, Mishra, and Ravishankar suggest that the Bank stood ready to negotiate a third economic restructuring loan for Karnataka in late 2003, but "the Government of India was not prepared to go ahead even then, given that Karnataka had not met its Fiscal Reform Facility targets" (a new innovation in the federal fiscal regime, discussed later in the chapter) (2008: 52). Andhra Pradesh, meanwhile, not only enjoyed continued access to World Bank borrowings, but claimed a disproportionate share of other centrally allocated resources, such as food aid, during the drought period (Aiyar and Menon 2002).

But simply chalking it up to a partisan resource allocation by the Centre ignores the Bank's own differing impulses in the two states. The Bank all along had regarded its big push in AP as a way of grabbing the attention of other states, while at the same time giving the central government additional political incentives to support the first focus state program. In Karnataka, since the Bank had not placed so much at stake – financially or in terms of reputation – it now found it easier to take a tough line with the Krishna government.

Following the withholding of the Bank's third adjustment loan in 2003, Karnataka dutifully trudged ahead on the reforms agenda, increasing the power tariffs and raising user fees for irrigation, transportation, water, and public hospitals; reducing consumption subsidies; and retrenching nearly 200,000 state employees through a Voluntary Retirement Scheme.

When the BJP called for national elections in April–May 2004, Krishna faced a difficult choice over whether to let his government run its full term through September – giving himself time to reap some benefit from a better run of weather that year – or to go for a concurrent election in the hope that he might ride the coattails of pro-Congress sentiment in the national polls. He committed to the concurrent option barely three months ahead of time, and only after the Congress Party national leadership decided it would be the best strategy. But while the Congress Party gained seats at the national level, and led the UPA coalition to form a new government at the Centre, it lost seats in the Karnataka State Assembly election.

Krishna at least could take comfort in the fact that his loss was not nearly as dramatic as Naidu's simultaneous ouster in AP. The Karnataka result was a hung Assembly, with an alliance between the Janata Dal (United) and the BJP scoring the highest number of seats (84), followed by the Congress Party (65 seats), the Janata Dal (Secular)(58 seats), and an assortment of smaller parties claiming the balance (17 seats). There was a brief discussion of Krishna reassuming power in a coalition with the JD(S), led by Deve Gowda, but the latter consented to allowing Congress to retain the state's top job only on the condition that it would be filled with someone else. The Congress Party and JD(S) formed a coalition on the thin reed of a common interest in keeping the BJP out of government, with N. Dharam Singh from the Congress Party as chief minister and the JD(S) laying claim to the state finance ministry and other key portfolios.

Initially, it looked like the World Bank and the new government might get on well – at least in comparison to the tense post-election atmosphere with the new Reddy government in Andhra Pradesh. The new Karnataka Finance Minister and Deputy Chief Minister, K. Siddharamaiah, presented a budget that projected the state's first revenue surplus in eight years. Cautiously asserting that Karnataka was "on the verge of fiscal correction," he promised to "complete the unfinished agenda of reforms" ("Control Fiscal Deficit" 2004). He gave the Krishna government credit, saying, "I have built upon the fiscal reform measures already adopted by the state government over the last few years"

(Roy 2004) – a far cry from Reddy's complaints in AP about having to "clean up the mess" left by Naidu. He also conceded that the end of the drought had now made the political conditions for reform a great deal easier.

But the rapprochement between Karnataka and the Bank was not to be. The Dharam Singh government lasted only until 2006, when the JD(S) abandoned the Congress Party for a Machiavellian alliance with the BJP. These two parties agreed to take turns at heading the government, but their deal broke down in 2007 and Karnataka was put under President's rule before the 2008 state election gave the BJP enough seats to form a government on its own. Remarkably, even in the face of such unstable and contentious politics, the state's budgetary position improved. Its interest in the World Bank waned, apart from continued project borrowing. The Bank was left to wonder what might have been, had its engagement with the state enjoyed different political circumstances.

### Uttar Pradesh

Of the Bank's three early-2000s focus states, the choice of Uttar Pradesh was the one that elicited the most incredulous reactions (and no small amount of cynicism) among observers of India's political economy. Uttar Pradesh (UP) is more commonly grouped with India's most "backward" states than alongside middle-income states such as AP and Karnataka. In fact, there was a pejorative shorthand often used to refer to the states of Bihar, Madhya Pradesh, Rajasthan, and Uttar Pradesh: BIMARU. Coined by demographer Ashish Bose in the mid-1980s (Ramesh 2000), the label works not only as a quasi-acronym, but also to connote a sense of "sickliness" in Hindi.[35]

UP's population of 166 million accounted for more than 16 percent of India's total population in 2001, making it the most populous state (even after a portion was hived off to form a new state, Uttaranchal, in 2000). The state's rate of GDP growth was considerably behind the national average in the 1990s, at a paltry 1.9 percent in 1991–3 and improving to 4 percent in 1993–8 (but against national averages of 4.1 percent and 6.7 percent for the same periods) (World Bank 2002a). According to Planning Commission figures, almost one-third of the state's population lived below the official poverty line in 1999–2000, compared to about one quarter of all Indians (Government of India 2001). UP's social indicators were very weak; on a composite Human Development Indicators (HDI) index for India's 15 largest states in 2001, only Bihar and Orissa performed worse (ibid.). The state's large territory encompasses great regional diversity, however, and disparities between the western and eastern extremes of the state are quite pronounced.

The importance of Uttar Pradesh to India's politics cannot be overstated. It provides fully 15 percent of the members of the national parliament, and has contributed eight of India's 13 prime ministers – beginning with Jawaharlal Nehru – since 1947. Once a bastion of Congress Party support, its electoral arena has evolved, with the rise of identity politics, into a tough three-way fight among the the Bahujan Samaj Party (BSP), the Bharatiya Janata Party (BJP), and the Samajwadi Party (Rahul Gandhi, the great-grandson of the "Nehru-Gandhi dynasty" patriarch, is now an MP from the state and his trying to restore the Congress Party as a credible contender there). Both the UP State Assembly and its 80-plus seats in the national parliament are fiercely contested by these parties, each of which has sought to appeal to particular segments of the electorate and encouraged an ethos of zero-sum competition over public resources – especially state jobs.

Though these characterizations risk over-generalization, they are still useful for understanding UP's complex politics: the BJP appeals predominately to the Hindu right, upper castes, and urban middle classes; the BSP mainly represents the historically marginalized *dalits* (formerly known as "Untouchables") and, more recently, some of the high-caste poor as well; the base of the Samajwadi Party includes "Other Backward Caste" (OBC) groups and Muslims. Since none of these parties (until 2007) had succeeded in fashioning broad enough support to win stable majorities in the State Assembly, UP tended to be governed by opportunistic coalitions that frequently broke down, necessitating new elections and perpetuating a near-constant condition of populist campaigning.[36]

Largely as a consequence of identity politics and unstable government, UP's ratio of current spending to capital spending was one of the highest in India, and development projects suffered from a chaotically high administrative turnover rate. Civil servants in UP have been subjected to reassignments on short notice, because political leaders wished to fill their ministries with members of a favored constituency. The top-level Indian Administrative Service (IAS) posts have been less subject to such crass partisanship, however, and it was largely on the efforts of the state's senior bureaucracy in the late-1990s that UP became an improbable focus state for the World Bank.

Sushil Chandra Tripathi, a career IAS officer with experience at the central government level, joined the state government as Principal Secretary of Finance in 1997 and became alarmed at the ongoing deterioration of its finances. Given the political context, Tripathi believed that it would require an external reform motivation to persuade UP's profligate leadership that adjustment was necessary, and he drew on his own unusual background to initiate a policy dialogue with the Bank, which by then was active in Andhra Pradesh (Tripathi 2003). Tripathi's prior experience in a central IAS post had afforded him an opportunity to interact with the international financial institutions in a manner not common among state-level administrators in India. During India's 1990–1 balance of payments crisis, he worked from the Indian embassy in Tokyo to complement the finance ministry's engagement with the World Bank and IMF, bridging the leadership change that accompanied the mid-1991 election. The experience persuaded him that at moments of crisis, the international institutions could tip economic policy in favor of reforms.

Not long after he took up his UP post, the Fifth Pay Commission effect led the state to raise pay for its employees, setting off a budget crisis that Tripathi viewed as a unique opportunity to press for fiscal and institutional reforms.[37] He specifically likened the state-level situation to the crisis that had faced the central government half a dozen years earlier. In his view, "The Fifth Pay Commission report was UP's 'external shock,' its 'Gulf War crisis'," which followed years' worth of unsound budget management. It offered a "strategic opening" to initiate a dialogue with the Bank and to convince the state's politicians that they had reached the limit of revenue deficit spending.

Chief Minister Kalyan Singh of the BJP supported Tripathi's initiative to engage the Bank. The government produced a White Paper on the state's finances intended to serve as a "plain-language primer, without bureaucratic jargon" on basic budgeting principles, aimed at persuading the state's politicians as well as the public. To reinforce the report's message that UP had no alternative but to undertake significant fiscal and institutional reform, in the weeks before the state government's presentation of its 1998–9 budget, Tripathi personally led seminars with groups of ministers and secretaries, sometimes lasting up to five hours.

The first meeting between the state government and the World Bank on the subject of a special reform-oriented relationship took place in January 1998. Both Ed Lim and the Bank's Washington-based Country Coordinator for India, Joëlle Chassard, recalled being impressed by the state's senior IAS officers – especially Tripathi and Chief Secretary Yogendra Narain – and judging that Kalyan Singh would provide political leadership for reform (Lim 2003; Chassard 2002). In March, UP was invited to a meeting in New Delhi organized by the Finance Ministry and billed as a forum for candidate focus states, with AP and Karnataka officials also attending.

The Bank proposed a comprehensive, multi-sector policy study of UP, similar to the 1997 "Agenda" report for AP – but, at Lim's encouragement, featuring an even more explicit focus on "governance." As in the AP and Karnataka cases, the Bank's analysis stressed the need for reform in the state's power sector as a key aspect of a necessary broader fiscal adjustment (transmission and distribution losses for the State Electricity Board were estimated at more than 40 percent, largely owing to nonpayment and theft). It further discussed governance in UP, and specifically argued that the high rate of civil servant transfers had adversely impacted development projects. As Sudha Pai observes, the Bank "saw the problem [in UP] as essentially one of poor governance, arising out of stagnation in revenue collection and low public investment, on the one hand, and low private investment on the other. Arguing that there was a close connection between fiscal deficit, poor governance and low economic growth, it identified three kinds of fiscal reform as crucial: reform of tax administration and policy to increase revenues; reprioritization of expenditure to control spending; and expenditure management for better utilization of scarce funds" (2005: 110).

In November 1998, at Tripathi's suggestion, the state government and the Bank presented the report as a "joint undertaking." The two sides then worked out the details of a broad reform program, including a medium-term fiscal framework, plans for restructuring the power sector, and governance targets such as reducing civil servant transfers (Tripathi 2003; Lim 2003). The following year, the Kalyan Singh government ended amid a squabble with the BJP national party leadership, and the elderly Ram Prakash Gupta took over. The turnover left most of the top bureaucracy intact, however, and if there were apprehensions on the Bank side as to whether Gupta would maintain the state's commitment to the reform program, these were dispelled in early 2000 when his government – with encouragement from the Centre – stood down a strike by 100,000 employees of the State Electricity Board (in protest of a plan to split it into separate enterprises for generation, transmission, and distribution, to lay the basis for privatization).

On April 26, 2000, the World Bank announced a US$511 million assistance package to "boost UP's ongoing fiscal and public sector restructuring program and spur critical reforms in the health and power sectors." Roughly half of the loan volume would fund the Uttar Pradesh Fiscal Reform and Public Sector Restructuring Loan/Credit, billed as "the first sub-national single tranche adjustment loan the Bank has provided in India" (World Bank 2000) – a result of the Executive Board's 1998 decision to approve the Sub-national Adjustment Loan (SNAL) instrument. Another US$150 million from IBRD would go for power sector restructuring, and the remaining US$110 million was an IDA credit for improvement of the state's primary health system. The piggy-backing of the power sector loan made it clear that the Bank regarded reform in this area as an integral part of the overall fiscal adjustment, and the additional simultaneous health loan was meant to demonstrate that states that had reached agreement with the Bank on a medium-term fiscal framework would also enjoy preferred access to more traditional kinds of project assistance as well. The state's total assistance from the Bank, US$1.35 billion in 2000–09, is shown in Table 2.3.

Though the state bureaucracy had initiated the engagement, the Bank saw in UP another strategic opportunity to ensure New Delhi's commitment to the focus states strategy. Whereas AP's political importance related mainly to Naidu's support for successive coalition governments at the Centre, UP's significance was more structural, as the most populous state in India. In a way, too, the sheer scale

**Table 2.3. World Bank Group Investment and Adjustment Loan Commitments to Uttar Pradesh, 2000–9**

| 2000 | *UP Fiscal Reform & Public Sector Restructuring Loan / Credit* | *$251 mn* |
|---|---|---|
| 2000 | UP Power Sector Restructuring Project | $150 mn |
| 2000 | UP Health Systems Development Project | $110 mn |
| 2002 | UP Water Sector Restructuring Project | $149 mn |
| 2002 | UP State Roads Project | $488 mn |
| 2009 | UP Sodic Lands Reclamation Project III | $197 mn |
| | *Total Adjustment Loans* | *$251 mn* |
| | GRAND TOTAL | $1.35 bn |

Note: Italics indicate adjustment loans (see endnote 4). All figures are in US$.
Source: Various loan documents. Online. <http://go.worldbank.org/63DY8HX2R0>. Retrieved on 06 July 2009.

of the challenge was seductive: as World Bank press releases were fond of pointing out, almost "almost one-tenth of the world's poor" lived in this single Indian state. The Bank, Lim now understood, could not just work with "outliers,"[38] as some saw AP and Karnataka with their high-profile IT sectors and distinctive chief ministers (Lim 2003).

Though the UP operations were controversial within the Bank (Howes et al. 2008), many staff shared Lim's newer perspective on the necessity of engaging the giant state. One official likened it to the principle of investing in a company whose stock you believe to be undervalued relative to its potential: "BIMARU" notoriety masked UP's potential under a reformist leadership and "good crop of bureaucrats" (Lal 2003). Another conceded that UP's extreme poverty was a key factor in its selection, and that its case showed how this "weakness" actually could be turned into a source of strength given the Bank's mission to alleviate poverty.[39] As Manor, the governance consultant, put it, "UP was chosen partly because the state government went to some lengths to cultivate the Bank and also because it is so big and so troubled. [The Bank] reckoned that it is a high risk state, where things may go wrong [...] but if you can turn it around you will have achieved something heroic" (Manor 2002). Lim himself put it perhaps most succinctly. Given both its extreme poverty and special political significance, he said, "UP was necessary for the long-term survival of the [focus states] strategy" (Lim 2003).

During the Bank's early policy dialogue with UP, the calculated risk appeared to be paying off. But some skeptics wondered how long the honeymoon could last. A prominent economic journalist, Swaminathan S. Anklesaria Aiyar, published a pair of columns commenting on the improbability of the Bank-UP relationship and offering "a guide to the World Bank" on navigating the treacherous politics of India's largest state. "My first reaction," Aiyar admitted, "was that UP politicians would surely take the Bank for a ride. However, a personal visit to the state has tempered my skepticism." Having met with the state's top civil servants, Aiyar noted that the reforms were "home-grown," and that the "driving force… is not the Bank but bankruptcy induced by the Pay Commission award." He argued, "The civil service and World Bank cannot hope to change the political culture. But bankruptcy may do the trick" (Aiyar 2000a). However, he cautioned, "A major danger to reforms is the possibility that aid from the World Bank will ease the hard budget constraint on UP, rescue politicians from the consequences of their bad ways, and so postpone a change in their mindset." With this in mind, he offered a set of "lessons for the Bank to succeed in UP," among them:

> Keep doling out modest sums to encourage change, but never be free with your purse. Let the state remain on the brink of bankruptcy. Focus on good advice, not on loan volumes […]
>
> Be firm but low-key. Keep emphasizing that you have no particular interest in lending money to UP; that you have many reservations and are going ahead only because local politicians say they want to reform and it is your job to support such change. If politicians no longer want to reform, there will be nothing for the Bank to support, and it must regretfully look elsewhere to more serious states.
>
> Do not give the impression that you have a mission to reform UP. Always give the impression that you are willing to walk away (Aiyar 2000b).

It would prove to be prescient advice. In late 2000, the state BJP undertook yet another leadership shuffle, replacing Gupta with a new chief minister, Rajnath Singh. Significantly, the civil servants that had been the driving force behind the reform program also departed around this time; as Tripathi put it, "The entire team disintegrated" (2003).

Initially, Rajnath Singh appeared to want to continue fiscal, power sector, and civil service reforms. In an interview he gave to a leading financial newspaper shortly after assuming office, he even wore the state's relationship with the Bank as a badge of honor:

> Yes, the economy is in bad shape. But this is the result of misrule of successive governments in the past. We failed to tap the reforms as southern states did. But things are changing fast.
>
> The trust that the World Bank has shown about Uttar Pradesh is remarkable. It is pumping more than [Rs. 220 billion] in the next seven years. Do you think that a Bank would do that if it does not have trust in UP's potential? Our fiscal situation is improving. The Center for

Monitoring the Indian Economy says so and the World Bank endorses this. The World Bank-funded projects in education, land development and health are probably the best-run projects on earth. The way the state has initiated reforms in power and administration is remarkable. This is not my statement; it's the statement of the World Bank. I hope this helps us in changing the perception of the state, which needs to be addressed first [...]

Uttar Pradesh adopted the reforms path late, but I can assure you that the breakneck pace of reforms will enable us to become the number one. There is a need for constant monitoring and follow up, which we are doing on a war footing. UP has tremendous potential (P. Bhattacharya 2000).

However, Singh soon dispensed with fiscal prudence in a bid to consolidate the BJP's vote bloc. In the run-up to state elections in 2002, his signature campaign promise was over 20,000 new jobs, aimed at siphoning *dalit* and backward caste votes away from the BSP and Samajwadi Party. He also froze the power tariff, promised to extend the Fifth Pay Commission's salary increases to UP teachers, and announced higher minimum support prices for farmers. As a result, the state's revenue deficit spiked upward again after two consecutive years of reduction.

The award of a high share of central assistance by the Eleventh Finance Commission in 2000–1 – combined with the windfall to the state budget provided by the Bank's own assistance package – reduced the state's sense of pressure to reform (Tripathi 2003). Reportedly, Singh's government even used part of the Bank's economic restructuring loan to pay state employees' salaries and other administrative costs. In December 2001 the Bank informed the state that it was freezing another major installment of budget support (Pai 2005, 2002), but the censure had no effect.

The Samajwadi Party and BSP, for their part, ran campaigns tailored to their own support bases. Mayawati Kumari, the *dalit* leader of the BSP, sought to out-do Singh with promises of government jobs for her constituents, but with an additional dimension of identity politics: she would force high-caste officials out of choice posts. Mayawati also promised to designate thousands of the state's villages as Dr. B.R. Ambedkar Villages, making them eligible for special projects and statues of the Indian freedom fighter and *dalit* hero. With each party making such promises to its slice of the electorate, none emerged from the election with a governing majority.

In April 2002, amid party brokering that would lead to a new government, the World Bank announced that it still could not commit to a second adjustment loan for UP. Manuela Ferro, a senior economist, evinced the increasingly dim view of the state's leadership. Ferro was particularly critical that "virtually no reforms were carried out" in the state's power sector under Rajnath Singh, and also cited corruption and a high rate of civil servant transfers. "Sympathies doled out at the time of polls are unfortunate," she said. "They hamper the growth and functioning of various [government] departments. So does bad governance… World Bank loans are directly linked with the pace of reforms. The faster you carry out the reforms, the sooner you get the remaining amount of fresh loans" (Shukla 2002).

In an unusual move, the state's centrally appointed Governor, Vishnu Kant Shastri, and the chairman of the UP Power Corporation, P.L. Punia, reached over the leadership to assure the Bank that the state would redouble its reform efforts. Finally, after what one report characterized as "a lot of pleading" by state officials, the Bank cautiously softened its stance (P. Tripathi 2002).

The BJP, which had won a plurality of seats, begrudgingly agreed to form a coalition government with the BSP – the price of which was Mayawati's assumption of the chief minister job. Ed Lim met with her to see if she intended to purse the power sector reforms. Lim even held out the possibility that the Bank could help fund Mayawati's pet projects under the Ambedkar Village scheme as a "carrot" (Lim 2003). According to a Bank official present at the meeting, Mayawati's "eyes lit up" at this and soon afterward she submitted an application to the central finance ministry. But when the project loan application was not approved, she became very agitated at the Bank.[10]

In mid-May, she publicly declared that she would not be bound by the Bank's "diktats" and that she would direct officials not to advance privatization in the power sector (Srivastava 2002). She also began to make good on her campaign pledge, transferring high-caste civil servants to new posts – often in backwater parts of the state – at astonishing rates: there were media reports of officers arriving at their new stations only to learn that they already had been transferred yet again. Having already withheld a second installment of adjustment support from the state, the Bank's only real leverage was to threaten to withhold project assistance from UP – which Lim did in a letter to Chief Secretary D.S. Bagga, Government of Uttar Pradesh, dated 1 August 2002. He complained:

> We have now learnt that project managers have been replaced within three weeks of assuming office. The project coordinator of the Diversified Agricultural Support Project has been changed twice in quick succession and at the moment there is no project coordinator. In the forestry project, numerous changes have been made over the past six months […]
>
> Such developments do not augur well for these time-bound projects that require consistently good leadership […]
>
> We will continue to closely monitor implementation and progress for all projects and if significant improvement is not made we may have to consider whether the Bank can continue to support these projects. I hope

you will review the situation and take appropriate steps to rectify the situation (quoted in P. Tripathi 2002).

The letter, which was leaked to the media, created a minor commotion in the UP State Assembly, though of a very different kind than the Andhra Pradesh house had witnessed two years earlier: opposition members aligned themselves *with* the Bank's criticism and *against* Mayawati's policies ("SP Accuses Mayawati" 2002). The issue even received mention in Britain's *Financial Times*, which anonymously quoted one government official as saying, "Mayawati is demonstrating to her Dalit support base that she can keep these higher-caste civil servants dancing around endlessly to her own whims. It does not appear to matter that no development work is getting accomplished" (Luce 2002).

The chief minister first responded by claiming that the leaked Bank letter was "a fake"; she later tried to portray it as "a misunderstanding" and "a routine correspondence" to which she had responded, implausibly, by explaining to Lim that the transfer of officials had been meant to accelerate the pace of work on Bank-supported projects ("Furor in UP Assembly" 2002). But she did not entirely relent in transferring civil servants.

Mayawati briefly feigned a commitment to fiscal rectitude for a few weeks after the debacle – she ordered a ban on new furnishings for government offices, purchase of new vehicles, and creation of new posts – but this was soon forgotten. In November 2002, the Bank issued a report entitled *Poverty in India: The Challenge of Uttar Pradesh*, which said that the state faced a "bleak future" unless it reversed its "deterioration in governance." The report also said that UP's poor increasingly were excluded from development that was supposed to benefit them, largely on account of official corruption (World Bank 2002a).

Soon after Ed Lim's showdown with Mayawati, he retired from the Bank and was succeeded by Michael Carter, who oversaw the Bank's transition from the "focus states" approach to the "lagging states" emphasis. UP endured yet another leadership change, with Mulayam Singh Yadav of the Samajwadi Party leading the government from September 2003 until Mayawati managed to form a BSP majority government after the 2007 State Assembly elections (following a campaign that saw her augmenting her *dalit* base with appeals to poor high-caste voters).

Sudha Pai argues that the main contrast between UP and the Bank's two southern focus states is that politics in AP and Karnataka are "characterized by three interlinked features that seem crucial to the successful execution of a reform programme: some degree of political stability, strong leadership, and competent administrative governance" (2005: 125). The account here has argued that UP *did* enjoy competent administrative governance at the outset of its reform program; indeed, if not for this factor, it is unlikely that reforms would have been initiated at all. But without stable political support, bureaucratic initiative could not be sustained.

Indeed, if one lesson that emerged from the Bank's Andhra Pradesh and Karnataka experiences was the importance of the political leadership's strategy for building a consensus for reform, then a lesson from UP was that no amount of bureaucratic competence – or financial assistance from outside – could compensate for a state's lack of political will. In Uttar Pradesh, Zoya Hasan has noted, "The lower castes are trying to make up for millennia of exclusion and humiliation. But in the process, economic development is completely lost" (2001).[41] A few years and many millions of dollars from the World Bank apparently had not been enough to change the electoral ethos in India's largest state. Whether for the BJP or the BSP, the World Bank was no match for the vote bank.

After the bumps of 2002, the Bank retained a limited project portfolio in UP, but the broader fiscal and governance dialogue essentially was lost. Still, after a period of continued fiscal deterioration (which Howes, Mishra et al. attribute to a one-time securitization of power sector dues in 2003–4; 2008: 55), UP's budget position began to improve in 2005–6 under a reformed central transfer regime. The new Mayawati government has taken a less confrontational attitude toward the Bank, and in 2007, at New Delhi's encouragement, approached the Bank for another adjustment loan. As of early 2009, however, this loan had yet to get past the discussion stage, and some of the same governance and power sector issues that had frustrated the Bank before were still in contention (Jainani 2009).

## Discussion: Did the "Focus States" Experiment Work?

Any appraisal of the Bank's "focus states" strategy for India must begin with the caveat that even a decade after its inception, and a half-decade after its phase-out in favor of a "lagging states" approach, it still may be too early to judge its relationship to sub-national growth and poverty reduction – if, in fact, causality ever could be established. We must bear in mind the inherently limited influence that any multilateral development assistance can be expected to have on growth and poverty outcomes in post-liberalization India, as the private sector has become the primary driver of economic activity. The next chapter will look more closely at the Indian states' varied economic experiences in the 1990s and 2000s.

Nevertheless, the ambitious goals that World Bank and Indian officials set for selective, sub-national policy-based lending invite an assessment. Here, we can conclude the "focus states" chapter with a reflection on political economy lessons that emerged from the reform experiences in Andhra Pradesh, Karnataka, and Uttar Pradesh, along with policy outcomes pertaining to some aspects of the broad fiscal, public sector, and governance programs that the Bank sought to encourage.

It should be pointed out that in terms of lending volume, sub-national adjustment assistance never took off to the extent that the Bank at one time had envisioned and the Indian government had endorsed. Over the ten-year period from 1996–7 to 2006–7, nine policy-based loans[12] to four Indian states – the three states discussed in this chapter, plus Orissa, discussed in the next chapter – totaled US$2.1 billion, whereas the 2001 *Country Assistance Strategy* had envisioned an *annual* volume of US$500–900 million for such loans (Howes, Mishra et al. 2008: 46). Even taking into consideration additional project assistance to the focus states, the selective aspect of the strategy did not reach the intensity first envisioned by Lim. Only after more than a decade of engagement with Andhra Pradesh had the Bank come close to committing the US$3 billion figure that Lim had floated to Naidu during their earliest negotiations.

In terms of political economy lessons, it is an understatement that sub-national politics in India have turned out to be more differentiated and complex than the Bank originally imagined. The economic reform experiences in just these three states diverged widely, despite a few underlying similarities.

Whereas Lim had put forward the idea that the Bank's sub-national strategy should be to favor states with the "best" policies, the realization turned out to be somewhat different. The states basically self-selected, and it turned out that the ones that perhaps best fit the Bank's market-friendly vision in the mid- to late-1990s – Maharashtra and Gujarat, for example – were not as interested in the Bank. With increasing access to private investment, they were microcosms of the Bank's "relevance" challenge in India as whole. If the World Bank had wanted to claim Gujarat, in any case, the Asian Development Bank beat it to the punch with a program loan in 1996. Later, Bank officials mildly criticized the ADB for "cherry-picking" Gujarat, but this view seemed to reflect some combination of lender rivalry and a new sensitivity in the early 2000s to the issue of inter-state disparities, after pressure from Indian finance ministry officials. The Bank's – or at least Lim's – original concept was unapologetic "cherry-picking." Interestingly, when Maharashtra's finances worsened in the early 2000s, the state government approached the Bank for an adjustment loan – well after the focus states strategy was underway elsewhere – but its request was denied by central officials who were rethinking the role of external assistance to the states ("Centre Axes Maharashtra Plea" 2003).

Thus, the focus states were middle-of-the-road cases, or even under-achievers, before beginning their partnerships with the Bank. Andhra Pradesh and Uttar Pradesh came to the Bank in dire budgetary straits, following years of election-driven subsidies and the building up of bloated public payrolls as parties distributed state jobs as patronage to their supporters. The Fifth Pay Commission shock, which led to a big increase in salary outlays for government workers, had been the final straw.

Still, these were two very different states, and their routes to Bank engagement were also dissimilar. In AP, the political leadership – namely Naidu – dominated the state's reform process and Bank relationship. In UP, the initiative came from the state's top bureaucrats, and the politicians were pulled along for a while before deciding to part company with the Bank.

Karnataka's leadership initiative followed a change of government in the state and the emergence of AP as the first focus state, suggesting that to some extent the hoped-for "demonstration effect" of the Bank's strategy did work. Yet even though this partnership looked promising at the beginning, the Bank and the Krishna government came to loggerheads over reforms in the power sector, and by the time they did reach an accord for another adjustment loan, the Centre's priorities were different.

The relationship with Naidu in Andhra Pradesh, in particular, illustrated the dangers of a reform program becoming too closely identified with the ruling party and with the World Bank itself, against the broader public interest. In AP, the opposition largely succeeded in defining the reform program as being externally imposed and anti-poor. There was much hypocrisy in the Congress Party's claims in AP: the same party, in the form of Krishna's government, pursued similar reforms in the neighboring state. But political traditions in AP and Karnataka are very different, as recent scholarship demonstrates (Manor 2004). That the Naidu and Krishna governments also "packaged"[43] reforms differently – the latter was more forthright with stakeholders, the former duplicitous – also contributed to the different reactions of the states' publics and opposition parties.

More generally, changes of government in the states presented challenges – and occasionally, opportunities – for the Bank. Krishna's arrival in Karnataka opened the door to a relationship that the Bank had already desired, but had been unable to consummate under the previous Patel government. But the electoral defeats of both Naidu and Krishna in 2004 were also big setbacks for the Bank.

The relationship with Andhra Pradesh eventually recovered as YSR modified his anti-Bank rhetoric, and the Bank learned to live with the fact that his government's priorities – particularly with respect to subsidies and public works for the rural sector – were different than Naidu's. (Time will tell if the leadership changes after YSR's death will significantly impact the state's relationship with the Bank, but the essential continuity after the relatively brief estrangement that followed the 2004 Naidu-to-YSR transition may be instructive.) In contrast, the Bank's broad-based partnership with Karnataka has not been resumed. This may be just as well for the state, as its budget position has markedly improved and its appetite for additional debt, other than limited project assistance from the Bank, has diminished.

In UP, extreme governmental instability undermined the state's reform program and eventually damaged its relationship with the Bank. A new majority government took power after the 2007 State Assembly elections. The sincerity of its reform intentions remains to be seen, even though a best-case survival scenario puts it already halfway through its term. It was not an auspicious sign for the Bank that Mayawati, with whom it so publicly clashed five years earlier, took charge of the state once again in 2007. Her government has pursued another adjustment loan from the Bank – at the Centre's encouragement – but the deal has yet to be finalized.

The example set by the focus states could also work against the Bank's ability to broaden the strategy's reach, as a situation involving the southern state of Tamil Nadu demonstrates. The state government, led by Jayalalithaa Jayaram, initiated a reform dialogue with the Bank in the early 2000s following the Bank's engagement in neighboring AP and Karnataka – another example of the positive "demonstration effect." A major adjustment loan proposal, for US$250 million, was readied for Executive Board approval. But after the 2004 elections, when Naidu and Krishna were sent packing, Jayalalithaa backpedaled. Her own party, the All India Anna Dravida Munnetra Kazhagam (AIADMK), was wiped out in the national parliamentary election, and though the next State Assembly election was not due until 2006, she began to fear a loss of public support, reneged on budgetary reforms negotiated with the Bank, and promised free electricity and other subsidies to the state's public. Her announcement of these policies came on 18 May 2004, the very day that the adjustment loan was to go before the Bank's board. According to Howes, Mishra, and Ravishankar, "It was only the 9.5 hour time difference between India and Washington that ensured that the announcements in India preceded the Board's discussion in Washington. Bank management decided to pull the operation from the board that morning." Candidly, they suggest, "The Bank probably had little alternative if it was to preserve its credibility" (2008: 53).

The challenge of reforming the states' power sectors merits particular attention. There have been several good studies of the Indian states' difficult reform experiences in this area (Howes, Mishra et al. 2008; Tongia 2007; Lal 2006; Kale 2004). The more deeply involved the Bank became at the state level, the clearer it became that reform in this sector was fundamental to addressing broader fiscal and governance issues. But Howes, Mishra, and Ravishankar concede that reforms in the sector "did not follow anywhere near along envisaged lines" (Howes, Mishra et al. 2008: 60). The privatization of distribution proved especially difficult, as did the ending of heavily subsidized or free electricity provision to key electoral constituencies. Only Orissa – which worked through a sectoral reform program with the Bank, discussed in the next chapter – completed privatization, and its experience was quite controversial.

In AP, the Bank essentially abandoned the privatization quest after the change of government in 2004. Howes and his Bank colleagues also say something very revealing about the Bank's learning curve with respect to the government's free power policies: "It became evident that the Bank was adopting what might be called a 'fig leaf' approach. States knew that the Bank wouldn't lend to them if they introduced free power. But practice showed that the Bank would lend even if they moved only a very small direction away from free power." States thus introduced tariffs but failed to collect them, or reimbursed farmers for them, or otherwise adhered to the letter but not the spirit of the reform program. "Over time it became obvious that [these moves] constituted a new equilibrium between the demands of the World Bank and the political imperatives of a largely rural democracy" (2008: 61).

In spite of the disappointing reform progress in the power sector, the states' budget positions have markedly improved from the calamitous position of the late 1990s and early 2000s. The consolidated (combined Centre and states) fiscal deficit has been *halved* relative to GDP – from almost 10 percent in 2001–2 to 5 percent in 2007–8 (it was expected to rise in 2008–9 in view of the global economic crisis). The combined fiscal deficits of the states – over 4 percent of GDP during 1998–2004 – has fallen to around 2 percent (Rao 2009). A variety of factors have contributed to the states' improvement, including economic growth and own-revenue enhancement (especially after the introduction of a state-level Value-Added Tax in 2005), and reforms in the central transfer regime (Howes, Mishra et al. 2008: 44; see also discussion below).

While the fiscal adjustment accomplishments of the Bank's focus states were highly variable during the 1998–2004 period discussed in the case studies, all eventually achieved their targets and performed better than states that did not receive policy-based loans from the Bank (Howes, Mishra et al. 2008: 54–9). Howes and his Bank colleagues concede, "It is unlikely that this large difference is explicable in terms of Bank influence on its selected states. Much more likely that between the Government of India and the Bank there was an effective screening process in place which considerably boosted the probability of winners being selected." Nevertheless, they suggest, "It is still likely that adjustment lending did, at the margin, induce reform, both fiscal and otherwise" in the focus states (2008: 58).

The broader fiscal improvement – for the states as a whole, and for the consolidated deficit – is one of India's most important reform accomplishments of the past several years, but the Bank's particular contribution here is also the most difficult to assess, because Indian fiscal federalism itself underwent changes during this time. In 2000, the Indian government asked the Eleventh Finance Commission to devise a "monitorable fiscal reform programme" that would link part of central grants to state governments to the latter's progress toward improved budget positions. A Fiscal Reforms Facility, with over US$2 billion in resources, was set up as an incentive fund for states meeting negotiated targets. By 2004–5, nineteen states had signed Memoranda of Understanding on fiscal reforms with the central government. The Twelfth Finance Commission recommendations went further toward institutionalizing a performance-based resource allocation, and phased out the Fiscal Reforms Facility in favor of a new Debt Consolidation and Relief Facility.

All this sounded a lot like what the Chidambaram-era finance ministry had envisioned for the World Bank's policy-based loans back in 1996. In fact, some Indian officials and public finance experts perceived a direct lineage from the fiscal conditionality in the Bank's state-level operations to the Centre's own criteria under the Fiscal Reforms Facility, though the use of revenue deficit, fiscal deficit, and expenditure quality indicators were obvious choices as criteria. The states' individual Memoranda with the Centre were confidential, but a former finance secretary for Uttar Pradesh, Sanjeev Ahluwalia, went so far as to say that his state's agreement with the Centre "directly emulated" its reform program with the World Bank, and that without the precedent of Bank conditionality it was "difficult to imagine" such a linkage of central transfers to UP's fiscal performance (2003). Some Indian states likely would have pursued fiscal reforms even if the Bank had not been part of the picture, but for "hard cases" like UP, the Bank may have helped spur action. However, it must be stressed that UP's progress is still fragile, and still could be derailed by its politics.

Thus, perhaps the original hope was realized – that the Bank's sub-national policy-based lending would help catalyze a broader reform process for India's states and intergovernmental institutions. Maybe the Bank did nudge these "second generation reforms" further along than they would have progressed in its absence. But with a gradual coalescence of forces – from growing state-level support for reforms, to private credit agencies rating the states' investment climates[11] – also pressing in the same direction, it is impossible to parse the exact contribution of the Bank. The discussion in this chapter, hopefully, has conveyed the inherently limited role that the Bank can expect to play in India – even at the sub-national level – in the era of liberalization, given the complexity of India's political process and the expanding variety of state, society, and market forces that shape economic policies.

If this was a successful "two-level game" outcome, whereby the Indian government used World Bank conditionality to help it bring about federal fiscal reforms, then by about 2003 New Delhi had had enough of this use for external assistance. Having established its own fiscal conditionality with the states, its priorities for the World Bank changed. The same "deliberately anti-egalitarian" quality that had driven the focus states strategy's inception under Lim and Chidambaram was now becoming a political liability. Rather than picking winners – if indeed that is what the Bank had been doing – India now desired that the Bank should turn its attention toward its most laggardly states.

# Chapter Three

# REASSERTING CENTRAL GOVERNMENT CONTROL, REORIENTING AID TOWARD "LAGGING STATES"

*The concentration of World Bank programs in a few reforming states carried with it the predictable risks of portfolio concentration in a highly politicized context, which resulted in significant swings in the volume of lending and spending on analytical work. Especially during the early years of shift to state-level engagement, the residual role of the World Bank at the national level was not well-defined and dialogue with the center suffered.*

World Bank, *Country Strategy for India* (2008b: Annex 4, p. 8).

*…a stage has come in our development where we should now, firstly, review our dependence on external donors. [...] While being grateful to all our development partners of the past, I wish to announce that the Government of India would now prefer to provide relief…*

The Honourable Jaswant Singh, Minister of Finance, Government of India, in his Budget Speech for 2003–4

*There could be multiple 'equilibrium points' in the Bank-India relationship [...] Organizations learn from the frontier, from the field. The Bank can be flexible and opportunistic.*

Dipak Dasgupta, Senior Economist, World Bank, New Delhi (2008)

This chapter considers two broadly contemporaneous developments in India's aid policies during the early 2000s. The first was a clear effort by the Indian government to signal the country's diminished need for external assistance, crystallized in a 2003 announcement by Minister of Finance Jaswant Singh that India no longer wished to receive bilateral aid from 22 donor countries. (India also began to reposition itself in the global pecking order by transitioning from a net recipient to a net contributor of aid; this development will be discussed in the final chapters). Though the announcement did not apply to multilateral donors such as the World Bank and the ADB – in fact, their role as main channels of assistance was reinforced by the bilateral provider exits – it demonstrated a new Indian confidence about its economic strengths and assertiveness about aid terms that continues to this day.

The second development, distinct from but related to the first, was a reassertion of central oversight with respect to the state-level operations of external assistance providers. The Government of India, following both bureaucratic and political impulses, began to reconsider its relatively permissive stance on the "focus states" strategies of the World Bank and other providers such as the Asian Development Bank (ADB) and Britain's Department for International Development (DFID). While both the multilateral and bilateral donors were affected by the recentralization policy, the central government concerns that led to it followed most directly from the World Bank's activities, given the scale and visibility of its state-level engagement (particularly in Andhra Pradesh).

On the one hand, the Centre sought to formalize the selection criteria for states availing multilateral program loans – an admission that the Bank's "focus states" selection had been *ad hoc*, and possibly politicized. The Centre sought to place an upper limit on the share of total lending represented by state-level program loans, therefore shifting the aid emphasis back to more traditional investment loans in the states as well as to central initiatives. It also issued clearer guidelines for states' use of multilateral program loans, so that the loans would not create perverse incentives to avoid reforms. In general, this thrust reflected the nascent strengthening of India's own fiscal federalism toward a more performance-based regime, and the Centre's desire that external assistance should not undermine these gains. To that extent, it indicated a mixed assessment of the Bank's state-level aid strategy so far: while it might have played a role in catalyzing state-level reforms and an improved central transfer system, its hitherto highly discretionary aspect also posed potential problems.

On the other hand, the Indian government also began to reconsider the very premise behind channeling aid toward the most reform-oriented states. As the Bank's program came to be perceived as favoring middle-income states in southern India, concerns about India's "lagging states" – especially the UP-Bihar-Jharkhand-Orissa corridor – led the Centre to put pressure on the Bank and the other agencies to overhaul their approach to working with states. Even if the donors had been inclined to disagree, they would have had little choice but to revise their strategies in line with Indian preferences.

In the case of the World Bank, as we will see, there was no significant resistance either to the recentralization initiative or to the shift from reforming states to lagging states. In part, this reflected a leadership change at the Bank's country office, but it also followed a more general impulse on the part of the Bank to be "flexible and opportunistic" – to do whatever was necessary to remain relevant to this large client that has less and less use for aid that does not fully support its own development goals.

The first part of the chapter will discuss India's revised aid policy, which first took shape during the NDA government. We will then look at the recentralization initiatives with respect to state-level program loans. The latter half of the chapter will track the World Bank's official strategy through 2004 to 2008 policy documents – from the end of the "focus states" experiment to a progressive emphasis on the poorest states. In assessing the early implementation of the "lagging states" approach, we will see that despite some successes, the Bank has had a predictably difficult time ratcheting up its lending share to a new target group of states that, by definition, exhibits the very weakest institutions and governance in India.

## India's Changing Aid Priorities: The Global Context

During April-May 2003, India's foreign exchange reserves – which had been next to nothing twelve years earlier – surged into the US$75–80 billion range, a record for the country. By year's end, the foreign exchange reserves crossed the symbolic US$100 billion mark, putting India in league with Asian neighbors China, Japan, South Korea, and Taiwan on this key indicator ("India Joins" 2003). Beginning in 2003–4, India's economy grew at an annual rate exceeding 8 percent, or almost 14 percent in real dollars (Panagariya 2008: xiv, xvi). Terms such as "rising power" and "emerging giant," long representative of India's aspirations, were now bandied about globally.

Buoyed by resources and optimism, the Minister of Finance for the NDA government, Jaswant Singh, announced in his 2003–4 Budget Speech[1] a change in India's aid policy intended to add to its global prestige (Price 2004: 4). India, Singh said, had come to a stage in its development where it both should "reconsider its dependence on external assistance," and "extend support to the national efforts of other developing countries." Though India was "grateful to all our development partners of the past," Singh said, it now wished to "provide relief" to several bilateral aid providers so that their resources might be transferred to NGOs or to more needy countries. In all, 22 donor countries would be asked to terminate their bilateral aid programs after concluding current projects; India would continue to accept bilateral aid from only the European Union, Germany, Japan, Russia, the UK, and the US. The rejected bilateral donors – which included Australia, Canada, Denmark,[2] France, the Netherlands, Sweden, and others – would have to channel future development assistance through NGOs, UN agencies, or multilateral institutions including the World Bank and ADB. Moreover, Singh announced, India would repay ahead of schedule its bilateral debt to 15 countries, totaling US$1.6 billion (remaining bilateral debt would stand at US$12.7 billion) (ibid., 7). India no longer would accept "tied aid" that linked assistance to purchases from the donor country.

The loan volume represented by the severed ties was not immense; part of India's rationale was to reduce the administrative costs it incurred by attending to a range of relatively small bilateral aid programs, each with their own particular procedures and requirements. The clear message was that when it came to aid, it was just too much trouble for Indian officials to spend time dealing with piddly partners.

Official Indian statistics from 2003 demonstrated the already dramatic reduction in reliance on aid. In the early decades after Independence, external assistance had comprised as much as 10 percent of India's total annual public sector investment. In 1991–2 – the year of the crisis that prompted IMF and World Bank interventions – external assistance was about 1.4 percent of GDP. Ten years later, in 2001–2, the figure was only about 0.5 percent of GDP, or US$3.57 billion. Total bilateral aid for the year was US$1.14 billion from 31 countries.[3]

At the same time as it sought to "relieve" some of its aid providers, Singh announced an "India Development Initiative" (IDI) to "leverage and promote [India's] strategic economic interests abroad." The IDI, he indicated, would become the major vehicle of India's own aid policy by providing grants and project assistance to other developing countries in Africa and South Asia. Moreover, India would align itself with the policies of the Group of Eight (G8) major industrialized countries and the Bretton Woods institutions by offering debt relief to the category of Heavily Indebted Poor Countries (HIPC) concentrated largely in sub-Saharan Africa. India, Singh said, had "fought against poverty as a country and as a people," and understood "the pain and the challenge that this burden imposes."

Singh's announcement was of a piece with other Indian initiatives on multilateral assistance. For 2002–3, India already had announced prepayment of US$2.8 billion in multilateral debt to the World Bank and ADB. Even more dramatically, having paid off its debt to the IMF three years earlier, India announced in June that it would become a donor to the Fund by subscribing 205 million Special Drawing Rights (SDR) – about US$300 million – to the Financial Transaction Plan facility, a reserve for bailing out poor countries in crisis ("India Becomes IMF Lender" 2003).

Taken together, the new policy represented an attempt to reposition India's relationship to development assistance, "from aid recipient to donor" (Price 2004). Analysts offered several possible explanations for the move, and in truth the government's policy probably stemmed from several motivations. But the common denominator was an apparent desire to project the image of a great power. Some of the excluded donors had suspended aid to India after its May 1998 nuclear tests – though so had other countries that still would be permitted to retain bilateral aid programs. (Jaswant Singh earlier had served as Minister for External Affairs for the NDA Government, and had shouldered the brunt of the diplomatic fallout from the nuclear issue). Additionally, several donors – particularly some of the Scandinavian countries – had criticized India harshly for the terrible communal violence that took place in Gujarat in 2002, which several independent observers had linked to malign neglect or even connivance on the part of the BJP-led state government (e.g. Human Rights Watch 2002).

Revealingly, as Price notes, critics whose aid still would be welcome included permanent UN Security Council members (America, Britain, and Russia), and leading fellow aspirants to permanent membership (Germany and Japan); the acceptable donor list was essentially the G8 (sans Canada, France, and Italy) plus the EU as a collective entity. Thus, India may have intended to signal which countries it perceived as its "peer group," and which countries' criticisms were an affront to its dignity.

Jaswant Singh's announcement surprised and disappointed some of the donors. The Netherlands, which recently had been the fourth-largest bilateral donor, had not expected to be treated so dismissively. India was the largest recipient in Sweden's aid portfolio, and that country was planning a five-year program worth US$25 million a year. Canada provided a similar amount of annual aid, and had been a donor to India since the 1950s (ibid., 5). It is particularly noteworthy that aid from the excluded Netherlands rivaled sums from some of the retained donors during the early 2000s (ibid., 6, Table 1). For countries such as the Scandinavian donors, whose aid relative to the size of their own economies was more generous than that of the retained G8 countries, the dismissal might have seemed particularly ungracious (the Dutch exit would prove particularly contentious; de Groot et al. 2008). But the donors understood the point of the message. A Swedish diplomat told *The Financial Times*, "It has nothing to do with money. It's about foreign policy" (Marcelo 2003).

In addition to great power diplomacy, the new aid policy reflected a preference by the NDA government to re-centralize decision-making with respect to external assistance. This reassertion of central control reflected a desire to consolidate the number of donors toward whom the government would have to devote ministerial and bureaucratic resources. As discussed below, it may have also reflected some misgivings among central bureaucrats over the recent extent of external involvement in India's states.

If the donors *non grata* greeted the announcement with some frustration, Indian responses to the new policy were mixed. While some expressed nationalist satisfaction, others were unsure. An editorial in *The Financial Express* called it "a sensible policy, implemented hamhandedly by officials who seemed to have a chip on their shoulder when dealing with donors" ("A Jaswant Singh Doctrine" 2003). The column went on to remark,

> While winding up small aid programmes and diverting such sums to NGOs, who often do better work than government agencies, is good policy, India cannot still afford to completely stop aid. Home to the world's largest number of poor people, it will attract aid flows from richer countries and can make use of low cost resources. Moreover, several state governments find aid funds bring in the extra cash required to keep development programmes going when government revenues get used up just paying salaries.
>
> [...] One thing should be clear to all: India will welcome aid that adequately impacts on development but is in no mood to cling on to funds that are costly to administer and come with sermons... (ibid.)

Harsh Sethi, writing for *The Hindu*, likewise wondered whether central officials had consulted with state governments or considered the implications of the policy for their aid-financed projects (it soon became clear that states had not been consulted in any systematic way). He also asked "what price hubris?" and suggested that it was foolhardy for Singh's finance ministry to imagine that it could contain the consequences of its abrupt dismissal of important bilateral donors. In the future, some of the countries that had been shown the door might argue against India's eligibility for concessionary multilateral financing, such as the World Bank's IDA credits:

> The Scandinavians, for instance, though minor donors in the Indian context, are the key donors for multilateral agencies. Will they be inclined to support Indian requests once they are told that their assistance is no longer required, ostensibly because India is now well on its way to becoming a prosperous country, possibly itself a donor nation? No matter how healthy our forex reserves currently look, there is no assurance of stability. Equally, while aid flows constitute a minuscule proportion of our GDP, there is little doubt that many of our programmes have been kick-started by aid and have managed an order of quality at least in part due to the interaction with the donors.
>
> Mr. Singh's grandiose announcement may please our unreconstructed *swadeshites* [economic nationalists]; it may bolster our pride that we are no longer a beggar nation. But, there is little doubt that it has alienated many of our external well-wishers and may land us with consequences that our political masters may not have thought of... (Sethi 2003).

These observations were prescient. In the next chapter, we will return to the issue of India' eligibility for concessionary IDA aid. Donor pressures to graduate India out of IDA indeed have intensified.

The NDA's aid policy, it should be noted, was modified somewhat by the successor United Progressive Alliance (UPA) government. When Chidambaram returned to the finance ministry he put the policy under review (Marcelo 2004). In September 2004, the finance ministry announced that India would accept bilateral aid from all G8 members and other EU members provided their packages were worth at least US$25 million a year (some re-invited donors declined to return; for a discussion of the Scandinavian exit, see de Groot et al. 2008). The new government, too, could seem proud almost to a fault on the subject of aid. After the devastating tsunami that struck the Indian Ocean region in December 2004, India refused aid (apart from long-term rehabilitation assistance from the World Bank and ADB), a move that again seemed calculated to project strength but may have also annoyed some donor countries (Chopra 2005).

## The Reassertion of Central Control Over the States' Borrowing

The various Indian aid policy announcements of 2003 and 2004 set the context in which the World Bank's updated Country Assistance Strategy (CAS) would emerge. Presented in September 2004, the new CAS covered the 2005–8 period. If the major innovation of the two previous Bank strategies had been the introduction and institutionalization of "focus state" lending, then the new CAS essentially ended that approach in favor of an emphasis on "lagging states." Though the altered strategy followed a change of leadership on the Bank side – "focus states" architect Ed Lim was replaced by new country director Michael Carter in late 2002 – the push for a new approach came from the Indian government. Essentially, the World Bank's lending strategy was caught in the dragnet of the Indian government's determination to diminish its reliance on aid, and to reassert its control over whatever external assistance it deemed worthwhile to retain.

In tandem with the new policy toward bilateral aid, India had informed donor countries that it wished also to reevaluate their engagement with the country's states. For example, as noted in the previous chapter, Britain's DFID developed its own focus states approach – often in partnership with the World Bank and ADB – and it became particularly involved with Andhra Pradesh in the early 2000s. At one point, in 2002–3, DFID's aid pledges to this single state exceeded the volume of its new commitments at the national level in India; in fact, its aid to AP at the time surpassed that to any other *country* in the British bilateral aid portfolio. The Indian government told DFID that the allocation was out of balance, and indicated that British aid should be split 50:50 between the states collectively and central projects and programs, even though the former spend more in critical sectors such as primary education and health. The Centre told DFID that its established focus state programs (in AP, Orissa, Madhya Pradesh, and West Bengal) could run their course. But it also indicated that in the future, it did not wish to see external donors making their own determinations as to which states were "doing well or badly," or "cherry-picking" the most reformist ones (House of Commons 2005).

Though overall the 2003 aid policy reaffirmed India's interest in multilateral as opposed to bilateral assistance, the World Bank's state-level operations essentially confronted the same changed Government of India attitude that impacted the bilateral programs. Several factors help to explain the Centre's wary bearing toward the "focus states" aid model: change in political leadership, bureaucratic backlash, and a general uneasiness at the development gaps that increasingly separated India's high-growth and lagging states.

### Change in Political Leadership

First, as detailed in the previous chapter, the Indian government that originally approved the Bank's focus states concept was the politically vulnerable United Front – a coalition without a strong central party. Further, the finance minister who signed off on the strategy, Chidambaram, was an enthusiastic liberalizer who harbored relatively few hang-ups about protocol, so long as the Bank understood that India retained ultimate control in the relationship. He and other central reformists hoped that the Bank might help catalyze sub-national and federal reforms that the government would have difficulty taking up on its own, given the constraints of its fractious coalition.

But by 1998, when the first state-level assistance program under the new strategy was ready to go on line, the United Front had been succeeded by the National Democratic Alliance, and Chidambaram had been replaced by Yashwant Sinha of the BJP. (Sinha was the NDA's first finance minister; in mid-2002, he swapped portfolios with Jaswant Singh, formerly the foreign minister). The change was significant in several respects. Though the NDA, too, was a coalition, its position was not quite as vulnerable as that of the United Front; thus, its perceived need for the Bank's assistance in pushing reforms was not as great. It was anchored by a national party – or, at least, a party with national aspirations – in the BJP. Though the NDA would continue to pursue economic liberalization during its six years at the helm, the BJP brought a more nationalist *swadeshi* (from Hindi, literally "own country," or self-sufficiency) orientation to the task.[4] The party had campaigned on a platform of economic nationalism, though its core agenda related less to economic policy than to Hindu identity politics and an assertive foreign policy. In power, the BJP leadership generally adopted a pragmatic, incremental approach to continuing India's economic reforms, but its fellow Hindu right organizations, particularly the Rashtriya Swayamsevak Sangh (RSS), continued to harbor deep misgivings. The upshot for the World Bank, as a "foreign" actor and standard-bearer of globalization, was eventual scrutiny of its perceived penetration into India's states.

Coincidentally, the very first loan under the focus states concept, the 1998 Andhra Pradesh Economic Restructuring Project, came along in a global-strategic context that gave the new NDA government a strong incentive to support it, irrespective of its other features: it was the first loan for India to come before the World Bank's Executive Board following the Indian nuclear tests in May 1998. The Board's June approval of the loan was far from certain, since the US and Japan had pledged to vote against all but "humanitarian" multilateral assistance to India, in line with their and other donors' decisions to impose economic sanctions as a punishment for the nuclear tests. Bank managers had already withdrawn energy and transport projects totaling US$1 billion from Board consideration, for fear that they would not be passed. Much to India's relief, the Board approved the US$543 million APERP, likely because the multi-sector project loan included health and education components that could be passed off as sufficiently "humanitarian" (ironically, had the APERP been a true adjustment loan such as the Bank later prepared for its focus states, it might not have passed, since there was disagreement within the Board as to whether such policy-based loans should be considered humanitarian). The humanitarian content of the Andhra Pradesh loan allowed donor governments to claim that the Board's approval "should 'in no way' be interpreted as a change in the official position on sanctions" punishing India for its nuclear adventure ("India Says Loans 'Rebuff' Critics" 1998).

Yet the loan's passage also let the NDA government claim victory: rightly or not, New Delhi heralded the approval as a sign of normalized relations with the great powers. Yashwant Sinha proclaimed, "This is a rebuff to those who've been claiming that we'll be severely hit by the sanctions" (ibid.). Sinha had been finance minister for only a short while, and a single World Bank loan that was being handled by ministry bureaucrats and was already in an advanced state of preparation might not have caught his attention – despite its unusual nature – before it was set to go before the Bank's Board. When it did, the NDA government's priority was to get a loan – *any* loan – approved; thus APERP did not stand out as the radically new development in the Bank-India relationship that it might have been seen as under more normal circumstances. In a circuitous way, then, the nuclear tests were another example of serendipity favoring Andhra Pradesh in its bid to become the first focus state.

As discussed in the previous chapter, Naidu's TDP had provided critical outside support to the NDA government after the 1998 elections. This gave the Centre additional incentive to support the Bank's early focus in AP; when it came to centrally managed resources, what Naidu wanted, his state usually got. The TDP's continued clout at the Centre was also a serendipitous development for its focus state program. Though the Bank had perceived Naidu's kingmaker role in the United Front as political "protection" when it first engaged the state in 1996, there was no way it could have known then that the TDP would be a pivotal supporter of the next central government as well. But Naidu was an NDA ally, and this disposed the new central leadership to keep the money flowing. The NDA also welcomed the later addition of Uttar Pradesh and Karnataka as focus states. UP, as India's most populous state and an important electoral arena for the BJP, was a good fit for the NDA in spite of its governance problems; what is more, a BJP chief minister led it at the time of its 2000 adjustment loan. Karnataka, with its global profile and competent government, was also acceptable in spite of its Congress party leadership.

In sum, then, the NDA inherited the World Bank's focus states strategy from the predecessor government, and while the BJP's *swadeshi* impulses encouraged it to take a less welcoming view of such sub-national engagement, other political factors aligned to encourage it to remain supportive of the approach – at least initially. But by 2002–3, the picture was beginning to change.

### The Bureaucrats Put on the Brakes

Whatever the BJP's nationalist leanings, the first reassertion of central control over the states' relations with the Bank came from finance ministry bureaucrats, not the political leadership. The Fund-Bank Division of the Department of Economic Affairs (DEA) is the Ministry of Finance unit that handles India's relations with the Bretton Woods institutions on a routine basis. Though the major reorientation of the World Bank assistance strategy had required the finance minister's (Chidambaram's) approval at the outset in 1996, ongoing management of the state-level operations was left with DEA bureaucrats, whose natural inclination was to establish standard operating procedures for sub-national program loans. But the Centre soon went beyond merely standardizing the selection criteria, to a more fundamental reconsideration of the purpose behind selective state-level development assistance.

The DEA was piqued when Andhra Pradesh received nearly one-third of all external assistance to the country for the 2001–2 and 2002–3 fiscal years. Department staff complained that a state with 7 percent of India's population should not be getting 31 percent of all aid – World Bank, plus DFID and other donors (Garg 2002). The DEA tried to withhold its approval of the AP adjustment loan by declining to forward the state government's Letter of Development Policy to the Bank, a required procedure. The state government was irritated because it had already assumed receipt of the loan in its budget projections. Chief Minister Naidu appealed over the heads of the central bureaucrats directly to Yashwant Sinha, who asked them to allow the loan to go through (P.V. Rao 2002).

The bureaucrats complied, but apparently they did not appreciate that their authority had been challenged by the appearance of partisan favoritism. The professional administrators at the DEA are generally top-flight Indian Administrative Service (IAS) officers, and they tend not to look favorably on political circumvention of the role they perceive for themselves, as custodians of fair and objective standards in the allocation of resources. It did not help that the Ministry of Finance was beginning to receive calls from leaders of other states, wondering what was behind the bounty of Bank assistance to Andhra Pradesh, and asking for a piece of the action.

In February 2002, DEA Secretary C.M. Vasudev even wrote a letter to World Bank President James Wolfensohn, to clarify India's position on the protocol that should be observed with respect to the Bank's state-level adjustment loans. It announced, "While the Government of India, in general, support the reform programme contained in the [Government of Andhra Pradesh] Letter of Development Policy, I would like to state that the approach to subsequent adjustment loans would be decided annually after discussions between the World Bank and Government of India" (World Bank 2002b: Annex A). Thus the bureaucrats would give up the fight over the AP adjustment loan, but they would prevail in the larger reassertion of oversight.

The announcement of formal selection criteria for state adjustment loans followed at the end of the year. The DEA decided it was time to standardize what previously had been an *ad hoc* process. In a December 2002 letter to state governments, the DEA said, "Since, in the past, there has been no uniformity in the Structural Adjustment Loans being taken up by the different States with the multilateral institutions like the World Bank, ADB etc., the institutions are being advised to ensure certain common criteria as a pre-requisite for accessing these facilities." Specifically, a state government would need to commit to a "credible medium-term fiscal plan" that would put it on track to: first, generate a revenue surplus and limit the fiscal deficit to less than 3 percent of state GDP within 3–5 years; second, eliminate or contain subsidies, especially in the power sector; third, reduce administrative costs and improve governance; and finally, reform public sector enterprises, potentially including disinvestment (partial privatization). Singh further stated that adjustment loans would comprise not more than 30 percent of total annual World Bank lending to India.[5] This essentially preserved the existing "high-end scenario" for adjustment lending – the upper limit of about one-third of the all-India loan volume mentioned in the Bank's 2001 CAS – but it was a noteworthy declaration because the Bank had proposed raising the share to 40 percent (Lim 2003).

In October 2005, the finance ministry revised these guidelines somewhat, and specified additional conditions for state-level adjustment loans (rechristened Development Policy Loans, or DPLs, by the World Bank) – which now were envisioned as *only 15 percent* of annual lending to India. Essentially, the Centre reduced the relative scope of this form of multilateral assistance, and went even further to subordinate what remained of it to India's own, modestly reformed federal fiscal regime. The new guidelines said that states wishing to avail such loans must enact Fiscal Responsibility and Budget Management (FRBM) Acts and present formal letters of commitment to the finance ministry – which, at its discretion, would forward them to the multilateral lenders.

The Centre wanted the states to compete for such loans, but it wanted to be the arbiter of which states would receive loans and which would have to wait – ostensibly, using the new objective standards for eligibiliy. Once a state received this form of quick-disbursing budgetary assistance, the Centre said, it must not be used to fund the state's revenue deficit. Though the Centre relaxed the requirement of generating a revenue surplus, a state still would have to make progress toward a zero revenue deficit by 2008–9. Moreover, though a state would be committing to a multi-year program, the external lender must disburse the assistance in a minimum of two separate tranches – contingent on the state's progress toward agreed benchmarks – to minimize moral hazard risk.

The state also would have to retire existing higher-cost debt equivalent to at least half of the loan proceeds, essentially making the adjustment loan a partial "debt swap." The revised guidelines were explicit that adjustment lending is *not* a form of "additionality" – it would be subject to states' centrally imposed annual borrowing limits, and therefore can only substitute for other forms of borrowing (World Bank 2007a: 4, Annex 7; Howes, Mishra et al. 2008: 64). Gone was the notion that multilateral program loans were some sort of "bonus money" or incentive fund outside the normal Centre-states transfer regime, intended to finance the cost of reforms. The Centre would closely monitor progress and supervise assistance transactions every step of the way – if states fell more than six months behind their budget targets, they risked forfeiting the balance of undisbursed loan money.

To some extent, this kind of development was probably inevitable. A few years earlier, the Indian government was an especially fragile coalition and the Bank's interlocutors in the finance ministry were supportive technocrats – some of whom, such as Montek Singh Ahluwalia and Shankar Acharya, had even worked at the Bank in the past. Now, a change of government and the normal rhythm of intra-agency turnover had changed the political context and brought in a new cadre of bureaucrats. The new authorities did not play a part in fashioning the focus states strategy, and they tended to perceive it through the traditional prism of safeguarding the Centre's authority. But the AP government and the Bank might have overreached, too; had the allocation to the state not been so disproportional, central bureaucrats might not have intervened as early on, or as extensively.

As the Bank's Sumir Lal, a political economist, put it in 2003, "The newer crop at DEA has slowed things down. They didn't author the focus states strategy, so they haven't 'owned it.' To them, it is intrusive, it does look like 'going around' GoI [Government of India]" (Lal 2003). Lal said that the DEA's new assertiveness was beginning to manifest in a variety of ways: "They don't want the Bank even to visit the states without permission. Even to organize a seminar in one of the state capitals, we're now having to go through much more red tape."

The recentralization initiative, if perhaps predictable, was nevertheless remarkable. If you were looking for "conditionality" in the arrangement, its most basic parameters emanated from the Government of India. Whatever role the Bank's focus states might have played in catalyzing a broader reform ethos among states, as far as India was concerned, the strategy had largely served its purpose. Sub-national adjustment lending by the Bank and the ADB was now just one tool in the kit for Indian reformers – and judging by the downward trend that they imposed on its share in the Bank's overall lending portfolio, they saw its importance diminishing rather than increasing.

However willing the Bank might have been to modify its strategy, the essential point is that it was *India's* decision to refashion the Bank's engagement with the states. In fact, as the discussion below of the 2004 Country Assistance Strategy will show, "modify" is an understatement; in effect, the Bank would officially abandon what arguably had been the single most innovative aspect of its India strategy for the previous half-decade. But the Bank apparently concluded that it had little choice but to respond to the government's wishes. It was not that the Bank and the finance ministry had significant disagreements over *policies*; both still desired to encourage the same basic fiscal and governance reforms in the states. But central authorities had come to harbor misgivings over *process*, and were more skeptical than their predecessors that the Bank's involvement could add much to India's own reform efforts. In fact, some believed that multilateral adjustment loans were becoming just another form of discretionary, politicized resource allocation to states – and that it was up to India, not to the external lenders, to tighten up the regime.

For India, the political and bureaucratic impulses to rethink the central government's encouragement of the focus states strategy sprang from different motives, but they became mutually reinforcing. Had the bureaucrats not taken issue with the pattern and process of state lending, then the central political leadership might not have bothered to scrutinize the arrangement, at least not in 2002–3. On the order of priorities for an Indian finance minister, the ongoing operations of the World Bank in India rank fairly low (it is telling that neither Yashwant Sinha nor Jaswant Singh, the two NDA finance ministers, have much at all to say about the Bank in their memoirs on their years in government; Singh 2007, Sinha 2007).[6] But once the DEA staff had reopened the issue, the political leadership was not as inclined to offer the degree of support it had shown a half-dozen years earlier – particularly now that the government's main priority for external assistance seemed to be further reducing India's use of it.

By the time Michael Carter took over for Ed Lim as the Bank's country director in 2002, it was apparent from a political standpoint that it was time for a changed approach. "The DEA said to us, 'Look, stop giving us this problem'," he recalled (Carter 2007). The department's task would be much easier if the external engagement with states were rationalized and routinized, so that they could stop fielding calls from various states for special dispensation. In a sense, Lim and Chidambaram's calculated "demonstration effect" had paid off – though it was not always clear that the message had gone through to other states that reform commitment rather than political connectedness was the *sine qua non* for eligibility.

The Bank's approach under Lim was "the right one for its time," Carter concluded. Though the Bank's strategy under Carter's direction would retain an emphasis on India's states, the Centre's changed orientation meant that the engagement would have to evolve. On balance, Carter said, he did not mind the central government's reassertion of its authority in "what ought to be a Bank-Centre-states relationship... The states should not be seen as doing something 'on the side'" (ibid.).

World Bank policy documents often stress the importance of a borrower country's "ownership" of the economic policy reforms that the Bank's assistance is meant to encourage. The Indian central government's policy changes with respect to state borrowing, beginning in 2002–3, certainly exhibited "ownership." But they also presented a dilemma for the Bank: the very strategy that it had articulated as a way of making itself more "relevant" to India was now being dialed down, only a half-decade into its implementation. Ultimately, relevance would follow from India's priorities. The Bank had been so concerned to retain the Centre's commitment to its "focus states" model that it acted in ways that were ultimately self-defeating, particularly by banking so heavily on the Naidu government in Andhra Pradesh and thus reinforcing the perception of an arbitrary, politicized state-level engagement. In the end, there was no avoiding the fact that the Government of India was the client; the Bank's sub-national engagement would follow its preferences.

## Domestic Politics: State-Level Economic Performance Under Liberalization

At the same time that bureaucratic and political factors were encouraging the Indian government to reconsider its support for the Bank's focus states strategy, the perennial issue of interstate economic inequalities started to attract more attention in Indian political and technocratic circles. India has always exhibited regional disparities in per capita income and poverty rates, and different economic growth and fertility rates have led these disparities to widen rather than narrow over time. As Amaresh Bagchi and John Kurian observe,

> For reasons of history and geography – the legacy of colonial policies as well as the sharp variations in physical features and resource endowments across regions – social and economic development has never been even in different parts of the country. During the colonial period, with agricultural productivity stagnating at low levels, the country as a whole remained abjectly poor and backward; and with industrialization occurring in a few isolated pockets, some regions were significantly more backward than others. Reducing these disparities through balanced regional growth has constituted one of the cardinal aims of planning – adopted as the strategy of development in India after independence. The need to address the problem of imbalances in development between regions was reiterated and stressed in successive plan documents. Yet, all key indicators show that far from getting diminished, the wide disparities in development levels and standards of living across states continued to persist even after several decades of planning (2005: 323).

Interregional inequalities confront all federal countries to some extent; both advanced industrialized federations, such as Germany and the US, and developing federal countries, such as Brazil and India, grapple with them – though the absolute deprivation that persists in the latter imparts a particular urgency to the problem. Regional economic disparities can be an especially sensitive political issue when they overlap with sub-national cleavages along ethnic and linguistic lines, as they do in India.[7]

In a democracy, it can be difficult to determine exactly what drives the political agenda at any given time, and why an ever-present issue such as regional inequality becomes more salient to decision-makers at some junctures than at others. In the mid-1990s, for Lim, Chidambaram, and other architects of the focus states strategy, the issue of interstate economic disparities seemed less important than the variation in policies and governance across states: the priority was to accelerate the sub-national reform process. For Lim in particular, increasing inequalities – to a point – even seemed desirable, if "demonstration effects" could motivate India's more backward states to emulate the high achievers. India's reformist political leadership did not disagree.

A half-decade later, the ethos clearly had changed – for Indian leaders, and consequently, for the Bank. One reason may have been the simple passage of time: a decade after the major 1991 liberalization offered more data and perspective on the regional dynamics of market-led growth than was available in the mid-1990s. Beginning in the late 1990s, a bevy of studies on regional economic trends in India appeared (for example, Cashin and Sahay 1996; Sachs, Bajpai et al. 1999; Ahluwalia 2000, 2002; Shetty 2003; Singh, Bhandari et al. 2003; Bhattacharya and Sakthivel 2007). Data limitations make comparisons challenging, and analysts have employed different estimation techniques that produce somewhat different indicators. But as Panagariya puts it, "the bottom line is that if we go by per-capita incomes across states, inequality has definitely gone up" (2008: 162). Similarly, according to Frankel, "The social consequences of economic reforms confirm trends suggesting the emergence of two economies. Economic performance disaggregated by states show substantially different outcomes" (2004: 603).

Montek Singh Ahluwalia – who, recall, served in the central finance ministry in the 1990s and supported the World Bank's focus states approach – presented a particularly influential set of studies (2000, 2002).[8] Though there are more recent studies that take into account newer data and have used different methodologies for comparison, Ahluwalia's work merits special attention here not only because of who he is, but also because the publication of his findings was contemporaneous to India's process of re-thinking the Bank's state-level engagement.[9]

Ahluwalia found a larger range of variation in growth rates among India's 14 major states during the 1990s than during the 1980s (the coefficient of variation was 0.27 in the post-reforms period, up from 0.15 in the earlier period). The trend was even more pronounced when expressed in terms of state growth rates per capita (an increase in the inter-state Gini coefficient from about 0.16 in 1986–7 to 0.23 in the 1997–8) (2002: 94, 97–8, n6). The growth rate of the combined Gross State Domestic Product (GSDP) for the 14 states increased from 5.2 percent in the pre-reform period to 5.9 percent in the post-reform period, but growth was increasingly concentrated in a small number of very high-achieving states. Gujarat and Maharashtra performed particularly well, with GSDP growth rates exceeding 8 percent, and per capita growth surpassing 6 percent in the 1990s. On the other hand, Bihar, Orissa, and Uttar Pradesh experienced sluggish 2–3 percent growth rates in the 1990s (compared to 4–5 percent to the pre-reform period), and in terms of GSDP growth per capita, they performed even more poorly at 1–2 percent (owing to relatively high population growth rates). Slightly behind Gujarat and Maharashtra, but also near the front of the pack, were West Bengal and Tamil Nadu. This, Ahluwalia pointed out, meant that high-growth states were sprinkled across India's west, east, and south – belying "simplistic perceptions about the role of geography in determining performance" (2002: 95). Still, the concentration of weak growth performance in the contiguous states of UP, Bihar, and Orissa, was difficult to ignore.[10]

Another kind of comparison reinforced the emerging image of "two Indias." The richest states in absolute terms – Maharashtra, Gujarat, Haryana, Punjab[11] – enjoyed GSDP per capita levels *four to five times greater* than the group of poor, lagging states. As Ahluwalia noted, "Balanced regional development has always been stated as an objective in India's plans, and although this objective has never been quantified in terms of rates of convergence of per capita GSDP, or a reduction in regional inequality to some specified target […], the objective surely implies that regional differences in per capita incomes should narrow with development, and in any case not widen" (2002: 96). He admitted that he and fellow economists had not expected such inequality trends: "There has always been an unstated assumption that inter-state differences would narrow with development" (2000: 1639; cited in Frankel 2005: 604).

There are surely many reasons for the income growth disparities, and it is not the intention here to review the substantial literature on the subject in detail. Some studies emphasize geographical factors and sector-specific productivity differences across states (Sachs, Bajpai et al. 2001). Ahluwalia, while not discounting natural comparative advantages based on geography and factor endowments, stressed variation in "the overall policy environment and the quality of governance" (2008: 117) across states. Still others take a regional political economy perspective and emphasize historical and institutional factors (Sinha 2005).

Moreover, Ahluwalia suggested, it was important to keep in mind what the GSDP growth data did *not* indicate. The data did not bear out the perception, as it was sometimes said, that the "rich states got richer and the poor states poorer" in an absolute sense: even the laggards exhibited positive (albeit very low) growth rates of per capita GSDP. Also, though Ahluwalia contended that there were important implications of growth for poverty, the relationship is complex.[12] What Planning Commission data *did* show was that even though there was a significant decline in poverty for all states (except Orissa) in the post-reform period, the level of poverty in some states remained very high; as Ahluwalia put it, "India's poverty problem is becoming increasingly concentrated" in the region of Bihar, Uttar Pradesh, and Orissa. In 1980, these three states had accounted for 37.5 percent of the total population below the poverty line in India, but 20 years later this had risen to 46 percent (2002: 101).

Public policy debates on regional growth and poverty trends in India tend to elide the caveats in the academic literature, and a technocrat like Ahluwalia had enough political acumen to recognize the "socially and politically explosive" implications of persisting low growth rates in some of India's most populous and poorest states (2000: 1462; cited in Frankel 2005: 605). Singh and Srinivasan have suggested that despite scholarly qualifications, "commonly held perceptions of growing inequality or unfairness may be enough to require policy attention" in India (2006: 355). Simply put, the political narrative was that many people, in some of India's largest states, were being excluded from the growth benefits of economic liberalization.

The strategy of the World Bank and other aid providers, which had deliberately favored "reforming states" and held non-reforming states at arm's length, became increasingly controversial in this context. The former Chief Minister of Madhya Pradesh, Digvijay Singh, articulated in 2003 what many political leaders in India – both at the Centre and in the states – were saying:

> In a country like India, which is highly unevenly developed, and where subsistence economies coexist with some of the 'best new economy' islands of the world, the word reform can mean very different things to different people […]
>
> […] We also need to be aware of the increasing inequalities between states in the post-liberalization era. States that were better endowed have been able to attract much of the national and foreign investment. Historical backlogs and national control of selected resources like minerals, forests and water have put states rich in natural resources like Madhya Pradesh, Orissa, or Bihar, at a disadvantage. We need to worry collectively about the fault line that is developing between the southern and western states, and the rest of India. *International donors are accentuating this divide in their newfound love for 'champion' states.* The test of any reform from the point of sustainability is in equalizing opportunities. I am afraid our reform process fails the test of an attempt to reduce interstate disparities (2003: 31, emphasis added).

In this view, the World Bank and other external assistance providers were part of the problem. This was from a leader perceived by many as one of India's most reform-minded chief ministers of the period (though, presaging Naidu and Krishna's experiences, he was voted out in 2003). Singh was a consistent advocate of decentralization, from a state that was fast shedding its "BIMARU" image as it experienced significant growth acceleration in the 1990s (though with a lesser reduction in poverty than hoped). Madhya Pradesh even had a public finance reform program with loan support from the Asian Development Bank – one of the very "international donors" contributing to the divide between the strong performers and the laggards.

The political winds had shifted; the "focus states" strategy of the World Bank and other external lenders would have to change.

## "Lagging States" in the Bank's Evolving *Country Assistance Strategy*

To emphasize leadership change, bureaucratic defensiveness, and federal politics on the Indian side of the relationship is *not* to suggest that the Bank had to be dragged reluctantly into a new engagement with the lagging states. In a way, the situation was the opposite of the one in the mid-1990s: whereas then the initiative for change had come from the Bank and found a receptive Indian government, now it was India driving the new strategy and the Bank finding good reasons to go along – not just to "get along," but to rededicate its country strategy to poverty reduction and improvement in social indicators. This is, after all, the institution that bears the motto, in bold lettering across one wall of the immense atrium in its Washington headquarters: "Our Dream is a World Free of Poverty." In the early 2000s, global dialogue around the Millennium Development Goals (MDGs) was reinforcing poverty concerns, and the Bank's analytic work was making it clear that India's – and the world's – ability to achieve the MDGs would be crucially influenced by the performance of Bihar, Orissa, UP and the like (World Bank 2004a). The Bank was rededicating itself to poverty reduction: the theme of its flagship *World Development Report* in 2004 was "Making Services Work for Poor People" (more recently, it was "Equity and Development"; 2006).

The Bank's India strategy is not only about ideas, but also about conjuncture of circumstances, experimentation, opportunism – and, not least, individual *people*. As the previous chapter argued, the alignment of Ed Lim at the Bank, Palaniappan Chidambaram and a cohort of technocrats at the Centre, and chief ministers such as Chandrababu Naidu at the state level, was critical to the momentum of the early focus states strategy. Now, in addition to turnover in the Indian government, the Bank's own players were different.

As noted above, Lim's successor, Michael Carter, was amenable to the Indian government's reassertion of its authority. Dipak Dasgupta, a lead economist for the Bank in India, reflected in 2008: "Lim was a maverick. He wanted to see which states would play golf with the Bank, and a chief minister like Naidu – he was a maverick, too, in a way. The problem for the Bank was, when so much is invested in the particular leadership, then you're a bit at sea if that goes away" (Dasgupta 2008).[13] Dasgupta's colleague V.J. Ravishankar characterized Lim as a "back-of-the-envelope kind of guy" (2008), suggesting his penchant for a highly personalized, instinctive decision-making process. One Bank staff member went so far as to say confidentially, "Lim staked his career in India on the focus states strategy." Carter, according to many Bank and Indian officials, was by nature more deliberative. Thus, the Bank's leadership change, along with the changing political context, seems to have encouraged a different course.[14]

Dasgupta suggested that there is an inherently contingent and path-dependent quality to the progression of the strategy – "There could be multiple 'equilibrium points' in the Bank-India relationship," he said. "In a sense, there is no such thing as 'the Bank,' or even 'the Bank in India.' There is no grand actor, but rather 50 different actors… much of this depends on who is in a position at a given point of time, and it often becomes understood and justified only in hindsight. Organizations learn from the frontier, from the field. The Bank can be flexible and opportunistic." Dasgupta even noted pointedly that he hails from Bihar, and though he did not go so far as to say that this drove the Bank's burgeoning interest in that state, he did suggest that it was inevitably a reinforcing factor. "A lot of Bank staff wouldn't want to go to Bihar," he said candidly. "But it is the cradle of India. If the Bank is not in Bihar, then what is its contribution?" (Dasgupta 2008).

However subjective, there is a Bank *strategy* – the *Country Assistance Strategy* (CAS), a formal, time-bound document produced by dozens of Bank staff across different functional units, following extensive dialogue with Indian government officials and hundreds of civil society "stakeholders." As a document, the CAS offers a window into the Bank's work and priorities in India for a 3–4 year period, and its iterative undertaking allows us to identify both major initiatives and incremental changes in the Bank's operations – and in the Bank-India relationship itself. In the remainder of this chapter, we will look at two successive such documents, the 2004 CAS (covering 2005–8 operations) and the new 2008 CAS (covering 2009–12).

The focus here will be on the changing framework for the Bank's engagement with India's states – one particular albeit encompassing element of the "strategy," rather than the complete *Strategy* document. State-level engagement is by no means the only important area of analytical and lending emphasis for the Bank. For example, there have been new initiatives to improve financial access for the rural poor.[15] There is an emphasis on support for rural women and disadvantaged communities through assistance to "self-help" cooperatives and employment organizations. The Bank is lending heavily for infrastructure such as national and state highways and rural roads. It has assisted local communities to restore traditional "tank" reservoirs for rain-fed agriculture. There are important national and state-level public health and nutrition initiatives. The Bank continues to support sector-specific policy and governance reforms, and has assisted some state governments with administrative modernization efforts such as computerizing land records. The list could go on. In short, the Bank's country portfolio encompasses a wide range of loans, and it increasingly supplements its lending operations with extensive "analytic and advisory activities" (AAA). The International Finance Corporation (IFC), the larger World Bank Group's private sector development arm, has become increasingly active in India (as discussed in Chapter 5).

The point is not to reprise the official strategy in detail. In any case, the Bank's CAS documents are readily available, and unlike some of its more technical project documents, they are fairly readable. This review is concerned more specifically with the major break in the 2004 CAS – from "focus states" to "lagging states" – and the development and implementation of the lagging states strategy over the past half-decade.

It is worth briefly recapitulating that exactly a decade earlier, Bank officials had worried that the CAS at that time was not really a "strategy" at all, but only a grab bag of projects and programs with no real integrating structure. Fearing loss of relevance, the Bank innovated the focus states approach to help push forward India's liberalization through state-level reforms, and to selectively concentrate its assistance in a few states where its impact might be greater than at the national level. In addition to special program loans for fiscal and governance reforms, the idea developed that focus states would also enjoy favorable access for more conventional project loans, on the "selectivity" principle that project outcomes would be more successful and sustainable where the overall policy environment was favorable. While the new CAS did not abandon the state-level focus, it certainly dramatically refashioned it, and it did do away with the focus state concept of bundling adjustment and investment lending in a select group of states with "good policies."

## The 2004 *Country Assistance Strategy*

In September 2004, the Bank presented a new *Country Assistance Strategy* document for India, which would cover the 2005–8 period. As we have seen, much had transpired since the previous CAS in 2001: Carter's accession as the Bank's new country director, the reassertion of central bureaucratic oversight, a renewed public conversation about interstate economic disparities, a new Indian posture toward foreign aid that projected great power aspirations – and, just months earlier, the election results that had ejected Bank-supported reformers in AP and Karnataka, given cold feet to another potential partner in Tamil Nadu, and replaced the BJP-led NDA government with the Congress Party-led UPA at the Centre.

Although the main substance of the Bank's new CAS had been negotiated during the NDA government, it would be naïve to suggest that the document did not take into account the changed political context to some extent. The UPA pledged "reforms with a human face" under the leadership of Prime Minister Manmohan Singh, the former finance minister. For many analysts, the message of the 2004 elections was that "India Shining" – the NDA's optimistic campaign slogan – had been "trumped by poverty" (Wallace 2007: 1), even if the normal anti-incumbency effect and other non-economic factors might also have contributed to the result. Indeed, the 2004 CAS acknowledged that it "coincides with a fresh governing cycle at the Center and in many states" (2004: 7). As ever, the Bank's challenge was to remain relevant; now, it had to tailor its appeal to an India that was increasingly intent on ending its need for international assistance, yet also progressively concerned about the widening gap between high-growth and lagging states.

Part of each new CAS document is devoted to a "self-assessment" of progress over the preceding CAS period. There is no pretense of objectivity; such an analysis is not intended to be impartial or critical in the same manner as reports by the Bank's Operations Evaluation Department (OED) or outside consultants. There is a natural self-serving quality to the self-assessment; even "lessons learned" can seem framed to minimize the Bank's own shortcomings and to justify some new role or function for the Bank going forward. Nevertheless, the discussion can be surprisingly candid at times.

The retrospective on the previous three years was significant, because the 2001 CAS had reinforced the commitment to the focus states strategy first articulated in 1997, and the three years that it covered included the high point of the strategy's implementation followed quickly by the unforeseen difficulties with reforms in all three focus states, as discussed in Chapter 3. The self-assessment reflected, "an important part of the rationale for [the focus states] approach was a view that comprehensive support across key sectors was more likely to yield sustainable positive development outcomes than a more sector driven approach" (2004b: 69). The CAS noted that over the previous three years, actual lending to AP, Karnataka, and UP had reached US$1.76 billion, or about 34 percent of total lending and 44 percent of state level lending, although this volume was on average less than one percent of the states' economic output. It had fallen slightly short of the 40 percent of total lending envisioned in the 2001 CAS.

The self-assessment found some "evidence of progress" in the focus states, both on their relevant policy indicators and growth and poverty outcomes relative to other states, although the Bank did not presume to take credit for the development achievements given the short time frame. (In any case, by the very rationale of the focus states approach, it was more likely that the Bank had selected states that were already on course to outperform their peers). The Bank suggested that its assistance had "played a role in mobilizing states to share and disseminate their reform experiences – although this is an area where more still needs to be done" (2004b: 71). The Bank also seemed "to have done well in sending a consistent signal on the link between adjustment lending and progress in reforms," particularly "when reforms went off track in UP early in the CAS period" – Lim's showdown with Mayawati. But standing its ground had come at a price to the Bank's country portfolio, as planned lending with a total value of about US$850 million – representing one adjustment loan each for AP, Karnataka, Orissa, and Tamil Nadu – had been "delayed by weaknesses in reform implementation in each state" (2004b: 69–70). Even so, the CAS suggested that the risk of "reform derailment" largely had been avoided.

The self-assessment acknowledged, "The Bank underestimated the volatility of the state level reform process in India, with often broad forward movement also marked by substantial policy delays and, sometimes, setbacks" (2004b: 69–70). The politics of reform had been more contentious than anticipated, and while this "[did] not necessarily bring into question adjustment support to states that are undertaking comprehensive reforms," the Bank did admit to difficulty in disengaging from slower-disbursing investment loans in states where reforms had gone off track (2004b: 70). This, as we saw in Chapter 3, had been the experience in UP, where the Bank withheld adjustment support but continued to disburse for substantial project loans even after the confrontation with the state government. But interestingly, rather than concluding with the lesson that the Bank *also* should find ways to discontinue project support in states where the fiscal and governance dialogue had gone south, the new CAS proposed decoupling state-level adjustment loans from complementary project investment – a concept that had been a key plank of the focus states strategy.

In sum, the self-assessment concluded, "Though the FY02–04 strategy was broadly appropriate, there are both important lessons of experience and shifts in the development context that suggest an evolution (rather than a fundamental rethink) of the strategy going forward" (2004b: 85). It plainly acknowledged the "common risk that the Bank Group faces in all large countries like India – namely the risk of becoming less relevant," but maintained, "This did not happen and the Bank Group has continued to play a strong supporting role in India's reform progress, particularly at the state level" (2004b: 84). Yet the 2004 CAS *did* signify a "fundamental rethink" of the focus states strategy. Again, the Bank's impulse was to "remain relevant" to an India that had clearly rethought the recent approach – and found it wanting.

The Executive Summary of the 2004 CAS cut right to the chase. It broadly described the new approach for engaging India's lagging states, in a passage that is worth citing in full:

Some important shifts are also being implemented in the approach to India's states. Since 1997, the CAS has included a focus on states undertaking comprehensive reforms, in order to support the leaders of change and serve as a catalyst to the state-level reform process. With the widening gulf between faster and slower growing states in India, leading to a concentration of poverty and poor social indicators in just a few states, some shifts in this approach are warranted. *Though the strategy will retain an essentially reform and performance-based approach to the states, it will also change in ways that are intended to go as far as possible in opening up new opportunities for engagement with these largest and poorest states*:

–First, in consultation with GoI [Government of India] and other partners, the Bank will seek to ensure that all of the largest and poorest states of India that so wish are engaged in a dialogue on cross-cutting reforms (fiscal management, governance, service delivery, the power sector and the investment climate).

–Secondly, the Bank will work proactively to try *to build a productive development relationship with four states where poverty is increasingly concentrated in India and where public institutions are considered to be at their weakest –* Bihar, Jharkhand, Orissa, and UP. This support could go beyond the basic dialogue on cross-cutting reforms noted above.

–Thirdly, state-level adjustment lending operations aimed at supporting achievement of the MDGs, are also expected to remain an important part of the Bank program. In addition to supporting state government efforts to reduce fiscal deficits, reform the power sector, strengthen governance and implement a range of actions to improve the investment climate – this lending would support cross-cutting actions to improve service delivery.

–Fourthly, *there is no longer an upfront decision to concentrate substantial state-level investment lending on "focus states" that are also receiving adjustment lending in support of cross-cutting reforms*. Instead, investment lending will be channeled more broadly to states that are able to comply with new 'guidelines for engagement' for the relevant sector. These guidelines attempt to clearly set out the sector-specific conditions that experience has shown to be necessary for project success. As described further in the CAS, in implementing these guidelines *the Bank will also seek, when possible, to provide its investment lending to states that have the greatest number of poor citizens, or weakest indicators, in order to maximize its impact.*

The overall impact of these changes is likely to be *a progressive shift in the share of lending that goes to the poorest states*, though dependent on the extent to which basic conditions for these projects can be met by those states (2004b: 2, emphases added).

Several elements of this strategy merit closer consideration. Though the wording was carefully parsed, and it somewhat softened the effective termination of the focus states strategy by saying that reform and performance-based criteria would continue to drive the Bank's state-level engagement, the other impulse – to openly favor the poorest states, with the "weakest institutions" – manifestly discarded the earlier approach.

The focus on Bihar, Jharkhand, Orissa, and UP followed directly from the findings of Ahluwalia and others that this band of states, running through north-central to eastern India, presented the densest concentration of poverty and weak human development indicators in the country. Given "the increasing concentration of poverty by region and by state," the CAS said, "It can be said that India occupies two worlds simultaneously [...] Bridging the gap between these two worlds is perhaps the greatest challenge facing [the Government of India] today" (2004b: 5–6). The key challenge would be accelerating economic growth in the lagging states. If these states continued to grow no faster than 5 percent a year, then for India to achieve the 6.5 percent annual growth target it projected for the Tenth Plan period (2002–7), its richest states would have to grow at near 10 percent a year on average – an "unlikely" scenario (2004b: 16). Though the CAS stressed that "a number of factors weakened the link between India's economic growth and poverty reduction" – including skewed ownership of productive assets, ineffective delivery of government programs, social discrimination, and patronage – it nevertheless argued that accelerating economic growth in the lagging states would be essential.

The idea that the Bank would go "as far as possible" to offer assistance to the lagging states, such as through sectoral lending that may or may not coincide with "cross-cutting" fiscal reform and governance programs, was a particularly significant break – in effect, a near total rejection of the focus states concept. Under the earlier approach, "maximizing impact" meant *avoiding* states where weak policies and institutions would dilute the impact of specific projects, however merit-worthy. Now, "maximizing impact" would mean giving preferential access to precisely such states.

There was a subtle shift in the meaning of "impact" across the two strategies. The focus states concept had accepted that given the inherent size limitation on the Bank's assistance to India, it could not really hope to have a significant direct impact on development outcomes; rather, it should encourage reforms that would facilitate growth and poverty reduction, and it should concentrate its efforts in the most reform oriented states and let "demonstration effects" pull the lagging states along. Now, the Bank would be leaving the relatively successful states to carry on without help, and pursuing a direct intervention for the laggards in the hope of impacting their growth and poverty reduction. State-level policy and governance reforms would still be the transmission belt to higher achievement, but there should be no illusion: the Bank was treading into new territory with a "selectivity" that deliberately targeted those states with the *worst* track records. In fact, it ran entirely opposite to the meaning of *ex post* "selectivity" in the cross-national aid literature, as articulated by Collier and others in the 1990s (see Chapter 3).

The risk to the country portfolio was obvious: the Bank was now turning toward states with weaker absorptive capacities for its loans. Already, for the 2003 fiscal year, the Bank's portfolio performance in India had declined, owing to projects that "clearly had not been ready for implementation at approval" (2004b: 19). New lending commitment actually fell below the "base case" envisioned in the 2001 CAS, partly owing to the slowdown in state-level reform progress – and this was with a focus on "lead reforming states."

What was more, the Bank had engaged India's states primarily through a sector driven approach before, prior to the late 1990s, and had become frustrated at its limited impact where the overall policy and governance environment did not favor strong growth and poverty performance. New "guidelines for engagement" and "self-regulating triggers" were meant to avoid badly run projects and abandoned reforms, but even the highest quality projects could not exist as islands of excellence in otherwise abysmally governed states. Cross-nationally, the Bank's past experiences in using conditionality to bring about policy change – rather than to encourage already committed reformers – had not been encouraging.

In short, though this was a "new" strategy for India, there was much in the lagging states paradigm that had a familiar feeling to it. If it would be too harsh a judgment to suggest that the Bank was going backwards, then at least it did seem to be drifting sideways. It was deliberately unlearning lessons about aid and influence from the 1980s and 1990s, driven by its own yearning for relevance and India's impulse to reframe political perceptions of the Bank's role in the states.

At the heart of the Bank's relevance dilemma was uncertainty over whether to favor the performers or the needy; even with a planned increase in lending volume, there would not be enough money to make significant contributions to both kinds of states. But if the Bank could not square this circle, it was because India itself was ambivalent as to the principles that should guide the multilateral lenders' engagement with the states.

Interestingly, the CAS explained that during background consultations for the new strategy, the Bank had put this very question to a cross-section of Indian government officials and civil society stakeholders: "What criteria [should] agencies such as the Bank Group adopt for lending strategies toward states – reform or need?" This question was included in a qualitative portion of a survey of "about 1,000 interlocutors in government, civil society, academia, media and the private sector," administered by a market research firm. In the 581 responses received,

> Karnataka, AP, Tamil Nadu and Maharashtra were perceived as reforming states, and were said to be more responsive and pragmatic in solving economic and social problems. The view was also that they were more disciplined and spent prudently. On the other hand, 'non-performing' states were characterized as having poor infrastructure, poor

governance, and an inability to make full use of their natural resources or allotted funds.

A clear majority [of respondents] said the first category of states was more likely to make good use of funds from agencies such as the Bank Group and should be targeted for more lending as an incentive to remain proactive and continue to show results. But a significant minority felt there were historical reasons for the condition of the non-performers and they should not be penalized by being denied funds. This group argued that to ignore the non-performers would lead to lopsided development, which would spawn its own set of problems.

A third stream of opinion was that a state's performance or need should not be the criterion, but rather there should be a focus on the likely impact of a particular project or program. These participants listed specific parameters for lending decisions, including earmarking for basic infrastructure like roads and power, health facilities, education, water and sanitation, and creating livelihood opportunities (2004b: 104).

The CAS argued that the importance of the lagging states to India's achievement of global development goals called for "further thinking about *how the Bank could best reconcile the conflict between needs and performance-based approaches to our work in India*" (2004b: 85, emphasis added). But what if the conflict could not be reconciled? Indeed, a careful reading of the 2004 CAS suggested that the Bank would attempt to have it both ways.

The Bank put forward a list of "twelve of India's 28 states [that] account for over 90 percent of India's poor" (2004b: 26) – AP, Assam, Bihar, Jharkhand, Karnataka, Madhya Pradesh, Maharashtra, Orissa, Rajasthan, Tamil Nadu, UP, and West Bengal – that would be of special interest to the Bank over the 2005–8 period. As literature on interstate comparisons has proliferated, the states have been bundled in a variety of ways. One of the most common groupings is of India's 14 or 15 "major states," a roster that basically encompasses the above states, minus Assam, plus Gujarat, Haryana, Kerala, and Punjab (Jharkhand has only existed since 2000, so earlier studies used the group of 14). (Left out of the "major" group are smaller states and union territories, the national capital of Delhi, and "special category states" entitled to exceptional central assistance owing to geographical disadvantage and other unique circumstances; this group includes Assam and the other northeastern hill states as well as Himachal Pradesh, Jammu and Kashmir, and Uttaranchal/Uttarakhand[16]).

The Bank's list of 12 was a curious construct, and though it was agreed upon in dialogue with the Indian government, it seems to have been constructed to convey the perception that the Bank was engaging with India's lagging states, while at the same time preserving and justifying engagement with states already strongly represented in the loan portfolio. At the core of the list, of course, were the four poor states specifically mentioned as candidates for special engagement by the Bank: Bihar, Jharkhand, Orissa, and UP. But the list also maintained AP, Karnataka, and Tamil Nadu, the southern states where it still had a legacy of loan commitments. By any conventional categorization, these were solidly middle-income states, even if they exhibited significant sub-regional concentrations of poverty. This pointed to another dilemma for both India and the Bank: should the focus of attention be on interstate disparities, on regional disparities *within* state boundaries, or on both?

While the 2004 CAS discussed both interstate and intrastate inequalities, the main emphasis, for practical purposes, was on the former. Still, as the Bank's rationale for state-level engagement shifted, so too did the way in which it characterized a middle-income state like Andhra Pradesh. As discussed in the Chapter 3, the Bank's consistent mantra during the Naidu era was that AP was India's "lead reforming state." The buzz was on Hyderabad and the coastal region; poverty in Telangana and other pockets of the state, though not entirely ignored, had received relatively little emphasis. But beginning with the Bank's 2004 report on AP, the accent shifted to its persistent poverty and *lack* of growth, despite the Naidu-era reforms. The Bank wanted to remain engaged in its former flagship focus state, but it needed to alter the rationale for doing so.

It is instructive to compare the Bank's list of 12 states with another list in the 2004 CAS, of seven states representing about 65 percent of the Bank's portfolio: UP (17 percent), AP (11 percent), Maharashtra (9 percent), Gujarat (8 percent), and Tamil Nadu, Rajasthan, and Karnataka (7 percent each) (2004b: 26). Note that all of these states, with the exception of Gujarat, were included in the 12 states that accounted for 90 percent of India's poor. The exclusion of Gujarat, one of the very wealthiest states in terms of per capita income, is perhaps understandable – but then how does one account for the inclusion of Maharashtra, with an even higher per capita income? It could be argued, quite correctly, that Maharashtra encompasses regions with significant concentrations of poverty. But given the new CAS emphasis on lagging states, there was a risk that "12 states accounting for 90 percent of India's poor" would lapse into the simplified nomenclature of "12 poorest states" – which, in fact, is how subsequent Bank literature has referred to the same dozen states (World Bank 2007a: Annex 6; 2008: Annex 4). A list of the 12 poorest states that includes Maharashtra – either the wealthiest or second-wealthiest state in India, depending on the ranking methodology – is bizarrely misleading. But, as noted above, Maharashtra was one of several states that had recently expressed interest in a closer relationship with the Bank.

At its margins, the Bank's list was somewhat arbitrary; though some states obviously had to be included, a different dozen states could have been cited as containing something very close to 90 percent of India's poor. Why not include middle-income Kerala? Likely because, like Gujarat, Kerala had been a focal state for the ADB, and the Bank was now keen to formalize the division of labor with other international lenders (though this consideration still does not fully explain the grouping, as Madhya Pradesh and West Bengal were also ADB program clients). Thus, in spotlighting a dozen states where its engagement could be justified on grounds of poverty, the Bank included the core "laggards," but was also careful to maintain a presence in states already strongly represented in the portfolio. This was understandable, but it does suggest an impulse by the Bank to hedge its bets with relatively reliable partner states, even as it turned its efforts to the hardest cases.

## Implementing the Lagging States Strategy

The focus states strategy had a run of at least seven years if we regard the 1997 CAS as its launch, or eight to nine years if we go from the mid-1990s when preliminary discussion of the approach first took place. By comparison, the lagging states emphasis is still relatively recent, though it has been reaffirmed (with only minor modifications) in the latest CAS for 2009–12. Moreover, though policy and governance reforms are still a priority for the Bank's state-level engagement, the true metrics of success will relate to poverty reduction and improvement in human development indicators; even though it will always be difficult to know the Bank's contribution to these outcomes, by their nature they are longer-term goals than the intermediate reforms that were the main priorities for the earlier focus states. For these reasons, and for brevity's sake, we will not attempt to analyze and compare experiences across lagging states as we did for AP, Karnataka, and UP in Chapter 3. Nevertheless, it is worth summarizing a few main issues, which point to the challenges that the Bank has taken on.

### Uttar Pradesh

Uttar Pradesh is an intriguing case, as one state that has spanned both the focus states era and the newer lagging states period. As we have seen, UP always was a rather unlikely "lead reforming state," and certainly it was a very different environment for the Bank than AP or Karnataka. It was chosen as a focus state partly because it had a "spell of reasonably good governance" (Chidambaram 2003) anchored by reformist senior bureaucrats for a few years, partly out of political realism on the part of the Bank, and partly because it was "so big and so troubled" that the Bank was drawn in by the prospect of helping to "turn it around" (Manor 2002). But UP's political economy seemed locked in a condition of nearly constant campaigning by parties using exclusionary appeals to caste and communal identities. In this unstable environment, the reform program went off track. The Mayawati government scoffed at the Bank's threat to withdraw budgetary assistance in 2002, though the Bank's threatened disengagement from investment loan projects turned out to be basically a bluff.

For a number of years the erstwhile reform dialogue was left in limbo, though UP did retain a significant share of project loans. In 2005, about 20 percent of the Bank's total net commitment in India was in UP, spread across five state-specific and 11 centrally sponsored multi-state projects. Only after Mayawati returned as chief minister in 2007 – this time with a governing majority – did the relationship resume. According to Bank officials, in her first meeting with Prime Minister Manmohan Singh after her return to power, Mayawati expressed interest in availing a program loan from the Bank. In public statements, she has sounded much more conciliatory toward the Bank than during her previous government – even citing the Bank's renewed interest in the state to burnish her developmental credentials. At the encouragement of the central government, the Bank has done new analytical and preparatory work toward another adjustment operation (a DPL) for India's most populous state.

The Bank thought it might have made a "breakthrough" with the new government. But as of 2009, the new adjustment loan had yet to materialize, and press reports suggested that the Bank might be skeptical of the government's commitment to improving the investment climate (Jainani 2009). The volume of project assistance to UP's largest state is likely to remain high, but the pace of reform may not accelerate as the Bank had hoped.

**Orissa** *(Note: This state was officially renamed Odisha in March 2011)*

If UP was the most visible case to straddle both the "focus states" and "lagging states" phases of the Bank's sub-national engagement strategy, Orissa has been a quieter – and considerably more successful – long-term case. Orissa is one of India's very poorest states, with an 85 percent rural population and a significantly higher tribal population than other states (about 22 percent, against a national average of 8 percent).

The Bank's engagement in Orissa began in the early 1990s, when it was the first state to adopt a Bank-sponsored restructuring plan for its troubled State Electricity Board (SEB). The program began with the Bank's withdrawal from a pending hydropower project in the state, and its insistence that further assistance to power projects in the state would require major structural reforms in the sector (Tongia 2007: 145). The sectoral restructuring culminated in 1999 with the first SEB privatization by any major state. The privatization is widely regarded as a failure, since even afterward "financial losses as well as theft and technical losses of electricity continued to swell" (ibid., 111). Orissa's disappointment somewhat chastened the Bank, and afterward it gradually softened its position that "privatization of distribution was a *sine qua non* of Bank engagement" in states' power sectors. Still, in its relationships with other states, the Bank did continue to press for SEB reform such as "unbundling" generation, transmission, and distribution functions; establishing independent regulatory authorities and advisory committees for tariff rates; and reducing power theft and losses (Howes, Mishra et al. 2008: 60–1).

In spite of the hard lessons over electricity, the Bank and Orissa maintained a close working relationship, which deepened in early 2000 with the election of a reformist government led by Chief Minister Naveen Patnaik. Orissa is a neighbor to Andhra Pradesh, and there was a clear element of wanting to follow in that state's footsteps, as well as some interesting similarities of circumstance across the two states. Patnaik's party, the regional Biju Janata Dal, was a BJP ally in the NDA coalition at the Centre. His government even produced a *Vision 2020* economic policy document – shades of Mahathir via Naidu. Like other Bank partners, Orissa sought relief from budgetary distress: salaries, pensions, and interest payments on a large debt stock (the largest of any state) consumed 100 percent of its revenues in 1999–2000, "leaving negligible room for development expenditure" (Howes, Mishra et al. 2008: 54). But over the next several years, Orissa achieved the largest fiscal correction of any state – from a deficit of about 10 percent of state GDP in 2001 to less than 1 percent in 2006. Even conceding that it had one of the furthest distances to travel to get back to fiscal health, this was a significant achievement (the Bank also credits reductions in non-developmental spending, improved tax administration, and increased central transfers).

Howes and his Bank colleagues consider Orissa the "surprise achiever" among the states that received adjustment loans (2008: 54). Its first such loan, for US$125 million, came in late 2004 – perfectly positioning it as a standard-bearer for the "lagging states" strategy in the new CAS. A second adjustment loan, for US$225 million followed in 2006 after the Bank's publication of a major 2005 report on Orissa's investment climate, optimistically sub-titled *Towards a High Performing State* (World Bank 2005). There have been additional projects in health, roads, irrigation, "rural livelihoods," and other areas. The state indicated its desire for a third adjustment loan in August 2008 ("Orissa to Seek $250 million World Bank loan" 2009). As of one year later there had not been any Bank commitment to this effect, though there had been substantial sectoral investments (three projects announced simultaneously in early 2009 amounted to US$444 million).

On balance, it has helped the relationship that Patnaik twice has been reelected to lead the state government (in 2004 and 2009), and that the Bank itself has drawn political economy lessons from its experiences elsewhere about the state leadership's need to pursue a gradual, incremental pace of reforms. The Bank considers Orissa a standout state in terms of prosecuting and convicting corrupt officials, a key governance issue (2007: Annex 6, p. 5). From a 1990s economic growth rate of about 4 percent, it improved to above 7 percent growth in 2003–6.

Still, Orissa remains far below the middle-income states on its human development indicators, and the shape of the Bank's continued engagement in the state remains to be seen. Project assistance continues, but plans for reform-based program support have been delayed. Unexpectedly, given the state government's relatively clean image, the Bank reports that a Detailed Implementation Review (DIR) of the Orissa Health Systems Development Project found "a range of administrative weaknesses that provide opportunities for fraud and corruption" in the Bank-assisted project (2008: Annex 8, p. 4) (The DIR, which also criticized four other Indian health projects, will be discussed in the concluding chapter).

Though Orissa has been a main beneficiary of the Bank's new lagging states emphasis, its experience also demonstrates the significant institutional challenges that remain in this group of states.

## Bihar

No discussion of the Bank's lagging states strategy would be complete without special attention to the case of Bihar. By almost any measure, the development experience of India's third most populous state has been abysmal in the post-1991 era, as other states have pulled far ahead of it. Its population is about 90 percent rural, its economy dominated by an anemic agricultural sector (it had significant mineral resources before losing part of its territory to Jharkhand in 2000, but in any case had not converted the wealth into significant income generation, for complex reasons). Its per capita income in the early 2000s was only about one-quarter of the national average. It contained one in seven people of India's below-poverty-line population; the poverty rate was about 39 percent, compared to 23 percent nationally (World Bank 2007a: Annex 6, p. 2). Social indicators were among the worst in India, with life expectancy the lowest in the country. In an accurate if somewhat ungainly formulation, the Bank characterized Bihar as "one of the most densely populated agglomerations of poor people anywhere in the world" (2008a).

Bihar's size and poverty make it more comparable to UP than to any of the other states where the Bank has had a deep involvement since the 1990s, though even this comparison only goes so far. Like UP, its recent politics have been dominated by a project of lower caste empowerment. But unlike that state (with its frequent alternation in power by several parties), Bihar was led by a continuous regime from 1990 to 2005: Lalu Prasad Yadav and his wife Rabri Devi. "Lalu" is one of the most colorful and controversial characters in all of Indian politics. His critics accuse him of gross corruption as chief minister, and a major scandal prompted him to resign in 1997. Thereafter, he served stints in prison and was perceived to govern by proxy through Rabri Devi, a political neophyte previously occupied with raising the couple's nine children.[17] Lalu seemed to relish his role as India's lower caste jester, and consistently maintained that corruption charges brought against him and his wife were a conspiracy by upper caste government and media elites threatened by the rise of peasant cultivator castes (such as his own Yadav community – an Other Backward Caste, or OBC, group). During the Lalu regime, backward caste candidates came to dominate the State Assembly, claiming more than half of its seats by the latter 1990s. Some scholarly analysts have contended that this transformation represented genuine lower caste emancipation from traditional subordination to the dominance of the upper castes, but even so, there has been an exceptionally corrosive effect on state institutions and development. As Jeffrey Witsoe suggests, "The political assertion of lower castes from the early 1990s resulted in a deep-seated conflict between a new lower caste political leadership and a largely upper caste bureaucracy, police, and judiciary. This is why the politics of caste empowerment resulted in a general breakdown of public institutions in Bihar" (2007). Lalu's Rashtriya Janata Dal found its electoral base in his "M-Y alliance" of Muslims and Yadavs, which "almost single-handedly kept the Hindu nationalist BJP at bay for fifteen years" (Witsoe and Frankel 2006: 2), even during the BJP's years of prominence at the Centre.

In 2005, Lalu became "a victim of the deepening aspirations – that he helped unleash" when a coalition of the Extremely Backward Castes (EBC), cobbled together by the Janata Dal-United and the BJP, won the State Assembly elections (ibid., 2–3) (In 2004, Lalu's party had done well enough in the national Lok Sabha elections that he joined the central cabinet as railways minister). A new chief minister, Nitish Kumar from the backward Kurmi caste, took over promising "all-inclusive growth at an accelerated pace" that would turn Bihar into "a developed state by 2015" – the target year for the global MDGs. The media tended to characterize the change as the displacement of caste politics by a new developmentalism, but as is so often the case in Indian politics, the truth was more nuanced. As Witsoe and Francine Frankel observe, "Nitish Kumar proved to be an ideal political figure to combine the themes of development and social justice, something Lalu had never managed to deliver in combination" (2006: 37).

The Bank's interest in Bihar predated the Kumar government, as the 2004 CAS attests. Hoping for a breakthrough, it had already undertaken a major analysis of the state's economy, policies, and governance, resulting in a report that was released in June 2005 during a six-month period when Bihar was under president's rule from the Centre (there were two State Assembly elections that year: the first, in February, produced a fractured verdict and led to Rabri Devi's resignation; the second, in November, produced a victory for Kumar's JD-U and allied BJP).[18] The report's title, *Bihar: Towards a Development Strategy*, was a frank admission that the state's previous leadership had not given priority to development, and Kumar approvingly referred to the study during the campaign to criticize the Lalu Yadav and Rabri Devi regime (World Bank 2007a: Annex 6, p. 2).

In addition to reaching out to the World Bank, Kumar forged a truce with the state's senior bureaucracy – by far the more important rapprochement, if it can last (Witsoe and Frankel 2006: 41). But there is still something of a disconnect between the national elite narrative about Bihar, and the perception of many of the state's people themselves: the former tended to see Bihar as India's "basket-case" and a global embarrassment, and saw the Lalu regime as a trauma inflicted upon what should have been a great state. But for much of the local backward caste population, the story is of a long-overdue social revolution. The state's identity politics remain complicated, not least as reflected in the awkward alliance between the JD-U and BJP.

The Bank's 2005 report marked the inauguration of what it hoped would be a broad-based engagement with Bihar, with emphasis on budget management and other reforms related to infrastructure, health, administrative decentralization, education, and private sector promotion. In 2007, the Bank committed a Rural Livelihood Project Loan of US$63 million and a Development Policy Loan of US$225 million. The DPL was probably the best illustration yet of why the Bank has hoped that its loan resources would be more meaningful at the state level than at the national level: at a time when total Bank assistance accounted for only 0.2 percent of India's central development budget, the Bihar adjustment loan was equivalent to *20 percent* of the state's revenue (2008b: 13). By late 2008, the state's share in the Bank's India portfolio was about 6 percent (2008b: Annex 8, p. 1), and there were indications that another adjustment loan operation was in the works.

The Bank is not alone in hoping that Bihar has turned a corner. Other donors – the ADB, DFID, and Japan's Official Development Assistance (ODA) – have coordinated with the Bank on a joint strategy for Bihar. Bihar also has much stronger civil society resources than its post-1991 achievements would suggest, especially among educated Biharis who left the state in droves while its development stalled. In January 2007, more than 600 non-resident Biharis from over 60 countries converged on the state capital of Patna for the grandly branded Global Meet for a Resurgent Bihar (Sridhar 2007: 113).

India as a whole needs Bihar to succeed. The state long derided as the poster child for "BIMARU" has become a key proving ground for the lagging states strategy. As the World Bank put it in 2008, "Bihar is a crucible in India's battle against poverty." Things have been so bad, the aid providers perceived, that the potential upside is tremendous: "Donors agree that the level of poverty and degradation in Bihar is so stark that if projects are implemented well they will show immediate results and create much bigger impact." Still, the Bank acknowledged, the investment risks are high: "The path ahead is likely to be fraught with many trials and tribulations for all those involved in Bihar's road to prosperity but if India is to prosper, Bihar will have to be reborn again, both in purpose and in the public imagination" (2008a).

## Postscript: The 2008 *Country Assistance Strategy*

In November 2008, the Bank presented a new *Country Assistance Strategy* for 2009–12. It is worth briefly considering the document here, for two reasons. First, as with earlier iterations, the newest CAS includes a Bank self-evaluation of the period just concluded (2005–8), which provides a fascinating window into how the Bank itself perceives recent developments. Second, the new CAS attempts to translate the lessons learned into new objectives, both for the immediate and longer-term future of the Bank-India relationship. As we will see in the next chapter, an underlying theme in the 2008 CAS is the looming possibility of a major transformation in the relationship, should India ascend to middle-income country status and lose eligibility for IDA grant aid. Here, we will confine the discussion of the Bank's latest strategy to the issue of state-level assistance.

The principle of "selectivity" – a mantra throughout the Bank's varied strategic approach to state-level engagement – is again invoked in the 2008 CAS: "Given India's size and diversity [...] selectivity remains a crucial goal if the World Bank is to make the most of its limited resources." Yet, the Bank acknowledged, "Previous strategies" – whether the focus states or the lagging states approach – "have largely failed to make sufficient headway toward this goal" (2008b: ii).

The further away from the focus states period the Bank gets, the more candid about the experiment it becomes. In the 2009 CAS, it reflects, "The concentration of World Bank programs in a few reforming states carried with it the predictable risks of portfolio concentration in a highly politicized context, which resulted in significant swings in the volume of lending and spending on analytical work. Especially during the early years of shift to state-level engagement, the residual role of the World Bank at the national level was not well-defined and dialogue with the center suffered" (2008b: Annex 4, p. 8). The CAS freely admitted that the shift to lagging states had reflected Government of India concerns, and recognized the perception that had emerged by 2003–4, with Tamil Nadu emerging as a new focus state alongside AP and

Karnataka: "Policy dialogue and new lending therefore concentrated on the three southern states, which, although home to large numbers of poor households, were generally regarded as having good prospects [...] this epitomized a tension between supporting reformers and focusing on poverty reduction" (ibid., 8; Annex 2, p. 2).

The self-assessment for the 2004 shift toward lagging states found "some success." The engagements with Bihar, Orissa, and UP all looked promising. But in Jharkhand, for which the Bank completed an economic report as a first step toward a reform program, the government "showed little interest in discussion or follow-up, partly as a result of political instability" (2008b: Annex 4, p. 10). By mid-2008 these core four lagging states, which were supposed to be such a Bank priority, had received single-state loans accounting for only 10 percent of the country portfolio – *less than their share in 2004*. Of the four states, only Bihar had seen an increase. In contrast, outstanding commitments to "three previous focus states" – AP, Karnataka, and Tamil Nadu – actually *increased* between 2004 and 2008, from 22 to 24 percent. The share of single-state loans to states *not* among the "dozen states representing 90 percent of India's poor" also increased slightly.

Did this mean that the Bank acted subversively – giving lip service to "lagging states" but continuing to favor its longtime friends and other states not among the most needy? Such an interpretation probably ascribes to the Bank more power and resolve than it actually possesses. The likely explanations are more mundane: the outcome reflected a combination of residual Bank affinity for the earlier focus states, and – as has been true across the period analyzed in this chapter – the preferences of the Indian government itself. The Bank had invested considerable resources – analytical and personal, let alone financial – in the earlier southern focus states, and it was natural that it would gravitate toward continued engagement with them. These states, and some others not among India's poorest, simply had developed stronger institutional capacities to qualify for Bank projects and programs – however much benefit of doubt the 2004 CAS sought to give to the lagging states. Ultimately, Bank loans still carry what can be fairly exacting technical and fiduciary covenants, which the lagging states are simply less capable of meeting even under an eased access regime.

But the slight drift of lending away from lagging states likely also reflected Indian impulses, as an engagement by the Bank with Himachal Pradesh – a northern hill state that is neither large nor poor – attests. Indian authorities encouraged this involvement, for what might be seen as broader political-strategic interests. Himachal Pradesh actually outperformed the national income per capita growth rate beginning in the 1990s, and its social indicators are relatively strong and improving. In fact, it has become something of a developmental darling in recent years – a bit like Kerala earlier – and has received academic and media attention for its achievements. The central government's interest appears to have been to use the Bank's resources to further understanding of the Himachal development model, so that other Indian hill states – some of which, in the northeast, are under threat from violent insurgencies – might benefit. Additionally, according to the 2008 CAS, "Himachal Pradesh was the first state in India to commit to a state-wide environmental action plan, and the Government of India expressed strong interest" in a program loan to the state, "in the hope that it could serve as an example for other mountainous, less developed states along India's border regions" (2008b: Annex 7, p. 2). This development, which had not been planned for in the 2004 CAS, reaffirmed that the Indian government basically views the Bank's state-level programs as a tool at its disposal for encouraging various kinds of development initiatives – the evolution from focus states to lagging states, and now a hill state – even if this risked spreading the loan resources thin.

In short, the CAS concluded,

The clear lesson is that a change in emphasis (e.g. toward the four poorest states) is easier said than done. The inertia in the World Bank program is considerable (given analytical gaps in new areas, project preparation lead times, established relationships, etc); therefore it takes determined effort and time to implement new priorities. There will also be, in the political economic context of India, pressures to deviate from any limited set of priority states, often for good reasons (2008b: Annex 4, p. 11).

Does such "inertia" contradict Dasgupta's staff-level perspective on the Bank's "flexibility and opportunism"? Not necessarily: the timing with respect to its engagement in Bihar, and its ability in Orissa to parlay a badly botched power sector reform program into a broadly successful fiscal reform and governance relationship, suggest that both serendipity and acumen do play important roles. But establishing good relationships with state governments takes time, loans require gestation and implementation periods, and it is unrealistic to expect the Bank's operations to turn on a dime – or even to keep pace with the winds of significant change brought on by a new grand strategy every three or four years.

Shifting from loan distribution to overall loan volume, the 2008 CAS reported, the share of state-level adjustment lending (DPLs) in total Bank lending to India had been *only 6 percent*. This fell below the targeted 15 percent for the 2005–8 period, which already was a major downward revision from the 30–40 percent that the Bank once talked about in the heyday of the focus states strategy. Clearly, state-level engagement has fallen well short of the major transformative development in the Bank-India relationship that the lender had hoped it would be (though the CAS maintains that the DPL tool "had a strategic importance" that went beyond the financial aspect, both for the Bank and for the Centre).

For the Bank, such loans still offered a toehold in state-level policies and provided an opportunity for wide-ranging analytical and advisory work, all of which could enhance the quality of other Bank projects in the states, and provide lessons for other states.

"From the viewpoint of the central government," the Bank maintained, "DPLs strengthen the Centre's own efforts to induce fiscally responsible behavior and improved governance in the states" (2008b: Annex 7, p. 4). This, of course, had been the Centre's position more than a decade earlier, when it first green-lighted the Bank's state-level adventure. But now, this interest had been significantly attenuated – by reforms in Indian fiscal federalism, by the central government's impulse to reassert control over external lenders' relations with states, and by growing concerns about inequality and poverty.

Going forward, the 2008 CAS retains the Bank's emphasis on lagging states for the 2009–12 period; it does not effect the same kind of strategic shift that the 2004 CAS represented compared to its "focus states" predecessors. But throughout the document, there is a sense that state-level engagement has not turned out to be the panacea for "relevance" that the Bank once hoped it could be.

Even seemingly secondary considerations are revealing. In the previous CAS, the Bank's Communications and Outreach strategy emphasized the establishment of four country websites for India – in English, Hindi, Kannada (spoken in Karnataka), and Telugu (Andhra Pradesh) – with a goal of providing translations in the relevant languages of "all press releases, summaries of most reports, and full text of major reports where possible" (2004b: 64). Subsequent development of local language content has been limited, however, and the 2008 CAS drops the mention of Kannada and Telugu communications – with no explanation. Certainly, given the large volume of documents that the Bank produces, translating material into multiple languages would be highly labor-intensive; while local talent is abundant and could readily handle plain-language literature intended for the public, translating official documents and technical reports would require more advanced skills. It might also be argued, reasonably, that many Kannada or Telugu – or Oriya or Tamil – speakers with Internet access would also be able to read English materials (in Bihar, UP, and other northern states, Hindi predominates, and the outreach is being maintained).

Whatever the reasons, the revised communications strategy is consistent with an overall image of the Bank backing down somewhat on state-level engagement, which once looked as if it would become almost as elaborate and multi-faceted as the Bank's relationships with individual countries. India's states, of course, are *not* countries – even if some are larger than most countries, and their political economies as differentiated. While the Bank has never presumed that it could relate to them as if they were countries, it has plainly become more restrained as the challenges of state-level operations have become clearer and as the Indian government itself has moved to exercise greater oversight.

In terms of lending operations, the planned share of state-level program loans (DPLs) in the overall country portfolio is revised downward yet again, to 10 percent. The central government's guidelines for such loans – issued in 2002 and updated in 2005 – have placed constraints on their use that could now limit their practicability. The Centre had converted their function from budgetary "additionality" for the states to debt-swap instruments; now, the Bank admits, "There is not much old expensive debt on the books of state governments, except for the National Small Savings Fund liabilities, which GoI is not willing to swap" (2008b: Annex 7, p. 5). The CAS also suggests that the Centre's two-tranche requirement – though intended to reduce moral hazard risk that states would renege of reform commitments – constrains the Bank from flexibility with respect to the timing and pace of its engagements with states. The Bank hopes that the Centre might reconsider the guidelines, but it will be the Government of India's decision.

The overarching theme of the 2008 CAS – "strengthening institutions for a middle-income India" – will be discussed in the next chapter. With respect to the states, the CAS is more explicit than ever that the Bank will have to pursue a "differentiated approach." The needs of the high- and middle-income states are very different than the poorest states, and indicators for India as a whole are pulling it toward a middle-income country status that may dramatically change the Bank-India relationship. If there is a key subtext in the 2008 CAS, it is of a World Bank that is bracing for changes that may challenge its relevance more than ever.

There is also a sense of resignation, and perhaps even some weariness, with respect to state-level engagement. It was always going to be challenging, but it has been even more difficult than envisioned back in the 1990s. Engaging with lagging states has proven particularly "difficult and resource-intensive" (2008b: 13). In some ways, the states have been worlds unto themselves – facing different development challenges, and with very different political economies. While there has been some degree of demonstration effect across states, and many more states have embraced the rhetoric of reform, there are deep structural reasons behind interstate growth and poverty disparities, which even the strongest political will is unlikely to overcome soon. And while the Centre's own interest in a partnership with the Bank over state-level reform has not ended, it has clearly changed in ways intended to ensure that the Bank and the states are not striking their own deals.

## Chapter Four

# A BITTERSWEET "GRADUATION" FROM AID: CAN IDA HOLD ON TO INDIA, AND WILL INDIA LET IT?

*A country with many poor but not a poor country.*

> His Excellency Mr. M. Hamid Ansari, Vice President of India
> (This quotation opens the World Bank's Country Strategy
> for India, 2009–12)

*Nothing will happen to India if the Bank were to disappear.*

> Rachid Benmessaoud, Operations Advisor, World Bank,
> New Delhi (2008)

*We are not dependent on the Bank. If it is available, we'll take it.*
*But, it is a very small amount of money.*

> M. Naga Raju, Director, Fund-Bank Division, Ministry of Finance,
> Government of India (2008)

*She (we gave her most of our lives)*
*is leaving (sacrificed most of our lives)*
*home (we gave her everything money could buy)*
*She's leaving home*
*After living alone for so many years (bye-bye)*

> John Lennon & Paul McCartney, "She's Leaving Home" (1967)

Graduation. Procession. *Pomp and Circumstance.* Credit hard-won achievement and recognize the devotion of time and resources by others that made it all possible. The graduate might face an uncertain future. But let that wait – first celebrate the milestone.

"Graduation" is the World Bank Group's jargon for its process of ushering a borrower out of eligibility for aid from the Bank's special soft-loan facility, the International Development Association (IDA), and into a new status as a "middle-income borrower" of only the Bank's standard loans, through the International Bank for Reconstruction and Development (IBRD). The end of aid – of access to IDA "credits" – is the essence of this graduation. The occasion is not marked by any special ceremony, just closed rounds of dialogue among IDA Deputies – donor representatives in the triennial IDA replenishment – followed by more closed dialogue among the Bank's Executive Directors. The local papers might not even carry the story.

India is not the first large developing country to confront graduation out of IDA; Egypt, China, Indonesia and a number of others have gone before it (with some dipping back into the IDA pool after experiencing economic setbacks). But the impact of India's exit will likely be the most profound, both for its relationship with the World Bank Group, and for the global development assistance regime generally.

The Bank and India face a critical juncture in their relationship. Right now, India alone among the giants of the developing world is still eligible for IDA assistance – the centerpiece of the Bank's engagement with poor countries for 50 years. The intersection of two trends in the Bank-India relationship – the coming IDA endgame, and the special emphasis on lagging states in the Bank's country strategy – poses a fascinating conceptual and practical tension for both sides.

IDA is unique. It was set up in 1960 – largely with India in mind – as a facility for long-term, low-interest development financing for the world's poorest countries. India *as a whole* is nearing the lower end of the Bank's middle-income range that will shift it to IBRD-only status, but enormous states such as Uttar Pradesh and Bihar are nowhere near this threshold. To the extent that the Bank can continue to offer a high share of IDA credits in its lending "blend" for India, it retains the interest of India's leaders, even in an era of abundant global liquidity (which, of course, contracted in the global economic crisis that began in late 2008). In recent years, however, IDA has come under increasing pressure by donor countries (which are, in turn, responding in part to NGO and activist pressure) to devote more of its resources to the world's poorest and most indebted countries, concentrated largely in sub-Saharan Africa. By contrast, deep deprivation in India's "lagging states" – several of which are more populous than entire African countries – receives almost no attention in the global poverty conversation.

For the Bank, India's graduation from IDA would be bittersweet, not only because the Bank and India have had such a long history together – a history of mutual influence, punctuated by occasional sharp tension, but recently settling into what officials on both sides refer to as a respectful "partnership" – but also because the Bank values India as a borrower and would like to keep a sizeable portfolio in the country. The Bank would like the vindication and legitimization that India's rapid, market-led growth might, as some would see it, bestow on the institution. (To be sure, the Bank also has many harsh critics among Indian and global civil society). The Bank – of the "Our Dream is a World Free of Poverty" credo – would also like to remain engaged in India's lagging states and sectors, even if India's own leaders have had to steer them toward this engagement of late. From a more prosaic perspective, the Bank also appreciates the hedge that India as a borrower provides to its global portfolio, given the country's perfect repayment record and ability to churn through a consistently high volume of projects.

But a big part of the Bank's appeal in India, since the country has experienced an explosion of private investment, has been the "blend" of IBRD and IDA terms in the Bank's lending. Currently, the ratio is about two-thirds in favor of IBRD, following a progressive "hardening" of loan terms, but one-third of annual borrowings in the US$3–4 billion range at no interest is still attractive from India's perspective. If India graduates from IDA, the cost of its Bank borrowing rises, and the additional "hassle factor" associated with extensive fiduciary controls and safeguard policies diminishes the Bank's appeal compared to commercial borrowing. The Bank will find it that much harder to stay relevant – that perennial quest in its largest borrower – after India's graduation from IDA.

India, apparently, anticipates that the graduation from IDA will be more sweet than bitter. As we have seen, India already has maneuvered to reduce its use of bilateral assistance, sending almost two dozen surprised donor countries packing in 2003. India is keen to gain a more prominent role in global governance, whether in the Bretton Woods institutions or in the UN Security Council, and its leaders apparently believe that its relationship to aid should be one of a donor, not a recipient. They are especially keen to follow the path that rival China trod over the previous decade: a blend IBRD-IDA borrower for nearly two decades, China graduated from IDA in 1999 and became a modest donor in 2007.

But as we have seen, India increasingly has sought to channel the Bank's assistance toward its poorest "lagging states"; indeed, this became a central thrust in the 2004 Country Assistance Strategy and the current CAS reaffirms the commitment. India as a whole may be nearing the low end of the Bank's broad "middle income" category of IBRD borrowers, but it is on the achievements of high-growth states such as Gujarat, Maharashtra, and Tamil Nadu. The agglomeration of north-central-eastern "lagging states" – and especially Bihar – have per capita incomes as low as one-fifth those of the frontrunners. The gap between these "two Indias" is one of the defining political economy challenges of the 21$^{st}$ Century; while one of these Indias is ready to leave IDA aid behind, the other exhibits some of the most pervasive poverty and weakest social indicators anywhere in the world.

If it is an irony that India itself has led the way toward the "lagging states" engagement with the World Bank even as it confronts intensified donor pressures to graduate out of IDA to make way for other borrowers, it is an even greater irony that India's aid mandarins seem to regard its prospective graduation as a badge of honor. India's IDA eligibility may not survive beyond the next replenishment (which runs from mid-2011 to mid-2014, with talks being conducted in 2010). India, and particularly its poorest states, would stand to benefit from continued access to IDA – as New Delhi itself has recognized. Yet Indian officialdom appears largely indifferent to the issue.

Some observers might judge this a misguided conceit; others might view it as the prerogative of an independent country that has made significant, if still only partial, progress toward reducing poverty. Perhaps India's stance is simply to make a virtue out of necessity – as its influence in the IDA replenishment process is, anyway, rather limited. I will sound a personal note here, because in the latter part of this chapter, I argue for another way forward: India should pursue a revolutionary reform of the IDA allocation regime, which would prorate its eligibility on a state-wise basis and thus retain IDA eligibility for Bihar, UP, and other laggards. However, I offer this suggestion not because I am particularly committed to seeing such a reform of IDA, but rather because it seems consistent with India's own stated objectives of both enlarging its role in global governance and giving special investment and reform priority to its poorest states. This would not be an easy reform to achieve, both because India's formal power in IDA governance is limited and because some donors and many NGOs likely would be hostile to a proposal that they would see as taking away IDA resources from Africa. But India has fought uphill battles before in the court of international opinion. It should not shrink from this argument.

I am personally agnostic on whether India should stay or go as far as IDA is concerned. It is for India to decide, though I do submit that it would be regrettable if the decision to sit satisfied, while IDA donors deliver the verdict, were to be made by a handful of Government of India bureaucrats rather than submitted to a more open discussion. Indian leaders may seek to follow China's path, in this as in other achievements, but the country's federal democratic political system should oblige at least some broader deliberation on the IDA graduation issue. Would many Indians care? Would many Biharis? Would many in India be glad to see the back of the Bank altogether? Let there be a debate. It would be boisterous, to be sure. But to borrow a formulation from journalist Edward Luce, "If intentions can be ascribed to nation-states, you could say that India has given a higher priority to stability than it has to efficiency. In many ways, the opposite could be said of China" (2007: 331). The growing gap between the "two Indias" threatens to undermine political and social stability, and thus erode the very foundations of India's recent impressive economic gains. IDA was created, in large part for India, two decades before China embraced the market and became a Bank borrower. It is as much India's facility as anyone's. Let there be a considered debate on when and how India should leave it.

If IDA were to offer such a prorated exception for India, would it not also have to offer it to other middle-income borrowers with lagging sub-national regions, such as China? Probably so, but it is not clear whether China would be interested, or how many other countries actually would stand to benefit. The devil would be in the details, and it would be for to the Bank and its member countries to work these out. But the upshot is that India could win continued access to the Bank's cheapest loans for its poorest states, while claiming credit for encouraging a major reform in the multilateral development assistance regime more broadly. Self-interest wrapped in moral advocacy for the developing countries has long been a theme in India's foreign policy; here, India could do well by doing good, bringing greater attention to the issue of sub-nationally concentrated poverty that challenges a number of pivotal developing countries.

What would the Bank's relationship with India look like, after its graduation out of IDA? Rachid Benmessaoud, the Bank's Operations advisor in New Delhi (who served as its acting Country Director in 2008–9), confessed, "Nothing will happen to India if the Bank were to disappear." Warming to this theme, however, he went on almost to argue against himself: "I know everyone keeps saying, 'The Bank needs India more than India needs it.' But you repeat it to yourself so much, and what does it really mean?" (2008). In the second decade of the 21$^{st}$ Century, as middle-income status beckons for one India while the other remains largely untouched by recent growth, the two sides will find out just how important the relationship remains for New Delhi.

This chapter will proceed as follows. The first section is rather technical and descriptive, but it is necessary to explain the difference between the World Bank's IBRD and IDA arms, what IDA "graduation" means, and some of the reasons why India's IDA graduation could significantly impact the Bank's overall business model. The next part looks more closely at India's current position in IDA, the implications of its "blend" status, and some of the politics behind recent donor pressure to graduate India from IDA. We then consider some of the Bank's general challenges in engaging middle-income countries, and what the Bank's role in India is likely to be as it reaches that level (even if India does not soon graduate from IDA, the Bank's engagement at the national level and in the better-performing states is increasingly following a middle-income model). The last part of the chapter proposes an IDA allocation reform that would maintain eligibility for India's poorest states, and argues that such an approach would be consistent with India's global governance goals as well as its domestic development objectives.

## A Brief Introduction to IDA: Financing, Governance and Borrowers

As noted in the Introduction, the two main lending arms of the World Bank Group are the original International Bank for Reconstruction and Development (IBRD), founded at Bretton Woods in 1944, and the International Development Association (IDA), established in 1960 "as an institution that could lend to very poor developing nations on easier terms" (World Bank 2007b: 17). Cumulative IBRD commitments are more than double those of IDA – over US$400 billion for the former compared to just under US$200 billion for the latter, as of 2008 – reflecting both IBRD's earlier inception and the two arms' dissimilar financial models. In new lending commitments for recent years, IBRD still surpasses IDA, but not by much. For fiscal 2008, IBRD worldwide commitments were US$13.45 billion compared to IDA commitments of US$11.24 billion. Since some committed funds go unutilized within the fiscal year, IBRD's actual gross disbursements were US$10.49 billion. But with credit reflows from past loans surpassing new lending, *net* IBRD disbursements were *negative* US$2.12 billion. IDA's gross disbursements for the year were US$9.16 billion, and its net disbursements were US$6.98 billion (World Bank 2008e).

The World Bank's IBRD and IDA arms share the same staff and physical facilities, report to the same managers, Directors and Governors, and generally apply common standards to evaluate prospective loans. But their financial models are fundamentally different. The Bank's IBRD loans are financed mainly through the sale of its AAA-rated bonds to private and institutional investors. These bonds are backed by guarantees provided by the Bank's wealthy member-states, in the form of capital "subscriptions." Countries do not actually pay these amounts to the Bank, apart a small fraction, which contributes to the Bank's operational capital. Rather, the subscriptions are retained as "callable capital" – "a kind of guarantee pooled together by the promises of all members" (Woods 2006: 196). In fact, the Bank does not need to draw on the capital subscriptions, since an overall strong record by borrowers in meeting their debt-service obligations has sustained the high bond rating. According to the Bank, "Even though IBRD does not maximize profits, it has earned a positive net income each year since 1948" (World Bank 2007b: 16).

Since this modest profit gives the Bank some operational independence, defrays its capital and staff expenditures, and in part cross-subsidizes IDA operations, the IBRD lending arm is critical to the Bank's overall business model.

IBRD loans to middle-income countries generally carry slightly lower interest rates than commercial borrowing – the Bank recently has made a special effort to price them below the market (World Bank 2007c: 4)[1] – though they carry extensive fiduciary, social and environmental, and broad policy conditions that create additional compliance costs for borrowers.

In contrast to IBRD's bond-backed loans, IDA credits and grants are financed mainly through contributions – "replenishments," in the Bank's lingo – from donor countries. IDA is replenished following a donor dialogue process every three years; the fifteenth replenishment, "IDA15," was finalized in December 2007 and runs through June 2011. Donor contributions have financed about 71 percent of IDA assistance since its inception, with the balance coming partly from IDA's own resources and transfers for other World Bank Group entities, mainly IBRD but recently the International Finance Corporation (IFC, the Group's private sector lender for developing countries) also. As of 2008, the five leading all-time donors were the United States (22.02 percent of cumulative subscriptions and contributions), Japan (19.38 percent), Germany (11.40 percent), the United Kingdom (10.30 percent), and France (7.36 percent). There has been some shift in donors' relative contributions in recent years. The same five countries topped the list of pledges for IDA15, though not in the same order: the UK was first (at 14.05 percent), followed by the US (12.19 percent), Japan (10 percent), Germany (7.05 percent), and France (6.50 percent). This group was followed by another five countries whose collective contributions represented a much larger share of their combined national incomes: Canada pledged 4 percent of the IDA15 total, followed by Italy (3.8 percent), Spain (3.14 percent), The Netherlands (2.99 percent), and Sweden (2.95 percent).[2]

The IDA15 replenishment saw a 42 percent increase in donor contributions over the previous go-round – the largest one-time increase in IDA's history – to about US$25 billion. This was in line with pledges by the Group of Eight industrialized countries, at the 2005 Gleneagles Summit in Scotland, to cancel remaining debt for the world's poorest countries and to double aid for Africa by 2010, mainly through grants. (Note that Britain, which under Tony Blair and Gordon Brown's leadership pushed the G8 initiatives, is the largest single donor for IDA15). Prior to this fifteenth replenishment, IDA's real growth had been about flat for almost two decades.

The implications of debt relief for IDA's operations are complicated. It has reduced the "reflows" (principal repayment and charges) from past loans that IDA otherwise would have expected for coming years. Repayments had become an important factor in the IDA financing picture only in the 1990s – given the long time horizon of IDA loans, it had taken that long for significant repayments from its earliest loans to begin accruing – but now the writing off of past loans implies again making IDA more dependent on donor pledges to finance the cost of new assistance. Under IDA15, donor commitments included US$6.3 billion for the Multilateral Debt Relief Initiative to help ameliorate the impact on IDA's finances.

Simply put, lowered reflows through debt relief have made IDA less self-sustaining. Thus, if the Bank does not wish to become increasingly dependent on donor commitments, it must hedge against this by transferring funds from IBRD and other in-house resources. For IDA15, total World Bank Group commitments to IDA were US$3.5 billion, mainly transfers from IBRD and IFC – a threefold increase from IDA14 (World Bank 2008e). In terms of percentage increase, the expansion of the Bank's own inter-entity financing for IDA actually exceeded the rise in donor commitments. If the Bank plans to keep up this model, it is essential that it continue to attract borrowers for IBRD loans.[3] Large and reliable IBRD borrowers – especially India – will be needed to help support continued IDA lending to poor countries.[4]

The Bank's internal contributions notwithstanding, the replenishment process every three years gives donor countries considerable leverage in IDA governance. In fact, it has been suggested that IDA replenishment is "the primary opportunity for donor nations to influence World Bank policymaking" (Weiss 2008: 5). Yet in spite of (or perhaps, because of) IDA's importance to the Bank's overall operations, the process is "highly informal" and not transparent. Jozef Ritzen, a former Vice President in the Development Economics Department at the Bank, calls this arrangement "a weak spot in the governance of the Bank" (2005: 85). Many World Bank processes *have* become much more transparent since the 1990s, owing mainly to pressure from external advocacy and watchdog organizations. For IDA replenishments, summary reports and policy documents are available, but detailed minutes from the meetings of donor IDA Deputies and the Bank's Executive Board are not. Transparency advocates and donor countries themselves have pressed the Bank for access to the minutes,[5] but they remain classified (Weiss 2008: 12). There is some hypocrisy in member country calls for greater transparency, since the politically sensitive nature of IDA replenishments – both for donors and borrowers – are a key reason for their continued classification.

In terms of formal decision-making, IBRD and IDA share the same Board of Executive Directors, as noted above. (Technically, under the IDA Articles of Agreement, the directors of the IBRD Board serve *ex officio* as IDA's Board). Countries' vote shares on the Board are weighted in accordance with their financial commitments to the Bank. The same five countries are the largest shareholders of both IBRD and IDA – and in the same rank order, though with some differences in their voting power. In IDA, as of mid-2009, the US had the single largest vote share (12.16 percent), followed by Japan (9.53 percent), Germany (6.30 percent), the United Kingdom (5.37 percent) and France

(4.04 percent).[6] The US voting power in IBRD is somewhat higher than in IDA, and the UK's marginally so. The other three big donors have slightly less power in IBRD than in IDA.

These five countries are each entitled to appoint Executive Directors to the Board. The Bank's 164 other member countries – which included 40 other IDA donors and 79 IDA borrowers in 2009 – elect 19 additional directors, usually to represent geographic groupings of countries (though China, Russia and Saudi Arabia enjoy "single country constituency" directors). India, along with Bangladesh, Bhutan and Sri Lanka, elects a director who wields 4.41 percent voting power in IDA. In all, IDA's "Part I" member countries – essentially, industrialized donor countries – have a voting power of 57.97 percent, as compared to 42.03 percent for "Part II" developing countries (not all of whom are IDA borrowers).[7]

Some discussions of the Bank's governance make too much of the weighted vote shares and other formal decision-making rules and procedures. The US still enjoys veto power for some types of high-level decisions requiring an 85 percent supermajority in IBRD, though recently this has ceased to be the case in IDA (as late as the IDA13 negotiations in 2001–2, the US had more than 20 percent share power). Collective European donor votes outweigh the US share, which would be significant if they coordinated their policy positions. In reality, decision-making is generally by consensus. Critics of the Bank might make the case that "consensus" is merely a euphemism for donor dominance and US hegemony in particular, though this is a somewhat oversimplified view.

The IDA replenishments, though nominally undertaken "every three years," are actually more like a continual process. Even the formal discussions among IDA Deputies take place over meetings spanning nearly one year (IDA15 talks opened in March 2007 and closed in December). The dialogue encompasses a range of technical and political economy considerations. It is important to recognize the influence of the Bank's own staff in the IDA replenishment process. While IDA may depend on donors for funds, these countries' IDA Deputies, and Executive Directors on the Bank's Board, depend on IDA itself for much of the data and technical background papers that shape their deliberations. This gives the organization's managers and staff subtle powers in framing issues for debate. However opaque it may remain, the IDA replenishment process is by its very nature a nuanced negotiation.

Donor countries bring different perspectives and priorities to the table: perhaps *the* key challenge confronting IDA, and the World Bank generally, is that its diverse shareholders and stakeholders want it to be so many different things at once. Recent US priorities have been to push a more performance-based allocation formula to promote responsible aid use, to raise the grant component of multilateral development assistance generally, and to increase IDA and World

Bank access for fragile and post-conflict states (especially countries perceived as critical to US security interests, such as Afghanistan). European donors have made debt relief and expanded aid for Africa a particularly high priority.

Donor countries vary in their engagement on particular issues. Peer perceptions of legitimacy among donors can vary widely, too. The formal voting power of the US, for example, should be seen as attenuated by America's declining contributions to IDA. American arrears – which stood at US$378 million even in 2008 – prompted three other donors to withhold a collective US$72 million from IDA12 and IDA13. The World Bank as an organization, not to mention other IDA donors, would not like to see a repetition of the pattern that has plagued the United Nations, where American nonpayment of dues has starved the institution of cash in an attempt to force compliance with US objectives. Though IDA never could have been established without US patronage in the first place, and though Washington remains highly influential, American power in IDA most certainly has declined. The recent falloff has been particularly precipitous, and though some of this can be understood in the context of the George W. Bush administration's global legitimacy deficit more generally, the American role in IDA governance likely will continue to attenuate as other donors become more assertive and new donors emerge.

In contrast to the American picture, the informal influence of some donors might be greater than their weighted voting powers would indicate. This is particularly true for some of the Scandinavian/Nordic and Benelux donors, whose aid contributions tend to represent a significantly higher share of their national incomes than aid from the largest donors. In addition, these countries tend to attach more importance to development assistance in general, as evidenced by the high-quality bureaucratic resources that they devote to their aid programs, including their bilateral portfolios. This class of donors thus exerts a moral authority surpassing its formal voting power.

Critics accustomed to seeing the World Bank as Washington's handmaiden might be surprised to learn that in recent replenishments it has been *other* donors who have led the way in pressing for India's graduation out of IDA, to free up resources for other borrowers. We will return to this issue below, but let us first consider the interests of IDA borrowers more generally.

Over the past several replenishments, IDA borrowers have come to play a somewhat more active role in the process – offering perspective papers, attending consultation sessions, responding to questionnaires, and giving other inputs. But the role of borrowers in IDA governance is still highly circumscribed. It is also attenuated by the trend of IDA Deputies – donor appointees – taking an ever-more substantive role in making important decisions during the replenishment talks, "subject to later validation by the Board with limited further debate" (Ahmed 2006: 92). In 2003, Indian Finance Secretary D.G. Gupta complained to the World Bank Development Committee, "IDA Deputies have moved from determining not only the generalities of IDA policies, but also the specifics, including policy conditionalities. But these actions have shut out the voice of its poorer members, which would have been expressed through the IDA Board" ("Enlarge Role for the Poor" 2003). Half a dozen IDA borrowers have been able to participate in recent IDA Deputy meetings as non-voting "observers," but this is an especially murky area – the published Chairman's Summary papers do not even list which countries received this privilege, for which meetings, and so on.

The appeal of IDA to borrowers is straightforward: IDA assistance comes on considerably softer terms than IBRD loans. IDA "credits"[8] are loans at no interest (though with a "service charge" of about 0.75 percent), with a 10-year grace period on repayment of principal, even beyond their long 25–40 year maturities. For some extremely poor states, IDA essentially still plays the role envisioned for it nearly 50 years ago: it lends to countries that are shunned by the private sector, or for whom market loans would be prohibitively costly. For these borrowers, there are few alternatives available. In contrast, for a large, relatively resourceful, and creditworthy borrower such as India, the biggest appeal of IDA lies in the cheap line of credit it provides for bridging finance gaps in infrastructure, social sector investment, and other development objectives.

Without limits on access to IDA, demand would far outstrip the available assistance. IDA addresses this problem in several ways. There is an annually updated operational cutoff for eligibility, based on countries' per capita incomes. For fiscal 2010, the threshold was US$1,135 Gross National Income per capita (based on 2008 accounts). Eligibility is linked not only to per-capita income, but also to creditworthiness: some countries with incomes below the operational income cutoff, but with adequate access to commercial and IBRD borrowing, do not receive IDA funds (International Development Association 2001a: 4). In addition to poverty and creditworthiness, the IDA allocation formula increasingly emphasizes "policy and institutional performance" as well, in an effort to encourage governance reforms and increase the effectiveness of aid.

While the multivariate allocation formula impacts the allocation of aid among IDA's dozens of smaller borrowers, for India and a few other large country borrowers the most direct determinant is a *fixed upper limit* on its access. India's "cap" under IDA15 is 11 percent of the total envelope (excluding arrears clearances). In comparison, Pakistan, with a population that is about 15 percent of India's, is entitled to 7 percent of IDA15 (International Development Association 2007a).

Given IDA's mandate as a "transitional arrangement," the list of borrower countries fluctuates over time, with implications for aid allocation. According to the World Bank,

IDA eligibility is a transitional arrangement that gives the poorest countries access to substantial resources before they are capable of obtaining the financing they need from commercial markets. As their economies grow, countries graduate from IDA eligibility. The repayments, or "reflows," that they make on IDA loans are used to help finance new IDA loans to the remaining poor countries (World Bank 2007b: 19–20).

More than 30 countries have "graduated" out of IDA eligibility, including Chile, Costa Rica, Egypt, Morocco, Thailand, and Turkey. However, there also have been cases of "reverse-graduation."[9] Indonesia is the most recent large country to exit IDA, graduating in 2008. (It had previously graduated in 1980, but reentered in 1999 after the Asian financial crisis). Some transitions are more momentous than others: the exit of a large country like Indonesia has a greater impact than that of Albania (a fellow 2008 graduate). Indonesia's World Bank Country Director, Andew Steer, marked the transition by saying, "It's very important not to think of IDA as something that will stay forever. That's not the point. The point is to put in place systems and programs that will make a difference in the lives of people and will be sustainable over the longer term."[10]

The case of China is likely to be particularly important to IDA's governance in the future. China, which joined the World Bank only in the 1980s,[11] was an IDA-IBRD "blend" borrower until 1999. A decade later, it has become a donor to IDA – contributing about one-tenth of one percent of the IDA15 replenishment. While this is a small start, the significance of China's transition has not been lost on India's own aid mandarins.

## The Elephant in the Pool

India, like China earlier, falls into the intermediate "blend" category of countries receiving a mixture of IBRD and IDA loans. After Indonesia's recent graduation, India is almost certainly next in line. It is by far the most populous country in the blend category, followed well behind by its neighbor Pakistan.[12]

In 2008, India's gross national income per capita was US$950, placing it below the operational cutoff for IDA eligibility.[13] But India does not have difficulty qualifying for IBRD loans or accessing private capital. To take one particularly striking indicator of its surging appeal as an investment destination, according to the Public-Private Infrastructure Advisory Facility (PPIAF, a multi-donor technical assistance facility managed by the World Bank Group), "India attracted more investment commitments to infrastructure projects with private participation in 2006 than any other developing country. Indeed, commitments in India were nearly twice those in its nearest rival, Brazil, and well ahead of those in China" (Harris 2008: 3). Private infrastructure investment in

India – almost non-existent in 1990 – has been on the rise since the reforms of the 1990s, with annual commitments reaching US$9 billion during 1996–7 before falling off somewhat at the end of the decade. A new surge began around 2004, and in 2006 private investors committed more than US$22 billion for almost 60 projects (ibid., 4).

This is not to suggest that there is no demand for the World Bank to lend in India – on the contrary, the country still faces major gaps and bottlenecks in infrastructure, particularly compared to China, and Indian leaders consistently stress the need for even greater investments to sustain their ambitious economic growth targets. There are critical needs in the rural sector – such as access to credit for small farmers – and a number of sectors where the Bank can contribute both in terms of lending and technical/analytical assistance. But it does mean that the World Bank is increasingly a relatively modest player in a very crowded investment field. As long as India continues to borrow from the Bank, almost by definition it will borrow relatively large sums in absolute terms. Yet as India's economy continues to grow, the Bank's contribution as a share of its developmental investment dwindles ever lower, forcing the Bank to work harder to remain relevant.

As noted in Chapter One, India's very acute needs for external assistance in the late 1950s were a key impetus for the very founding of IDA in 1960. But as more newly independent developing countries became borrowers, India's position as a huge IDA borrower presented a problem. The Bank stepped up aid to India after the 1966 devaluation imbroglio – both to mend ties with the important client, and to fulfill its increasingly poverty-focused mission during the McNamara period – but the more IDA aid that India claimed, the less was available for other IDA borrowers. Even in the 1960s, the Bank had to place fixed limits on IDA assistance to India (and Pakistan) to reserve access for others.

The Bank's longtime General Counsel, the late Ibrahim F.I. Shihata, relates a discussion from the fifth IDA replenishment in 1977, for which the office of the Bank's president (then McNamara) prepared a memorandum on "the criteria underlying the allocation of IDA credits which would provide a basis for review by the IDA Executive Directors." In interpreting the IDA Articles of Agreement, the president's note reiterated that in order to be eligible for IDA funds, borrowers must be relatively less developed, lack creditworthiness for conventional lending, and be in a position, as indicated by their economic performance and absorptive capacity, to use IDA effectively (Shihata 2000: 557). The note went on to discuss other issues impacting IDA access, and made special mention of India with respect to population size:

> Population size is a basic criterion for allocating IDA resources among eligible countries. However, allocations on the basis of population alone

would result in a heavy concentration of IDA resources in a few countries; India would account for over one-half of the allocations to the currently IDA eligible countries. It could be argued that aid efforts, including those of IDA, are essentially aimed at people rather than nations and, accordingly, that the per capita criterion should be given a predominant position. However, a strict allocation of IDA resources according to population size would, for example, considerably reduce the share of some of the sparsely populated countries of Sub-Saharan Africa. These countries face problems that justify more generous allocation of concessionary assistance. Those problems include limitations in trained manpower, wide dispersion of small populations over wide areas and small market size that cannot support broad-based industrialization efforts. These factors along with minimum project size and the requirements of a continuing lending program have introduced the so-called "small country bias" in IDA lending. *The Association has thus achieved a much wider geographical diversification of operations than would have resulted from strict adherence to the criterion of population* (ibid., 558; emphasis in original).

That this was deliberated over 30 years ago demonstrates that limiting India's IDA access, in order to ration assistance for African and other borrowers, is nothing new. But allocation issues became particularly significant in the 1980s as donor contributions to IDA stagnated in real terms, and even more so since the 1990s as HIPC and other debt initiatives have made relief to Africa a high priority.

The flip side of the "small country bias" is what Michael Lipton and John Toye, in a 1990 study of aid to India, call the "large country effect." They explain that donor countries would like to "appear as generous in as many different countries as possible, and can win friends in twenty medium-sized poor countries… by economizing on aid to one large country like India" (1990: 3). This effect has implications not only for India's IDA share and other multilateral assistance, but also for its aid volume overall. In per capita terms, the contrast between India and other developing countries was striking even a quarter-century ago: Lipton and Toye show that total 1985 aid to India worked out to around US$1.90 person, versus US$16.20 for other developing countries (not including China; ibid., 3). (Of course, as we have seen, there are also demand-side historical reasons for India's unusually low aid dependency).

In 1993, John P. Lewis noted that country-size parameters "greatly distort" the per capita distribution within IDA. At the time, China and India together accounted for more than two-thirds of the IDA-eligible world population, but were permitted only a combined 30 percent of the distribution. On the other hand, sub-Saharan African countries received at minimum 45 percent of IDA credits (1993: 33).

The Indian position in IDA presents a double bind for the World Bank. On the one hand, given India's size and share of the world's poor – and its relatively sound aid administration, at least compared to many other low-income borrowers – it conceivably could generate projects and programs that would take up the entire pool of IDA resources. On the other hand, this great size is precisely the problem. Allowing India to dominate IDA on the merits – or even allocating its aid on something closer to per-capita parity with other low-income countries – would mean denying donors the opportunity to "win friends" in dozens of smaller needy countries. If that formulation sounds too cynical, it is worth pointing out that if donors truly were motivated to limit India's aid mainly in consideration of the objective needs of other recipients – rather than by political-diplomatic impulses – another approach would be simply to increase their aid commitments all around. But until very recently, they have not done so.

The "blend" status has been the Bank's solution for handling giant IDA borrowers like India (or, for a time, China). Having large, still poor, but relatively creditworthy countries borrow both from IBRD and IDA has suited their interests as well as the Bank's. For the blend borrower, the interest-free cost basis of IDA credits means that even under the "blend" scenario, the Bank's loan packages are priced very competitively compared to private sector alternatives, thus offsetting their higher bureaucratic costs and carrying the additional benefit of the Bank's technical and analytical work. This arrangement retains India's interest (in both senses of that word) in IBRD. But if IDA credits were to fall to a very low share of the Bank's assistance to India – or to disappear altogether – then its financial appeal is greatly diminished. Simply put, the Bank needs IDA to keep itself engaged in India.

But the blend category also functions as a kind of halfway house out of IDA; at some point, as it enters the middle-income range, a blend country eventually will graduate to IBRD-only borrower status. IDA graduation is a process, not a sudden event. But for a process that more than 30 countries have undergone, it remains surprisingly informal. In theory, there is little ambiguity in the IDA charter that it is intended as a transitional facility for the poorest countries; once a borrower crosses the income threshold for eligibility, its exit from IDA should be relatively straightforward. But in fact the process is more subjective. The Bank's 2008 Country Assistance Strategy for India notes, "Under current IDA graduation policies, if a country's GNI per capita exceeds the IDA operational cutoff for at least two years in a row, a case-by-case determination is made by IDA management" (2008b: ii). The CAS also observes that India's growing per capita income could put it over the cutoff as early as 2010 or 2011, though it suggests that this is less likely if growth slows in the context of the global economic downturn.

There are precedents for country graduation below the cutoff, however. For example, when China graduated a decade ago (fiscal 1999) its per capita income was US$860, less than the operation cutoff of US$925 at the time. But it had "strong export earnings and large reserves, and a demonstrated track record of successfully borrowing on the international commercial markets to meet much of [its] capital needs" (International Development Association 2001a: 12). Graduates tend not to be altogether reluctant in their departure; by the time they go through the process, their Bank borrowings usually represent such a small share of their development investment that the loss of easy money from IDA is a transition that they can bear. There is also the political symbolism of achievement in the process – even if the country still exhibits significant levels of poverty, as do China, Indonesia, and other recent graduates.

In this as in other contexts, India's leaders are driven by a sense of competition with Asian neighbors; following China, Indian officialdom sees graduation from IDA as a mark of achievement and prestige. But at the same time, India's recent developmental objectives – particularly the goal of improving economic performance and poverty reduction in "lagging states" – have led it to place a higher emphasis on IDA than might be expected of a soon-to-be graduate. Usually, in the years before graduation, a country's volume of IDA borrowing tapers, and the composition of the Bank's loan blend is progressively "hardened" toward a higher share of IBRD loans. What is interesting in India's case is that while there *has* been a hardening of the blend toward IBRD terms, its absolute level borrowing from IDA has stayed about the same or even slightly increased in recent years, as its Bank borrowings overall have expanded. Thus, India is bucking the usual trend (Basu 2007).

In the early 1990s, the Bank's assistance to India contained a higher IDA component – about two-thirds – than IBRD. As noted in Chapter Two, this "softness" was criticized by IDA donors, and led some to call even then for India's graduation. In 1995, India's IDA borrowing exceeded China's (US$944 million to US$630 million), and the combined share of the Asian giants drew criticism in the US Congress and even merited an article in the *Los Angeles Times* (Mann 1996). During the late 1990s, India's IBRD-to-IDA blend came closer to 50:50 (with a slight bias still in favor of IDA), in the context of total annual commitments ranging from about US$1.5 billion to US$2 billion. Beginning around 1999–2000 the blend gradually hardened to the current level of about 70 percent IBRD – basically an inversion of the early 1990s ratio – but in the context of an overall expansion of annual commitments to US$3–4 billion.[14]

By any measure, India is still a very substantial IDA borrower. In fiscal 2008, its US$837 million in borrowing was the second-highest share among all IDA recipients, behind only Vietnam (US$1.2 billion) and ahead of Bangladesh (US$735 million), Ethiopia (US$711 million), and Nigeria (US$572). (The next four highest borrowers were all African, and Nepal rounded out the top ten). The Bank's 2008 Country Strategy for India envisions an IDA contribution equivalent to US$4.41 billion over the three-year fiscal period (2009–11). By comparison, *total* IDA resources for the fifteenth replenishment are US$41.6 billion; thus, India will claim about the 11 percent of total IDA resources that its cap permits.

The hydra-headed Bank's "attitude" about India's potential graduation from IDA is difficult to characterize in simple terms. The country team itself has little connection to the replenishment dialogue process that will ultimately determine when and how India goes, and it is clear from the 2008 CAS that they are bracing for change by trying to articulate a "middle-income country partnership" that would resemble the Bank's relations with China, Brazil, and other large countries (more on this below).

But from a broader operations standpoint, it is clear that the Bank is reluctant to see India leave IDA. To be sure, the Bank has many priorities – which not infrequently are in conflict with one another – but there is little reason to suspect that its basic position has changed very much from what it said about India's IDA membership in a 2001 policy paper. Noting that India and Indonesia were "two large IDA countries for which the issue of graduation and IDA eligibility has arisen on several occasions" – a passive construction that should not obscure the point that *donors* have raised the issue during replenishment talks – the IDA staff argued,

> India is home to 300 million poor, more than in all of sub-Saharan Africa. India has 36 percent of the world's poor, and 32 percent of the world's children not enrolled in primary education [...]
>
> The great bulk of IDA support [in India] goes for the social sectors and rural poverty reduction projects. IDA funds are used, for example, to support the Bank's largest education and nutrition programs, both targeted at girls. IDA also supports a large number of health programs, in order to combat AIDS, malaria, and leprosy. Without IDA, the Bank would not be able to lend to social sectors, because of the Government's reluctance to borrow non-concessional funds for "soft" sectors. Moreover, although at the macro level, IDA funding means little to India, IDA's impact has greatly increased by adopting a state focus.
>
> India makes effective use of IDA resources [...] (International Development Association 2001a: 14)

The policy note went on to point out that a pending Operations Evaluation Department analysis (Zanini 2001) found that the "relevance" of Bank's country strategy in India recently had "improved substantially... through a more sharpened focus on poverty reduction, a more selective approach to state assistance and greater attention to governance and institutions."

The IDA document practically pleaded that India should not be graduated just as the Bank – as the staff saw it – was revitalizing its relationship with the borrower:

> To reduce IDA assistance at this particular juncture *would marginalize the Bank* and threaten the progress made in the last few years in promoting reforms [...]
>
> Given the fact that India has the largest concentration of the poor in the world, a reduction in IDA resources would not be desirable. The country's increasing creditworthiness could be reflected in a hardening of the blend through increased IBRD lending relative to IDA, rather than a decline in its IDA allocation (ibid., 15; emphasis added).

But some donors are ready to see India out of IDA *now*. Especially since Indonesia has undergone re-graduation, all eyes are on India when it comes to finding ways to free up IDA resources, for Africa in particular.

Tellingly, ahead of IDA15, a Bank technical analysis for the Executive Board ran through a hypothetical "graduation scenario" that singled out India for illustration (Pakistan and Vietnam were also discussed, though with later hypothetical exits). It showed that on income criteria alone and disregarding creditworthiness, India would graduate from IDA by 2014–15 if its future growth rate of income per capita matched the recent average, and by 2016 even under a slower 4 percent growth scenario (International Development Association 2007a: 22). This analysis was not intended to *predict* when India would graduate (note also that it offered a more conservative projection than in the 2008 Country Strategy). But it nevertheless gave donors something to focus on. If creditworthiness was taken into account, donors could make a case for India's graduation even before it crosses the income threshold.

The opacity of the triennial IDA replenishment process makes it impossible to know exactly which donors have pushed India's graduation, and for what specific reasons, though the general issues are clear enough. Even many Bank staff, whose work would be substantially impacted by the change, are not privy to the details of the replenishment talks and must gather what information they can from water cooler conversation and other informal means. Without access to the minutes that would reflect individual donor positions, it is impossible to verify the accounts of Bank staff and Indian finance ministry officials. But the rumors themselves are revealing, and educated inferences from known facts make it possible to piece together a plausible basic account.

According to one former official from the Indian finance ministry's DEA, the "Scandinavian donors" in particular have led recent calls for India's graduation (Tewari 2008), even during IDA14 talks in 2005. The donors' basic position, as he characterized it, was "Why does India need IDA?" This makes sense because, as discussed in Chapter Three, the Scandinavian donors were among those most impacted by India's surprise termination of bilateral aid programs in 2003. The IDA14 replenishment was the first such dialogue after India's announcement, and it also followed soon after India's controversial post-tsunami aid diplomacy in December 2004-January 2005. As noted, some Indian analysts had predicted at the time that the government's "hamhanded" handling of the 2003 aid policy announcement would come back to haunt India in multilateral settings, and it appears that indeed it did reverberate.

The former DEA official's account about Scandinavian pressure is plausible also in that these countries place special emphasis on aid for Africa and post-conflict states (Haarder 2004), and may see India's share of IDA resources as impinging on these priorities.[15] The Executive Director for the Nordic and Baltic countries – whose constituency is Denmark, Estonia, Finland, Iceland, Latvia, Lithuania, Norway, and Sweden – holds 5.28 percent voting power in IDA, though as noted, the special engagement and relatively high aid-to-national income contributions of some of these countries gives them a greater importance in IDA governance than the vote share would imply.

The Bank's Nordic-Baltic Office, perhaps not surprisingly, did not comment on its position with respect to India's status in IDA.[16] Nor is it the point to single out this constituency on the basis on an unverifiable account (unverifiable because of IDA's non-disclosure of the pertinent records). These donors almost certainly were joined by others in calling for India's graduation. The US does not appear to be leading on the issue; and it is not obvious what its position would be. On the one hand, there were calls in the US Congress to oust China and India more than a decade ago; on the other hand, the concern then might have been more about China than India, and such criticisms were before the major strategic engagement between India and the US that emerged at the end of the Bill Clinton presidency and accelerated during the George W. Bush administration. Japan may be an exception to the donor pressure; in the past, it reportedly resisted calls by others for China and India to graduate IDA, both out of a sense of advocacy for Asian neighbors and to support its own export interests (Mann 1996).

Again, donors want IDA to be many things, and India's large IDA share is apparently seen as serving less pressing priorities than debt relief and expanded aid for Africa and post-conflict areas. It is an understandable view, given the image that India itself has increasingly put forward in recent years for what are essentially reasons of pride and politics.

If India still cares about borrowing from IDA – and the recent priorities it has articulated for development assistance suggest that it should – then it has not done much to help its own case. Some Indian officials even expect that the graduation issue is important enough to the Bank itself that it will advocate for India's continued IDA access – so why should they go to the trouble? Before concluding with a critical analysis of India's own strangely passive stance on the pending graduation issue, let us consider in more detail some of its implications for the World Bank.

### Toward a Middle-Income "Partnership"?

With India's years as an IBRD-IDA blend borrower appearing numbered, the Bank is positioning itself for a future relationship with the country that may come to resemble the ones it has with China, Brazil, Indonesia, Mexico, and other large middle-income countries that borrow from the IBRD facility but not from IDA. Yet the combination of India's great size and deeper history with the Bank (its cumulative borrowings surpass even China's)[17] makes its impending graduation from IDA by far the most significant the Bank has ever considered.

The 70-odd "middle-income" borrowers of the World Bank are a highly heterogeneous group of countries, with per capita annual incomes ranging from around US$1,000 to US$10,000. Nearly 70 percent of the world's poor (below the US$2 a day threshold) live in these countries, so by any standard the Bank believes it must actively engage with such countries if its "world without poverty" dream is to have any meaning. But the Bank has found it difficult to articulate a strategy for middle-income borrowers that aligns with its ambition to remain a leading force in global development and poverty reduction efforts. Perhaps more than any other area of its operations, this is where we find the Bank pulled – perhaps irreconcilably – in competing directions by its diverse shareholders and stakeholders.

Starting in the 1990s, under pressure by NGOs and donors and on the defensive against a diverse but strident anti-globalization movement more generally, the Bank adopted ever-greater safeguards and procedures that significantly raised the "hassle factor" in its loans. Borrower governments, particularly in large countries like China and India, bristled at what they saw as intrusive lecturing on their economic, social, and environmental policies, and resented what looked to them like the Bank giving too much credence to critical views of their own development priorities.

Journalist Sebastian Mallaby, the author of an in-depth study of the World Bank during the Wolfensohn presidency, generalizes from the case of South Africa some dilemmas confronting the organization in its relationships with middle-income developing countries. Initially, the post-Apartheid government in South Africa declined to borrow from the Bank at all. (Since 1997, South Africa has worked with the Bank on fewer than a dozen projects, mostly in an advisory capacity; it has borrowed only a little over US$60 million from IBRD).[18]

> The South Africans objected that the Bank was an infuriating business partner: it was bureaucratic and slow-moving, and it required its borrowers to make repeated trips to Washington. Even if the World Bank's market-based loans were slightly cheaper than those from private banks, the hassle of dealing with it was more than the South Africans could stomach…

Mallaby then spins out a rather apocalyptic scenario, from the perspective of the Bank's self-interest in preserving its organizational integrity, professionalism, relevance, and sense of legitimacy. While it may seem overstated, it accurately reflects anxieties that Bank managers and staff perceive:

> The Bank's cumbersome bureaucracy could deprive it of strong clients, countries like Brazil, India, and China, which are home to the majority of the world's poor, but which increasingly have the option of borrowing on private capital markets. The Bank's morale and professionalism – its clear superiority over UN agencies – depend on retaining those strong borrowers, because the small profits that the Bank collects on its market-based operations pay for a large part of the institution. If strong developing countries defect, and the Bank becomes mainly a provider of soft IDA credits, its financial independence will erode and it will depend increasingly on handouts from its shareholders. In a worst-case scenario, it could decline, gradually but inexorably, into the cash-strapped dependency of the United Nations. Its best people will drift off, and its professionalism will fade – accelerating the defection of the South Africas of the world, and sucking the Bank into a vicious downward spiral (Mallaby 2004: 111, 120).

Political scientist Ngaire Woods notes several factors that have driven up the real costs of World Bank resources, and have made the Bank less attractive to borrowers with other options. Firstly, donors reduced their real contributions to IDA over time, limiting the size of this facility and the ability to couple IDA credits with IBRD loans for stronger clients (though, as noted, IDA15 saw a substantial increase in pledges). Secondly, and more to the point for creditworthy borrowers, Woods notes, "an increasingly onerous bureaucratic process has grown up within the World Bank." Between the mid-1970s and the mid-1990s, the Bank's average administrative costs per project *doubled* (the Bank recently has made a concerted effort to reduce costs, with uncertain results). Thirdly, and relatedly, the "conditions attached to loans have grown in breadth and depth" as the Bank has sought to leverage changes in borrowers' economic policies and to apply social and environmental safeguards to projects.

"The result of the three forces," Woods says, "is that developing countries are displaying a diminishing appetite for borrowing from the World Bank" (2006: 189). The IBRD arm, she argues, suffers especially from the so-called "hassle factor" associated with Bank loans, which "has begun to push away some of the Bank's most successful borrowers" (ibid., 200). Beginning in the mid-1990s – with the exception of a lending spike in 1998 and 1999, associated with the Asian/emerging markets financial crisis – the Bank's IBRD lending to middle income borrowers dropped, slowly but consistently, from US$13.21 billion in gross disbursements in 1996, to US$10.11 billion in 2004 and US$10.49 billion in 2008 (Mallaby 2004: 209; World Bank 2008e). As noted above, repayment on past IBRD loans exceeded new disbursements by more than US$2 billion in 2008. This decline in IBRD lending occurred even as private capital flows greatly expanded (though with volatility in their composition; Goldin and Reinhart 2006: 84), and lending by regional multilateral development banks also has increased.

Simply put, the World Bank now must work harder to retain the major developing countries that it would like to have as its largest and most reliable IBRD borrowers – countries like Brazil, China, India, Indonesia, and Mexico. But from the other side, the Bank has come under increasing scrutiny and pressure from donor governments and NGOs, raising the costs of doing business with it in more ways than one. Particularly significant has been the ever-expanding social and environmental safeguards carried by the Bank's project loans – the "bread-and-butter" infrastructure investments that IBRD funds in sectors such as water and roads. Only very recently has the Bank been able to arrest the secular decline in infrastructure lending, with a huge boost expected in 2009–10 as the Bank works to provide counter-cyclical capacity in the global financial crisis and economic contraction. The onset of the global crisis late in 2008 will lead to a lending spike for the Bank, but the effect likely will be temporary even if more pronounced than that of the 1997–8 Asian and emerging markets crisis.

Johannes F. Linn, a Brookings Institution fellow and former World Bank Vice President for Europe and Central Asia, noted in 2006 that the substantial drop in World Bank lending had taken place in all regions *except* South Asia (2006: 87–88) – implying that India, and to a lesser extent Pakistan, had been a significant bulwark against the Bank's declining financial relevance globally.

Linn poses a sensible question: "Why would one worry about this declining trend in World Bank lending to MICs [middle-income countries]? Is it not a good thing if the Bank works itself out of a job in countries that, one might think, should in any case stand on their own feet?" (2008: 88). But contrary to the perception that middle-income countries should be largely self-sufficient, Linn notes that many of them still face significant development challenges, particularly at the lower end of the wide "middle-income" range. Linn argues that the decline in Bank lending to middle-income countries is a problem not only for these borrowers and for the Bank itself, but it also has implications for IDA operations and non-loan assistance to poorer countries:

> The World Bank's package of financial and advisory support through IBRD loans (along with its free-standing analytical and advisory services) is in principle well suited to supporting the structural and institutional changes along with investments in physical, social, and environmental infrastructure that are needed in the MICs [...]
>
> The Bank's role as 'transmission belt' carrying low-income countries through middle-income status into the ranks of high-income countries may well be at stake. This is somewhat ironic, because, on balance, the Bank has probably been more successful in helping middle-income than low-income countries. Part of the 'transmission belt' function of the Bank is to convey the lessons of MIC development experience to low-income countries [...]
>
> The ability of IBRD to continue making sizeable contributions to the Bank's soft loan and grant window – the International Development Association (IDA) – and for transfers to the debt reduction initiative for the poorest heavily indebted countries will be endangered, because these financial windows are financed in part from the income generated by IBRD loan charges. This would mean a sizeable reduction in financial flows to the poorest developing countries [...]
>
> *If the Bank is no longer seriously engaged in supporting MICs, its role as a global development organization that helps address global economic, social, and environmental challenges on a worldwide scale will be at risk. No other organization can currently perform this function credibly* (2006: 89–90).

Such a perspective is obviously self-serving to a large extent. But there is no gainsaying the claim that no other single development organization possesses its range of knowledge and financial resources. The point here is not so much to evaluate the objective merit of claims that continued World Bank engagement is essential to middle-income country development, but rather to recognize that *the Bank* certainly believes that this is true, and sees itself as under intensifying pressure to evolve its entire way of doing business to remain relevant. And the Bank's engagement with India, as the country transitions from low-income to middle-income status, will be the single most important borrower relationship contributing to this broader goal.

Several developments over the past decade help to illustrate the challenge that the Bank faces in lending to middle-income countries, and even to relatively self-reliant countries that aren't quite there yet – with India foremost among them. In 2002, the Bank's Board of Directors weathered a significant storm with large borrowers over safeguards in loans for water infrastructure projects. In the view of China and India, [19] standards that the Bank had adopted under pressure from anti-dam activists "demanded so many precautions and perambulations that they amounted to a virtual ban" (Mallaby 2004: 357) leading the Executive Directors for the two Asian giants to demand that the Bank reassess its standards. The China and India directors reminded the Bank's managers that "between the two of them they spoke for more than 2 billion people, or one in three members of the human race" (ibid., 361).

Of course, from the perspective of many critics of the Bank, these governments do *not* give "voice" to citizens adversely impacted by development projects. This is especially true of the authoritarian Chinese regime, but democratic India, too, comes in for criticism by the activist community – most infamously in the Narmada River context. But this is precisely the Bank's dilemma: it faces increasing scrutiny from NGOs and their allies in donor country governments, but its clients are developing country governments who enjoy expanded access to capital and who do not delight in the Bank's cumbersome conditionality and safeguards.

Over the past several years, the Bank has undertaken a major initiative under the banner of "Strengthening Middle Income Country Engagement," and the current World Bank Group President Robert B. Zoellick (2007–) has given the program a high priority. It has not been an easy road. There are a number of aspects to the program, and the issues are too many to summarize here.[20] But two aspects merit specific mention.

First, the Bank has explicitly recognized the "hassle factor" that had come to plague its relationships with many countries. Responding to the kinds of frustrations expressed by China, India and other independent-minded borrowers, the Bank has experimented with allowing projects to follow national social and environmental policies rather than the Bank's own safeguards. In 2004, it initiated a pilot project along these lines in Mexico. But while the Bank maintained that this approach would not result in a weakening of social and environmental safeguards, nearly 200 Northern and Southern NGOs submitted an open letter from "international civil society" to the Bank's Executive Board, which blasted the Bank's middle-income strategy and the Mexican pilot project for doing exactly that (Bank Information Center 2004). The Bank subsequently reaffirmed its interest in experimenting with deferring to national standards (it did not phrase it that way, of course). As the Bank tries to be both "client centered" and responsive to its many critics, this remains a strongly contested issue (Park and Vetterlein 2010).

Second, even as it seeks to reverse the decline in lending, the Bank's strategy for middle-income clients increasingly calls on its "knowledge bank" function. This is nothing new. At least since the mid-1990s, the Bank "has made knowledge sharing an explicit objective and has increased its efforts to organize its knowledge sharing activities in a systematic way so that information can have the broadest possible impact" (World Bank 2007b: 72). Scholarly analysts have repeatedly emphasized this aspect of the Bank's identity (e.g. Gilbert, Powell et al. 2000; Pincus and Winters 2002). Even critics of the Bank acknowledge its knowledge capabilities (Meltzer 2000), though some argue that Bank effort would be better spent supporting research and learning efforts within developing countries themselves (Kapur 2006).

The Bank's middle-income country strategy hopes to trade increasingly on its "AAA" (Analytic and Advisory Activities) and "non-lending solutions" (basically policy and technical advice) in its relations with middle-income clients. Financial and advisory services from the IFC, the World Bank Group's private-sector lending arm – are also expected to expand and more closely align with IBRD operations in middle countries (IFC's "global advisory portfolio" has grown tenfold, to nearly US$1 billion, since 2001).

If talk of "non-lending solutions" sounds like consultancy jargon, it is. By positioning itself not only as a lender and therefore bringing a value distinct from what major private banks can do for middle-income borrowers, the Bank is increasingly moving onto another playing field crowded with global private management consultancies such as McKinsey & Company, Accenture, Deloitte, Bain & Company, Boston Consulting Group – not to mention, in India, top homegrown companies such as Tata and Infosys.

The Bank's official line is that its knowledge resources are unparalleled, given the cross-national breadth and historical depth of its work in the field of development. As noted above, it is fair to say that no other single entity can match its spectrum of capabilities. But that does not prevent others from cultivating specific niche competencies, and in private, some Bank staff admit that to de-couple lending and analytical services would be to head into uncharted territory. "Historically, and even still, so much the Bank's analytical services are 'bundled' with its loans," points out Parmesh Shah, a senior rural development specialist for South Asia. "What is the market value of the advice? We don't really know. The Bank has to learn to compete in the 'advice marketplace' with the McKinseys of the world" (2007).

On balance, most Indian officials seem to believe that the Bank brings valuable knowledge resources to the table, distinct from its lending contribution. Thus, this will be an important basis for a "middle-income strategy" in India, just as it has been in the Bank's relations with other large developing countries. Mallaby is right to point out, "Brazil's government – or India's government or China's – is stuffed full of first-rate technocrats who know their country far better than any foreigner." But he also maintains, "There is still a role for a friendly outside institution that can distill global experience and provide technical advice – an analysis of rival models of pension privatization, for example, or of malaria control or high-altitude road construction" (2004: 290).

### *The 2008 Country Assistance Strategy (Reprise)*

The Bank's 2008 Country Assistance Strategy (CAS) for India, first mentioned in Chapter Three, offers up the image of a Bank that is increasingly pulled in different directions by "the two Indias." The strategy explicitly calls for a "differentiated" approach beginning in the 2009–12 assistance period. In the middle-income states, and at the national level, the Bank basically will begin to engage India as the middle-income country that, for Bank classification and IDA eligibility purposes, it likely soon will become. This is new territory, and there is a strong sense, both in the CAS document and in conversations with Bank and Indian officials, of what might be called "crossing the river by feeling the stones" – to borrow the famous Deng Xiaoping phrase about China's economic reforms.

Indeed, a number of Bank and Indian officials cited the Bank's relationship with China as one they are looking at very closely for clues as to where their engagement might be headed in coming years. To that end, it is worth briefly noting the Bank's perspective on a question it asked itself in a 2006 document on IBRD relationships with middle-income countries: "Why is China a client of the World Bank Group?"

> The Government of China values the WBG's [World Bank Group's] work in China for the ideas, innovations, and knowledge that it brings. It sees the WBG as a neutral objective partner that can be trusted to act in China's best interest in learning from international experience. WBG activities build on a long-term partnership based on a shared

commitment, and pragmatic cooperation that aims to develop and implement sustainable solutions tailored to pressing development problems. Though modest in scale, WBG activities often have large impacts, helping to scale-up policy and institutional reform, technological innovation and improved project management. The WBG has contributed to a stronger focus on high-quality poverty analysis; financial sector reform, including interest rate reform and IFC issuance of a local currency denominated "Panda" bond; and greater awareness of resource scarcity and environmental challenges and how to manage them.

China remains interested in new IBRD borrowing because it values the nonfinancial services that IBRD provides as part of its loan package and that are not readily available from the private sector. IBRD typically makes a commitment to remain involved until the issues are resolved, at a cost that is limited to the loan charges. Similarly, Chinese private companies work with IFC because they value the services IFC delivers with financing. As a trusted partner, IFC plays a unique role in piloting initiatives that lead to further economic opening and adoption of international norms. MIGA [the Bank Group's Multilateral Investment Guarantee Agency] helps China by complementing existing insurance capacity and thus helping attract foreign direct investment. It also provides mediation support to clients when investment disputes occur. (World Bank 2006b: 7, Box 4).

In some ways, this description may be to gaze a decade or more into the future of the Bank's relationship with India, when non-lending services will be more important than the Bank's financial footprint.

But just as there are many important differences between India and China, there likely will be – and *should* be – important differences in the Bank's engagement with the two countries. In the context of a federal democratic polity, it is not clear how well India will manage the social tensions that are likely to intensify if the gaps between its high-achieving states and lagging states, and between urban and rural areas, continue to widen. (For that matter, it is not certain that China will be able to contain social pressures either, but that is a subject for a different book).

Pulling against the "middle-income" theme of the Bank's India strategy is the focus on "lagging states" – especially the UP-Bihar-Jharkhand-Orissa agglomeration that represents one of the most significant concentrations of poverty anywhere in the world. Whatever other goals might crowd the Bank's perennially over-ambitious agenda, this "other India" is where it must remain engaged if it is to contribute to the realization of the Millennium Development Goals. And it is not just the Bank that sees it this way; as demonstrated in Chapter Three, Indian leaders themselves led the reorientation of the Bank's Country Strategy *away* from the middle-income reforming states and toward the poorest ones.

## The IDA Endgame: *Pride and Poverty* or *A Tale of Two Indias?*

In one sense, the recent path that has led to the "lagging states" emphasis in the Bank's strategy for India illustrates, more than ever, the essential asymmetry in the Bank's relationship with its largest borrower. As the simple saying goes, the Bank needs India more than India needs it. The Bank set out in the mid-1990s to do whatever it had to do in order to remain relevant, and it has progressively bent to India's preferences in redesigning its assistance strategy – from an initial focus on reformist states to spur others along by example, to a much more direct engagement with the hard-case states as regional inequalities have only accentuated.

But the lagging states agenda also exposes, as never before, an uncomfortable ground reality in states like Uttar Pradesh, Bihar, Jharkhand, and Orissa – and the growing gap between "the two Indias." This hard truth does not align well with the image of a "rising power" that India presents to the world. As its aggregate indicators edge toward the lower range of the Bank' "middle income" category that will preclude its access to IDA, India's deepening concern about poor growth performance and persistent poverty in lagging states belies the projected indifference or pride about its graduation from aid.

Kapil Kapoor, Principal for the South Asia Region on the Bank's Public Sector Governance Board, argues that the Bank's recent assistance strategy in India "has boosted its relevance and legitimacy," but suggests that the divergence between "the two Indias" has become the defining challenge in the relationship. "India as a whole may 'graduate' from IDA before Bihar, Orissa, and UP do," he pointed out. "And these are huge states, bigger than many African countries" (2008).

As we have seen, despite recent unprecedented economic growth, deprivation in India persists on a massive scale. India's largest and poorest states *are* more populous than many African countries, and their development indicators rank alongside that continent's weakest. The population of Uttar Pradesh alone is nearing 200 million; if it were an independent country, it would be the fourth or fifth most populous in the world. Poverty rates in rural Bihar and Orissa are comparable to in Burundi, and worse than in Ghana and Malawi (Murgai, Pritchett et al. 2006: 2) – all recent IDA and HIPC or Enhanced-HIPC borrowers. As Fareed Zakaria observes, "[India] might have several Silicon Valleys, but it also has three Nigerias within it – that is, more than 300 million people living on less than a dollar a day. It is home to

40 percent of the world's poor and has the world's second-largest HIV-positive population" (2008: 133). Given the incongruity between this reality and external perceptions of India's economic success and rise to great power status, it might also be said that India has an international image problem that is partly its own creation.

Quite simply, without IDA, a lagging states strategy for India makes little sense – for either the Bank or for India. India and the Bank could choose to ignore the contradiction of an exit from IDA in the midst of the new assistance strategy. Officially, at least, this seems to be the course they are on. The default outcome, then, would be for India to graduate out of IDA within the next replenishment or two, in which case the lagging states agenda would probably wither, as other Bank strategies have done before. The Bank would then be back to the place it started out from fifteen years ago: drifting along without a clear sense of purpose, demoralized at its diminished relevance to India's economic reforms and development. India's lagging states would still face yawning gaps in infrastructure and institutional constraints on faster growth and poverty reduction.

The other possibility would be to fundamentally transform the IDA allocation methodology to maintain access, at least for India's poorest states. Even with IDA, the Bank probably will not have much impact on the fundamental problems of development confronting the lagging states; in the end, it is for their peoples and their leaders to commit to exceedingly hard tasks. But there are signs of increased willingness to do so, especially in places like Bihar and Orissa. With IDA, at least, the Bank can offer India and her lagging states a cheap line of credit for important investments, thereby reducing the future debt burden they will carry and somewhat diminishing the Centre's need to redirect resources away from high-performing states.

This high-level institutional reform would require innovative thinking by all parties: the World Bank itself, donors, and – perhaps above all – India. The country's leaders would have to muster the political courage to articulate a new kind of "global power" identity for India – one that does not disregard the lagging states challenge in order to save face, but rather embraces it as a defining task for this great civilization in the new millennium. By pursuing a change in the IDA allocation criteria to permit continued lending for India's poorest states, New Delhi could encourage new thinking about the multilateral development assistance regime more generally – thus contributing to the expanded role in global governance that it seeks for itself.

The details of a new allocation scheme would have to be worked out in the next IDA replenishment talks – for IDA16 (2011–14) – given the possibility of India's graduation during its fiscal period. The most straightforward approach would be to disaggregate India into low-income states eligible for

IDA or an IBRD-IDA blend, and middle-income states eligible for IBRD loans only. One potential sticking point is that the Government of India is the legal borrower on the Bank's sub-national loans, with the states designated as beneficiaries. But the same kinds of on-lending agreements that the Centre already adheres to could be used to ensure that the borrowing would be used for the benefit of low-income states. In fact, Kapil Kapoor said, the Bank had suggested to the Indian finance ministry that it should begin setting aside the entirety of India's IDA borrowings for projects and programs in the lagging states, to build a case for continued IDA access. "The poverty and development indicators are aggregated on this basis," he observed, "so that's the story that India can tell the world" (2007).

The same indicator that has been cited in so many recent studies of regional income divergence in India, Gross State Domestic Product (GSDP) per capita, could be used to sort out the states for IDA eligibility purposes. What would be the access implications for the states? Consider that against the contemporaneous IDA14 operational cutoff of US$1,025, Bihar's 2006–7 per capita income at current prices was Rs. 9,702 – only a little over US$200 (using an average 2006 currency exchange rate of Rs. 45/US$1). In Andhra Pradesh, the figure was Rs. 29,074 (about US$646), in Gujarat, Rs. 37,532 (about US$834), and in Delhi Rs. 66,728 (US$1,483)[21] – demonstrating the incredible variance both across states and across the rural-urban dimension (Delhi, of course, is a metropolitan area). However, by 2008–9 Gujarat's per capita income had risen to Rs. 45,773 – about US$964 at current exchange rates. This dramatic trajectory demonstrates why it is really only some states – like Haryana and Punjab in the northwest, Gujarat and Maharasthra in the West, the unusual hill state of Himachal Pradesh, and Kerala and Tamil Nadu in the South – that are nearing the income threshold that would preclude a role for IDA. They may surpass it in a few years, and on the strength of their achievements, India in the aggregate will, too. But under a prorated allocation, even states like Andhra Pradesh – the Bank's decade-long darling – likely would still be IDA-eligible on a per capita income basis for a number of years. Of course, the core lagging states, like Bihar, still have much farther distances to travel, and could remain IDA-eligible for well more than a decade.

India's recent borrowing has *not* seen a systematic allocation of IDA resources for the lagging states along the lines Kapoor suggests. There has been, at best, a limited informal movement in this direction. To be sure, there have been a number of IDA-only loans in the lagging states, such as the US$82.4 million Orissa Rural Livelihoods Project approved in 2008. But the respective 2007 and 2008 Development Policy Loans for Himachal Pradesh (US$200 million) and Bihar (US$225 million) were both two-thirds IBRD in their composition, under the one-size-fits-all DPL policy that the central government itself has encouraged. This is in spite of the great income differential between these two states. As noted in Chapter Three, the Himachal operation was a priority for the Centre on the grounds of encouraging the state's sustainable development policy, but such an *ad hoc* use of IDA funds risks undermining the lagging states rationale. In general, India's preference for IDA use has been to combine state-wise and sector-wise allocation criteria, which has meant IDA-only investments in priority sectors even in relatively well-off states, such as a US$154 million IDA-only rural water supply and sanitation loan for Punjab – one of the very richest states – as recently as 2006.

Loans for central projects in India would pose a special issue under a prorated IDA graduation scenario, but those for which India would like to avail IDA assistance could be handled by targeting implementation in lagging states. Some existing projects come close to this model. For example, in 2008 the US$521 million National Vector Borne Disease Control and Polio Eradication Support Project was entirely IDA funded, and used a combination of state-wise and district-level targeting for 50 highly disease-burdened districts across Andhra Pradesh, Chhattisgarh, Jharkhand, Madhya Pradesh and Orissa (World Bank 2008d: 6) – all of which, excepting AP, are low-income states. These kinds of details are for India and the Bank to work out, and no doubt they will create constraints on the design of some kinds of national projects with distribution across richer and poorer states (though for such projects, an IBRD-IDA blend might make sense).

In April 2007, while the IDA15 replenishment talks were underway, the Bank presented an *IDA at Work* note – prepared in consultation with Indian officials – entitled "India: Using IDA Effectively in a Large Country." It was a somewhat colorless bureaucratic product – a missed opportunity to make an explicit case for continued IDA access for states such as Bihar. But between the lines, the document revealed that despite their posturing, Indian leaders believe the country would benefit from continuing IDA aid. It argued that improving lives among India's approximately 300 million people below the poverty line would be critical for achieving global development goals, and highlighted the "increasingly sharp picture" of "two Indias" – one "on a rapid development trajectory," the other "caught in a low-level development trap, progressing much more slowly" (International Development Association 2007b: 3).

It also exhibited the mixed attitude of the Indian government – pride at India's own capabilities, yet continued interest in IDA assistance for lagging states – that has led to India's curiously passive non-policy on its IDA graduation. On the one hand, the document maintained, "Because India has substantial resources of its own, IDA's impact has been less financial than intellectual" (ibid., 4). On the other hand, it argued,

Investment needs are particularly acute in the most populous states of India where close to two-thirds of India's poor are located – Bihar, Uttar Pradesh, Orissa, Jharkhand, and Chattisgarth.

These states should eventually follow the more successful Southern states of India in developing their own capacities and resources for meeting development goals. IDA assistance can help lagging states access central government resources by creating development programs they can successfully implement. Because capacity-building takes time and *resources that the central government does not currently have, IDA's sustained development programs play a crucial role improving institutional capacity at the state level* (ibid., 8–9; emphasis added).

The note concluded, "IDA assistance will be essential, especially to leverage domestic spending and improve its effectiveness, thereby helping India – and the world as a whole – meet the MDGs" (ibid., 10). But nowhere did it mention the issue of India's graduation from IDA, let alone draw the explicit connection to the "other India" left behind by post-liberalization growth achievements in the most successful states.

It is worth noting that there does not appear to be any obstacle in the IDA charter to disaggregating a large country for prorated eligibility. To the contrary, Article I of the Articles of Agreement of IDA describes its purpose as "to promote economic development, increase productivity and thus raise standards of living in *the less developed areas of the world* included within the Association's membership… (cited in Shihata 1995: 374–5, emphasis added). (IBRD Article III, Section 4 similarly stipulates "The Bank may guarantee, participate in, or make loans to any member *or any political sub-division thereof*…").[22] Though the phrase "less developed areas" generally has been interpreted as synonymous with "less developed countries," it could in principle include lagging sub-national divisions of large, developmentally mixed countries.

There are also precedents for exceptions to the cutoff rule for IDA access. Beginning in the mid-1980s, IDA began an exception for "small island economies" whose per capita incomes were above the mark. Over the years almost a dozen micro-countries – Cape Verde, Dominica, Grenada, Kiribati, Maldives, Samoa, St. Kitts and Nevis, St. Lucia, St. Vincent and the Grenadines, Tonga, and Vanuatu – have benefited from this exception. In addition to the "small island exception," credit problems confronting other borrowers (such as Macedonia and Bolivia) have led to exceptions permitting IDA borrowing even after their incomes passed the cutoff mark. Apart from the obvious issue of scale, there is no reason why similar exceptions could not be applied to India's lagging states.

One potential objection to this approach may come from India itself. Given the lingering protectiveness toward India's economic sovereignty that New Delhi's recent policies on aid use have exhibited, it is not clear that Indian leaders would be comfortable with a state-wise prorated IDA eligibility arrangement. One Bank staff member suggested that given its strong predilection to control states' external borrowing, New Delhi might not like the symbolism of "disaggregating India" in the context of such a high-level governance process of the World Bank.[23] Interviews with Indian DEA officials in 2008 suggest that this is probably an accurate assessment. But there is no substantive reason why this should be the case, or why it should have repercussions for India's treatment in other global governance settings. And as the evolution of the Bank's state-level engagement has shown, there is little risk of New Delhi losing control over the states' relationships with the Bank.

From the perspective of the donor countries, a broader impediment to such a major restructuring of the IDA eligibility criteria might be that, presumably, what was offered to India also would have to be offered to other Bank borrowers. As if India were not already the elephant in the IDA pool, what would it mean to have some of its most populous states remain – only to be joined by poor regions of other countries that had already graduated IDA? Would recently re-graduated Indonesia, for example, send some of its poor provinces back?

The impact might not be as great as imagined. For example, middle-income Brazil, which has never been an IDA borrower, is famous for its regional income inequality. But even its poorest Northeastern states, such as Piauí, would not qualify for IDA under an operational cutoff comparable to the current IDA15 level. The biggest question mark would be for China, where Guizhou and some other provinces might be eligible for IDA under a prorated allocation, depending on where the cutoff was drawn. But it is not clear that China would care very much to come back to IDA, more than a decade after graduating (and more recently, becoming a donor). Moreover, the political economy context of regional disparity in China differs significantly from that of federal, democratic India.

Thus, India could pursue a new IDA allocation regime that serves its own stated developmental goals for its lagging states, while framing this self-interest in the context of a transformed aid regime that embraces the challenge of sub-national poverty in the giants of the developing world (even drawing attention to the issue in rival China). Self-interest wrapped in a broader advocacy for the less developed countries has been a hallmark of India's foreign policy for decades, and the IDA regime is an area where its assertiveness could make a significant impact.

The plight of India's lagging states – and of concentrated sub-national backwardness generally – is almost invisible in high-level multilateral talks about global poverty reduction, including the triennial IDA replenishment dialogue. If it is remarkable that donor countries should ask why India would need IDA, it is in part because for all the talks on aid and poverty reduction in recent years, the conversation remains two-dimensional – dominated largely by the related focuses on Africa and debt relief. Nor do transnational activists and NGOs devote nearly the same energy to the cause of poverty in India as in Africa. Bihar does not have Western celebrities sounding the alarm on its development emergency.

But it is also because Indian leaders themselves have gone out of their way not to disabuse global observers of a somewhat superficial view of economic change in India, so as not to threaten the image of a rising great power. India's recent growth surge has only intensified pressure on the Bank from donor countries to graduate India out of IDA. And though India would benefit from continued access to IDA, officials in New Delhi are seemingly content to allow this to happen – a passive stance in the guise of a proud aid policy.

India's leadership has always looked to the day when the country would assume its rightful place among the great powers. Despite significant political change and the evolution of a broad consensus in favor of economic liberalization, Indian leaders are as defensive of India's sovereignty and policy autonomy today as ever; indeed, the recent growth and international recognition has created an "exaggerated self-confidence" in India's statecraft (Ganguly and Pardesi 2007). New Delhi's great power aspirations and prideful-to-a-fault aid diplomacy have led to a pervasive dissonance in global perceptions of India's economic picture.

This discussion would be merely academic if *India itself* had not asked the Bank to deepen its engagement with its lagging states. Indian officials are entirely aware of the incongruity that an "IDA without India and India without IDA" would present, especially at this juncture. But remarkably, even though the power to pursue continued IDA access is concentrated among a relatively small cadre of Indian officialdom – in the finance ministry in New Delhi, and in the office of India's Executive Director at the Bank in Washington – there appears to be no consensus as to what India's position on its own graduation should be.

For some, the topic is a source of pride. There is also a sense that IDA's global importance would be diminished if it stopped aiding India. M. Naga Raju, Director for the finance ministry's DEA Fund-Bank Division, asked rhetorically, "If IDA is not lending to India, then what is its contribution?" (2008) – almost daring the Bank to make the eligibility case on India's behalf. A former DEA official suggested that India should still pursue access to IDA, but should undertake strategic maneuvering *now*, to prepare for the coming intensification of donor pressure to graduate. "Let there be no talk of 'graduation' until at least 2015," he maintained. He suggested that India should become a simultaneous borrower *and* donor to IDA, following its recent IMF contributor status, and in line with its dual donor/recipient identity in other aid institutions such as the International Fund for Agricultural Development (a specialized UN agency, where the official now happened to work; Tewari 2008). Becoming a donor even as it continued to draw on IDA resources, he suggested, would send a powerful signal about India's external capabilities but also about the value it placed on IDA and the Bank for helping it to address continuing internal challenges of development. But Naga Raju dismissed this suggestion, maintaining that India had "no interest" in becoming an IDA donor (2008).

There is a feeling in New Delhi – both in the finance ministry and at the Bank – that the issue is more important to the Bank than it is to India. "India's attitude toward the IDA dialogue has been, 'We can take it or leave it'," said a Bank senior economist. "India doesn't really need it. The bigger question is for IDA, and for the Bank if India graduates IDA" (Dasgupta 2008). Naga Raju concurred: "We are not dependent on the Bank. If it is available, we'll take it. But, it is a very small amount of money" (2008).

Indian officials seem content to be pulled along by the thread that IDA graduation would weave into the "great power" tapestry they wish to display. They fully recognize India's financial interest in continued access to soft loans, and the special value that IDA assistance represents in supporting the lagging states. Still, they appear content to play a waiting game with the Bank: since the loss of the "blend" status for India could have knock-on effects for the Bank's entire business model, they are prepared to let the Bank make the first move. Why should they grovel for aid if the Bank will do it for them? Certainly, the Indian government has no interest in presenting itself as an aid supplicant.

One problem with this view is that it does not appreciate how hard it would be for the Bank alone to make the case for India's continued IDA access, when India itself has so thoroughly cultivated the impression that it has "arrived." Witness Fareed Zakaria's description of India's decadent public relations campaign at the 2006 conference of the World Economic Forum in Switzerland:

> In the twelve years that I've been going to Davos, no country has so captured the imagination of the conference or dominated the conversation as India did in 2006 [...]
>
> As you got off the plane in Zurich, you saw large billboards extolling *Incredible India!* The town of Davos itself was plastered with signs. "World's Fastest Growing Free Market Democracy," proclaimed the local buses. When you got to your room, you found a pashmina shawl and an iPod

shuffle loaded with Bollywood songs, gifts from the Indian delegation. When you entered the meeting rooms, you were likely to hear an Indian voice, one of dozens of CEOs of world-class Indian companies in attendance. And then there were the government officials, India's "Dream Team" – all intelligent and articulate, and all intent on selling their country. The forum's main social event was an Indian extravaganza, with a bevy of Indian beauties dancing to the pulsating rhythms of Hindi tunes against an electric blue Taj Mahal. The impeccably dressed chairman of the forum, Klaus Schwab, donned a colorful Indian turban and shawl, nibbled on chicken tikka, and talked up the country's prospects with Michael Dell. *India Everywhere* said the logo. And it was (2008: 130–1).

As similarly ebullient Indian campaigns have rolled through international capitals and financial centers, is it any wonder that rich countries are again raising questions about India's need for IDA aid?

If the Bank itself were to advocate for an exception to maintain IDA access for India, it would be a significant enough precedent that it would likely require the sponsorship of the Bank's president; self-serving staff advocacy probably would not move donors. While it is only conjecture, Jim Wolfensohn might have been the Bank leader to make this case. Shortly before his departure in 2005, in an op-ed for *The Times of India*, Wolfensohn recognized the emergence of "two Indias," and the significance for global poverty efforts:

When I think of India, I see a civilisational force that can and must be a voice of weight and reason on the global stage. The international community is already recognizing India's potential to play this role [...]

But when I think of India, I also see a very critical role for this country in a much more immediate fight – the global fight against poverty. The simple fact is that the world cannot win this fight if India does not win it. Despite the impressive gains made by India in the assault on poverty in the last two decades, more than a quarter of India's one billion people are still below the official poverty line; that amounts to more than 250 million people, about a quarter of all the worlds' poor, living here in India (Wolfensohn 2005: 517).

Paul Wolfowitz and Robert Zoellick, Wolfensohn's successors, are more conservative (in disposition as well as in economic ideology), and have weathered a rough patch in Bank-India relations, as we will see in the concluding chapter. (A Wolfowitz loan cancellation so irritated India that it threatened to pull out of the Bank, leaving the more genial Zoellick to engage in repair efforts after the former's disgraced resignation in 2007). Wolfowitz placed a high priority on aid for Africa and post-conflict states, and seemed ready to hasten India's transition to middle-income status. At the World Bank-IMF annual meetings in Singapore in 2006, he told Indian journalists – incorrectly – that India was "going toward smaller levels of World Bank lending," and stressed that the Bank's main contribution was technical assistance ("The Future of World Bank in India" 2006). Zoellick, for his part, already appears to think of India in middle-income terms, judging by comments at the 2009 Bank-Fund spring meetings in Washington: "India may be a country a little bit like Brazil, where we could probably help with infrastructure investments that would both put people to work and deal with some of the growth bottlenecks for the next stage of India's growth." He made no mention of IDA specifically, but did suggest,

> Over time – and I do stress "over time" – it will be helpful for India to look for ways where it can help other developing countries, and this may be in direct resources, indirect resources. And if we are thinking about building a sturdy multilateral system for the future, we should also look for the growing developing economies to contribute to some of their poor neighbors (Zoellick 2009).

Clearly, the suggestion was that India should become a donor. It should give more to poorer developing countries, not impinge on their share. Reportedly, Zoellick did press India to make a contribution to IDA15.[24] It did not. As noted, Indian officials are divided on this – presumably, not so much over whether they should become a donor, but rather when and how. But India could also make a "contribution" to IDA in the form of a serious proposal for reform of its allocation. And it could do more to assist global poverty reduction efforts by looking out for its own lagging states than by contributing to the hat pass for Africa.

## Toward a Debate Worthy of India's Democracy

Another problem with Indian officialdom's seeming indifference to IDA graduation is that there has been almost no broader debate on the issue in India. A few officials are steering – or rather, letting drift along – a policy that could have implications for millions of India's people, particularly in the lagging states. Besides being a strangely inert response to donor country pressures to graduate – do Indian officials really think it enhances their country's prestige if the Bank submits to donor demands while India sits silent? – it is an undemocratic arrogation of bureaucratic power not to solicit a more open discussion of India's interest in IDA. Even though the Centre is constitutionally empowered to manage the states' external borrowing, the insulated decision-making on this issue seems not to serve India's own developmental interests – as the government itself has defined them through the lagging states emphasis. Likely, the issue will get a broader hearing at some point. The question is whether it will come too late.

As noted in Chapter Two, India's states lobbied the Centre for years to pass on external assistance to the states on "back-to-back" terms, so that they might realize the full cost benefit of an IDA grant (the Centre's policy was to pass on World Bank and other external assistance on 70:30 loan-to-grant basis). Only in 2005, after the Twelfth Finance Commission weighed in with a recommendation supporting the states' position, did the Centre agree to "back-to-back" on-lending terms (with the caveat that the states themselves bear the foreign exchange risk; the Bank's loans are dollar-denominated).

Having fought to realize the full cost benefit of IDA borrowings, the states are unlikely to let the graduation issue pass without opposition; what central officials regard as a trifling issue, the states might care much more about. State-level finance officials are sophisticated enough to see the writing on the wall, and central officials interviewed in 2008 conceded that some states were beginning to raise questions about IDA. But there had been no systematic discussion involving state leaders. The states will likely resent in the extreme the hubris of a few officials in New Delhi in Washington, who would hold open the door while donors pushed India out of IDA, in the belief that doing so somehow burnished India's great power prestige. And it likely would not be only the lagging states – the ones most directly impacted by losing IDA, under the Bank's assistance strategy – that would object. The richer and less aid-dependent states might prefer to see their poorer neighbors continue to tap IDA, to somewhat reduce the burden they seem them imposing on India's fiscal federalism. Already, there are tensions between richer states that want more central transfers on account of their better fiscal management, and poorer states that want more money to compensate for lack of resources and private investment.

Besides state-level interest, there is remarkably little public discussion in India of the IDA graduation issue. A rare exception is N.K. Singh, a former Indian Administrative Service official who has held numerous central and state-level posts (including in the DEA's Fund-Bank Division) and frequently contributes a column to *The Indian Express*. Even in late 2004, as Chidambaram prepared to attend the annual IMF-World Bank meetings in Washington for the first time since returning to the finance ministry earlier that year, Singh offered a list of advice, including the warning,

The resources of the International Development Assistance (popularly known as IDA) remains rather meagre as we move from the XIII to the

XIV replenishment cycle. Attempts to cap India's access at modest levels or worse to graduate us out of IDA resources must be firmly resisted. Higher growth rates of the 1990s have certainly brought down the incidence of poverty to say 19% or 22% or some other figure depending on the preferred methodology. In absolute terms, however, given our population, the number of people living below the poverty line still remains very large. India clearly qualifies to receive IDA resources and we can assure the international community that given our improved disbursement procedures, the head-room for IBRD/ IDA or a blend that is available would be more fully utilized (2004).

On the other hand, S. Venkitaramanan, another former IAS officer and 18th Governor of the Reserve Bank of India (at the time of the 1991 liberalization), wrote in *The Hindu* in 2006 that "India must kick the World Bank habit" altogether – end borrowing from both IDA and IBRD – and no doubt there would be others who would agree, if for very different reasons. In the book's conclusion, we will see the context in which Venkitaramanan offered this suggestion: in fact, India may have come close to severing ties with the World Bank altogether, in a particularly stormy episode during the ill-fated Wolfowitz presidency.

In 2007, there was an important step toward a broader dialogue about the future of India's relationship with the Bank, when a number of civil society organizations convened the Independent People's Tribunal on the World Bank in India. The Tribunal, held over a long weekend at Jawaharlal Nehru University in New Delhi, brought over 200 "deponents" to give "testimony" on the impact of Bank policies and programs to a "jury" comprised of interdisciplinary scholars, several former justices (including a former Supreme Court of India justice), a former Indian government official who had represented the country in international trade talks, and celebrity activists including the ubiquitous Arundhati Roy (the Bank itself declined to participate, saying it "did not agree with the format of a 'tribunal' established with juries and judged to 'try' the Bank"; World Bank 2007d).

Unfortunately, this looks to have been the kind of event where the outcome was all but predetermined. After hearing almost uniformly negative testimonies – selected precisely to be so – about the Bank's impact in India, the 13-panel jury submitted,

> Our conclusion based on these testimonies is that the majority of World Bank sponsored projects do not serve their stated purpose, nor do they benefit the poor of India. Instead in many cases, they have caused grievous and irreversible damage to those they intend to serve. The evidence we

have heard adds up to a disturbing picture of the World Bank's underlying agenda and operations, as it benefits those privileged with capital but pushes to despair the already vulnerable. We recommend that the World Bank should compensate those it has harmed gravely through its policies, projects, and neglect in carrying out its own environmental and social safeguards. Unless there are instituted clear and transparent mechanisms through which World Bank activities and policies can be independently monitored and audited, it would be better for the World Bank to quit operations in India.

From the testimonies a pattern became visible. The World Bank does not act in isolation. It has worked in collaboration with the other international financial institutions, as well as with the private sector agendas from powerful nations, in perpetuating an economic system that has benefitted these stakeholders disproportionately, almost invariably at the cost of the poor.

Additionally, we find the Indian government an equally responsible party in perpetrating this state of affairs. It became apparent in the course of these deliberations that in India now there is little difference between the thinking of its policy makers and the World Bank. We hold the Indian government equally responsible and call for a reversal of its policies (2008: 23).

The Bank, as this book has amply demonstrated, has committed numerous errors of judgment in its operations in India over the years. But this group of critics got the relationship exactly backwards: the Indian government, at this point, is by far the stronger power. If there is little policy difference between India and the Bank, it is not because the Bank has imposed its agenda on India – or even because of the "revolving door" that shuttles senior Indian officials back and forth between New Delhi and the Bretton Woods institutions – but because India's leaders have embraced the market. They have embraced it on their own terms, and both Indian leaders and the World Bank understand that it is for the Bank to reconcile to India's terms if it wishes to remain relevant. The perspective on the World Bank embodied in this Tribunal event is so outdated it can hardly be taken seriously, despite its grave tone.

At least one Independent Tribunal panelist seemed to have sensed this, however, demonstrating that strong opposition to the Bank's philosophy is not incompatible with a realistic perspective on the Bank's role in India's liberalization and the balance of power in the Bank-India relationship. Ramaswamy R. Iyer – a former government official and research professor at the Centre for Policy Research in New Delhi, who had helped investigate the

Sardar Sarovar Project in the early 1990s (see Chapter One) – submitted a lengthy qualification to the jury's conclusion. For its uncommon common sense, it is worth quoting in full:

> I am neither an apologist for the World Bank nor a believer in neo-liberal economic philosophy. I have no disagreement with the [Independent Tribunal] Report on its findings of serious adverse effects on the country, and in particular on the poor, of various economic policies and programmes. However, I find it necessary to qualify my endorsement of the report with the following observations.
>
> First, I do not see why we should ask the World Bank to quit. *It is as much our bank as any other country's. India has contributed to its funds. If we feel that it is too much under American control, we must try to fight that control rather than let go of the WB.*
>
> Secondly, the policies that all of us criticize – SEZ [Special Economic Zones], alienation of good agricultural land, giving of large areas of land to the corporates, agricultural policies that lead to farmers' suicides, development policies that marginalise the poor further, urban renewal policies that drive the poor out of their homes and livelihoods, dam projects that displace large numbers of people, the privatisation of utilities and water, the dilution of environmental clearance processes or coastal zone policies in the interest of domestic and foreign industrial/commercial investment, and so on – are the policies of our elected governments, Central and State, including 'communist' governments such as West Bengal. They have adopted those policies not necessarily at the bidding of the World Bank, but because they – and many in academia, the media and the intelligentsia – subscribe to neo-liberal economic thinking. There are many who sincerely believe that this is the right path, and that those who oppose it are wrong. That is where the fight – a difficult one – lies.
>
> I am aware that the World Bank and IMF have been criticised even by some of their own former officials for prescribing standard Structural Adjustment Programmes to a number of hapless countries and causing all kinds of problems. *India, however, is not a weak or small country that can be bullied by the WB or IMF. If the Government of India adopts certain policies, it cannot be allowed to say that it did so under the pressure of the World Bank; it must take the responsibility for its decisions.*
>
> Thirdly, capitalism (including its neo-liberal form), was not invented by the World Bank. It is the dominant economic philosophy of the world today. Not merely America but even China and Russia subscribe to that philosophy. Globalisation, liberalisation, privatization – these are the

widely proclaimed slogans of today. Challenging that philosophy, and not just demonising the World Bank, is what we need to do.

I am not saying that the WB should be absolved of all guilt. It can be criticized if it goes beyond the call of duty in promoting its official philosophy and tries to arm-twist a member country into adopting certain policies or taking certain actions against its inclinations. It can also be criticised if individual officials of the World Bank throw their weight about or hector and bully the officials or politicians of a member country. For instance, the World Bank's advocacy of the privatisation of water services often amounts to pressure; and its Delhi office certainly seemed to show undue interest in seeing Price Waterhouse Cooper selected as consultant to the Delhi Jal Board for the reorganisation of its water-supply activities. There is also reason to believe that in 2000–01 the World Bank worked actively to sabotage the Report of the World Commission on Dams. In other words, we can blame the WB not for making certain recommendations or advocating certain policies, or even for stipulating certain conditions, but for carrying its 'persuasion' too far, applying pressure and arm-twisting. That distinction is not adequately made in the Report (2008: 24–5; emphasis added).

This is the kind of contribution that a serious debate on India's relationship with the World Bank deserves. The World Bank *is* as much India's as anyone's. If there is a broader internal consensus that India should part ways with IDA or even with Bank borrowing altogether, then it should do so. But if it does remain a Bank borrower, and if it wants to see a special Bank engagement in the likes of Bihar and UP, then it makes sense to find a way for these states to be able to borrow on IDA terms – whatever other reforms its many critics would like to impose on it.

In the world's largest democracy, should these questions be left to a handful of unelected officials? India is running out of time to hold this kind of broader discussion – which would need to include state-level leaders and a balanced representation of civil society perspectives. The next IDA replenishment talks get underway in 2010, and will decide the principles governing the fund's allocation into 2014. If India does not take ownership of the IDA issue for its lagging states – this time getting out in front of the inevitable donor impulse to graduate the country *in toto* – then the outcome likely will be a *fait accompli* graduation at some point in the next few years. If Indian leaders choose to look at this outcome as a badge of honor, then that is their prerogative. But it is doubtful that millions of India's poor would see it that way, or even that the ephemeral celebration of an arbitrary milestone – entry into the World Bank's "middle-income" crowd – would do much for India's international prestige or seriously bolster its case for more representative global governance institutions. A non-event with lasting financial implications, even if relatively modest ones for India, seems like a dubious accomplishment.

India has already impressed the world with its economic growth. Should it not embrace the principles of equity and non-discrimination that have guided its foreign policy for over 60 years? The poor in Bihar and Uttar Pradesh should have as much right to benefit from IDA as the poor in Benin and Uganda. If they are invisible to donor governments, it is the fault of the donors themselves and the transnational activist community as much as India's swaggering self-image. But the primary responsibility for presenting a more balanced picture to the world rests with India, and in so doing India could help to transform the very architecture of World Bank assistance – surely a more meaningful accomplishment.

## Chapter Five

# COMMENCEMENT: INDIA'S CHANGING RELATIONSHIP TO GLOBAL DEVELOPMENT ASSISTANCE

## Weathering the Latest Storm

Paul Wolfowitz picked the wrong fight. The former US Deputy Secretary of Defense, a key figure behind the George W. Bush administration's decision to go to war in Iraq in 2003, was always going to be a controversial tenth president of the World Bank Group when he succeeded James Wolfensohn in June 2005. Like his predecessor, Wolfowitz resolved that fighting corruption would be a top priority for the Bank under his leadership. This would set him up for charges of rank hypocrisy when, just two years later, he was forced to resign amid a personal ethics scandal[1] and widespread opposition from Bank managers (DeYoung and Kamen 2007).

But well before his presidency ended on that sour note, Wolfowitz committed a key tactical error by provoking an unnecessary crisis in the Bank's relationship with India. In 2005, Wolfowitz unilaterally suspended a loan for a major health project in India – US$850 million for the second phase of an ongoing Reproductive and Child Health (RCH-II) project – in response to allegations of fraud and corruption in the procurement process (Padmanabhan 2006). Summing up the significance and the boldness of the move, Sebastian Mallaby wrote in *The Washington Post*, "This is a vast sum, and India is one of the bank's most formidable clients: It borrows a lot, has a good economic record and tells development organizations to get lost if they behave condescendingly. But Indian politicians were said to have their hands on the health funds, so Wolfowitz blocked the loans anyway" (Mallaby 2006). The Bank also put several other health projects in India on hold in early 2006, and suspended components of an unrelated urban transport project in Maharashtra over concerns related to the resettlement and rehabilitation of displaced residents ("Maharashtra" 2006).

The financial impact of these decisions was noteworthy: in the fiscal year immediately preceding Wolfowitz's arrival, the Bank had approved a then-record US$2.9 billion in new lending, whereas in the year following his arrival the volume dropped to US$1.1 billion (Padmanabhan 2006). The fallout for the Bank-India relationship would have less to do with money, however, than with the Bank's decision-making process, and its president's perceived disrespect of the Indian government. The tip-off about corruption in the predecessor RCH project had reportedly come through an Indian NGO (ibid., 2006), and the Bank's Department of Institutional Integrity undertook an investigation. The Government of India was aware of the inquiry, but was taken aback by Wolfowitz's decision to pull RCH-II from consideration by the Bank's Executive Board after the internal investigation found "grave" problems – including bribery, collusion, and fraud – in the first phase of the project. (The Integrity unit's report was not made public, but the editorial page of *The Wall Street Journal*, which supported Wolfowitz's decision, eventually posted a leaked copy) ("World Bank Corruption" 2007). Tensions over the decision were widely reported in the international news media. Michael Carter, the Bank's Country Director for India at the time of the loan suspensions, told America's National Public Radio that Wolfowitz and his inner circle had engaged in "no consultations" over the health project loans with Bank staff in New Delhi, and that he believed that the management's handling of the issue was "seriously flawed" (Gjelten 2007).[2] Carter eventually resigned, and was one of 42 former Bank managers who signed an open letter, published in the *Financial Times*, calling for Wolfowitz's resignation to prevent the institution's "credibility" from becoming "fatally compromised" ("Text of World Bank Letter" 2007).

According to interviews with Bank staff and Indian officials in New Delhi, the unilateral, top-down approach risked seriously undermining the sense of "partnership" that the Bank and India had worked to establish over the previous decade. The insularity of the decision-making process made it difficult even for Bank staff to understand exactly what transpired between the Bank president and senior Indian officials, but the *Financial Times* reported that according to Indian officials, Minister of Finance P. Chidambaram had "considered cutting ties" with the Bank to protest the perceived affront (Guha and Yee 2007). Even if the story is apocryphal, it says much about how the Bank-India relationship looks from inside the Indian government. Chidambaram sent a "firm note" to Wolfowitz in April 2006, urging him to avoid "further strain" in the relationship between the Bank and India, and explicitly asking the Bank not to link the review of health sector projects to assistance for the Mumbai Urban Transport Project (Dhoot and Ranjan 2006).

As in past discordant episodes in the Bank-India relationship, the government indicated that it was prepared to proceed with the projects in question with or without the support of the Bank. A senior finance ministry official told

*India Today*, "It is not the money. We are capable of funding the [RCH-II] project [...] from other sources, but we are keen to clear our position." The magazine suggested, "It is probably for the first time in 62 years that the relationship between India and the World Bank has soured to this extent" (Padmanabhan 2006). This might have been an overstatement – given the depth of antipathy over, say, the 1966 devaluation debacle, or the Narmada imbroglio of the early 1990s – but Wolfowitz's decision-making did demonstrate a disregard for India's clear trajectory of diminished aid dependency and improved growth prospects, for the major improvement in strategic relations between India and the US that was underway at the time,[3] and most importantly, for the Bank's decade-long effort at enhancing its relevance in India and the country's importance in the Bank's global portfolio and operations.

Wolfowitz's intention may have been to send a clear signal that the Bank under his leadership would show no tolerance for corruption, but his inept handling of issue proved self-defeating. He even managed to offend Britain, whose DFID aid agency was a partner on the Indian health program and had been satisfied by steps taken by the Indian government to add new project safeguards, but still was unable to move the Bank president to resume assistance. (Reportedly, this strained Wolfowitz's relationship with the British development minister, Hilary Benn, and ensured that his patron, Chancellor of the Exchequer and future Prime Minister Gordon Brown, would not support the beleaguered president's efforts to stay on at the Bank in 2007) (Weisman 2007). The episode created an unnecessary and largely negative public spectacle for the Bank, and Indian officials were more adept than Wolfowitz and his inner circle at managing public perceptions. C.M. Vasudev, India's previous Executive Director[4] to the Bank, protested, "There is no justification for holding up RCH-II on account of some misdeeds in the preceding project, especially since the Indian Government has assured the Bank that the guilty will be punished. Ultimately, the people, who are the potential beneficiaries, will suffer" (ibid., 2006). The last point might have been gratuitous, especially if India intended to carry on with or without the Bank's help on the project, but Wolfowitz had inadvertently handed Indian leaders an opportunity to demonstrate such righteous indignation – whether or not it was deserved.

The rift with India also made it difficult to secure its leaders' support for the Bank's broader "governance and anti-corruption" drive. Wolfowitz attempted to make this agenda the focal point of the Bank-IMF meetings in September 2006, but ended up in an "embarrassing climbdown" when leading finance ministers on the Bank's Board of Governors asserted that the Bank's Executive Board would maintain careful oversight of the president's initiatives

(Duncan 2006). But even this reassurance left India and some other borrower countries disgruntled at the process, threatening to finally crack their already eroding support for the Bank's US-centric governance pattern. Chidambaram was a particularly vocal critic at the conference, telling *The Times* of London, "Development cannot wait for improved governance and a corruption-free world. Both must go hand in hand" (ibid., 2006). (Around this same time, according to a former World Bank official, China informed the Bank that it was considering stopping its borrowing because the Wolfowitz Bank was "exceeding its mandate" by pursuing the anti-corruption agenda with such zealotry) (Phillips 2009: 131, note 27).

The Bank president eventually may have recognized his botched handling of the Bank-India relationship. In an April 2006 interview with *India Today* he sounded conciliatory notes, saying that he "would not like to bracket India" alongside countries like Chad and Congo on the issue of corruption. He went on to explain,

> I would like to put this issue in a better context. India's development record over the past 15 years has been spectacular. It has brought an incredible improvement in the lives of the poorest. It has made India the envy of many other countries in terms of its hi-tech and advanced economic activity. It is providing inspiration to the countries that have been told that the only way to develop is through dictatorial rule. India is the biggest demonstration that one can have a pluralistic democratic society and still bring in development. So, if we have problems in one or two of the 63 projects, people ought to see it in that context. It is not the Bank's fight. It is India's fight. We are both concerned about it and are looking at solving this (ibid., 2006).

The framework of a shared Bank and Indian fight against corruption would provide a basis for fence mending, but the repair work would take place mostly after the embattled Wolfowitz's departure. Ultimately, the health projects corruption issue would become so embarrassing for both sides that it made sense to lower tensions and work together to contain the public fallout. The problems in the RCH-II project, and allegations of similar fraud, collusive contractor practices, and official corruption in other health sector projects in India, prompted the Bank's Department of Institutional Integrity in 2006 to open up a wide-ranging investigation into five Bank-supported projects spanning 1997 to 2003. It was the largest investigation the department had ever undertaken. Separately but concurrently, in February 2007, Wolfowitz and the executive board asked an independent panel, chaired by former US Treasury Secretary Paul Volcker, to review the work of the Integrity department in the context of its contribution to the Bank's Governance and Anticorruption strategy. The Volcker panel's fairly critical report was released in September (Volcker 2007).

The Integrity department's Detailed Implementation Review (DIR) was made public in early 2008. It found serious problems in five Bank-assisted health projects, representing a total investment of about US$570 million. Indian officials had given preferential treatment to certain bidders for government contracts, sharing bid estimates and technical specifications with bidders and failing to provide justification for the award of contracts. Some bidders submitted patently fraudulent documents, and there was collusion between major corporate contractors such as BASF and Bayer to split or rotate contracts and to inflate prices. Some NGO contractors turned out to be fictional or to exist only to create fraudulent invoices. Most damning for the Indian government, officials in charge of project supervision had submitted false completion reports for project activities that were incomplete or exhibited known major deficiencies. Most damning for the Bank, the DIR found that its own systems for project design, supervision, and evaluation had failed to prevent and address egregious corruption (Department of Institutional Integrity 2007; Wierzynska 2008).

The human cost of the wide-ranging problems was clear. In one US$194 million AIDS project, companies reportedly had provided HIV test kits that gave erroneous or invalid results. Some of the worst offenses occurred in the US$82 million Orissa Health Systems Development Project. As noted in the previous two chapters, Orissa has been one of the Bank's partner states through both the "focus states" and "lagging states" phases of sub-national engagement. Generally, the Bank has regarded its administration as comparatively competent and clean. But many of the 55 hospitals connected to the project exhibited appalling conditions: raw sewage exposure, leaky roofs, crumbling concrete, moldy walls, non-functional water and electrical systems. In one case, an improperly grounded piece of neonatal equipment risked exposing infants and medical personnel to electrical shocks.

By the time of the report's release, Wolfowitz had been succeeded by Zoellick, who pursued a damage-control strategy, emphasizing that the Bank and the Indian government took seriously "the unacceptable indicators of fraud and corruption" in the health projects and had "joined forces" to mount a vigorous response. This would result in an Action Plan, which dutifully promised new safeguards and procedures to increase transparency and prevent fraud and corruption – and which reasonable skepticism might regard as adding to the "hassle factor," thus further decreasing the appeal of World Bank project loans for borrowers such as India, with uncertain effectiveness against corruption.

The reliably aid-skeptical *Wall Street Journal* editorial page weighed in on the scandal, under the headline "World Bank Disgrace." The paper continued to support Wolfowitz's confrontational approach toward the Indian government, saying he had "shown real spine" in the earlier RCH-II project intervention and lamenting that "lending to Indian health projects resumed the moment he departed last year." As for the new leadership, the paper opined, "Credit Robert Zoellick for knowing how to put the best face on a profound embarrassment." But it criticized Zoellick for not giving strong enough backing to Suzanne Rich Folsom, the Wolfowitz appointee who led the Department of Institutional Integrity during the DIR, in the face of opposition Bank staff. Instead, the *Journal* huffed, Zoellick had thrown his support behind Bank Managing Director Ngozi Okonjo-Iweala, whose public statements emphasized India's "strong resolve" to deal with corruption ("World Bank Disgrace" 2008). The Bank's press release that accompanied the publication of the DIR noted, "The Government of India will take the lead in pursuing indicators of wrongdoing that emerged in the DIR" (World Bank 2008c).

Behind the carefully parsed public declaration of a joint anti-corruption effort with India in the lead, there was still tension in the Bank-India relationship over the imbroglio. In March, ahead of an important Executive Board meeting to review the unpleasant findings, the Indian health ministry issued a report responding to the DIR, which conceded some of the findings but challenged others. A ministry official complained to the press that the "one sided" and "unfair" DIR was creating a mistaken impression that corruption and fraud were endemic to India's health sector, thus doing "incalculable damage to the credibility of successful disease control programmes" such as a national tuberculosis initiative. (Indeed, *Mint*, an Indian business newspaper, reported that some donors, including the Geneva-based Global Fund to Fight AIDS, Tuberculosis and Malaria, had become "jittery" over corruption in Indian health projects, and were closely watching events at the Bank).

The Bank leadership must have sensed the need to extend a larger olive branch. A Bank spokesman told *Mint* that the DIR "would have been a stronger document if GoI [Government of India] had been given an opportunity to provide its comments on the report before it was issued," but the Bank stood by the findings of serious fraud and corruption (Shrivastava 2008). The Executive Board commended India for a "constructive and swift" response to the allegations – a clear nod to the sovereignty-sensitive perspectives of India and other strong borrowers on the board. The Bank stressed that its own failings had "allowed possible indicators of wrongdoing to go unnoticed," and Zoellick reiterated the Bank's cooperative intentions going forward (Wroughton 2008). Ultimately, the Bank sounded the right conciliatory notes, and the two sides moved on.

The *Wall Street Journal* editorialists were not the only observers to criticize the Bank's efforts at assuaging India's indignation. *The Economist* cited Amir Attaran, a law professor and immunologist at the University of Ottawa, who suggested that Bank managers were too cozy with their clients in India to conduct a proper investigation: "This is a corrupt party investigating itself" ("Dirty Linen" 2008). Devesh Kapur, director of the Center for the Advanced Study of India at the University of Pennsylvania and a coauthor of a comprehensive history of the World Bank (Kapur, Lewis et al. 1995), offered this uncompromising censure:

> The revelations go beyond details of the specific programs, revealing more about the World Bank and India [...]
>
> Since the bank has made poverty its raison d'être and no country has more poor people than India, the two have obvious reasons for deep engagement. But the World Bank–India relationship is unique, stemming both from India being the bank's largest borrower and the perceived sophistication of Indian policymakers and their ability to articulate programs, as distinct from ability or willingness to implement them [...]
>
> If a country is unwilling to act vigorously on its own behalf in matters of primary education and health, that country is clearly uninterested and deserves little support from the international community. And if a country is unable to undertake these basic tasks, then the problem is much deeper [...]
>
> The abject failure of the Indian state to improve the quality of life of hundreds of millions of its citizens is as unconscionable as it is deeply rooted in the country's political economy. Any solution squarely lies there. Perhaps the biggest error the bank has made in India has been not to walk away earlier and realize that non-lending might serve the country – especially its poor – better (Kapur 2008).

The corruption exposed in the India health projects DIR was an outrage, and Kapur is right to suggest that its handling says much about the overall relationship between the World Bank and India. But the scandalous findings should be put in the broader context of that relationship, which has endured for 60 years and which encompasses a wide range of lending and non-lending interaction, across many developmental sectors and policy areas. The kind of corruption uncovered in the health projects DIR would exist in India's public sector even if the World Bank did not exist.

Is the Bank culpable when its staff looks the other way out of concern not to offend a most prized borrower? Certainly. But as we have seen, the Bank has worked hard to remain relevant in India over nearly two decades of economic liberalization, and it is understandable that many staff would not want to jeopardize what they perceive as significant progress toward a partnership that gives the Bank a closer engagement with the states, the key sub-national arenas of developmental policy in India today.

The example of Orissa illustrates why. As we have seen, it is one of India's very poorest states. Its public health sector was deeply implicated in the DIR findings of fraud and corruption. And yet, as we have also seen, the state government has effected one of the largest fiscal corrections in India between 2001 and 2006, a period partially overlapping with the transgressions in the health sector noted in the DIR. A decade ago, on the advice of the Bank, the state government undertook India's first privatization of a State Electricity Board – a reform that, though significantly flawed, required real resolve and a willingness on the part of its leaders to run political risks. Orissa's government has amassed a relatively strong record of fighting corruption, in spite of the documented abuses. The state's overall rate of economic growth has improved considerably from the 1990s; it has significantly outperformed poor peers such as Bihar. We cannot know what the state's achievements would have been without the Bank's financial, analytical, and advisory support. Certainly, the relationship with the Bank may have led to problems in some areas, such as the unsuccessful electricity reforms and the abetting of abuses in health projects. But on balance, it seems to have been a constructive relationship, and the Bank might be forgiven for wanting to maintain it.

### In Crisis, Opportunity or May You Live in Interesting Times

The confrontation between the World Bank and India over corruption in health projects offers a fitting episode with which to conclude this study, because its ultimate denouement indeed does say much about the Bank-India relationship. The Bank, under Wolfowitz's leadership, risked alienating one of its most important borrowers, almost to the point of losing it. It was not that Wolfowitz was wrong to take a hard line against corruption. Indeed, his predecessor, Wolfensohn, had tried to do much the same – with mixed results – but without provoking such a strong negative reaction from borrower governments and Bank staff. (This is not to say that Wolfensohn's agenda was entirely embraced, but his successor's reception was disastrous). The editorialists at *The Wall Street Journal* may be loath to admit it, but atmospherics are important in politics, and Wolfowitz simply had no credibility as a crusader against corruption. In part, this was because of his rank personal hypocrisy, given the ethical lapses in his personal affairs that eventually came to light. But the legitimacy deficit also stemmed from his unilateral decision-making style, and reflected the simple truth that many Bank member governments and staff saw him from the beginning – fairly or unfairly – as proxy for a US administration that they perceived as arrogant, incompetent, and contemptuous of multilateral institutions. The irony is that George W. Bush himself proved to be one of the most pro-India American presidents in history, advancing a major US-India nuclear agreement in cooperation with the Manmohan Singh government and deepening the "strategic partnership" between the world's two largest democracies. Wolfowitz simply failed to respect the Bank-India relationship, and by the time he realized his tactical error, it was too late.

Zoellick's rebuilding effort has been generally successful, suggesting that the relationship remains durable if occasionally contentious. The Bank and India have weathered rough patches before, and undoubtedly they will do so again. It is also revealing that though India reportedly considered cutting ties with the Bank over its treatment in the health sector corruption issue, Chidambaram's finance ministry evidently thought the better of it. It is one thing to make a fair point about the respect that India deserves as one of the Bank's founding members, and as a borrower with a generally good track record. But it would have been another thing entirely to precipitously end an engagement that has endured for so long, and which, on balance, still serves India's interests.

Recent developments in the global economy attest to the World Bank's continued relevance in a world very different from the one it was born into more than six decades ago – a world in which access to capital markets for developing countries has seen a heady two-decade expansion. But if the lesson had not been learned already in the Asian financial crisis of 1997–8, the new global financial crisis that began in 2008 serves as a harsh reminder that the availability of private capital to emerging markets may be subject to sudden shifts. There is still a role for a major public institution like the World Bank to offer continued access to development finance – even for, and especially for, a budding lower-middle income country like India, particularly in areas such as infrastructure investment. It is telling that India recently has led calls within the Group of Twenty (G20) major developed and developing countries for a significant expansion of the World Bank's capitalization, to avoid a contraction in its global lending (Mukul 2009). New Delhi has secured a Bank pledge to greatly expand lending to India over the next three years, including funding for major infrastructure initiatives and recapitalizing state banks (Reuters 2009; Sharma 2009).

Even Indian observers who just a few years ago crowed about India's financial independence and asserted that it had little use for the Bank, have taken note of the major assistance push over the past year. Former Reserve Bank of India (RBI) Governor S. Venkitaramanan, who wrote in 2006 that "India must kick the World Bank habit" altogether – "Withdrawing from the World Bank is the proper response to the hyperactive do-gooders at

Washington, who are trying to mould the world's governments in their self-perceived perfect image" (Venkitaramanan 2006) – wrote approvingly of the single-day announcement of US$4.3 billion in new loans for India in September 2009:

> The World Bank's initiative is a vote of support to the stimulus programme of the Government for further economic growth. The substantial relief offered in regard to the borrowing requirements of the Government through this loan would mean a reduction in pressure on domestic resources. This will lessen the crowding-out impact of the hefty Government borrowing from domestic sources. The monetary authority, the RBI, which is managing the borrowing requirements of the Government should perhaps heave a sigh of relief [...]
>
> There is a strong pro-India feeling in the World Bank hierarchy even at present, perhaps because of the increasing economic strength of this country. The World Bank's pro-India attitude continues to be robust. This indicates the Government's success in convincing the World Bank and US Administration of the nature of its just demands. It is obvious that this is due to India's strong record of good governance and sound economic management during the recent decades (Venkitaramanan 2009).

In simple terms, for the Bank's relevance to its largest borrower, the global financial crisis has been good for business. In the thirteen months spanning October 2008 to October 2009, the Bank's board has approved a record US$8.14 billion in new lending for India – more than double the recent annual loan volume. According to press reports, the Bank envisions US$14 billion in infrastructure investment (about US$9.6 billion in IBRD loans and US$4.4 billion in IDA credits), focusing especially on India's poorest states, over the next three years (Rangan and Goyal 2008). In a single day in September 2009, the board approved US$4.3 billion – a sum comparable to the entire annual assistance volume that had been envisioned in the 2008 Country Assistance Strategy, before the crisis. The biggest-ticket loans so far have been a Banking Sector Support Loan (US$2 billion), a "public-private partnership" loan to support India Infrastructure Finance Company Limited (IIFCL) (US$1.2 billion), and the national Fifth Power System Development Project (US$1 billion). There also have been major new project loans for Andhra Pradesh, Haryana, Madhya Pradesh, and UP, in addition to a multi-project package for Orissa that had just preceded the crisis-context lending push.

Apart from the impact on the Bank's assistance program in India, the crisis also has the potential to bring about significant rebalancing in global economic governance generally, and in the governance of the World Bank

Group in particular. This book has not been primarily about India's role in the Bank's governance, and it is still too early to assess what the long-term significance of the crisis will be. But recent developments portend potentially far-reaching changes.

The issue must be set in a broader context. If the World Bank did not already exist, something like it might well have been invented in response to the most serious crisis in the world economy since the Great Depression. But the World Bank, alongside other organizational pillars of global economic governance, does exist, which is part of the current challenge. Were it to be invented today, its power and decision-making structures probably would be quite different from those of an institution fashioned more than six decades ago (in the case of IBRD, or five decades in the case of IDA). India is far from the only major developing country that is calling for major changes in World Bank governance, though its voice is likely to be one of the most strident and influential.

In October 2009, a high-level external commission, led by former Mexican President Ernesto Zedillo, issued a report that saluted the Bank's response to the global crisis but urged major reforms in the institution's governance. Representing India on the eleven-member panel was Montek Singh Ahluwalia, Deputy Chairman of the Planning Commission; other countries and entities represented (by officials or former officials) included Brazil, China, Ghana, Goldman Sachs, Japan, the UK, the UN, and the WTO (World Bank 2009a).

In its Executive Summary, the report said that although the crisis has reaffirmed the World Bank Group's indispensability, its effectiveness is undermined by its hierarchical governance structures, in which the American and European roles remain too dominant and many member countries find too few opportunities for voice and participation. Interestingly, among other specific reform recommendations, the commission suggested *reducing* the size of the Board of Directors from 25 to 20 chairs, to create a more "compact, efficient, and effective" body and to reduce the significant "overrepresentation" of European countries on the board (currently, about a third of the body). In addition, the panel suggested abandoning the historical conventions that linked countries' IMF quotas with their shareholding and voting power in IBRD, as well as the gentlemen's agreement that has traditionally given the US the right to name the World Bank president and the Europeans the right to select the IMF head. (Reform of the Fund was not in the panel's purview, but it suggested that in important respects, the issues were inseparable). The Zedillo report stressed that the most urgent priorities were to expand the Bank's capital base in order to ensure adequate capacity to respond to the crisis, and to pursue a package of reform measures referred to collectively as "voice reform": Executive Board consolidation, the discontinuation of single-country appointed chairs in favor of all elected chairs representing multi-country constituencies, and a number of interlocking measures to reallocate voting power (Zedillo 2009).

It should be noted that at the September 2009 summit of the G20 countries in Pittsburgh – the third G20 meet since the onset of the crisis – world leaders committed to a number of global governance reforms, including a 3 percent reallocation of World Bank vote shares in favor of developing countries (bringing their total collective share to 47 percent), a pledge that was reaffirmed at the Bank-Fund Annual Meetings in Istanbul in early October (World Bank 2009b). But already, the Zedillo commission report has framed a far more ambitious agenda for Bank governance reform, and we are likely to witness more significant developments. Already, the Pittsburgh summit is being hailed as a major turning point, not least because world leaders agreed that going forward, the G20 will be the new permanent council for international economic cooperation, largely supplanting the G8 (which excluded major emerging markets).

In Istanbul, the Indian finance minister, Pranab Mukherjee, offered a plenary address in which he announced, "Resistance to the overdue change will only detract from the legitimacy, credibility and effectiveness" of the international financial institutions. He warned, "The Fund and the Bank cannot emerge from the crisis unchanged. They have to enhance their legitimacy to perform their expanded roles and mandates effectively." Much of his address was focused on the IMF, for which Mukherjee advocated at least a 7–8 percent shift in quota shares in favor of developing countries, against a G20 commitment of 5 percent in Pittsburgh. With respect to the Bank, Mukherjee advocated at least a 6 percent vote share reallocation, double the G20 pledge. (Prime Minister Manmohan Singh in Pittsburgh had advocated a 7 percent reallocation for Bank votes shares, which would have taken the developing countries' collective share to over 50 percent; "China, India" 2009). Mukherjee also called for a fundamental reform of the methodology for determining vote shares, giving primacy to a country's economic weight measured in GDP at purchasing power parity (PPP) exchange rates ("India Pitches for Governance Reforms" 2009). Such a reform, which at the moment appears a rather remote possibility, would increase India's voting power tremendously.

So far, G20 talks have given a higher priority to the Bank's Bretton Woods sister, the IMF, than to the Bank. After the April 2009 G20 meet in London, which looked like a "jamboree" for the Fund, *The Economist* lamented that the Bank looked like the "forgotten sibling":

Since January Mr Zoellick has lobbied hard for Western governments to put aside a small fraction – 0.7% – of their stimulus packages to help fund programmes in poor countries. But though there was endorsement in the G20 communiqué for the bank's proposed "Vulnerability Framework", there was no hard cash. The IMF, however, emerged from the meetings with a promised tripling of its capital [...]

Some think that Mr Zoellick blundered by focusing on the vulnerability fund, rather than securing a lump sum at the summit. But that may be unfair. The bank is one of the multilateral development banks that will help disburse up to $100 billion of new lending promised by the G20. Mr Zoellick himself says the bank does not need new capital but he does emphasise the need to turn "commitments into tangible financial support".

The bigger issue is that poor countries, when it comes to access to funds, complain that they have been pushed even further down the global pecking order because of a problem that was not of their making. They fear that rich countries' debt problems will mean that less money is available for poor ones. The bank's economists reckon that the crisis could push 53m more people into extreme poverty in poor countries, but some of those countries feel the bank itself could help more and will make that point loudly ("Forgotten Sibling" 2009).

India has been one of those "loud" countries. Yet ironically, after an initial contraction in private investment, India has seen a flood of capital in recent months, as global investors have been attracted by its relatively strong growth: an annualized 6.1 percent in the second quarter of 2009, and projected 2010 growth second only to forecasts for China ("A World Apart" 2009; "Economic and Financial Indicators" 2009). For a country that has sought to carefully manage its capital markets throughout the course of its economic liberalization, embracing foreign investment while avoiding the potential rush of "hot money" will be a key challenge in coming years.

From India's perspective, there is a subtext to the calls for reform of global economic governance that is as much about international political competition as about economic need: beneath the common narrative of an overdue power shift from the global North to the global South, there are dimensions of South-South competition as well. An analysis of proposed Bank and IMF reforms in *Business Line*, an Indian financial daily, summed up the issue that preoccupies a large segment of India's strategic elites: "This could imply gains for India and China, which are being seen as the main gainers of the proposed change, but China is likely to gain more" ("China, India" 2009). This reality, of course, only befits China's greater economic weight, and the preoccupation is ultimately counterproductive. India will not soon lay legitimate claim to the same stake in global economic governance that China is beginning to assert, and to focus primarily on the formal dimensions of decision-making is to buy into rules that will inevitably favor China. India would do better to embrace the considerable power it already enjoys in its own large assistance program with the Bank, and to selectively engage on key broader issues – such as making the "lagging states" access case in the coming IDA16 replenishment talks – out of enlightened self-interest. Interestingly, another subtext to the present global power shift is a concern in some quarters that a greater role in global governance for major emerging markets such as China, India, and Brazil could lead to a marginalization of Africa. After the Pittsburgh G20 summit Tom Hart of the ONE campaign, the advocacy organization cofounded by Irish rock icon Bono of U2, cautioned,

> Moving from the G8 to the G20 is a seismic shift: it brings many more of the world's people to the table, but the new expanded world body must now start addressing the needs of the poorest countries, especially in Africa. For nearly a decade now, Africa has been squarely on the G8's agenda, even if delivery on their commitments has been mixed. During this transition time, African development must not fall through the cracks (Simmons 2009).

It is a safe bet that the ONE activists will be single-minded in their focus on expanding development assistance and debt relief for Africa when the IDA16 replenishment talks open. Are Indian officials prepared to make the case for lagging states like Bihar, Orissa, and Uttar Pradesh? In August 2008, just weeks before the bottom fell out of the global financial system, *The Times of India* carried a striking report on a new set of World Bank global poverty estimates, which suggested that fully one-third of the world's poor – defined as those living on less than US$1 a day – were Indian. Moreover, India's population contains an even higher proportion of the highly vulnerable – those living on less than US$2 a day – than sub-Saharan Africa. This is the global poverty that a campaign such as ONE – misleadingly monikered but highly effective in persuading donors – passes over in its singular focus on Africa, however great the continent's problems. If India does not make its case to the world, who will?

## Summary and Significance of Findings

This book has shown that there is much to learn from the evolution of the World Bank-India relationship, and particularly over the last 15 or so years, as sub-national engagement has emerged as a key pillar of the assistance strategy. The story that emerges has significance for lender and borrower alike, and for the political economy literature on development assistance, market reform, and states in the global economy.

This book's historical background chapter, "The First Half-Century: From Bretton Woods to India's Liberalization Era," established the context for understanding the World-Bank India relationship through the 1990s. This history showed how in many ways, India and the World Bank have grown up together. Yet it also made clear that for most of their shared six decades, the Bank has confronted significant challenges in terms of its influence on India's economic policies. Not long after India's independence, the country emerged as a leading borrower of the Bank, as the institution shifted its mission from postwar reconstruction to development assistance. As the Bank came to know India, and underwent transformations of its own, it also took a more critical view of some aspects of its *dirigiste* economic policies. As early as 1966 the Bank undertook an ill-fated experiment in policy-based lending to encourage liberalization in India – a full decade-and-a-half before the "structural adjustment" era that came to define the Bank in the 1980s. Chastened by reform backlash in this sovereignty-sensitive client, the Bank retreated from policy-based lending in India for long after, entering an awkward phase of expanded lending for Indian projects even as it became increasingly unsympathetic toward India's state-led and autarkic development model. India, for its part, demonstrated its willingness and capability to pursue alternative sources of developmental finance when it did not agree with the Bank's loan conditions. India's 1991 macroeconomic liberalization, while supported by stabilization and structural adjustment loans from the IMF and the Bank, proved to be something of a false start for the renewed relevance of the Bank.

Chapter Three, "Remaining Relevant: The Reform Strategy for an India of States," analyzed a major innovation in the Bank's country assistance strategy for India, beginning in the mid-1990s. The Bank resolved to disaggregate the large federal country, and to focus its assistance on India's lead reforming states with a view to encouraging powerful "demonstration effects" that would encourage non-reforming states to embrace similar changes in policies, institutions, and governance. From the Bank's perspective, this new strategy of "selectivity" was a concession to the maxim, "India is too big for the Bank," and a bid to remain engaged in the liberalization process. Essentially, the new "focus states" approach took structural adjustment lending to the sub-national level, and though the Bank also developed a similar concept for other large, federal borrowers – including Brazil, Mexico, Nigeria, and even Russia – the approach was most fully articulated and institutionalized in India, with Andhra Pradesh, Karnataka, and Uttar Pradesh comprising the initial group of focus states. Critically, however, India's central government was an integral partner – and saw itself as the senior partner – in the focus states strategy. In a "two-level game" strategy, New Delhi embraced the Bank's proposal for sub-national reform lending, since it would encourage state-level policy changes that the central government desired anyway, but could not bring about on its own. The state governments, eager to maximize their budgetary resources and to advertise market-friendly governance to potential private investors, competed for access to the Bank's focus states assistance.

As the chapter's case studies of the three focus states showed, however, the three states proved to be very different animals. Bank officials, and even the Government of India, had to feel their way through disparate reform experiences with individual states, with mixed outcomes that never quite aggregated to the national impact originally envisioned. And yet, on the key issue of fiscal improvement, India's states as a whole and the Bank's focus states in particular were showing real progress by about 2005 – just as the focus states experiment was being wound down by the Government of India.

Chapter Four, "Reasserting Central Government Control, Reorienting Aid Toward 'Lagging States'," discussed the impasse that had begun to confront the focus states strategy by around 2004, and the reasons for yet another significant shift in the Bank's approach. The first broad reason for the shift was that the Bank's initial process for selecting states was perceived as too *ad hoc*. Some non-participant states began to complain, and with some justification, of political bias – particularly since the Bank's flagship focus state of Andhra Pradesh, ruled by the flamboyant N. Chandrababu Naidu and his regional Telugu Desam Party, happened to be a key supporter of the coalition government in New Delhi at the time of its selection. At the peak of the focus states experiment, Andhra Pradesh came to receive nearly one-third of all external assistance to India. However, the evidence presented in this section of the book demonstrated that the Bank essentially acted on its own initiative in devoting so much assistance and publicity to the state, as a way of politically "locking in" the central government's commitment to the sub-national lending focus. This preemptive tactic backfired when bureaucrats in the central finance ministry began to resent a single state's capture of a large share of aid, and they directed the Bank to come up with a more formal and transparent process for selecting focus states.

The second broad reason for the shift in strategy was that the political narrative about the states' relationship to India's economic reforms and growth began to change, from the latter 1990s to the early 2000s. Having begun to address the challenge of state-level reforms and fiscal deficit reductions, the Indian government turned attention to a different concern: the widening gaps in per-capita income and poverty rates among India's richest and poorest states. The central government and the Bank became vulnerable to the criticism that they were "picking winners" among the states – favoring the better-off states and ignoring the needs of the poorest and most populous states. Though the charge was not strictly accurate, the perception nevertheless crystallized as a political reality, even before the narrative of widening disparities became a major theme in India's 2004 elections. At the behest of the Indian government, the World Bank's Country Assistance Strategy embraced the new concept of "lagging states," and proclaimed that the Bank's state-level lending would place a special emphasis on those states with the highest concentrations of poverty and the lowest human development indicators.

Chapter Four, "A Bittersweet Graduation: Can IDA hold on to India, and Will India Let It?" discussed a critical juncture *now* confronting the Bank-India relationship. The Bank's new emphasis on lagging states has brought into sharp relief "the two Indias," in which the per-capita incomes between the wealthiest states, such as Gujarat and Maharashtra, and the poorest states, such as Bihar and Jharkhand, diverge by as much as five to one. Put differently, India today contains both Malaysia and Malawi, and disparities in income growth and poverty reduction are among the most urgent political economy issues confronting the country. Moreover, the persistence of poverty in large parts of India matters globally. Though India's poorest states rarely receive the attention that the international activist community and media have devoted to sub-Saharan Africa in recent years – Bono and Bob Geldof have not lobbied the G8 on behalf of Bihar – these states comprise a substantial proportion of the world's poor. Progress toward the UN Millennium Development Goals requires much further poverty reduction in this other India.

But on the wings of its recent rapid economic growth, India as a whole now stands at the cusp of ineligibility to borrower from the Bank's IDA facility for low-income countries. Some of the donor countries that fund IDA appear especially eager to devote a greater share of its resources to Africa. Were India to "graduate" from IDA, its relationship with the Bank likely would become more like that of Brazil, China, and other large middle-income countries who borrow from the Bank on market terms, and who increasingly have turned to alternative sources of financing that carry less of a "hassle factor" than World Bank loans.

For material reasons, the Bank would stand to suffer a significant loss of financial and operational autonomy if it loses India as its largest borrower, and the change could also have significant implications for the Bank's self-image and legitimacy. India's own perspective on its possible graduation out of IDA is strangely ambivalent. On the one hand, India would like to maintain access to low-cost, long-term financing, especially for its poorest states. On the other hand, it likes the symbolism of "arrival" as a global power, and would prefer not to have to make the case that it is still so poor that it needs IDA. This would run counter to the image that India is intent on advancing, and might undermine its efforts to gain greater formal decision-making influence in global governance, both within the Bretton Woods institutions and in other international arenas. Creative approaches to maintaining India's IDA eligibility might exist – for example, disaggregating its income and poverty measures on a state-wise or regional basis – but such innovation, even if it could secure the support of the donor countries, looks likely to founder on Indian sensitivities over sovereignty.

What are the implications of this book's findings and arguments for the Bank, and for India? There are important – albeit different – implications for both sides. For the Bank, one significant point is that its enthusiasm for "relevance" in India can lead it to conduct itself in ways that actually *diminish* its room for maneuver, and ultimately its impact, amid the constraints imposed by a complex federal political economy. In other words, sometimes the Bank tries too hard to be politically savvy, its "apolitical norm" notwithstanding, and is simply overwhelmed by the complexities and contingencies of India's politics.

Here, the example of the Bank's relationship with the AP government led by Chandrababu Naidu from 1998 to 2004 again comes to mind. Though Naidu presented himself as India's leading state-level reformer, his significance to the Bank lay at least as much in the pivotal position his Telugu Desam Party (TDP) held vis-à-vis successive coalition governments at the Centre. It was not enough for the Bank that the central finance ministry had endorsed its "focus states" strategy before the specific engagement in AP even unfolded, since the Centre held the prerogative to reverse its support for the approach at any time. So to give central officials additional incentives to stay friendly toward the strategy, the Bank's senior leadership in New Delhi perceived that an engagement with Naidu's government would be good politics – even apart from the "good governance" and fiscal reform goals that the state government claimed to hold dear. When Naidu's reform rhetoric and the policy reality diverged, the Bank was willing to indulge its star reformer with abundant continued lending – to the point of encouraging resentments both from other states and from central officials. Ultimately, both Naidu and the Bank overreached in their engagement, and central officials moved quickly to rationalize the Bank's state-level assistance programs – limiting the approach to only a fraction of the scale that the Bank had intended such lending to reach.

There is another key lesson for the Bank that emerges out of its focus states experiences – not only in AP, but also in Karnataka, in UP, and others. The seemingly simple notion that it somehow would be easier to engage the states than to deal with India as a whole, turns out to be an illusion. In feeling their way through disparate state-level reform experiences, World Bank officials, and even Indian leaders themselves, have turned out to be like the proverbial blind men and the elephant, trying in vain to aggregate an analytical framework and strategy for the country as a whole. Yet it is increasingly apparent that the states are not unlike small countries, in terms of the tremendous variations in their political economies: their party systems are different, their governance institutions and political traditions are different, their human capital and resource endowments are different, their post-liberalization productivity propensities are different – the list could go on. It may be true, as is sometimes said, that Tamil Nadu provides a more fitting and inspiring development model for Bihar than, say, Taiwan does. But it is not clear that Bihar can easily replicate Tamil Nadu's recent achievements, given the great differences that separate the two states. It will follow its own path, and the Bank's engagement with the state will be keenly watched.

Apart from the purported "demonstration effects" that its focus states would generate, another rationale for the Bank's selective engagement was the idea that it would be easier to disengage from particular states, should they backtrack on reforms, than to exert tough-minded leverage in its lending at the national level. Here, the record has been mixed; certainly, a large state like UP – more populous than many African countries – exerts its own kind of gravitational pull on the Bank, not least because of its political importance at the national level. In some ways, the fact that the Bank's state-level operations in India must navigate a three-sided negotiation – with the central government in a pivotal position – makes them even *more* challenging than country-level relationships in other parts of the world.

The implications of all this are at least as important for India as they are for the Bank. This study provides significant additional evidence to support arguments against "the myth of the shrinking state" in India (Nayar 2009), and in favor of more nuanced notions such as Lloyd and Susanne Rudolph's formulation of "shared sovereignty in a federal market economy" (2001). As studies of India's engagement with other global economy institutions have suggested, India's federalism shapes its interactions with the World Bank in important ways, and is in turn impacted by such interactions in a process of mutual transformation (Jenkins 2003, for example, makes a similar point about India's engagement with the World Trade Organization). The Indian national state is very much alive – if not always well – and it is undergoing a "thickening" of its "federal institutional structure" (ibid., 616).

More than two decades ago, the Rudolphs offered another perspective which seems even more relevant today: they described India's as a "weak-strong state," a paradox that arises from its location "on a shifting continuum between constrained and autonomous" vis-à-vis India's complex and increasingly mobilized society." But "the international environment," they argued, "is far less salient for explaining Indian economic or political development than is the case for other Third World countries, unless it is salient in a negative sense, as an environment to exclude or keep at bay" (1987: 1, 13, 3). The Indian government has proven itself quite strong in its dealings with the most powerful global development agency. But it remains often all too weak in basic tasks of development, particularly in its poorest states.

On balance, the mixed record of World Bank engagement at the state level has tended to favor the central government's development policy goals, which have evolved from bringing about broad improvement in state-level finances to securing reform promises – if not always performance – from the most laggardly states. That the Indian leadership would perceive the Bank's engagement as a complement to its own authority and reform efforts, and not as a threat to economic sovereignty, says much about state power and ideational change in today's India. But the flip side of the Bank's self-defeating tendencies is the Centre's penchant for micromanaging development assistance allocation across the states. India thus may be losing out on additional opportunities for innovation that a more relaxed regime might allow for. This, of course, is the paradox of liberalization and growth generally, from the standpoint of national economic management – sometimes getting more means doing less. The Government of India has at times appeared more willing to cede control over the regional distribution of private investment than over much more modest flows of official development assistance. This is philosophically defensible, if a key goal of an institution such as the World Bank is to facilitate access to investment resources where private lenders fear to tread. But India could articulate a clearer position on its continuing interest in Bank borrowing, especially with respect to IDA and the most developmentally challenged states such as Bihar.

## Conclusion: Unfinished Tasks

Existing academic models of change in international organizations are inadequate to the task of analyzing how the World Bank, the premier multilateral development assistance institution, has been profoundly impacted by its relationship to India, its largest cumulative borrower. Against a state-centric theoretical tradition in International Relations that assumes international organizations exist to solve collective action problems for states and essentially do the bidding of the most powerful among their masters, recent constructivist theories have assumed that international organizations develop missions, cultures, and interests of their own, which may diverge from the interests of their state sponsors. Yet there is still inadequate attention to the influence that the largest developing countries wield – as borrowers in the Bretton Woods institutions, in particular.

What is needed is a synthetic approach that treats *the World Bank as an actor –* however sprawling it might be – with goals distinct from those of its member states, relating to its own finances, operations, continuance, and what might be characterized as "self-actualization": its desire to be relevant. The constraints and compulsions that the Bank's member states create for it should not be discounted; rather, instead of an almost exclusive focus on the power of donor countries, the *influence of borrowers* must also be recognized. For it is clear that a large, creditworthy country such as India – and especially India – can bend the Bank to its own purposes, simply by demanding that the Bank continuously innovate in order to bring something valuable to the table. The history of the Bank's strategy in India, and the coming revolution in Bank-India relations that IDA graduation may portend, demonstrate how donor constraints, the Bank's self-preservation and "relevance" impulses, and the preferences of a proud but still-poor borrower are all converging to produce a critical juncture in the international development assistance regime.

The significance of this investigation goes beyond scholarly interest. The World Bank could still play an important role in India's development – and therefore in the reduction of poverty on a global scale – for many years to come. Its contribution is not only in the cross-national experience and technical expertise it has to offer; indeed, the emergence of a new global financial crisis suggests that there is still a role for public sector development assistance, to smooth access to investment capital and budgetary support when private lenders draw back. As India makes further progress in poverty reduction, and narrows the gap between its high-income and "lagging states," it might decide that it can dispense with World Bank borrowing altogether, as it has done with many previous bilateral aid sources. The Bank would be forced to adjust; its global role would be considerably diminished. But at least it could be satisfied with the sense of accomplishment that such poverty reduction would represent. If the Bank effectively quits India soon, forced by donors to "graduate" a country that still houses a massive proportion of the world's poor – or if India preemptively quits the Bank, out of some misplaced sense of pride – the relationship would be ending well short of such an accomplishment.

Pandit Jawaharlal Nehru, just before death on 27 May 1964 ended his long service as India's first prime minister and the key architect of its developmental and foreign policies, scribbled a few lines at his bedside table.[5] They were from the poem by Robert Frost, "Stopping by Woods on a Snowy Evening":

*The woods are lovely, dark and deep.*
*But I have promises to keep,*
*And miles to go before I sleep,*
*And miles to go before I sleep.*

# NOTES

## Introduction

1 In 2007–8, an active year for the Bank in India after an unusual dip in lending the preceding year, India was the largest IDA borrower and second-largest IBRD borrower (in that particular year, Argentina was the largest IBRD borrower and China the third-largest).

2 Ziegler is not credited with a byline for "Banyan," per the magazine's convention, but he is officially cited as the author of Banyan on *The Economist* website, at <http://www.economist.com/mediadirectory/listing.cfm?journalistID=26>. Retrieved on 18 September 2009.

3 Specific arrangements for subnational lending in federal countries depend on borrower country institutions. In Brazil, for example, the World Bank has lent directly to state governments, subject to the federal government's guarantee (which is a requirement of the Bank's charter). In India, the designation of Government of India as "borrower" and the relevant state government as "beneficiary" reflects both the constitutional constraints on sub-national borrowing and the central government's preferences.

4 The notion of an empathic outsider's "insider" perspective is a modified borrowing from Gilbert and Vines (2000: 11), who admit to a "deliberately sympathetic view of the Bank's purposes and activities." I may be on the mistaken side of the longstanding debate over the distinction between *sympathy* and *empathy*, but I use the latter to suggest intellectual appreciation of Bank and Indian government interests, as opposed to agreement or "fellow feeling" with those interests.

5 Similarly, David Moore favors drawing inspiration from Gramsci's studies on hegemony for "unsheathing the constant interplay between strategies of consent and coercion as the world's most important 'development' institution [the World Bank] vacillates between façades while it attempts to create consensus around capitalism's mission in the Third World" (Moore 2007, 2). David Williams goes so far as to say that the Bank's pursuit of a "good governance" agenda over the past two decades signals "the declining significance of sovereignty as a way of organizing relations between developed and less developed states" (2008: 3).

6 Technically, India is a "blend country," meaning part of its Bank borrowing is on concessionary IDA terms, and part is on market terms through the International Bank for Reconstruction and Development (IBRD), the Bank's facility for middle-income borrowers.

7 On the methodological concept of "crucial cases," see also Gerring 2007.

8 Michael N. Barnett and Martha Finnemore, "The Politics, Power, and Pathologies of International Organizations," *International Organization* Vol. 53, No. 4 (1999), pp. 699–732; p. 704.

9  Ruttan (1996) argues that the Bank should be seen as occupying a position at the center of a *two*-part "principal-agent" relationship, in which donor countries provide the Bank with funds and delegate to it the power over how to lend them, and the Bank then lends these funds to developing countries, requiring them to fulfill certain obligations in exchange. In both relationships, he suggests, asymmetries of information imply a privileged position for the Bank, vis-à-vis both donor and borrower countries. Even so, this formulation ignores the possibility that at least some borrowers—the largest and least resource-dependent ones—might also act as Bank principals in some contexts." (Miller-Adams 1999: 12).

10 Putnam's original essay described two different kinds of "two-level games," the other being the strategic use of domestic constraints to enhance policymakers' bargaining position in international negotiations. This is where national authorities say to their international counterparts, "We wish we could go along with you on this agreement, but we could never get constituency X at home to accept it; what else can you offer us?" Putnam says relatively little about the converse phenomenon, in which national authorities use international agreements to achieve domestic objectives, but this is the sense in which I use the term here. Subsequent theorists have developed the concept further; see for example Snidal and Thompson 2003.

  Though he does not frame in terms of the "two-level game" metaphor, Killick notes that "The money and support of donor agencies can be used as *a political resource by reformers* within a government and this may be decisive when reformers and their opponents are fairly evenly balanced. In such situations, the fact that reformers can enlist the staffs of the IFIs and other donor agencies as supporters may give them additional clout in the Cabinet and other legendary smoke-filled rooms where policy decisions are taken. That they can unlock access to large amounts of finance gives them a further standing which is likely to be decisive in circumstances of economic crisis. Conditionality, then, can be seen as strengthening the hands of those within government who support the approach to policy favoured by the donor community. That often amounts to supporting those who place a larger weight on economic, as against political rationality; and upon improved economic performance in the longer term as against the avoidance of short-term political discomfort" (1998: 15).

11 Even African relationships with the Bank might exhibit considerably more nuanced influence politics than the passive-aggressive subversion notion captures, their aid dependency notwithstanding; see Whitfield 2008.

12 To the author's knowledge, the last independent scholarly monograph to offer a broad political economy perspective on India's relationship with the World Bank was published three decades ago (Bhambhri 1980), and only in India. Almost as surprising, there has been *no* book-length political economy treatment of the relationship between China and the World Bank by an independent scholar. Jacobson and Oksenburg (1990) study China's participation in the Bretton Woods institutions (including the General Agreement of Tariffs and Trade, or GATT), but their volume is now two decades old. Recently, June Park (2009) offers a promising preliminary attempt at understanding the evolution of China's relationship with the Bank, "from debtor and beneficiary to partner," in an unpublished paper.

13 John Ruggie, adapting an earlier observation by Karl Polanyi, argued that the postwar international political economy had been constructed by the capitalist Western allies on an historic compromise that sought to balance external openness to trade with an internal social contract favoring low unemployment, welfare provision, and other domestic priorities (Ruggie 1982). As it proceeds along its own "great transformation," India could be seen as working out its own versions of the political compromises that "embed" economic liberalism in its society.

# Chapter One. The First Half-Century: From Bretton Woods to India's Liberalization Era

1 Oral history interview, Leonard Rist, July 19, 1961, p. 47, *Oral Hist. 44:* Fonds 01, Columbia University Project; WB IBRD/IDA 44 Oral Histories; World Bank Group Archives. Quoted in Alacevich (2009: 10).

2 IBRD Article V, section 5(d); cited in Mason and Asher (1973: 31).

3 See for example Gilpin (2001: 309). India's development strategy was in line with Keynesian orthodoxy and emerging "Big Push" ideas about state-led development, typified by the Harrod-Domar growth model, which held that raising capital investment was the key to economic growth.

4 P.N. Dhar, an economist and later advisor to Indira Gandhi's government, reflected in 1966, "At the same time as aid exercised a softening effect [on India's balance-of-payments position], it obliterated from view, or, at any rate, blurred the real character of a developing situation… The question really is whether India's growing need for aid is not an indication that the Indian economy is drifting into a vicious circle of needing more and ever more aid because of a faulty deployment of resources" (2003: 54). Dhar went on to stress "the urgent need for agricultural development" (ibid., 59–63).

5 Author's interview, August 2003, New Delhi.

6 See Kapur et al. (1997: 12). On the creation of IDA, Mason and Asher (1973: 380) explain, "India, Pakistan, and some other major borrowers were piling up external debt so rapidly as to call into question their creditworthiness for loans on Bank terms. The creditworthiness of newly independent countries in Africa for interest-bearing loans was also questionable. IDA, in short, had to be invented to keep the Bank preeminent… in the growing complex of multilateral agencies attempting to facilitate international development." India was further implicated in IDA's creation in at least two important ways. As early as 1949, a UN Subcommission on Economic Development, chaired by India's V.K.R.V. Rao, had suggested a new agency that would provide financing at lower interest and longer terms than IBRD. The US at the time was not in favor, preferring a greater reliance on private capital and IBRD itself. But nine years later, after the US began to amass considerable rupee and other nonconvertible local currency holdings as payment for food aid under Public Law 480 (discussed below in the text), US Senator A.S. "Mike" Monroney (D-Oklahoma) introduced the idea of an International Development Association as an agency to which the US could transfer such currencies for the purpose of lending them back to the aid recipient countries (ibid., 389). Though the IDA that was established in 1959 differed significantly from this proposal (which ultimately was deemed unworkable), the history shows that its creation should be understood as a result of overlapping borrower, donor, and World Bank interests.

7 Quoted in Mason and Asher (1973: 677).

8 Quoted in Nayar (2001: 94).

9 This section draws significantly from two outstanding recent articles by historians (Cullather 2007; Muirhead 2005).

10 Also, whereas over time US and multilateral aid became more "programmatic" (i.e., supporting India's balance of payments), Moscow's assistance was almost exclusively public sector project-centered (Chaudhry and Vanduzer-Snow 2008: 48) or in barter form (Duncan 1993: 37).

11 US Department of State, "Soviet Economic Offensive in India," 1959, declassified 25 January 1983; cited in Chaudhry and Vanduzer Snow (2008: 50).

12 Such concerns were minor chords in Rostow's modernization symphony; ultimately, he was a pragmatic optimist, and an effective salesman for both dynamic developmental theories and active aid policies. But the pessimistic notion that India's softer democratic state sheltered (largely intractable) traditional social and institutional orders that were antithetical to development would be taken up more forcefully a few years later by Gunnar Myrdal in his magisterial *Asian Drama* (1968), even if the Swedish economist stopped somewhat short of arguing that only a ruthlessly efficient state could lead India to developmental take-off (Lankester 2004, 292).

13 World Bank Archives, Box 53, file: India – Consortium Meetings, January–March 1963, Central Files 1946–71, Operational Correspondence, India, Escott Reid to Burke Knapp, "India and Pakistan Consortia," January 30, 1963. Cited in Muirhead (2005: 6).

14 Word Bank Archives, Box 55, file: India – Consortium Meeting, September–December 1963, Central Files 1946–71, Operational Correspondence India, King to Stevenson, October 24, 1963. Cited in Muirhead (2005: 21, n41)

15 For a detailed account, see Bjorkman 2008 [1980].

16 Quoted in Kux (1993: 243).

17 Quoted in Kux (1993: 251).

18 Kux's source for the quote is Bowles (1971: 526).

19 Quoted in Panagariya (2008: 50).

20 Quoted in Pedersen (1993: 106). Though, in another context, Jha put it somewhat differently. "Laughing merrily," he told Lewis that while agricultural reform "reflected mainly Indian ideas and Indian initiatives," devaluation "was what [World Bank President] George Woods told us we had to do to get aid" (1995: 136).

21 Quoted in Frankel (2005: 298).

22 Quoted in Mukherji (2000: 383).

23 Quoted in Kux (1993: 24).

24 Jagdish Bhagwati and T.N. Srinivasan note, "By 1969–70, the liberalization appeared to have been largely reversed. The import premium was back to 30 to 50 percent on the average, export subsidies were reinstated and were up to high levels, industrial de-licensing amounted to little, especially because of continuing quantitative restrictions (QRs), automatic protection with QRs was still the order of the day, and the picture looked very similar to that which obtained during 1962–5" (1975: 30; quoted in Mukherji 2000: 379). The authors also comment, "The Indian experience... is instructive for the political timing of a devaluation: foreign pressure to change policies, if brought to bear when a government is weak... can be fatal. Indeed, there is much to be said, if the aid relationship is to be mature and relatively free from frictions... for the donor's influence to take the form of advice rather than prescription. In this regard, it is well worth noting that the Soviet practice of confining scrutiny to the performance of aid-financed projects, and not attempting to evaluate and influence the whole plan or set of policies of the recipient country, has helped to avoid the kind of adverse reaction the Western donors have provoked, however well intentioned their pressures may have been. Here we have the paradox of political economy: that a program approach, which makes much sense from an *economic* point of view, makes little sense from a *political* point of view" (ibid., 153, emphasis in original).

25 See for example Mosley et al. 1991: 29; Kapur et al. 1997: 466–7.

26 Recently released transcripts from the US National Security Archives reveal the extent to which US-India relations had plummeted by 1971. Nixon, conferring with his National Security Advisor, Henry Kissinger, expresses his unhappiness at India's intervention in Pakistan's civil war by saying, "What the Indians need is a mass famine." After calling

Mrs. Gandhi "a bitch" and the Indians "such bastards" and "such a treacherous and slippery people," Nixon and Kissinger agree that it would be desirable for China, then on the cusp of rapprochement with the US, to "make a move" militarily against India, though no such intervention took place. A more complete reversal of Kennedy-era US perceptions of India could not be imagined. National Security Archives, <http://www.gwu.edu/~nsarchiv/news/20050629/>. Accessed 22 June 2009. Quoted in Luce (2007: 264–5).

27  See Lele and Bumb (1995: 69–96).

28  The authors note that some of these same officials, such as Manmohan Singh and Montek Singh Ahluwalia, would go on to lead the policy team that ushered in India's 1991 liberalization program. Frankel (2005: 585) describes "the rudiments of the new policy" in connection with the IMF loan as "placing some 100 items of open General License; granting 'automatic licensing' to 20 major industries; lifting price controls on steel and cement, and providing incentives for Indian business firms to enter into technical collaboration with foreign corporations to acquire state of the art manufacturing facilities."

29  Namboodiripad (1991); quoted in Frankel (2005: 591–2).

30  In a recent memoir, Sinha (2007:1–24) has defended his role as India's "original reformer," though this is a partisan argument. Manmohan Singh, Sinha's successor in the 1991 Congress Party government, was involved in earlier reform dialogue that shaped the Sinha budget through his leadership role at the Planning Commission and as an economic advisor. It would be fair to say that policymakers from several parties recognized the serious nature of the external crisis and the need for far-reaching economic reforms. Sinha would return to the job of finance minister in the BJP-led NDA government in 1998, handing the portfolio over to party-mate Jaswant Singh in 2002 (see Chapter 4).

31  World Bank 1996: xvii; quoted in Nayar (2001: 130).

32  Government of India 1992: 27; cited in Alamgir (2007: 256–7).

33  Monier Williams, *Sanskrit-English Dictionary.* Available online at: <http://www.sanskrit-lexicon.uni-koeln.de/monier/>. Retrieved on 03 June 2009.

34  "Narmada River." *Encyclopædia Britannica.* 2009. Encyclopædia Britannica Online. <http://www.britannica.com/EBchecked/topic/403526/Narmada-River>. Retrieved on 03 June 2009.

35  *Sarovar* means "lake" in Hindi; *Sardar* is a common honorific title, meant in this case as a tribute to Sardar Vallabhbhai Patel (1875–1950), a leading figure in the Indian nationalist movement and the first Home Minister after independence.

36  Author's observation.

37  Lori Udall, "The World Bank and Public Accountability: Has Anything Changed?," November 1995 draft chapter for Fox and Brown, *The Struggle for Accountability*; cited in Keck and Sikkink (1998: 147).

38  See Mallaby (2004: 361–2). For an analysis of China's Qinghai project, see also Sanford and Change (2003: 119–56).

39  During the 1980s, the Bank increasingly pushed for far-reaching economic reforms in its lending to many clients in Latin America and sub-Saharan Africa. Though the Latin American debt crisis, intensified by Mexico's default in 1982, was a major contextual factor, both the early 1980s "structural adjustment" agenda and the later 1980s "good governance" agendas were more proximately rooted in the Bank's experiences in sub-Saharan Africa. The 1981 Berg Report, focused on Africa, "was the first World Bank report to argue openly that one of the key reasons for development failure was a lack of reliance on the market mechanism to allocate economic resources" (Williams 2008: 50). Likewise, "the concepts of 'governance' and 'good governance' were first publicly

introduced by the World Bank in a 1989 report, *Sub-Saharan Africa: From Crisis to Sustainable Growth*. The report argued that 'underlying the litany of Africa's development problems was a crisis of governance'" (ibid., 69).

40  The phrase "dividing the leviathan" is borrowed from Sinha 2005.

## Chapter Two.  Remaining Relevant: The World Bank's Strategy for an India of States

1  At present, India is comprised of 28 States and 7 Union Territories.

2  Author's interview, 2002.

3  Per India's designation as a "blend" borrower in the World Bank, such loans have been either a 50:50 ratio of IBRD loans and IDA credits, or approximately 70:30 loan-to-credit blend (in fact, engagement at the state level has enabled the Bank to gradually "harden" the financing blend for India to reflect a higher loan component; this issue will be discussed in greater detail in Chapter Four). Initially, the central government transferred funds to the states at a 70:30 loan-to-grant ratio regardless of the composition from the World Bank (Howes et al. 2008: 48). Over time, the Centre and the states argued over this arrangement, with the states complaining that the Centre pocketed part of the concessionary component to its advantage, the Centre countering that this was a fair trade for its bearing of the currency risk. After 2005, following the recommendations of India's Twelfth Finance Commission, the Centre agreed to "back-to-back" terms that would make to Bank-to-GoI and GoI-to-states financing blend the same, with the foreign exchange risk to be borne by the states (ibid., 48).

4  Howes et al. point out the technical distinction between adjustment lending *per se*, "which is quick-disbursing and not earmarked for any particular sector," and the more general term "policy-based lending" to encompass both adjustment lending and investment lending in the context of an "agreed overall policy framework" (ibid., 43, *n*1) Some loans to India's states, such as the Andhra Pradesh Economic Restructuring Project (APERP) in 1998, were technically investment loans – prior to the Bank-wide approval of a Sub-national Adjustment Loan (SNAL) instrument in 2000 – but nevertheless included such a significant reform-conditional component that they should be understood as "policy-based loans." A similar point could be made about the Bank's power sector restructuring loans to the states, essentially "sub-national sectoral adjustment loans" within an agreed policy framework.

  Again, for the purposes of this study, the point of interest is that prior to the mid-1990s, the Bank had never incorporated an overall fiscal framework, public expenditure, state enterprise reform, or governance conditionality into its state-level operations in India; state-level engagement was entirely project-centered using investment loans. The introduction of a broad policy framework, beginning in 1998 in Andhra Pradesh, marked the operational beginning of the Bank's new strategy for what I call "an India of states." Here I also note post-1998 project lending in the relevant states, because an implicit dimension of the "focus states" concept was that in addition to policy-based loans, these states might also enjoy favored access to investment loans relative to non-focus states.

5  Relevant studies of power sector reforms are noted below. For a comparison of governance reforms in the three Bank focus states, see Beschel 2003.

6  Jairam Ramesh, an economic advisor to the Congress government, asserts that Singh did not favor the idea of policy-based lending by the Bank to the states (Ramesh 2002).

In any event, Singh later professed to support the strategy as a complement to central government reform efforts (M. Singh 2003).

7 The Asian Development Bank has made policy-based loans to Assam, Kerala, and Madhya Pradesh, in addition to Gujarat, but "typically on the basis of only one operation per state" (Howes et al. 2008: 48, *n*8). The UK Department for International Development (DFID) co-financed World Bank and ADB policy-based loans in Andhra Pradesh, Madhya Pradesh, and Orissa for several years, but discontinued the practice (ibid., 48, *n*8).

8 Both World Bank and ADB officials raised this point in interviews. But ironically, in 2004 when West Bengal and the ADB agreed to a technical assistance project for public expenditure management and other policy reforms, it was financed mainly by a grant from DFID in Britain – the former colonizer itself (Asian Development Bank 2004).

9 Lim reflected on how experiences with the Chinese and other Asian cases of economic reform had shaped his perspective on growth and inequality, and how Indian leaders had tended to be more concerned with distributive issues:

"In 1987, as part of our program of economic dialogue and assistance through conferences […], the Chinese authorities asked us to organize a conference on plans and markets, mainly to understand how Asian countries managed their economies. The main interest then was the Republic of Korea, with which China had no direct relationship but whose experience in state-directed growth was the object of much curiosity from Chinese policymakers. So we organized a conference in Bangkok, Thailand, with all participating countries obviously giving it quite a bit of importance. […] From India came Dr. Manmohan Singh, then [deputy] chairman of the Planning Commission, and Montek Singh Ahluwalia, the economic advisor to the prime minister. The large Chinese delegation was headed by the vice minister for the System Reform Commission, the agency responsible for formulating the reform process and strategy.

After the other delegations presented their experiences in managing a market economy, the Chinese vice minister presented an outline of the Chinese reform program. At the end of this presentation, Manmohan Singh, in his usual gentle but forceful tone, asked, 'Would not what you are trying to do result in greater inequality in China?'

To that the vice minister replied, with firm conviction, 'We would certainly hope so!'

As economists, we have all struggled with the issue of equality and growth. Many of us would see a degree of equality as an end in itself; empirical evidence also shows that economic growth can be sustained only if the benefits of growth are fairly distributed among different segments of the population.

There are, however, instances in which greater inequality has to be possible to create the incentives necessary for work and entrepreneurship" (2005: 99–100).

10 For a range of perspectives on the states' role in India's economic reforms, see Howes, Lahiri et al. 2003).

11 Policies varied by state. Cheap inputs for farmers were especially prominent in Punjab. Andhra Pradesh exemplified how food subsidies ostensibly intended for the poor could be captured by others; by the mid-1990s, the government's rice subsidy covered 85 percent of the state's population (World Bank 1997a).

12 See especially Singh and Srinivasan 2006; Rao and Singh 2005; World Bank 2004c; McCarten 2003; Khemani 2002; Vithal and Sastry 2001; Kletzer and Singh 2000.

13 The Reserve Bank of India (RBI) plays a role as "debt manager and banker to the State Governments," ands its Ways and Means Advances (WMA) facility is meant to meet "temporary mismatches" between receipts and expenditure (Reserve Bank of India 2000).

In the late 1990s, several states became habitual users of the WMA and overdraft facilities of the RBI; see for example the discussion of Andhra Pradesh later in this chapter.

14  According to Swaroop (2000), the central government's expenditure/investment choices were unaffected by external assistance. The implication for donors such as the World Bank was that even though their development projects may generate high rates of economic return, "they could be assisting the central government in financing something very different at the margin."

15  World Bank, *The World Bank Group Country Assistance Strategy for India, 1998–2001*, p. 9; quoted in Howes, Mishra et al. (2008: 45).

16  World Bank, *CAS for India, 1998–2001*, p. iii; quoted in Howes et al. (2008: 47).

17  Established in the early 1970s, the Central Pay Commissions, like other advisory panels to the government, are made up of both technical specialists and political or semi-political personalities. The Finance Commission provides terms of reference for the Pay Commission's deliberations on categories and levels of pay for central government employees. The central government is not legally bound to accept the panel's recommendations, but they can provide leverage to public employees' unions and in practical terms can be difficult for the government to reject.

18  External assistance figures from Lok Sabha Unstarred Question No. 1967, 01 August 2003.

19  On the rise of NTR, see Kohli 1988.

20  NTR's government turned a revenue surplus of 1.33 billion rupees (Rs.) in 1982–83 into a deficit of Rs. 1.69 billion by 1984–85. The fiscal deficit, previously just over 2 percent of GSDP, swelled to 6.3 percent by the mid-1980s.

21  Naidu briefly served as AP finance minister following NTR's reelection as chief minister in 1994, but soon led an intra-party revolt against the patriarch over the widowed NTR's decision to marry a much younger woman, whom he had allowed to emerge as an extra-constitutional power center. For a more detailed discussion of Naidu's conversion, see Sen and Frankel (2005). The author provided research assistance and served as associate editor for this publication.

22  See Sen and Frankel (2005: 4).

23  The *Vision 2020* document asserts that "knowledge-led growth" in fields such as IT services, biotech, and pharmaceuticals – along with other select "growth engine" sectors such as agro-industry, mining, and tourism – would by 2020 permit the state to achieve "a level of development that [would] provide its people tremendous opportunities to achieve prosperity and wellbeing and enjoy a high quality of life." See Government of Andhra Pradesh (1999).

24  This poll has been cited in a number of sources, and referred to by Naidu himself in public speeches. See for example Rudolph and Rudolph (2001: *n*4).

25  An Indian Administrative Service (IAS) officer from Andhra Pradesh, V. Govindarajan, was a senior secretary in the Fund-Bank Division of the Department of Economic Affairs, the Finance Ministry unit that handles India's relations with the Bretton Woods institutions. Though Govindarajan never made himself available to the author for an interview, several World Bank and Indian officials said that he was instrumental in arranging the meeting between Naidu and Wolfensohn. Lim (interview, 2003) maintained that Govindarajan was a "good, upstanding IAS officer" who probably had become uncomfortable at the suggestion that any improper influence had been used to favor AP's access to the Bank, given that by 2002–3 this impression was beginning to crop up in complaints by other states. Chidambaram approved of the meeting between Naidu and the Bank leadership, though he did not participate in it. "I trusted that Naidu and his team wouldn't make a bad impression," he recalled (2003).

26  For a similar argument about Naidu's "new populism," albeit one that is more critical of its "neoliberal" underpinnings, see Reddy (2002).

27  World Bank, undated Web content, "India: Power Sector Reform in Andhra Pradesh," *Participation in Macroeconomic Policies: Case Studies.* Online. <http://www.worldbank.org/participation/web/webfiles/indiapower.htm>. Retrieved on 10 June 2005.

28  The Minister of Power, K. Subbarayudu, did not score high marks for public relations when he retorted that copies of the documents were available on the World Bank's website, since this defense only invited an opposition rejoinder about the government's technological elitism.

29  Even in 2000, before the drought, AP had accounted for 385 of 480 cases reported across India. Though analysts attribute these tragedies to multiple factors, state policies were substantially implicated in a recurring scenario: indigent and lacking access to formal credit, many of the victims had taken on large personal debts to local moneylenders in order to purchase fertilizer, pesticide, and other inputs – the prices of which, like power tariffs, increased as Naidu's government withdrew subsidies to meet its fiscal adjustment targets.

30  In 2000, Naidu's AP government, along with leaders from Kerala, Maharashtra, and Tamil Nadu, protested the Eleventh Finance Commission's revenue transfer formula as giving too much money to states with more poverty, faster population growth, worse public finances, and worse infrastructure (Mukherji 2002: 69–70).

31  For another account of Karnataka's electoral history through 1999, see Gould 2003.

32  Author's confidential interview with a World Bank official, New Delhi, August 2003.

33  Nor did other assistance providers like ADB and DFID bandwagon behind the Bank in Karnataka, as the government might have expected based on the early competition between ADB and the World Bank. Karnataka's share of total multilateral and bilateral external assistance to India (11 percent in 2001–3), while more than double its share of India's population (5 percent), was in absolute terms much smaller than AP's take.

34  Author's confidential interview with a Government of Karnataka finance department official, Bangalore, August 2002.

35  The acronym has always been somewhat misleading; for example, it does not include Orissa, which is India's second-poorest state after Bihar. Moreover, in the late 1990s Rajasthan and Madhya Pradesh experienced growth rates above the national average; see Ahluwalia (2002).

36  The transformation of UP politics has been such a fascinating train-wreck that it has attracted considerable scholarly interest; the literature on the state is too vast to review here, but Zoya Hasan's body of work has been particularly noteworthy, and the following sources also merit attention: Rai 2003; Chandra 2004, 1999; Chhibber 1999, Chapter 6; Van Dyke 1999.

37  This account draws freely on the author's interview with Tripathi, who at the time was back in a central IAS post as Secretary of the Ministry for Human Resource Development in New Delhi. The account was checked against the recollections of other participants in the Bank-UP dialogue, in conversations with the author in August 2003. These include, on the Indian side, former UP Chief Secretary Yogendra Narain, central Planning Commission advisor N.J. Kurian, and former Secretary, Planning Commission Ajit Mazoomdar; on the World Bank side, V.J. Ravishankar, Sumir Lal, and another official who did not wish to be named.

38  Lim singled out the ADB's efforts in Gujarat for criticism, saying that its selection of this state, which already exhibited on of the highest per capita income levels in the country, amounted to "cherry-picking."

39  Author's confidential interview with a staff member of the South Asia Poverty Reduction and Economic Management (PREM) Unit, The World Bank. New Delhi, 20 August 2002.

40  Author's confidential interview with a World Bank official, 08 August 2003, New Delhi.

41  For a fascinating experimental study that suggests that a preference for "spiteful" resource allocation may shape development policies in Uttar Pradesh, see Fehr et al. 2008.

42  This figure includes the APERP investment loan and three subsequent adjustment loans to Andhra Pradesh, two adjustment loans to Karnataka, one adjustment loan for Uttar Pradesh, two adjustment loans for Orissa, and one adjustment loan for Tamil Nadu that was withdrawn from the Bank's board at the last minute (see discussion in the text).

43  For a similar comparison of "reform packaging" in Andhra Pradesh and Tamil Nadu, see Kennedy 2004. Pani (2006) offers an interesting perspective on Krishna as a reformist "icon" in Karnataka.

44  It has become commonplace to rank India's states on economic and policy indicators in ways similar to the systems used by the World Bank, UN Development Program, and others – including a proliferation of private sector analysts – typically use to compare countries. The Confederation of Indian Industries (CII) ranks state-level investment climates. Debroy, Gangopadhyay, and Bhandari present an innovative "economic freedom index" ranking the states on a composite of indicators designed to point to economic freedom as "the unfettered ability of an individual to make economic choices" (2004: 563). They find Tamil Nadu, Maharashtra, and Gujarat to be the most free of 20 major Indian states, and Bihar, Chattisgarh, and Jharkhand to be the least free.

## Chapter Three.  Reasserting Central Government Control, Reorienting Aid toward "Lagging States"

1  The 2003–4 Budget Speech is available online. <http://www.indiabudget.nic.in/ub 2003-04/bs/speecha.htm>. Retrieved on 13 July 2009.

2  An earlier episode involving Danish aid may have presaged the 2003 policy. Denmark, like other donors, suspended aid programs in India after the 1998 nuclear tests. In 2000, it was ready to resume bilateral aid with new initiatives on the private sector, health, human rights and democracy, and several other focus areas. The Indian finance ministry informed the Government of Denmark that democracy and human rights were "the concerns [...] of the Indian polity" and that India "would not like to avail ourselves of external funding for these sectors" (quoted in Mathew 2007: 282). Still, India utilized almost US$11 million in Danish aid in 2003–4, before discontinuing the relationship (Price 2004: 6, Table 1).

3  National Planning Commission figures released in 2003; cited in de Groot et al. 2008: 16.

4  Yashwant Sinha, though not a Hindutva hardliner by any means (in fact, he has recently spoken out against what he takes to be the party's captivity to the RSS), even titled his 2007 memoir *Confessions of a Swadeshi Reformer* (Sinha 2007). The BJP's relationship to the *swadeshi* concept, and to India's integration in the global economy, was complex; see Malik 2007, Nayar 2007b.

5  Letter from Finance Minister Jaswant Singh to State Chief Ministers; cited in *Jal News*, 11 December 2002. Online. <http://www.angelfire.com/in/jalnews/2002/11122.htm>. Retrieved on 21 February 2005.

6  Where Sinha does discuss the Bank, it is generally in the context of anecdotes about international meetings that he attended or chaired. The following passage is representative,

and demonstrates the high priority that he attached to using such forums to advance India's global prestige:

"In the IMF and World Bank meetings held in Prague in 2000 we had a joint meeting of the Development Committee and the IMFC [International Monetary and Finance Committee], which was headed by Gordon Brown [then the UK Chancellor of the Exchequer]. The duty of presiding over the joint meeting was shared by both of us. The IMFC and the Development Committee continued to meet separately as well. I presided over the meetings of the committee held in April 2001 in Washington, the annual meeting in October 2001 in Ottawa and the spring meeting in April 2002 in Washington. *This position gave India a very high profile in the international financial institutions.* One Government of India official, a veteran of these meetings, once told me that he had never seen India have such a high profile in these forums" (Sinha 2007: 193, emphasis added).

7  A 2005 World Bank Policy Research Paper examined inequality in "five great federations" – China, India, the US, Brazil, and Indonesia – from 1980 to 2000. All three Asian giants exhibited increasing inequalities, both across and within regions. The largest states/provinces of India and China exhibited particularly divergent incomes. (China is often treated as "federal" by economists, given the importance of sub-national governments in economic policy implementation, but from a political science perspective it is generally not regarded as federal since it is not democratic and since sub-national units enjoy little constitutional power, however much *de facto* autonomy they might have. Nor is Indonesia truly federal in its politics). See Milanovic 2005.

8  But note that Shankar Acharya (2002), Ahluwalia's former colleague, suggests that Ahluwalia's analysis did not give sufficient attention to the performance of individual states, or to non-growth dimensions of "performance" such as life expectancy and literacy. Moreover, apart from a two-sector disaggregation (agriculture and non-agriculture), the study placed little emphasis on the composition of economic growth. Various other studies have looked more closely at these kinds of issues.

9  By 2002, Ahluwalia had gone to Washington to direct a new independent evaluation office at the IMF. He returned to the Indian government after the 2004 elections.

10  In 2000, the political geography of this region was altered when three new states were created: Uttaranchal was hived off from UP, Jharkhand from Bihar, and Chhattisgarh from Madhya Pradesh. Madhya Pradesh, though once grouped alongside other "backward" or "Bimaru" states, was a relatively strong growth performer during the post-reforms period. The three new states, particularly Jharkhand, have continued to struggle.

11  Though not the fastest growers in the post-liberalization period, "breadbasket" states Haryana and Punjab achieved high average incomes in earlier decades, following the Green Revolution.

12  As with the literature on state-level growth performances, it is not the intention here to review the substantial work on poverty in India. For a good discussion of the state of the debate as it looked in 2002, see Deaton and Drèze 2007 [2002]. Note also that it is important not to conflate per-capita GSDP, poverty, and human development indicators. Singh and Srinivasan 2006 compare state-level measures from the Planning Commission's National Human Development Index (HDI) – which takes into account per-capita expenditure, head count poverty ratio, literacy rate, formal education enrollment, infant mortality rate, life expectancy, access to safe water, and access to "pucca" (reasonably permanent) housing – and find modestly *decreasing* inequality in HDI from the 1980s to the 1990s. See also the discussion in Panagariya 2008: 162.

13  A Karnataka finance secretary who had dealt with the Bank during Lim's tenure offered, "Lim had a way of throwing his weight around – he wanted you to know that he had a

lot of authority over what the Bank was going to do. Some of us didn't mind it, but that's traditionally not the way it's done in dealing with government officials in India." A Bank staff member who had worked under Lim said, "He had a habit of making off-the-cuff promises" of assistance to officials at the state level. "Then we would hear from the DEA bureaucrats, 'What pisses us off is that states get a promise from your country director, then complain to us' [if a loan does not work out]" (2008).

14 Several Indian officials offered high praise for Carter's deep knowledge of and respect for the country; Anirudh Tewari, a former DEA director, said, "I have yet to meet a person of non-Indian origin who understands India better than Michael" (2008). Tewari did not interact with Ed Lim, who left the Bank almost two years before he joined the Department. He did volunteer an opinion about Lim's widely publicized confrontation with Mayawati, the UP chief minister, in 2002 (see Chapter 3), saying, "It is not the role of the World Bank's country director to be so visible."

15 For an important analysis of relevant issues in this sector, see Basu 2006.

16 This former hill region of Uttar Pradesh was established as the new state of Uttaranchal in 2000, and in 2007 its name was changed to Uttarakhand, a term that appears in Sanskrit scriptures.

17 For a somewhat more nuanced and sympathetic perspective on Rabri Devi, see Joseph 2001.

18 Voters evidently had poll fatigue: the turnout in the November election was only about 46 percent, the lowest in Bihar in nearly 50 years (the February turnout had been only slightly higher) (Witsoe and Frankel 2006: 39).

## Chapter Four. A Bittersweet "Graduation" from Aid: Can IDA hold on to India, and Will India Let It?

1 In 2006–7, the Bank reduced the cost of IBRD loans. In India, this translated into a reduction of roughly a quarter of a percentage point in pricing on IBRD's variable spread and fixed spread loan products, against an average cost of loans to the Indian government of 2.25 percent the year before. The new pricing put IBRD rates in line with the London Interbank Offered Rate, a reference rate used by commercial banks (World Bank 2007c).

2 International Development Association, "IDA Donors and Partners." Online. <http://go.worldbank.org/DG0REG38A0>. Retrieved on 27 July 2009.

3 Early in IDA's history, IBRD transfers represented as much as 15–18 percent of donor contributions. This soon fell to the single-digit range, though beginning with IDA11 in the 1990s, IBRD transfers spiked again to almost 15 percent of donor contributions before leveling off at around 9–10 percent for IDA12 through IDA14.

4 Note that Adam Lerrick argues that the claim that IBRD operations help to support IDA aid is "a fiction." Lerrick, a former private financial executive, is a scholar at the Tepper School of Business at Carnegie Mellon University, who served as senior advisor to the International Financial Institution Advisory Commission (known as the "Meltzer Commission") commissioned by the US Congress in 1998. The Commission's report (Meltzer 2000) recommended major restructuring of the World Bank and other international financial institutions, including an end to Bank lending in middle-income countries and a focus on its knowledge role and provision of grants to poor countries. Some critics of the report interpreted its agenda as *de facto* dismantling the IFIs, and reactions split largely on partisan/ideological lines.

Lerrick asserted in 2005, "There is a basic fallacy in this argument [that IBRD lending is necessary to subsidize IDA credits and grants]. The Bank makes no money at all on its loans to middle-income countries. The Bank charges the same interest rate to all its borrowers regardless of credit risk, and this interest rate is simply the Bank's own cost of funds plus the spread of 0.5 percent per annum to cover the Bank's administrative costs. But where does the Bank actually make its money? The Bank doesn't make it on its lending, the Bank makes it on the investment income on its zero interest capital. The Bank currently holds almost $40 billion in cash on its balance sheet that it pays no remuneration on. This is the original initial paid-in capital from its members and the accumulated retained earnings. The investment of this pool of funds generates between $1.5 and $3.5 billion per year depending on the level of interest rates. It would generate the same net income whether it's used as lending and financing for middle-income countries or it was simply invested in AAA Government Bonds in the capital markets. This is why the Bank's net income depends on the level of interest rates. If the Bank's net income were derived from its lending activities, it would make the same net income whether interest rates were at 1 percent or interest rates were at 15 percent because the lending interest rates are simply a spread above the Bank's own cost of funds" (deFerranti, Lerrick et al. 2005).

This merits a considered response, and the reader is invited to verify Lerrick's claims against publicly available financial statements from the Bank (such as in its annual reports). First, the Bank's argument that IBRD provides a necessary cross-subsidy to IDA may have been truer in the past than it is today. Lerrick is describing a Bank that has progressively had to compete on a cost basis with private sector lenders, even as its own administrative costs surged during the 1990s and early 2000s. It is still the Bank's official position that IBRD operations are essential to its business model and to cross-subsidize IDA, and it is that conviction of its managers and staff (which seems to find sympathy among donors, apart from conservatives in the US) that is important to the argument here because it provides an underlying incentive for the Bank to want to retain large, reliable borrowers such as India. On that point, there is no disagreement with Lerrick, who says the idea "that the Bank actually wants countries to graduate from its lending programs" is another "fiction" – "Unfortunately, the Bank thinks of itself as a bank and not as a development agency. No bank wants to lose its best clients, and because the Bank charges the same interest rate to all of its borrowers, it has every incentive to lend to its best lowest-risk clients and retain their business" (ibid., 2005). This is especially true of India.

5  A July 2009 report by the US Senate's Committee on Foreign Relations, chaired by John Kerry (D-Mass.), called on the Bank to "implement transparency reforms" in the latest IDA replenishment, "including disclosing Board minutes" (Senate Report 111–50: 2009).

6  World Bank, "International Development Association: Voting Power of Member Countries." Online. <http://go.worldbank.org/VKVDQDUC10>. Retrieved on 27 July 2009.

7  Technically, the "Part I" and "Part II" designations do not perfectly correspond to donor and borrower rosters; the nomenclature actually refers to whether countries choose to pay their contributions to IDA in freely convertible currency (Part I countries) or local currency (Part II countries). The designations are commonly used shorthand for donors and borrowers, however. In practice Part I countries are almost all industrialized and donors; Part II countries are almost all developing countries, a few of whom are IDA donors.

8  IDA also administers a smaller number of "grants" to highly debt-distressed countries; this does not apply to India.

9  For example, Egypt originally graduated in 1981 but reentered a decade later, and graduated again in 1999. Nigeria graduated in 1965, but its downward economic spiral brought it back in 1989.

10 International Development Association, "IDA Borrowing Counries." Online. <http://go.worldbank.org/83SUQPXD20>. Retrieved on 27 July 2009.

11 China's membership in the Bank was represented by Taiwan until 1980. Mainland China (the People's Republic of China), initiated relations with the institution soon after launching its economic reforms in 1978; see Lim 2005: 101.

12 The other blend countries in 2009 were Armenia, Azerbaijan, Bolivia, Bosnia-Herzegovina, Dominica, Georgia, Grenada, St. Lucia, St. Vincent, Uzbekistan, and, inactively, Zimbabwe.

13 World Bank indicator, using Atlas method, from "India at a Glance." Online. <http://go.worldbank.org/63DY8HX2R0>. Retrieved on 23 July 2009.

14 The composition is loan-specific; some project loans are still 50 percent IDA. India itself has developed guidelines stipulating that IDA resources should be directed toward sectors significantly impacting on its achievement of the Millennium Development Goals – particularly in the lagging states. In the country's middle-income states, and at the central level, some loans will be entirely on IBRD terms during 2009–11 (2008b: 21). The Bank's state-level adjustment loans (DPLs) have been an important part of the shift toward a harder blend, since they are about two-thirds IBRD/one-third IDA. They have not been the only factor, especially since this kind of lending never reached the 30–40 percent share of the Bank's India portfolio that Lim had envisioned. An increase in IBRD assistance for infrastructure projects has also contributed.

15 According to Lewis, "Since the inception of their aid programs, the Nordic countries have considered poverty alleviation their guiding principle and have deliberately channeled a high percentage of Official Development Assistance to the poorest groups in the least developed countries. When the World Bank was revising the formula for aid allocation to IDA countries, the Nordic countries pressed the Bank to give pro-poor elements greater weight in the performance criteria" (1993: 36).

16 The Nordic-Baltic Office did not respond to an interview request by the author to address its position on India's status in IDA. Author email to World Bank EDS20, "Request to Interview ED/Alternate or Senior Staff" (27 May 2009).

17 As of 2006, China's cumulative borrowings from the World Bank totaled US$40.9 billion (of which US$30.9 billion was IBRD, and US$9.9 billion IDA), compared to India's total US$65.7 billion (US$33.6 billion IBRD, US$32.1 billion IDA); World Bank 2007b: 62–3.

18 According to the World Bank web site for South Africa, "Projects & Programs." Online. <http://go.worldbank.org/0V0IPMVXT0>. Retrieved on 30 July 2009. For more than thirty years beginning in the Apartheid era, the Bank did not lend to South Africa.

19 Mallaby narrates an episode from the Bank's lending in China, reminiscent of the earlier Narmada controversy in India, to demonstrate why larger, more creditworthy borrowers might wish to avoid IBRD borrowing in favor of commercial alternatives. As noted in Chapter One, in 1999, an irrigation project in the western province of Qinghai, which borders Tibet, became the target of a major protest campaign by Western activists opposed to population resettlement aspects of the project. The debate became particularly acrimonious after the activists recruited US Congressional support and the US threatened to cut payments to the next replenishment of IDA (even though the Qinghai project loan would have been entirely through IBRD, suggesting how closely linked IBRD operations can be to the IDA replenishment process). American pressure, in turn, led

President Wolfensohn to activate the Bank's Inspection Panel (established in 1993 after the Narmada controversy in India). The Panel's report was critical, and the Bank's management response proposed another year's worth of studies, leading the Chinese government to withdraw its request for World Bank assistance (Mallaby 2004: 270–81).

20 See World Bank 2006b; de Ferranti 2006.

21 Andhra Pradesh GSDP per capita figure is an advance estimate from the State Government's website, <http://www.aponline.gov.in/quick%20links/apfactfile/apfactfile_4.html>, retrieved on 03 August 2009. Bihar, Delhi, and Gujarat figures are from media reports; see "Bihar Lowest in Per Capita Income," *Rediff India Abroad* (23 October 2008), online <http://www.rediff.com/money/2008/oct/23bihar.htm>, retrieved on 03 August 2009; see also "Gujarat's Per Capita Income Increases, Along with Debt," *The Times of India* (08 July 2009).

22 Both IBRD and IDA are enjoined by their charters to secure sovereign guarantees for sub-national lending, with IDA enjoying slightly greater discretion in this regard. In some federal countries such as Brazil, the Bank lends directly to sub-national governments with a central guarantee, in contrast to the intermediary role that the Centre plays in India.

23 Author's interview with a former External Affairs Officer for the World Bank in India, Washington, DC, July 31, 2007.

24 See European Network on Debt & Development, "Lowdown on World Bank and IMF Annual Meetings 2007" (23 October). Online. <http://www.eurodad.org/whatsnew/articles.aspx?id=322&item=1758>. Retrieved on 04 August 2009.

# Chapter Five.  Commencement: India's Changing Relationship to Global Development Assistance

1 Wolfowitz was romantically involved with a senior World Bank staffer, Shaha Riza, before assuming the presidency. He initially tried to arrange for her to remain on staff in spite of an ethics rule prohibiting romantic relationships between Bank supervisors and subordinates; later, he dictated the terms of her external assignment to the US Department of State, including a substantial increase in her tax-exempt World Bank salary.

2 In an interview with the author in 2007, after his retirement from the Bank, Carter reiterated these points and added that Wolfowitz "really blew it" by picking on India, but suggested that his successor Robert Zoellick now had "a fabulous opportunity to rebuild the relationship" (Carter 2007b).

3 In two separate interviews in 2008, an Indian finance ministry official and a World Bank official – neither of whom wished to be named, given the speculative nature of their comments – said that one widely circulated theory about Wolfowitz's conduct was that the former Bush administration insider was, in fact, attempting to signal that he was "his own man" by challenging India over the health project corruption, given that during 2005–6 the US administration and the Indian government were pursuing a high-profile "strategic partnership." The centerpiece of this diplomacy was a proposed path-breaking agreement on civilian nuclear cooperation that would effectively legitimize India's possession of a nuclear weapons program outside the bounds of the Nuclear Nonproliferation Treaty. This may be to read too much into Wolfowitz's motives, however.

4 As previously noted, the Indian ED also represents Bangladesh, Bhutan, and Sri Lanka.

5 This well-known story is told with typical panache in Shashi Tharoor's excellent biography of Nehru (2003: 214).

# BIBLIOGRAPHY

## Published Sources

Acharya, Shankar. 2003. *India's Economy: Some Issues and Answers*. New Delhi: Academic Foundation.

————. 2002. "Comment: State-Level Performance under Economic Reforms," in Anne O. Krueger, ed, *Economic Policy Reforms and the Indian Economy*. Chicago: University of Chicago Press. 122–5.

————. 2000. *India's Economy: Some Issues and Answers*. New Delhi: Academic Foundation

Ahluwalia, Montek Singh. 2002. "State-level Performance Under Economic Reforms in India," in Anne O. Krueger, ed, *Economic Policy Reforms and the Indian Economy*. Chicago: University of Chicago Press. 91–122.

————. 2000. "Economic Performance of States in Post-Reforms Period," *Economic and Political Weekly* (06 May).

Ahmed, Masood. 2006. "Votes and Voice: Reforming Governance at the World Bank," in Nancy Birdsall, ed, *Rescuing the World Bank*. Washington, DC: Center for Global Development, 87–94. Electronic format version of book, online. <http://www.cgdev.org/content/publications/detail/9957>. Retrieved on 03 August 2009.

Aiyar, Swaminathan S. Ankelsaria. 2000a. "World Bank Bets $4B on UP." *The Economic Times* (13 July).

————. 2000b. "A Guide to the World Bank for UP's Reform." *The Economic Times* (16 July).

Alacevich, Michele. 2009. *The Political Economy of the World Bank: The Early Years*. Palo Alto, CA: Stanford University Press for the World Bank.

Alamgir, Jalal. 2007. "Nationalist Globalism: The Narrative of Strategic Politics and Economic Openness in India," in Baldev Raj Nayar, ed, *Globalization and Politics in India*. New Delhi: Oxford University Press. 245–66.

Asian Development Bank. 2007. "Evaluation of the Gujarat Public Sector Resource Management Program in India." Online. <http://www.adb.org/Documents/PPERs/IND/29458/29458-IND-PPER.asp>. Retrieved on 07 July 2009.

————. 2004. "Technical Assistance (Financed by the Government of the United Kingdom) to India for West Bengal Development Finance." TAR IND: 35213 (August). Manila and New Delhi: Asian Development Bank.

Babb, Sarah. 2009. *Behind the Development Banks: Washington Politics, World Poverty, and the Wealth of Nations*. Chicago: The University of Chicago Press.

————. 2004. *Managing Mexico: Economists from Nationalism to Neoliberalism*. Princeton: Princeton University Press.

Bagchi, Amaresh and John Kurian. 2005. "Regional Inequalities in India: Pre- and Post-Reform Trends and Challenges for Policy," in Jos Mooij, ed, *The Politics of Economic Reforms in India*. Thousand Oaks, CA: Sage Publications, 322–50.

Bank Information Center (BIC). 2004. "World Bank's proposed middle income country strategy threatens to weaken social and environmental standards. 186 organizations sign letter in protest" (07 June). Online.<http://www.bicusa.org/en/Article.1469.aspx>. Retrieved on 31 July 2009.

Banyan. 2009. "India's Hamstrung Visionary." *The Economist* (08 August), p. 40.

Bardhan, Pranab. 1998 [1984]. *The Political Economy of Development in India*, Expanded Edition. New Delhi: Oxford University Press.

Barnett, Michael and Martha Finnemore. 2004. *Rules for the World: International Organizations in Global Politics*. Ithaca, NY: Cornell University Press.

Basu, Priya. 2006. *Improving Access to Finance for India's Rural Poor*. Washington, DC: The World Bank.

Becker, Elizabeth. 2005. "Similar Résumé, a Different Decade; For McNamara and Wolfowitz, a War and then the World Bank." *The New York Times* (22 March). <http://query.nytimes.com/gst/fullpage.html?res=9D05E1DB1F3CF931A15750C0A9639C8B63&pagewanted=all>. Retrieved on 22 June 2009.

Bendix, Reinhard. 1977 [1960]. *Max Weber: An Intellectual Portrait*. Berkeley: University of California Press.

Beschel, Jr., Robert P. 2003. "Civil Service Reform in India: Perspectives from the World Bank's Work in Three States," in Stephen Howes, Ashok K. Lahiri and Nicholas Stern, eds, *State-level Reforms in India: Towards More Effective Government*. New Delhi: Macmillan India. 233–56.

Bhaduri, Amit and Deepak Nayyar. 1996. *Intelligent Person's Guide to Liberalization*. New Delhi: Penguin Books India.

Bhambhri, Chandra Prakash. 1980. *World Bank and India*. New Delhi: Vikas Publishing House.

Bhagwati, Jagdish N. and T.N. Srinivasan. 1975. *Foreign Trade Regimes and Economic Development: India*. New York: Columbia University Press for the National Bureau of Economic Research.

Bhattacharjee, Subhomoy. 2004. "World Bank May Cut Off State Loans." *Rediff.com* (9 August).

Bhattacharya, B.B. and S. Sakthivel. 2007. "Regional Growth and Disparity in India: Comparison of Pre- and Post-Reform Decades," in Baldev Raj Nayar, *Globalization and Politics in India*. New Delhi: Oxford University Press, 458–76.

Bhattacharya, Prajnan. 2000. "Interview: 'People Should be Prepared for a Hard Budget'," *The Economic Times* (26 December).

Bjorkman, James W. 2008 [1980]. "Public Law 480 and the Policies of Self-Help and Short-Tether: Indo-American Relations 1965–1968," in Lloyd Rudolph and Susanne H. Rudolph, eds, *Making U.S. Foreign Policy Toward South Asia: Regional Imperatives and the Imperial Presidency*. Bloomington: Indiana University Press. 359–424.

"Blend of Reforms Needed." 2000. *The Statesman* (Calcutta)(09 November).

"Booting Up in Andhra Pradesh: The State Election to Watch in India." 1999. *The Economist* (11 September).

Boquérat, Gilles. 2003. *No Strings Attached? India's Policies and Foreign Aid 1947–1966*. New Delhi: Manohar/Centre de Sciences Humaines.

Bowles, Chester. 1971. *Promises to Keep: My Years in Public Life, 1941–1969*. New York: Harper & Row.

Callaghy, Thomas M. 1989. "Toward State Capability and Embedded Liberalism in the Third World: Lessons for Economic Adjustment," in Joan Nelson (ed), *Fragile Coalitions: The Politics of Economic Adjustment.* Washington, DC: Overseas Development Council, 115–38.

Cashin, Paul and Ratna Sahay. 1996. "Regional Economic Growth and Convergence in India." *Finance & Development* (March): 49–52.

Caufield, Catherine. 1996. *Masters of Illusion: The World Bank and the Poverty of Nations.* New York: Henry Holt & Company.

"Centre Axes Maharashtra Plea on World Bank Loan." 2003. *The Financial Express* (27 May).

Chakrabarty, Bidyut. 2006. *Forging Power: Coalition Politics in India.* New Delhi: Oxford University Press.

Chandra, Kanchan. 2004. *Why Ethnic Parties Succeed: Patronage and Ethnic Head Counts in India.* New York: Cambridge University Press.

———. 1999. "Post-Congress Politics in Uttar Pradesh: The Ethnification of the Party System and its Consequences," in in Ramashray Roy and Paul Wallace, eds, *Indian Politics and the 1998 Election.* Thousand Oaks, CA: Sage Publications. 55–104.

Chaudhry, Praveen K., Vijay L. Kelkar, and Vikash Yadav. 2005 "The Evolution of 'Homegrown Conditionality' in India: IMF Relations." *Journal of Development Studies* 40, No. 6 (August): 59–81.

Chaudhry, Praveen K. and Marta Vanduzer-Snow, eds. 2008. *The United States and India: A History Through Archives, The Formative Years.* Thousand Oaks, CA: Sage Publications.

Chhibber, Pradeep, and Irfan Nooruddin. 2004. "Do Party Systems Count? The Number of Parties and Government Performance in the Indian States." *Comparative Political Studies,* 37, No. 2 (March): 152–87.

Chidambaram, P. 2007. *A View from the Outside: Why Good Economics Works for Everyone.* New Delhi: Portfolio/Penguin Books India.

"China, India Will Get More Weight at IMF, World Bank." 2009. *Business Line* (27 September).

Chopra, Mannika. 2005. "India Resists Tsunami Aid, Reveals New Identity." *The Boston Globe* (24 January). Online. <http://www.boston.com/news/world/asia/articles/2005/01/24/india_resists_tsunami_aid_reveals_new_identity/>. Retrieved on 13 July 2009.

Collier, Paul. 1997. "The Failure of Conditionality," in Catherine Gwin and Joan Nelson, eds, *Perspectives on Aid and Development.* Washington, DC: Overseas Development Council. 51–78.

"Control Fiscal Deficit to Ensure Rapid Progress." 2004. *The Hindu* (05 August).

Corbridge, Stuart, Glyn Williams, Manoj Srivastava, and René Véron. 2005. *Seeing the State: Governance and Governmentality in India.* New York: Cambridge University Press.

——— and John Harriss. 2000. *Reinventing India: Liberalization, Hindu Nationalism and Popular Democracy* Cambridge, UK: Polity Press.

Cullather, Nick. 2007. "Hunger and Containment: How India Became 'Important' in US Cold War Strategy." *India Review* 6, no. 2 (April–June): 59–90.

Das, Gurcharan. 2002. *India Unbound: From Independence to the Global Information Age,* revised and updated edition. New Delhi: Penguin Books India.

Deaton, Angus and Jean Drèze. 2007 [2002]. "Poverty and Inequality in India: A Re-examination," in Baldev Raj Nayar, ed, *Globalization and Politics in India.* New Delhi: Oxford University Press, 408–57. First published as "Poverty and Inequality in India: A Re-examination," in *Economic and Political Weekly* (07 September): 3729–48.

Debroy, Bibek, Shubhashis Gangopadhyay, and Laveesh Bhandari. 2004. "An Economic Freedom Index for India's States," in Bibek Debroy, ed, *Agenda for Improving Governance.* New Delhi: Academic Foundation in Association with the Rajiv Gandhi Institute for Contemporary Studies, 563–652.

de Ferranti, David. 2006. "The World Bank and Middle Income Countries." Brookings Institution Papers. Washington, DC: The Brookings Institution.

_____, Adam Lerrick and Lawrence MacDonald (moderator). 2005. "Who Needs the World Bank: The Future of China, India and the Middle-Income Countries?" Transcript (23 September). Panel discussion at *The Future of the World Bank: A Center for Global Development Symposium*. Washington, DC: Center for Global Development.

de Groot, Albert, C.K. Ramachandran, Anneke Slob, Anja Willemsen, and Alf Morten Jerve. 2008. *Managing Aid Exit and Transformation: India Country Case Study*. Joint Donor Evaluation Commissioned by Sida, Netherland's Ministry of Foreign Affairs, Danida, Norad and the authors (May). Online. <http://www.sida.se/exitevaluation>. Retrieved on 12 July 2009.

Department of Institutional Integrity. 2007. *Detailed Implementation Review: India Health Sector 2006–2007*, Vol. I and II. Washington, D.C.: The World Bank Group (December). Online at <http://go.worldbank.org/YVLEFEQKZ0>. Accessed on 02 November 2009.

Desai, Meghnad. 2005. *Development and Nationhood: Essays in the Political Economy of South Asia*. New Delhi: Oxford University Press.

DeYoung, Karen and Al Kamen. 2007. "Wolfowitz Apologizes for 'Mistake'." *The Washington Post* (13 April). Online at <http://www.washingtonpost.com/wp-dyn/content/article/2007/04/12/AR2007041201188_pf.html>. Retrieved on 12 October 2009.

Dhar, P.N. 2003. *Evolution of Economic Policy in India: Selected Essays*. New Delhi: Oxford University Press.

Dhoot, Vikas and Amitav Ranjan. 2006. "Chidambaram Sends a Firm Note to Bank: Let's Not Strain Ties." The Indian Express (05 April). Online at <http://www.indianexpress.com/news/chidambaram-sends-a-firm-note-to-bank-lets/1822/>. Retrieved on 12 October 2009.

"Dirty Linen." 2008. *The Economist* (19 March). Online at <http://www.economist.com/world/international/displaystory.cfm?story_id=10880573>. Retrieved on 01 November 2009.

Drezner, Daniel (ed). 2003. *Locating the Proper Authorities: The Interaction of Domestic and International Institutions*. Ann Arbor: University of Michigan Press.

Dugger, Celia W. 1999. "Even the Poor Pay Heed to the Esoterica of India's Riches." *The New York Times* (10 September).

Duncan, Gary. 2006. "Wolfowitz Reined in by Ministers: Wealthy Nations Assert Their Right to Oversee the World Bank President's Anti-Corruption Campaign." *The Times*, London (19 September).

Duncan, Peter J.S. 1993. "The Soviet-Indian Model: Continuity in a Changing Environment," in Margot Light, ed, *Troubled Friendships: Moscow's Third World Ventures*. London: British Academic Press for the Royal Institute of International Affairs. 29–51.

Eckstein, Harry. 1975. "Case Study and Theory in Political Science," in Fred I. Greenstein and Nelson W. Polsby (eds), *Handbook of Political Science*, Vol. 7. Reading, MA: Addison Wesley, 79–138.

"Economic and Financial Indicators." 2009. *The Economist* (31 October), p. 109.

Einhorn, Jessica. 2001. "The World Bank's Mission Creep." *Foreign Affairs* (September/October): 22–35.

"Electricity Might Determine the Fate of TDP." 2004. *Indo-Asian News Service* (16 April).

"Enlarge Role for the Poor: India." 2003. *Business Standard* (23 September).

Evans, Peter B., Harold K. Jacobson, and Robert D. Putnam (eds). 1993. *Double-Edged Diplomacy: International Bargaining and Domestic Politics*. Berkeley: University of California Press.

Fehr, Ernst, Karla Hoff, and Mayuresh Kshetramade. 2008. "Spite and Development." Policy Research Working Paper 4619 (May). Washington, DC: The World Bank, Development Research Group, Macroeconomics and Growth Team.

Finnemore, Martha. 1996. *National Interests in International Society*. Ithaca, NY: Cornell University Press.

"Forgotten Sibling." 2009. *The Economist* (23 April). Online. <http://www.economist.com/research/articlesBySubject/displaystory.cfm?subjectid=526358&story_id=E1_TPV NRNQN>. Retrieved on 02 November 2009.

Frankel, Francine R. 2005 [1978]. *India's Political Economy, 1947–2004: The Gradual Revolution*, 2nd Edition. New Delhi: Oxford University Press.

"Furor in UP Assembly Over World Bank Letter." 2002. *Financial Express* (29 August).

"The Future of World Bank in India." 2006. *The Indian Express* (17 September).

Ganguly, Sumit and Manjeet S. Pardesi,. 2007. "India Rising: What is New Delhi to Do?" *World Policy Journal* XXIV, No. 1 (Spring): 9–18.

_____, Larry Diamond, and Marc F. Plattner (eds). 2007. *The State of India's Democracy*. Baltimore: The Johns Hopkins University Press.

Gavin, Michael and Dani Rodrik. 1995. "The World Bank in Historical Perspective." *American Economic Review, Papers and Proceedings* 85: 329–34.

Gerring, John. 2007. "Is There a (Viable) Crucial Case Method?" *Comparative Politics Studies* 40, No. 3:231–53.

Gilbert, Christopher L. and David Vines. 2000. "The World Bank: An Overview of Some Major Issues," in Christopher L. Gilbert and David Vines, eds, *The World Bank: Structure and Policies*. Cambridge: Cambridge University Press, 10–36.

Gilbert, Christopher L., Andrew Powell and David Vines. 2000. "Positioning the World Bank," in Christopher L. Gilbert and David Vines, eds, *The World Bank: Structure and Policies*. Cambridge: Cambridge University Press, 39–86.

Gilpin, Robert. 2001. *Global Political Economy: Understanding the International Economic Order*. Princeton: Princeton University Press.

Gjelten, Tom. 2007. "Wolfowitz Feels the Heat at the World Bank." National Public Radio (13 April). Online at <http://www.npr.org/templates/story/story.php?storyId=9558497>. Retrieved on 12 October 2009.

Goldin, Ian and Kenneth A. Reinhart. 2006. *Globalization for Development: Trade, Finance, Aid, Migration, and Policy*. New York and Washington, DC: Palgrave Macmillan and The World Bank.

Goldman, Michael. 2005. *Imperial Nature: The World Bank and the Struggles for Social Justice in the Age of Globalization*. New Haven: Yale University Press.

Gould, Harold A. 2003. "Political Self-Destruction in Karnataka, 1999," in Paul Wallace and Ramashray Roy, eds, *India's 1999 Elections and 20th Century Politics*. Thousand Oaks, CA: Sage Publications. 94–140.

Government of Andhra Pradesh. 1999. *Andhra Pradesh: Vision 2020*. Hyderabad: State Secretariat.

Government of India. 2001. *National Human Development Report*. New Delhi: Planning Commission, Government of India.

_____.1992. *Economic Survey 1991–92*. New Delhi: Ministry of Finance, Government of India.

Guha, Krishna and Amy Yee. 2007. "World Bank Loans to India Climb 170%." *Financial Times* (5 July).

Guha, Ramachandra. 2007. *India After Gandhi: The History of the World's Largest Democracy*. New York: HarperCollins.

Guhan, S. 1995a. "Federalism and the New Political Economy in India," in Balveer Arora and Douglas V. Verney, eds, *Multiple Identities in a Single State: Indian Federalism in Comparative Perspective.* New Delhi: Konark Publishers. 237–71.

———. 1995b. "The World Bank's Lending in South Asia." *Brookings Occasional Papers.* Washington, DC: The Brookings Institution.

Gupta, Shekhar. 2007. "Foreward," in P. Chidambaram, *A View from the Outside: Why Good Economics Works for Everyone.* New Delhi: Portfolio/Penguin Books India. ix–x.

Gurumurthi, S. 1995. *Fiscal Federalism in India.* New Delhi: Vikas Publishing House.

Haarder, Bertel. 2004. Statement by the Hon. Bertel Haarder, Governor of the [World] Bank for Denmark, on behalf of the Nordic Countries, at the Joint Annual Discussion. Press Release No. 10 (03 October). Board of Governors, 2004 Annual Meetings of the International Monetary Fund and World Bank Group, Washington, DC. <www.imf.org/external/am/2004/speeches/pr10e.pdf>. Retrieved on 31 July 2009.

Haas, Ernst. 1990. *When Knowledge is Power: Three Models of Change in International Organizations.* Berkeley: University of California Press.

Harris, Clive. 2008. "India Leads Developing Nations in Private Sector Investment." *Gridlines* Note No. 30 (March). Washington, DC: Public-Private Infrastructure Advisory Facility, in Care of The World Bank.

Hasan, Zoya (ed). 2002. *Parties and Party Politics in India.* New Delhi: Oxford University Press.

———. 2001. "Transfer of Power?: Politics and Mass Mobilization in UP," *Economic and Political Weekly* (24 November).

Hawkins, Darren G., David A. Lake, Daniel L. Nielson and Michael J. Tierney. 2006. "Delegation Under Anarchy: States, International Organizations, and Principal-Agent Theory," in Darren G. Hawkins, David A. Lake, Daniel L. Nielson and Michael J. Tierney (eds), *Delegation and Agency in International Organizations.* New York: Cambridge University Press, 3–38.

"He Knows His Friends, Foes, and Priorities." 1999. *The Economic Times of India* (08 October).

"Heels Over Head: YSR Turns Pro-World Bank." 2005. *The Economic Times* (18 May).

House of Commons. 2005. *International Development—Third Report* (09 March). London: International Development Committee, House of Commons, Parliament, United Kingdom. Online. <http://www.publications.parliament.uk/pa/cm200405/cmselect/cmintdev/124/12402.htm>. Retrieved 13 July 2009.

Howes, Stephen, Ashok K. Lahiri and Nicholas Stern, eds. 2003. *State-level Reforms in India: Towards More Effective Government.* New Delhi: Macmillan India.

Howes, Stephen, Deepak Mishra and V.J. Ravishankar. 2008. "A Decade of World Bank Sub-National Policy-Based Lending to India: A Retrospective," in Raghbendra Jha, ed, *The Indian Economy Sixty Years After Independece.* Houndmills, Basingstoke, UK: Palgrave Macmillan. 41–68.

Human Rights Watch. 2002. "'We Have No Orders to Save You': State Participation and Complicity in Communal Violence in Gujarat." Volume 14, No. 3(c). Online. <http://www.hrw.org/legacy/reports/2002/india/>. Retrieved on 23 July 2009.

Independent People's Tribunal on the World Bank in India. 2008. "Findings of the Jury: Verdict of the Independent People's Tribunal Held at Jawaharlal Nehru University, New Delhi, India, 21–2 September 2007" (11 September). Online. <http://www.worldbanktribunal.org/judgement.html>. Retrieved on 02 August 2009.

"India Becomes IMF Lender." 2003. *BBC News* (30 June). Online. <http://news.bbc.co.uk/2/hi/business/3031568.stm>. Retrieved on 13 July 2009.

"India: Cabinet Decides Against Power Tariff Hike." 2001. *The Hindu* (14 September).

"India Joins the $100-Billion Club!" 2003. *Rediff.com* (21 December). Online. <http://www.rediff.com/money/2003/dec/21forex.htm>. Retrieved on 13 July 2009.

"India Pitches for Governance Reforms." 2009. *Business Line* (07 October). Online. <http://www.thehindubusinessline.com/2009/10/07/stories/2009100751611500.htm>. Retrieved on 02 November 2009.

"India Says Loan Rebuffs Critics." 1998. *The Financial Times* (03 July): 6.

"India: State's 'Admirable' Plans Praised." 2000. *The Hindu* (10 November).

International Development Association. 2007a. "The Demand for IDA15 Resources and the Strategy for Their Effective Use." Washington, DC: International Development Association/The World Bank.

———. 2007b. "India: Using IDA Effectively in a Large Country." Washington, DC: International Development Association/The World Bank. Online. <http://go.worldbank.org/S0ORROSSO0>. Retrieved on 02 August 2009.

———. 2007c. "IDA's Long-Term Financial Capacity." Washington, DC: International Development Association/The World Bank.

———. 2001a. "IDA Eligibility, Terms and Graduation Policies" (January). Washington, DC: International Development Association/The World Bank.

———. 2001b. "New Options for IDA Lending Terms" (September). Washington, DC: International Development Association/The World Bank.

Jacobson, Harold K. and Michel Oksenburg. 1990. *China's Participation in the IMF, the World Bank, and GATT: Toward a Global Economic Order.* Ann Arbor: University of Michigan Press.

Jafri, Syed Amin. 2000. "AP House Rocked by World Bank Official's Statement." *Rediff.com* (5 September). Online. <http://www.rediff.com/news/2000/sep/05ap.htm>. Retrieved on 28 February 2003.

Jainani, Deepa. 2009. "Promises are Fine, but Deliver Too: World Bank Message to UP Govt," *The Financial Express* (18 January).

Jakobeit, Cord. 2005. "Enhancing the Voice of Developing Countries in The World Bank: Selective Double Majority Voting and a Pilot Phase Approach," in Ariel Buira (ed), *Reforming the Governance of the IMF and the World Bank.* London: Anthem Press, 213–34.

"A Jaswant Singh Doctrine on Foreign Aid." 2003. *The Financial Express* (06 June). Online. <http://www.financialexpress.com/news/a-jaswant-singh-doctrine-on-foreign-aid/75614/1>. Retrieved on 13 July 2009.

Jayal, Niraja Gopal. 2006. *Representing India: Ethnic Diversity and the Governance of Public Institutions.* New York: Palgrave Macmillan.

Jenkins, Rob. 2004. "Introduction," in Rob Jenkins (ed), *Regional Reflections: Comparing Policies Across India's States.* New Delhi: Oxford University Press, 1–26.

———. 2003. "How Federalism Influences India's Domestic Politics of WTO Engagement (and is Itself Affected in the Process)." *Asian Survey* 43, No. 4: 598–621.

———. 1999. *Democratic Politics and Economic Reform in India.* New York: Cambridge University Press.

Joseph, Ammu. 2001. "Rabri Devi Revisited." *The Hindu* (09 September). Online. <http://www.hindu.com/2001/09/09/stories/1309078b.htm>. Retrieved on 23 July 2009.

Joshi, Vijay. 1998. "Fiscal Stabilization and Economic Reform in India," in Isher Judge Ahluwalia and I.M.D. Little, eds, *India's Economic Reforms and Development: Essays for Manmohan Singh.* New Delhi: Oxford University Press. 147–68.

Joshi, Vijay and I.M.D. Little. 1996. *India's Economic Reforms 1991–2000.* New Delhi: Oxford University Press.

Kahler, Miles. 1992. "External Influence, Conditionality, and the Politics of Adjustment," in Stephen Haggard and Robert R. Kaufman (eds.), *The Politics of Adjustment: International Constraints, Distributive Conflicts, and the State*. Princeton: Princeton University Press, 89–136.

Kale, Sunila S. 2004. "Current Reforms: The Politics of Policy Change in India's Electricity Sector." *Pacific Affairs* 77, No. 3 (Fall): 467–91.

Kamarck, Andrew M. 1996. "The World Bank: Challenges and Creative Responses," in Orin Kirshner, ed, *The Bretton Woods-GATT System: Retrospect and Prospect after Fifty Years*. Armonk, NY: M.E. Sharpe. 106–27.

Kamath, Shyam J. 1992. "Foreign Aid and India: Financing the Leviathan State." Cato Policy Analysis No. 170 (6 May). Washington, DC: Cato Institute. Online: http://www.cato.org/pubs/pas/pa-170.html (accessed 15 June 2009).

Kapur, Devesh. 2008. "Developing Countries Worse Off Than Once Thought—Part II." *YaleGlobal* (13 Febrary). Online at <http://yaleglobal.yale.edu/display.article?id= 10345>. Retrieved on 01 November 2009.

————. 2006. "The 'Knowledge' Bank," in Nancy Birdsall, ed, *Rescuing the World Bank*. Washington, DC: Center for Global Development, 159–70. Electronic format version of book, online. <http://www.cgdev.org/content/publications/detail/9957>. Retrieved on 03 August 2009.

————, John P. Lewis, and Richard Webb. 1997. *The World Bank: Its First Half Century*, vol. 1, *History*. Washington, DC: Brookings Institution Press.

Keck, Margaret E. and Kathryn Sikkink. 1998. *Activists Beyond Borders: Advocacy Networks in International Politics*. Ithaca, Cornell University Press.

Kennedy, Loraine. 2004. "The Political Determinants of Reform Packaging: Contrasting Responses to Economic Liberalization in Andhra Pradesh and Tamil Nadu," in Rob Jenkins, ed, *Regional Reflections: Comparing Politics Across India's States*. New Delhi: Oxford University Press, 29–65.

Khan, Mushtaq H. 2002. "Corruption and Governance in Early Capitalism," in Jonathan R. Pincus and Jeffrey A. Winters, eds, *Reinventing the World Bank*. Ithaca: Cornell University Press, 165–84.

Khemani, Stuti. 2003. "Partisan Politics and Intergovernmental Transfers in India." World Bank Policy Research Working Paper No. 3016. Washington, DC: The World Bank.

————. 2002. "Federal Politics and Budget Deficits: Evidence From the Indian States." World Bank Policy Research Paper No. 2915. Washington, DC: The World Bank.

Killick, Tony with Ramani Gunatilaka and Ana Marr. 1998. *Aid and the Political Economy of Policy Change*. New York: Routledge.

Kirk, Jason A. 2007. "Economic Reform, Federal Politics, and External Assistance: Understanding New Delhi's Perspective on the World Bank's State-Level Loans," in Rahul Mukherji, ed, *India's Economic Transition: The Politics of Reforms*. New Delhi: Oxford University Press, 265–99.

————. 2005. "Banking on India's States: The Politics of World Bank Reform Programs in Andhra Pradesh and Karnataka," *India Review* 4, No. 3–4: 287–325.

Kletzer, Kenneth and Nirvikar Singh. 2000. "Indian Fiscal Federalism: Political Economy and Issues for Reform," in Satu Kähkönen and Anthony Lanyi, eds, *Institutions, Incentives, and Economic Reforms in India*. Thousand Oaks, CA: Sage Publications. 37–76.

Kohli, Atul. 1996. "Can the Periphery Control the Center?: Indian Politics at the Crossroads." *The Washington Quarterly* 19, No. 4 (Autumn): 115–28.

————. 1988. "The NTR Phenomenon in Andhra Pradesh.

Krasner, Stephen D. 1985. *Structural Conflict: The Third World Against Global Liberalism*. Berkeley: University of California Press.

Krishna, S.M. 2002. Government's Budget Speech Delivered to the State Assembly of Karnataka (21 March). Online. <http://www.kar.nic.in/finance/bud2002/part-a.htm>. Retrieved on 06 July 2009.

Kurian, N.J. 2002. "Growing Inter-State Disparities." *Seminar* 509 (January). Online. <http://www.india-seminar.com/2002/509/509%20n.j.%20kurian.htm>. Retrieved on 03 July 2009.

Kurmanath, K.V. 2005. "Pace of Reforms Has Slackened in Last One Year: World Bank." *Business Line* (04 May).

Kux, Dennis. 1993. *Estranged Democracies: India and the United States, 1941–1991*. Washington, DC: National Defense University Press.

Lal, Sumir. 2006. "Can Good Economics Ever Be Good Politics?: Case Study of India's Power Sector. World Bank Working Paper No. 83. Washington, DC: The World Bank.

Lankester, Tim. 2004. "'Asian Drama': The Pursuit of Modernization in India and Indonesia." *Asian Affairs* XXXV, no. III (November): 291–304.

Lele, Uma and Balu Bumb. 1995. "The Food Crisis in South Asia: The Case of India," in K. Sardar Lateef, ed, *The Evolving Role of the World Bank: Helping Meet the Challenge of Development*. Washington, DC: The World Bank. 69–96.

Lewis, John P. 1995. *India's Political Economy: Governance and Reform*. New Delhi: Oxford University Press.

———. 1993. *Pro-Poor Aid Conditionality*. Policy Essay No. 8. Washington, DC: Overseas Development Council.

Lim, Edwin. 2005. "Learning and Working with the Giants," in Indermit S. Gill and Todd Pugatch, eds., *At the Frontlines of Development: Reflections from the World Bank*. Washington, DC: The World Bank. 87–120.

Lipton, Michael and John Toye. 1990. *Does Aid Work in India?: A Country Study of the Impact of Official Developmental Assistance*. New York: Routledge.

Luce, Edward. 2007. *In Spite of the Gods: The Strange Rise of Modern India*. New York: Doubleday.

———. 2002. "State's Antics Bring World Bank Warning," *The Financial Times* (UK)(03 September).

"Maharasthra, World Bank Working to Resolve Issues." 2006. *Business Standard* (07 June).

Malik, Ashok. 2007. "The BJP, the RSS Family, and Globalization in India," in Baldev Raj Nayar, ed, *Globalization and Politics in India*. New Delhi: Oxford University Press, 288–309.

Mallaby, Sebastian. 2006. "Wolfowitz's Corruption Agenda." *The Washington Post* (20 February). Online at <http://www.washingtonpost.com/wp-dyn/content/article/2006/02/19/AR2006021901137.html>. Retrieved on 12 October 2009.

———. 2004. *The World's Banker: A Story of Failed States, Financial Crises, and the Wealth and Poverty of Nations*. New York: The Penguin Press.

Mann, Jim. 1996. "World Bank Poverty Loans Bestowing Billions on Prospering India, China." *Los Angeles Times* (05 February). Online. <http://articles.latimes.com/1996–02–05/ news/mn-32640_1_world-bank-s-ida?pg=1>. Retrieved on 03 August 2009.

Manor, James. 2004. "Explaining Political Trajectories in Andhra Pradesh and Karnataka," in Rob Jenkins, ed, *Regional Reflections: Comparing Politics Across India's States*. Cambridge: Cambridge University Press. 255–84.

Marcelo, Ray. 2004. "India Blurring the Policy Lines on International Aid." *The Indian Express* (28 September). Online. <http://www.indianexpress.com/oldStory/55959/>. Retrieved on 13 July 2009,

———. 2003. "India Opts to Decline Aid from All but Six Countries." *The Financial Times* (08 July): 9.

Mason, Edward S. and Robert E. Asher. 1973. *The World Bank Since Bretton Woods*. Washington, DC: The Brookings Institution.

Mathew, George. 2007. "The Indian View of Danish Aid." *International Journal of Rural Management* 3, No. 2: 269–86.

McCarten, William J. 2003. "The Challenge of Fiscal Discipline in the Indian States," in Jonathan Rodden, Gunnar S. Eskeland, and Jennie Litvack, eds, *Fiscal Decentralization and the Challenge of Soft Budget Constraints*. Cambridge, MA: The MIT Press. 249–86.

McKeown, Timothy. 2004. "Case Studies and the Limits of the Quantitative Worldview," in Henry E. Brady and David Collier (eds), *Rethinking Social Inquiry: Diverse Tools, Shared Standards*. New York: Rowman & Littlefield Publishers, 139–68.

McNamara, Robert S. with Brian VanDeMark. 1996. *In Retrospect: The Tragedy and Lessons of Vietnam*. New York: Vintage.

Meltzer, Allan H. (Chairman). 2000. *Report of the International Financial Institution Advisory Committee*. Washington, DC: United States Congress. Online. <http://www.house.gov/jec/imf/ifiac.htm>. Retrieved on 03 August 2009.

Menon, Parvathi. 2004a. "Loan as Lever." *Frontline: India's National Magazine* 21, No. 23 (19 November).

————. 2004b. "Karnataka's Agony." *Frontline: India's National Magazine* 18, No. 17 (18 August).

Messias, Lionel. 2000. "World Bank Praise for AP." *Gulf News* (10 November).

Milanovic, Branko. 2005. "Half a World: Regional Inequality in Five Great Federations." World Bank Policy Research Working Paper 3699 (September). Washington, DC: World Bank and Carnegie Endowment for International Peace.

Miller, Susan K. 1992. "World Bank Admits Mistake Over Dam." *New Scientist* 134, no. 1827 (June 27): 4.

Miller-Adams, Michelle. 1999. *The World Bank: New Agendas in a Changing World*. New York: Routledge.

Mitchell, J. Clyde. 1984. "Case Studies," in R.F. Ellen (ed), *Ethnographic Research: A Guide to General Conduct*. Orlando: Academic Press, 237–41.

Mooij, Jos. 2005. "Introduction," in Jos Mooij (ed), *The Politics of Economic Reforms in India*. Thousand Oaks, CA: Sage Publications, 15–45.

————. 2003. "Smart Governance? Politics and the Policy Process in Andhra Pradesh, India." Overseas Development Institute Working Paper No. 228 (October).

Moore, David (ed). 2007. *The World Bank: Development, Poverty, Hegemony*. Scottsville, South Africa: University of KwaZulu-Natal Press.

Morris, Errol (director). 2003. *The Fog of War: Eleven Lessons from the Life of Robert S. McNamara*. Sony Pictures Classics.

Morse, Bradford. 1992. *Sardar Sarovar: Report of the Independent Review*. Ottawa: Resource Futures International.

Mosley, Paul, Jane Harrigan, and John Toye. 1991. *Aid and Power: The World Bank and Policy-Based Lending*, vol. 1, *Analysis and Policy Proposals*. New York: Routledge.

Muirhead, Bruce. 2005. "Differing Perspectives: India, the World Bank and the 1963 Aid-India Negotiations." *India Review* 4, no. 1 (January): 1–22.

Mukherji, Joydeep. 2002. "The Indian Economy: Pushing Ahead and Pulling Apart," in Alyssa Ayres and Philip Oldenburg, ed, *India Briefing: Quickening the Pace of Change*. Armonk, NY: Asia Society and M.E. Sharpe. 55–90.

Mukherji, Rahul (ed). 2007. *India's Economic Transition: The Politics of Reforms*. New Delhi: Oxford University Press.

————. 2000. "India's Aborted Liberalization—1966." *Pacific Affairs* 73, no. 3 (Autumn): 375–92.

Mukul, Jyoti. 2009. "India to Push for Expansion of World Bank Capital." *Business Standard* (21 August). Online at <http://business.rediff.com/report/2009/aug/21/india-to-push-for-expansion-of-world-bank-capital.htm>. Retrieved on 31 August 2009.

Murgai Rinku, Lant Pritchett, and Marina Wes. 2006. *India Development Policy Review: Inclusive Growth and Service Delivery: Building on India's Success.* Washington, DC and New Delhi: The World Bank.

Myrdal, Gunnar. 1968. *Asian Drama: An Inquiry Into the Poverty of Nations,* Vol. 1–3. New York: Pantheon.

Naidu, N. Chandrababu with Sevanti Ninan. 2000. *Plain Speaking.* New Delhi: Viking Books India.

Namboodiripad, E.M.S. 1991. "The Present Economic Situation, Policy Alternatives." *JANATA* (October 13).

"Narmada River." *Encyclopædia Britannica.* 2009. Encyclopædia Britannica Online. <http://www.britannica.com/EBchecked/topic/403526/Narmada-River>. Retrieved on 03 June 2009

Nayar, Baldev Raj. 2009. *The Myth of the Shrinking State: Globalization and the State in India.* New Delhi: Oxford University Press.

————. (ed). 2007a. *Globalization and Politics in India.* New Delhi: Oxford University Press.

————. 2007b. "The Limits of Economic Nationalism in India: Economic Reforms under the BJP-led Government, 1998–9," in Rahul Mukherji, ed, *India's Economic Transition: The Politics of Reforms.* New Delhi: Oxford University Press. 202–30.

————. 2001. *Globalization and Nationalism: The Changing Balance in India's Economic Policy, 1950–2000.* Thousand Oaks, CA: Sage Publications Inc.

Nielson, Daniel L. and Michael J. Tierney. 2005. "Theory, Data, and Hypothesis Testing: World Bank Environmental Reform Redux." *International Organization* 59, No. 3: 785–800.

————. 2003. "Delegation to International Organizations: Agency Theory and World Bank Environmental Reform." *International Organization* 57, No. 2: 241–76.

"No Conditional Loans from World Bank, Says Rosaiah." 2004. *The Hindu* (25 October).

Operations Evaluation Department. 2004. *Brazil: Forging a Strategic Partnership for Results—An OED Evaluation of World Bank Assistance.* Washington, DC: The World Bank.

"Orissa to Seek $250 million World Bank Loan for OSEP." 2009. *Business Standard* (07 August). Online. <http://www.business-standard.com/india/news/orissa-to-seek-250-million-world-bank-loan-for-osep/44292/on>. Retrieved on 22 July 2009.

Paarlberg, Robert. 1985. *Food Trade and Foreign Policy: India, the Soviet Union, and the United States.* Ithaca, NY: Cornell University Press.

Padmanabhan, Anil. 2006. "Aiding Acrimony." India Today (17 April). Online at <http://archives.digitaltoday.in/indiatoday/20060417/business2.html>. Retrieved on 12 October 2009.

Pai, Sudha. 2005. "Populism and Economic Reforms: The BJP Experiment in Uttar Pradesh," in Jos Mooij, ed, *The Politics of Economic Reforms in India.* Thousand Oaks, CA: Sage Publications, 98–129.

————. 2002 "Electoral Identity Politics in Uttar Pradesh: Hung Assembly Again," *Economic and Political Weekly* 37, No. 14: 1334–41.

Pal, Mahendra. 1985. *The World Bank and the Third World Countries of Asia (with Special Reference to India).* New Delhi: National Publishing House.

Panagariya, Arvind. 2008. *India: The Emerging Giant.* New Delhi: Oxford University Press.

Pani, Narendar. 2006. "Icons and Reform Politics in India: The Case of S.M. Krishna," *Asian Survey* 46, No. 2: 238–56.

Park, June. 2009. "The Evolution of China's Relationship with the World Bank: From Debtor and Beneficiary to Partnership." Paper presented at the 2009 Convention of the International Studies Association, New York, NY (15–18 February).

Park, Susan and Antje Vetterlein. 2010. "Owning Development: Creating Global Policy Norms in the IMF and the World Bank," in Susan Park and Antje Vetterlein, eds., Owning Development: Creating Global Policy Norms. Cambridge: Cambridge University Press (forthcoming).

Patnaik, Prabhat. 2003. *The Retreat to Unfreedom: Essays on the Emerging World Order.* New Delhi: Tulika Books.

———. 2000. "Economic Policy and its Political Management in the Current Conjuncture," in Francine R. Frankel, Zoya Hasan, Rajeev Bhargava, and Balveer Arora (eds), *Transforming India: Social and Political Dynamics of Democracy.* New Delhi: Oxford University Press, 231–53.

———, and C.P. Chandrasekhar. 2007. "The Indian Economy under 'Structural Adjustment'," in Rahul Mukherji, ed, *India's Economic Transition: The Politics of Reforms.* New Delhi: Oxford University Press. 52–86.

———. 1998. "India: *Dirigisme*, Structural Adjustment, and the Radical Alternative," in Dean Baker, Gerald Epstein, and Robert Pollin (eds), *Globalization and Progressive Economic Policy.* Cambridge: Cambridge University Press, 67–91.

Pedersen, Jørgen D. 1993. "The Complexities of Conditionality: The Case of India," in George Sørenson, ed, *Political Conditionality.* Portland, OR: International Specialized Book Services. 100–9.

Phillips, David A. 2009. *Reforming the World Bank: Twenty Years of Trial – and Error.* New York: Cambridge University Press.

Pincus, Jonathan R. and Jeffrey A. Winters. 2002. "Reinventing the World Bank," in Jonathan R. Pincus and Jeffrey A. Winters, eds, *Reinventing the World Bank.* Ithaca: Cornell University Press, 1–25.

Prasad, R.J. Rajendra. 2000. "WB Chief's Remarks General: gov't.," The Hindu (06 September). Online. <www.hinduonnet.com/thehindu/2000/09/06/stories/0406 201e.htm>. Retrieved 10 June 2005.

Press Trust of India. 2009. "India Seeks $3.2 bn from World Bank to Recapitalize PSU Banks." *livemint.com* (07 August). Online at <http://www.livemint.com/2009/08/ 07160853/India-seeks-32-bn-from-World.html>. Retrieved on 28 August 2009.

Price, Gareth. 2004. "India's Aid Dynamics: From Recipient to Donor?" Asia Programme Working Paper (September). London: Chatham House.

Putnam, Robert. 1988. "Diplomacy and Domestic Politics: The Logic of Two-Level Games," *International Organization* 42 (Summer): 427–60.

Ramesh, Jairam. 2000. "The State of States," *India Today* (28 July).

Rai, V.K. 2003. "A Profile of Uttar Pradesh: Stability in Instability," in Paul Wallace and Ramashray Roy, eds, *India's 1999 Elections and 20th Century Politics.* Thousand Oaks, CA: Sage Publications, 287–310.

Rangan, M.C. Govardhana and Kartik Goyal. 2008. "World Bank Plans $14 Billion India Lending Program." *Bloomberg.com* (12 December). Online at <http://www. bloomberg.com/apps/news?pid=20601091&sid=az_DUsyY5If0&refer=india>. Retrieved on 02 November 2009.

"Ransom State." 2002. *India Today* (27 May): 21–5.

Rao, M. Govinda. 2009. "The Fiscal Situation and a Reform Agenda for the New Government," *Economic and Political Weekly* XLIV, No. 25 (20 June): 77–85.

————. 1997. "Indian Fiscal Federalism: Major Issues," in Sudipta Mundle, ed, *Public Finance: Policy Issues for India.* New Delhi: Oxford University Press, 224–58.

Rao, M. Govinda and Nirvikar Singh. 2005. *Political Economy of Federalism in India.* New Delhi: Oxford University Press.

Reddy, G. Krishna. 2002. "New Populism and Liberalisation: Regime Shift under Chandrababu Naidu in AP." *Economic and Political Weekly* 37, No. 9 (2–8 March): 871–83.

Reserve Bank of India. 2000. *State Finances: A Study of Budgets 1999–2000.* Mumbai: Reserve Bank of India.

Reuters. 2009. "World Bank, India Agree on \$2 Bln Loan for Banks" (24 August). Online at <http://in.reuters.com/article/economicNews/idINIndia-41933820090824>. Retrieved on 31 August 2009.

"Riding Two Horses." 2000. Editorial. *The Hindu* (04 June).

Ritzen, Jozef. 2005. *A Chance for the World Bank.* London: Anthem Press.

Rodden, Jonathan A. 2006. *Hamilton's Paradox: The Promise and Peril of Fiscal Federalism.* New York: Cambridge University Press.

Rodden, Jonathan, Gunnar S. Eskeland, and Jennie Litvack, eds. 2003. *Fiscal Decentralization and the Challenge of Soft Budget Constraints.* Cambridge, MA: The MIT Press.

Rostow, W.W. 1990 [1960]. *The Stages of Economic Growth: A Non-Communist Manifesto,* Third Edition. New York: Cambridge University Press.

Rothermund, Dietmar. 2008. *India: The Rise of an Asian Giant.* New Haven: Yale University Press.

Roy, Subir. 2004. "'I Want to Show that Good Politics is also Good Economics'," *Business Standard* (11 August).

Rudolph, Lloyd I. and Susanne Hoeber Rudolph. 2008 [2002]. "New Dimensions of Indian Democracy," in Lloyd I. Rudolph and Susanne Hoeber Rudolph, *Explaining Indian Democracy: A Fifty-Year Perspective, 1956–2006,* Vol. 2, *The Realm of Institutions: State Formation and Institutional Change.* New Delhi: Oxford University Press, 312–26. Originally published as "New Dimensions of Indian Democracy," *Journal of Democracy* 13, No. 1 (January 2002): 52–66.

————. 2001. "Iconisation of Chandrababu: Sharing Sovereignty in India's Federal Market Econom." *Economic and Political Weekly* XXXVI, No. 18 (05–11 May): 1541–52.

————. 1987. *In Pursuit of Lakshmi: The Political Economy of the Indian State.* Hyderabad: Orient Longman Limited under license from The University of Chicago Press.

Ruggie, John. 1983. "International Regimes, Transactions, and Change: Embedded Liberalism in the Postwar Economic Order." *International Organization* 36, No. 2 (Spring): 379–415.

Ruttan, Vernon W. 1996. *United States Development Assistance Policy: The Domestic Politics of Foreign Economic Aid.* Baltimore: The Johns Hopkins University Press.

Sachs, Jeffrey D., Nirupam Bajpai, and Ananthi Ramiah. 2001. "Understanding Regional Economic Growth in India." Paper presented at the Asian Economic Panel meeting, Seoul (25–6 October).

Sáez, Lawrence. 2002. *Federalism Without a Centre: The Impact of Political and Economic Reform on India's Federal System.* Thousand Oaks, CA: Sage Publications.

Sanford, Jonathan and Michelle Chang. 2003. "World Bank Lending: Issues Raised by China's Qinghai Resettlement Project," in Elisabeth P. McLellan, ed, *The World Bank: Overview and Current Issues.* New York: Nova Science Publishers. 119–56.

Sen, Sumantra and Francine Frankel, eds. 2005. "Andhra Pradesh's Long March Toward 2020: Electoral Detours in a Developmentalist State, *Doing Business in India: Political,*

*Social and Cultural Overview* (Spring). Philadelphia: Center for the Advanced Study of India, University of Pennsylvania.

Senate Report 111–50. 2008. "World Bank International Development Association Replenishment Act of 2009" (16 July). 111th United States Congress, 1st Session. Senate Committee on Foreign Relations, John Kerry (D-Mass), Chair. Washington, DC: US Government Printing Office.

Sengupta, Mitu. 2008. "How the State Changed Its Mind: Power, Politics and the Origins of India's Market Reforms." *Economic and Political Weekly* 43, No. 2 (24 May): 35–42.

Sethi, Harsh. 2003. "What Price Hubris?" *The Hindu* (20 June). Online. <http://www.hindu.com/2003/06/20/stories/2003062000191000.htm>. Retrieved on 13 July 2009.

Sharma, Shantanu Nandan. 2009. "Plan Panel Okays $5bn Loan from World Bank." *The Economic Times* (23 August). Online at <http://economictimes.indiatimes.com/Economy/Plan-panel-okays-5-bn-loan-from-WB/articleshow/4923995.cms>. Retrieved on 31 August 2009.

Shetty, S.L. 2003. "Growth of SDP and Structural Changes in the State Economies: Interstate Comparisons," *Economic and Political Weekly* (06 December): 5189–200.

Shihata, Ibrahim F.I. 2000. *The World Bank Legal Papers*. Boston: Martinus Nijhoff Publishers.

———. 1995. *The World Bank in a Changing World*, Volume II, *Selected Essays and Lectures*. Boston: Martinus Nijhoff Publishers.

Shrivastava, Bhuma. 2008. "World Bank sticks to corruption charges ahead of key meeting." *Mint* (13 March). Online at <http://www.livemint.com/2008/03/13010108/World-Bank-sticks-to-corruptio.html>. Retrieved on 01 November 2009.

Shukla, Srawan. 2002. "World Bank Puts Loan Part on Hold," *The Economic Times* (05 April).

Simmons, Virginia. 2009. "ONE's Reaction to the Pittsburgh G20 Communique" (25 September). *The ONE Blog*. Online. <http://www.one.org/blog/category/non-governmental-organizations/imf/>. Retrieved on 02 November 2009.

Singh, Jaswant. 2007. *In Service of Emergent India: A Call to Honor*. Bloomington, IN: Indiana University Press.

Singh, Manmohan. 1964. *India's Export Trends and Prospects for Self-Contained Growth*. Oxford: Oxford University Press.

Singh, N.K. 2005. "World Bank Needs India as Much as We Need It." *Indian Express* (28 August). Online at <http://www.indianexpress.com/oldStory/77103/>. Retrieved on 18 September 2009.

———. 2004. "Coffee, Tea or International Aid?" *Indian Express* (03 October).

Singh, Nirvikar, Lavesh Bhandari, Aoyu Chen, and Aarti Khare. 2003. "Regional Inequality in India: A Fresh Look." *Economic and Political Weekly* (15 March): 1069–73.

Singh, Nirvikar and T.N. Srinivasan. 2006. "Indian Federalism, Economic Reform, and Globalization," in Jessica S. Wallack and T.N. Srinivasan, eds, *Federalism and Economic Reform: International Perspectives*. New York: Cambridge University Press, 301–64.

Sinha, Aseema. 2005. *The Regional Roots of Developmental Politics in India: A Divided Leviathan*. Bloomington, IN: Indiana University Press.

Sinha, Yashwant. 2007. *Confessions of a Swadeshi Reformer: My Years as Finance Minister*. New Delhi: Viking Penguin.

Shihata, Ibrahim F.I. 1994. *The World Bank Inspection Panel*. New York, Oxford University Press.

Snidal, Duncan and Alexander Thompson. 2003. "International Commitments and Domestic Politics: Institutions and Actors at Two Levels." In Daniel W. Drezner (ed), *Locating the Proper Authorities: The Interaction of Domestic and International Institutions*. Ann Arbor: The University of Michigan Press, 197–239.

"SP Accuses Mayawati of Misleading House on World Bank Letter." 2002. *The Press Trust of India* (02 September 2).

Sreedharan, Divya. 2003. "WB Loath to Release Funds for Reforms in Power Sector," *The Hindu* (05 May).

Sridhar, V. 2007. "Waiting for Deliverance." *Frontline: India's National Magazine* (23 February): 113–18.

————. 2000. "Brutal Crackdown." *Frontline: India's National Magazine* (16 September).

Sridharan, Kripa. 2003. "Federalism and Foreign Relations: The Nascent Role of the Indian States," *Asian Studies Review* 27 (December): 463–89.

Srinivasan, T.N. 2000. *Eight Lectures on India's Economic Reforms*. New Delhi: Oxford University Press.

Srinivasulu, Karli. 2003. "Party Competition and Strategies of Mobilization: An Analysis of Social Coalitions in Andhra Pradesh," in Paul Wallace and Ramashray Roy, eds, *India's 1999 Elections and 20th Century Politics*. Thousand Oaks, CA: Sage Publications. 141–66.

————1999. "Regime Change and Shifting Social Bases: the Telugu Desam Party in the 12th General Election," in Ramashray Roy and Paul Wallace, eds, *Indian Politics and the 1998 Election*. Thousand Oaks, CA: Sage Publications. 210–34.

Srivastava, Archana. 2002. "No 'New Privatisation' in Energy: CM," *The Economic Times* (14 May).

Stiglitz, Joseph. 2007. "Democratizing the World Bank." *Brown Journal of World Affairs* 13, No. 2: 79–86.

Suri, K.C. 2005. "The Dilemma of Democracy: Economic Reforms and Electoral Politics in Andhra Pradesh," in Jos Mooij, ed, *The Politics of Economic Reforms in India*. Thousand Oaks, CA: Sage Publications, 130–68.

————. 2002. "Democratic Process and Electoral Politics in Andhra Pradesh." Overseas Development Institute Working Paper No. 180 (September).

Surin, Kenneth. 2003. "Hostage to an Unaccountable Planetary Executive: The Flawed 'Washington Consensus' and Two *World Bank Reports*," in Kumar, Amitava (ed), *World Bank Literature*. Minneapolis: University of Minnesota Press, 128–39.

Swaroop, Vinaya, Shikha Jha, and Andrew Sunil Rajkumarb. 2000. "Fiscal Effect of Foreign Aid in a Federal System of Governance: The Case of India." *Journal of Public Economics* 77, No. 3 (September): 307–30.

Tatke, Sukhada. 2009. "Most of India's Urban Poor are in Maharashtra." *The Times of India* (22 September). Online at <http://timesofindia.indiatimes.com/news/india/Maharashtra-has-more-urban-poor-than-UP/articleshow/5039995.cms>; accessed on 25 September 2009.

Tendulkar, Suresh D. and T.A. Bhavani. 2007. *Understanding Reforms: Post 1991 India*. New Delhi: Oxford University Press.

"Text of World Bank Letter." 2007. *The Financial Times* (22 April). Online at <http://www.ft.com/cms/s/0/ef67a7e6-f0d3-11db-838b-000b5df10621.html?nclick_check=1>. Retrieved on 12 October 2009.

Thakur, Ramesh. 1998. "A Changing of the Guard in India." *Asian Survey* 38, No. 6 (June): 603–23.

Tharoor, Shashi. 2003. *Nehru: The Invention of India*. New York: Arcade Publishing.

Tongia, Rahul. 2007. "The Political Economy of Indian Power Sector Reforms," in David Victor and Thomas C. Heller, eds, *The Political Economy of Power Sector Reform: The Experiences of Five Major Developing Countries*. New York: Cambridge University Press, 109–75.

Van Dyke, Virginia. 1999. "The 1998 General Election: The Janus-faced Policies of the BJP and Religious Mobilization at the District Level in Uttar Pradesh," in in Ramashray Roy and Paul Wallace, eds, *Indian Politics and the 1998 Election*. Thousand Oaks, CA: Sage Publications. 105–28.

Venkitaramanan, S. 2009. "World Bank Loan to India—We Have Everything to Gain." *Business Line* (30 September). Online. <http://www.thehindubusinessline.com/2009/09/30/stories/2009093050640800.htm>. Retrieved on 02 November 2009.

———. 2006. "India Must Kick the World Bank Habit." *Business Line* (17 April). Online. <http://www.thehindubusinessline.com/bline/2006/04/17/stories/2006041700710900.htm>. Retrieved on 02 November 2009.

Vithal, B.P.R. and M.L. Sastry. 2001. *Fiscal Federalism in India*. New Delhi: Oxford University Press.

Volcker, Paul A. (Chair). 2007. *Independent Panel Review of the World Bank Group Department for Institutional Integrity*. Washington, D.C. Online at <http://siteresources.worldbank.org/NEWS/Resources/Volcker_Report_Sept._12,_for_website_FINAL.pdf>. Retrieved on 31 October 2009.

Vreeland, James. 2003. *The IMF and Economic Development*. New York: Cambridge University Press.

Wade, Robert. 1996. "Japan, the World Bank, and the Art of Paradigm Maintenance: *The East Asian Miracle* in Perspective." *New Left Review* 217: 2–36.

Wallace, Paul. 2007. "Introduction: India Shining Trumped by Poverty," in Ramashray Roy and Paul Wallace, eds, *India's 2004 Elections: Grass-roots and National Perspectives*. Thousand Oaks, CA: Sage Publications. 1–8.

Weaver, Catherine. 2008. *Hypocrisy Trap: The World Bank and the Poverty of Reform*. Princeton: Princeton University Press.

Weinraub, Bernard. 1991. "Economic Crisis Forcing Once Self-Reliant India to Seek Aid." *The New York Times* (29 June). Online. <http://www.nytimes.com/1991/06/29/world/economic-crisis-forcing-once-self-reliant-india-to-seek-aid.html>. Retrieved on 23 June 2009.

Weisman, Steven R. 2007. "'Second Chance' at Career Goes Sour for Wolfowitz." *The New York Times* (18 May). Online at <http://www.nytimes.com/2007/05/18/washington/18worldbank.html?pagewanted=1>. Retrieved on 12 October 2009.

Weiss, Linda (ed). 2003. *States in the Global Economy: Bringing Domestic Institutions Back In*. New York: Cambridge University Press.

Weiss, Martin A. 2008. "The World Bank's International Development Association (IDA)." Report for Members and Committees of the United States Congress. Order Code RL33969. Washington, DC: Congressional Research Service.

Whitfield, Lindsay. 2008. "Aid and Power: A Comparative Analysis of the Country Studies" and "Conclusion: Changing Conditions?" in Lindsay Whitfield (ed), *The Politics of Aid: African Strategies for Dealing with Donors*. New York: Oxford University Press, 329–79.

Wierzynska, Aneta. 2008. "How is the World Bank Reacting to Recent Reports of Corruption in its Projects?" Transparency International. Washington, D.C.: Transparency International USA (April). Online at <http://www.scribd.com/doc/6701394/India-DIR-Review-TI-USAApr081>. Retrieved on 02 November 2009.

Williams, David. 2008. *The World Bank and Social Transformation in International Politics: Liberalism, Governance and Sovereignty*. New York: Routledge.

Wibbels, Erik. 2005. *Federalism and the Market: Intergovernmental Conflict and Economic Reform*. Cambridge: Cambridge University Press.

Witsoe, Jeffrey. 2007. "Challenges and Opportunities Facing India's Poorest State." *India in Transition* (20 August). Philadelphia: Center for the Advanced Study of India, University of Pennsylvania. Online. <http://casi.ssc.upenn.edu/node/139>. Retrieved on 23 July 2009.

———. (senior researcher) and Francine Frankel (editor). 2006. "Social Justice and Stalled Development: Caste Empowerment and the Breakdown of Governance in Bihar." *India in Transition: Economics and Politics of Change* (Spring). Philadelphia: Center for the Advanced Study of India, University of Pennsylvania.

Wolfensohn, James D. 2005. *Voice for the World's Poor: Selected Speeches and Writings of World Bank President James D. Wolfensohn, 1995–2005*. Washington, DC: The World Bank.

Woods, Ngaire. 2006. *The Globalizers: The IMF the World Bank, and Their Borrowers*. Ithaca, NY: Cornell University Press.

———. 2005. "Making the IMF and the World Bank More Accountable," in Ariel Buira (ed), *Reforming the Governance of the IMF and the World Bank*. London: Anthem Press, 149–70.

"A World Apart." 2009. *The Economist* (31 October), pp. 83–4.

World Bank. 2009a. "Outside Review Supports World Bank Group Reform," Press Release No.2010/109/EXT (21 October). Washington, DC: The World Bank Group. Online at <http://go.worldbank.org/2I98FYWNJ0>. Retrieved on 02 November 2009.

2009b. "Zoellick Opening Remarks, Development Committee Press Conference, Annual Meetings 2009 (05 October). Istanbul: Annual Meetings of the IMF and World Bank Group, 2009. Online. < http://go.worldbank.org/S6P7K723L0>. Retrieved on 02 November 2009.

2008a. "Can Bihar Get Out of the Poverty Trap?" Washington, DC: The World Bank. Online. <http://go.worldbank.org/BMOBAQYZN0>. Retrieved on 23 July 2009.

———. 2008b. *Country Strategy for India, 2009–12*. Report No. 46509-IN. Washington, DC: The World Bank.

———. 2008c. "Government of India and World Bank Group Join Forces to Stamp Out in Health Sector Projects." World Bank Press Release. Washington, D.C. (11 January). Online at <http://go.worldbank.org/YVLEFEQKZ0>. Retrieved on 1 November 2009.

———. 2008d. India: National Vector Borne Disease Control and Polio Eradication Support Project, Project Appraisal Document (26 June), Report No. 43572-IN. Washington, DC: The World Bank.

———. 2008e. *World Bank Annual Report 2008: Year in Review*. Washington, DC: The World Bank.

———. 2008f. "World Bank Group Pledges $3.5 Billion for Poorest Countries." News Release No. 2008/078/EXT. Washington, DC: The World Bank.

———. 2007a. *Country Strategy Progress Report for India for the Period FY2005–2008*. Report No. 39796-IN. Washington, DC: The World Bank.

———. 2007b. *A Guide to the World Bank*, 2nd edition. Washington, DC: The World Bank.

———. 2007c. *The World Bank in India* 6, No. 3 (November). New Delhi: The World Bank.

———. 2007d. "World Bank Statement on the Independent People's Tribunal on the World Bank in India" (24 September). Online. <http://go.worldbank.org/LHI56RPYY0>. Retrieved on 01 August 2009.

———. 2006a. *India—Inclusive Growth and Service Delivery: Building on India's Success*. World Bank Development Policy Review. New Delhi: Macmillan India for the World Bank.

———. 2006b. "Strengthening the World Bank's Engagement with IBRD Partner Countries" (07 September). Washington, DC: The World Bank.

————. 2004a. *Attaining the Millennium Development Goals in India*. Washington, DC: South Asia Region Human Development Unit, the World Bank.

————. 2004b. *Country Strategy for India*. Washington, DC: The World Bank Group.

————. 2004c. *State Fiscal Reforms in India: Progress and Prospects*. Report No. 28849-IN (10 November). Washington, DC: The World Bank, Poverty Reduction and Economic Management Sector Unit, South Asia Region.

————. 2004d. *Unlocking Andhra Pradesh's Growth Potential: An Agenda to Achieve the Vision 2020 Growth Targets*. Washington, DC: The World Bank.

————. 2002a. *Poverty in India: The Challenge of Uttar Pradesh*. Washington, DC: Poverty Reduction and Economic Management Unit, South Asia Region, The World Bank.

————. 2002b. Report and Recommendation of the President of the World Bank Group on the Andhra Pradesh Economic Reform Loan/Credit. Report No. P7508-IN (15 February). Restricted circulation.

————. 2000. "World Bank Provides $511 Million to Accelerate Growth and Fight Poverty in Uttar Pradesh, India's Most Populous State." News Release No. 2000/318/SAS (26 April). Washington, DC and New Delhi: The World Bank.

————. 1999. Project Agreement, Andhra Pradesh Economic Restructuring Project (04 February). Online. <http://go.worldbank.org/FSKJBGBCS0>. Retrieved on 03 July 2009.

————. 1998. "World Bank to Assist Human Development Needs in India's Lead Reforming State," News Release No. 98/1850/SAS, Washington and New Delhi (25 June).

————. 1997a. *Andhra Pradesh: Agenda for Economic Reforms*. Report No. 15901-IN. Washington, DC: The World Bank.

————. 1997b. *A Guide to the World Bank*, 2nd edition. Washington, DC: The World Bank.

————. 1996. *India: Five Years of Stabilization and Reform and the Challenges Ahead*. Washington, DC: The World Bank.

"World Bank Corruption (editorial)." 2007. *The Wall Street Journal* (04 September). Online at <http://www.opinionjournal.com/editorial/feature.html?id = 110010557>. Retrieved on 12 October 2009.

"World Bank Disgrace (editorial)." 2008. *The Wall Street Journal* (14 January). Online at <http://online.wsj.com/article/SB120026972002987225.html>. Retrieved on 01 November 2009.

Wroughton, Lesley. 2008. "World Bank, India Approve Steps to Fight Corruption." Reuters (13 March). Online <http://www.reuters.com/article/bondsNews/idUSN1334804620080313>. Retrieved on 01 November 2009.

"YSR Death Triggers Ugly CM Race." 2009. *The Times of India* (04 September). Online at <http://timesofindia.indiatimes.com/news/india/YSR-death-triggers-ugly-CM-race/articleshow/4969560.cms>. Retrieved on 04 September 2009.

Zakaria, Fareed. 2008. *The Post-American World*. New York: W.W. Norton & Co.

Zanini, Gianni. 2001. *India: The Challenges of Development—A Country Assistance Evaluation*. Washington, DC: The World Bank, Operations Evaluation Department.

Zedillo, Ernesto (Chair). 2009. *Repowering the World Bank for the 21st Century: Report of the High-Level Commission on Modernization of World Bank Group Governance* (October). New Haven:Yale Center for the Study of Globalization. Online. <http://go.worldbank.org/2I98FYWNJ0>. Retrieved on 02 Novemeber 2009.

Zoellick, Robert B. 2009. "Opening Press Conference: World Bank-IMF 2009 Spring Meetings" (23 April). Washington, DC. Online. <http://go.worldbank.org/D7N30ZB780>. Retrieved on 02 August 2009.

# Interview Sources Cited in the Text

(For a list of additional persons interviewed on background, see Acknowledgements.)

Basu, Priya. 2007. Author's interview with Lead Sector Specialist, Finance and Private Sector Unit, World Bank. Washington, DC (31 July).

Benmessaoud, Rachid. 2008. Author's interview with Operations Advisor, the World Bank. New Delhi (06 June).

Bhattacharya, B.K. 2002. Author's interview with the former Chief Secretary, Government of Karnataka. Bangalore (02 August).

Carter, Michael. 2007b. Author's telephone with former Country Director for India, World Bank, by telephone to Mr. Carter's home in England (17 July).

Chassard, Joële. 2002. Author's interview with the Country Coordinator for India, World Bank. Washington, DC (17 July).

Chidambaram, Palaniappan. 2003. Author's interview with the former Minister of Finance (1996–8), Government of India. New Delhi (10 August).

Dasgupta, Dipak. 2008. Author's interview with Lead Economist, World Bank. New Delhi (04 June).

Garg, S.C. 2002. Author interview with Director, Fund-Bank Division, Department of Economic Affairs, Ministry of Finance, Government of India. New Delhi (05 September).

Harshe, Rajen. 2001. "Stakeholder Participation in Andhra Pradesh Reform Process." Draft report submitted to the World Bank as an internal document, shared with the author by Rajen Harshe.

Kapoor, Kapil. 2007. Author's interview with Principal for the South Asia Region, Public Sector Governance Board, World Bank. Washington, DC (31 July).

Lal, Sumir. 2003. Author's interview with External Affairs Officer, The World Bank. New Delhi (11 August).

Lim, Edwin. 2003. Author's interview with the former Country Director for India (1996–2002), World Bank. Osterville, MA (14 July).

Manor, James. 2002. Author's e-mail correspondence with the Director, Civil Society and Governance Programme, Institute of Development Studies, Sussex, UK (16 September).

Naga Raju, M. 2008. Author's interview with Director, Fund-Bank Division, Department of Economic Affairs, Ministry of Finance, Government of India. New Delhi (04 June).

Ramesh, Jairam. 2002. Author's interview with Head of Economic Cell, Indian National Congress Party, and former economic advisor to the Ministry of Finance, Government of India. New Delhi (21 August).

Rao, P.V. 2002. Author's interview with the former Chief Secretary, Government of Andhra Pradesh (2000–2). Hyderabad (26 August).

Ravishankar, V.J. 2008. Author's interview with Senior Economist, World Bank, New Delhi (05 June).

Shah, Parmesh. 2007. Author's interview with Senior Rural Development Specialist, South Asia Region, World Bank. Washington, DC (31 July).

Singh, Manmohan. 2003. Author's interview with the Leader of the Opposition, Rajya Sabha, and former Minister of Finance (1991–6), Government of India. New Delhi (10 August).

Subbarao, Duvurri. 2002. Author's interview with the former Finance Secretary (1993–8), Government of Andhra Pradesh. Washington, DC (26 September).

Tewari, Anirudh. 2008. Author's interview with former Director (2004–6), Department of Economic Affairs, Ministry of Finance, Government of India. New Delhi (03 June).

Tripathi, Sushil Chandra. 2003. Author's interview with the former Principal Finance Secretary, Government of Uttar Pradesh. New Delhi (05 August).

Zagha, Roberto N. 2002. Author's interview with the Sector Director, South Asia Poverty Reduction and Economic Management Unit, World Bank. Washington, DC (26 September).

# INDEX

Note: Page references in *italics* refer to illustrations.

Lightning Source UK Ltd.
Milton Keynes UK
UKOW051722230911

179184UK00001B/26/P